International Impact of Colonial Rule in Korea, 1910–1945

Edited by YONG-CHOOL HA

CENTER FOR KOREA STUDIES PUBLICATIONS

The Northern Region of Korea: History, Identity, and Culture
Edited by Sun Joo Kim

Reassessing the Park Chung Hee Era, 1961–1979: Development, Political Thought, Democracy, and Cultural Influence
Edited by Hyung-A Kim and Clark W. Sorensen

Colonial Rule and Social Change in Korea, 1910–1945
Edited by Hong Yung Lee, Yong-Chool Ha, and Clark W. Sorensen

An Affair with Korea: Memories of South Korea in the 1960s
By Vincent S. R. Brandt

South Korea's Education Exodus: The Life and Times of Study Abroad
Edited by Adrienne Lo, Nancy Abelmann, Soo Ah Kwon, and Sumie Okazaki

Spaces of Possibility: In, Between, and Beyond Korea and Japan
Edited by Clark W. Sorensen and Andrea Gevurtz Arai

Beyond Death: The Politics of Suicide and Martyrdom in Korea
Edited by Charles R. Kim, Jungwon Kim, Hwasook Nam, and Serk-Bae Suh

International Impact of Colonial Rule in Korea, 1910–1945 edited by Yong-Chool Ha has been supported by the Northeast Asian History Foundation.

In addition, The Center for Korea Studies Publication Series has been supported by the Academy of Korean Studies Grant funded by the Korean Government (MEST) (AKS–2011–BAA–2101).

이 논문 또는 저서는 2012년도 정부(교육과학기술부)의 재원으로 한국학중앙연구원의 지원을 받아 수행된 연구임 (AKS-2012-BAA-2101).

The Center for Korea Studies Publication Series is dedicated to providing excellent academic resources and conference volumes related to the history, culture, and politics of the Korean peninsula.

Clark W. Sorensen | Director & General Editor | Center for Korea Studies

International Impact of Colonial Rule in Korea, 1910–1945

Edited by

YONG-CHOOL HA

A CENTER FOR KOREA STUDIES PUBLICATION

International Impact of Colonial Rule in Korea in Korea, 1910–1945
Edited by Yong-Chool Ha
© 2019 by the Center for Korea Studies, University of Washington
Printed in the United States of America
22 21 20 19 5 4 3 2 1

All rights reserved. No part of this publication may be reproduced or transmitted in any form or by any means, electronic or mechanical, including photocopy, recording, or any information storage or retrieval system, without permission from the publisher.

CENTER FOR KOREA STUDIES
Henry M. Jackson School of International Studies
University of Washington
http://jsis.washington.edu/Korea

CATALOGING-IN-PUBLICATION DATA IS ON FILE WITH THE LIBRARY OF CONGRESS
ISBN (HARDCOVER): 978-0-295-74670-8
ISBN (PAPERBACK): 978-0-295-74669-2
ISBN (EBOOK): 978-0-295-74671-5

The paper used in this publication meets the minimum requirements of American National Standard for Information Sciences–Permanence of Paper for Printed Library Materials, ANSI Z39, 48-1984.

Contents

Acknowledgments | vii
List of Illustrations | ix

Introduction | 1
YONG-CHOOL HA

Part I: Colonial Policies for Forging Korea's Image

1. A Devil Appears in a Different Dress: Imperial Japan's Deceptive Propaganda and Rationalization for Making Korea Its Colony | 19
HAKJOON KIM

2. Establishing Japanese National Identity and the "Chosŏn Issue" | 49
SANG SOOK JEON

3. Japanese Propaganda in the United States from 1905 | 73
ANDRE SCHMID

Part II: Colonial Korea's Perception of Foreign Societies

4. The Impact of the Colonial Situation on International Perspectives in Korea: Active Imaginations, Wishful Strategies, and Passive Action | 105
YONG-CHOOL HA and JUNG HWAN LEE

5. Modern Utopia or "Animal Society"? The American Imaginaries in Wartime Colonial Korea, 1931–1945 | 139
YUMI MOON

PART III: FOREIGN SOCIETIES' PERCEPTIONS OF COLONIAL KOREA

6   The British and American Perceptions of Korea during the Colonial Period | 179
    DAEYEOL KU

7   Russian Perception of Koreans and the Japanese Colonial Regime in Korea during the First Quarter of the Twentieth Century | 219
    SERGEY O. KURBANOV

8   Chinese Understandings of Colonial Korea in Modern Times, 1910–1945: Observations and Reflections | 239
    KEZHI SUN

9   Publicizing Colonies: Representations of "Korea" and "Koreans" in *NIPPON* | 259
    NAOKO SHIMAZU

Bibliography | 285

Contributors | 315

Index | 318

Acknowledgments

The idea of studying the international impact of Japanese colonial rule in Korea has not been a popular one. It took many years to develop the idea into a concrete project. It was Professor Yong Duk Kim, president of Northeast History Foundation in 2007, who understood the importance of the project and decided to support the project. Without his understanding and support this book would not have been possible. The University of Washington Center for Korean Studies organized an international conference in November 2010. This book is one of the outcomes of that conference. As often is the case with international conferences much time has been spent in editing the papers, which were originally read and discussed at the conference. Along the way the Northeast History Foundation has been generous in allowing more time and providing extra financial support. The editor would like to thank the past presidents of the Northeast History Foundation, Dr. Jae Jung Chung, Dr. Hak-Joon Kim, and Dr. Hosup Kim, and the current president, Dr. Do Hyong Kim, who understood what it takes to a produce a book from an international conference. If it were not for their patience and support this book would have never been published.

As the project involved multi-year cooperation from many individuals, the Northeast Foundation patiently and generously supported the project until it grew into the present volume. I would like to express my sincere thanks to Dr. Woo Seung Min, who played an important liaison role at the beginning of the project, and the many other researchers at the Foundation who provided valuable input to make this volume better through personal advice and the review process. I also wish to thank the authors of this volume who were patient throughout the arduous editing process and to the late Professor Hongyung Lee and Professors Don Hellmann, Ken Pyle, Hwasook Nam, and Madeline Dong at the University of Washington Henry M. Jackson School of International Studies for their participation in the conference.

I also would like to express my appreciation to Professor Clark W. Sorensen, Chair of the Center for Korean Studies at University of Washington who understood the importance of the project and was willing to publish this book as part of the Center for Korean Studies Publications Series. Turning the first draft papers into publishable products was such a time-consuming job and without the diligent and dedicated editing by Tracy Stober this book indeed could not have seen light. I would also like to thank Dr. Young Sook Lim, who rendered all of the possible administrative assistance at every critical juncture of the project.

As with long-term projects I am indebted to many students for their research and technical support. Dr. Kyung Jun Choi, Dong Hee Han, and Dong Hui Park did not mind helping me collect data and bibliographical citations.

Illustrations

Tables

4.1 Distribution of editorials on international affairs, *Chosŏn ilbo* (1920–30) 110
4.2 Number of editorials related to international affairs in the *Chosŏn ilbo* (1920–30) 111
4.3 Percentage of *Keijō Nippō* editorials related to international affairs (1920–30) 112
4.4 Number of editorials related to international affairs in the *Keijō Nippō* (1920–30) 113

Figures

9.1 Cover of the Korea issue, NIPPON, Volume 18 (July 1939) 269
9.2 Korean women carrying pots, NIPPON, Volume 18 (July 1939) 273
9.3 Korean artisans' tools, NIPPON, Volume 18 (July 1939) 279

Introduction

YONG-CHOOL HA

Scholars have studied issues related to the Japanese Colonial Period in Korea (1910–45) in detail, but there is no gainsaying that their attention has been heavily skewed toward the domestic aspects of colonial rule.[1] Arguments have mainly centered around whether Japanese colonial rule was modernizing or exploitative. These questions have often been treated under the assumption of a closed empire model. The impact of international influence has seldom been considered, or at most indirectly recognized, in the context of discussions about economic changes in Korea. Thus, international aspects of Japanese colonial rule have not received full attention. Indeed, study of early twentieth-century Korea has been so influenced by the context of Japanese imperialism that little is actually known of how the extra-imperial world was perceived and understood in Korea society during this period.[2]

Such scanty attention to the international impact on Korea during the Colonial Period seems natural because many considered Korea to not exist legally as a separate international entity.[3] However, the fact that Korea was not an active member of the international community at that time should not preclude international affairs having an effect on Korea during colonial rule. More importantly, further research is necessary to understand how the worldview of Korean elites, whether in Korea or abroad, was affected by the colonial situation. This edited volume is a preliminary effort to fill this gap in the understanding of the various ways international affairs impacted colonial rule and the colonized situation. The specific goals of this volume are the following: (1) to introduce the various facets of Colonial Period international affairs that have seldom received attention and how they impacted colonial rule; and

(2) to provide a platform for understanding not only what happened during the Colonial Period but also for analyzing the long-term implications of the international impacts on the Colonial Period in Korea and how that relates to the present time.

The scope of the international impact on colonial rule is quite broad. The patterns of impact can take several paths including: external-internal, external-external, or internal-external directions. The areas of impact can be political, economic, social, and cultural in nature. In terms of status, this text covers both the elites and the masses. The chapters in this volume are not intended to cover all of the complex areas of international impact. However, the coverage is wide enough to demonstrate the complexity of the international impact on colonial rule.

Several patterns of analysis emerge from the contributions in this volume in terms of the direction of impact. Part one "Colonial Policies for Forging Korea's Image," chapters 1, 2, and 3 by Hakjoon Kim, Sang Sook Jeon, and Andre Schmid respectively, discuss the impact of Korea on Japan. Kim and Schmid follow the impact lines on the international stage while Jeon details the domestic connections between the two states. Part two "Colonial Korea's Perception of Foreign Societies" showcases two chapters (chapter 4 by Yong-Chool Ha and Jung Hwan Lee and chapter 5 by Yumi Moon) that discuss Korea's view of global affairs. Finally, chapters in Part 3 "Foreign Societies' Perception of Colonial Korea" take the opposite view and discuss Korea and the colonial situation from the British, US, Russian, and Chinese perspectives (chapters 6, 7, and 8 by Daeyeol Ku, Sergey Kurbanov, and Kezhi Sun). Chapter 9 by Naoko Shimazu reveals the Japanese perceptions of the peninsula.

The chapters cover both the elites and the masses, although they are considerably skewed toward elite levels. Also, for the most part the chapters focus on the political aspects. However, a few chapters provide mixed analyses by including social, cultural, and economic aspects (for example see chapter 5 by Yumi Moon, chapter 7 by Sergey Kurbanov, and chapter 8 by Kezhi Sun). The chapters also vary in terms of the time covered. For details of the time prior to the annexation (1910) see chapters 1, 3, 7, and 8. For the early part of the Colonial Period (1900–30s) see chapters, 3, 7, and 8. Two chapters discussed specific decades. For details on the 1930s see chapter 5 by Yumi Moon; for the 1920s see chapter 4 by Yong-Chool Ha.

Beyond demonstrating the patterns of international impact of the colonial rule, this volume addresses the following thematic questions: (1) How did Japan try to present colonial Korea to Koreans and the outside world? (2) How did Japan strategically view Korea in establishing its new international identity? (3) How did the perceptions of Korea, formed during colonial rule, affect the future status of Korea? (4) How should we understand elite divisiveness in terms of international perspectives and their implications on post-Liberation elite struggles in Korea? (5) What views are distinctly colonial in relation to world perspectives? (6) What Korean strategic thinking and action programs, formed during the colonial era, are still relevant to present-day Korea? (7) How did historical, ideological, and geopolitical factors affect neighboring countries' perceptions of colonial Korea? And finally, (8) how should we understand the passive international status of colonial Korea from international perspectives?

Based on the analyses of the above questions several broad observations can be made. The international circumstances of the first three decades of the twentieth century forced Japan to justify their colonial rule in East Asia to the rest of world. Japan's colonial discourses about Korea were so negative that their impact has been far reaching both in time and scope. Painting Korea as uncivilized and historically dependent has had a tremendous impact on the future international status of Korea. It also has caused controversies regarding the interpretation of Korean history and thereby affected Korean-Japanese relations.

These chapters show that Japan was a highly insecure colonial power, and this in turn pushed officials to work harder to justify colonization to the international community. At the same time colonial Korea was more than a mere colony to Japan: it was one of the strategic geopolitical pieces Japan needed to become a continental power. This dual nature of colonial Korea led Japan to adopt unrealistic policies such as quick assimilation. Finally, being colonized caused Korean intellectuals to become passive about taking concrete actions. This led to unrealistic expectations about possibilities for international relations to change the status quo, and thus caused a huge gap between perception and action.

Hakjoon Kim's chapter, "A Devil Appears in a Different Dress: Imperial Japan's Deceptive Propaganda and Rationalization for Making Korea Its Colony" focuses on the attempts by Japanese colonial authorities to justify their colonial rule over Korean people and society. These discourses were both extensive and intensive; they covered numerous areas and were implemented with tenacity and consistency. They targeted both the elites and the masses. According to Kim, "[i]n simple terms, they attempted to create an image of Korea as that of a 'hopeless country,' one which needed Japan's protection and guidance."[4] Ultimately the colonial authorities aimed to inculcate fatalism and nihilism among the Korean people.

At an ideological level, Social Darwinism and the idea of a Great Eastern Union (*daitō gappō*) were constantly drawn upon. The former, that was interpreted in Asia as a struggle between nations in which only the fittest would survive, was used to instill the idea of a weak Korea, one which could not survive in the world where the strong eat the weak. The idea of a Great Eastern Union was used to promote the idea that the ultimate goal of Japan's colonial rule was simply to establish a peaceful order in East Asia.

Historical and geopolitical distortions were frequently used to justify the inevitability of colonial rule. The former included the argument that what Japan calls Mimana on the Korean peninsula (K. Imna) was a Japanese colony from AD 100–500, and that Japan introduced rice culture to Korea (when the opposite is more likely).[5] Japanese historians claimed Korea, as a tributary state of China, lacked experience in independence throughout its entire history. The geopolitical ambition of Russia combined with a weakened China made Korea, according to Japan, ripe for the picking and justified annexation by Japan as Japan's only means for survival. Along with these distortions of history Koreans were repeatedly reminded of their weak and corrupt leaders who did not care about the Korean people. This technique served as a means to separate the masses from the elites, while Japanese propaganda embellished the leadership quality of Japanese colonial authorities, noting that they were beneficial to Korea and would make Korea civilized and enlightened.

As a way to allay the fear of the Koreans, the colonial authorities' frequently cited racial affinity between the Japanese and Koreans claiming they share the same ancestry and the same roots. The relationship between the two peoples was often compared to that of teeth and lips.[6] The Japanese mobilized all of these tactics to plant an inferiority complex in the Korean people, the immediate visible impact of which divided the elites, but a more far reaching result was the development of colonial historiography, which became a source of debate in the post-colonial era and a target to be overcome in Korean society since Liberation.

Sang Sook Jeon's approach to the international impact of colonial rule in chapter 3 "Establishing Japanese National Identity and the 'Chosŏn Issue'" is rather unusual in that she analyzes the locus and the weight of Korea in the context of Japan's international and regional strategies and developmental plans. Rather than follow the conventional interpretation that Korea and the Korean peninsula only gradually became the focus of Japanese imperialism, Jeon argues that, from the beginning of the Meiji regime, Korea formed the cornerstone of Japan's attempt to become a continental power and modern nation state. In other words, Japan's vision and strategies in confronting Western imperial powers were based on Korea being an essential element in building Japan's national identity. As such Japan perceived every possible change that occurred on the Korean peninsula as affecting Japan's security and its scheme to become a continental power.

Jeon traces the historical origins and the development of Japan's perception of Korea. According to Jeon, it all started when Russia's move eastward began to awaken Japan's anxiety. Based on the conceptual distinction between a "sovereignty line" and an "interest line" Japan developed a strategy where the latter (Korea) needed to be defended in order to secure the former (Japan). Ideologically Japan countered the Western idea of Yellow Peril within their own idea of Asianism in which common racial origins and affinity were emphasized between the Koreans and the Japanese. Annexation of Korea thus became an inevitable and essential part of Japan's quest to become a continental and internationally recognized imperial power. Through this lens, the Korean peninsula was understood to be the core foundation capable of changing Japan's identity from an island state to that of a continental nation.

Japanese officials had two different approaches to Korea. Their first tactic regarded Korea as a bridge across which Japan could advance into Manchuria and beyond, while the other approach viewed Korea to be a beachhead from which Japan could establish a foothold on the mainland. Differences between the two concepts of how best to use the Korean peninsula were stark. In the first case Japan would concentrate its efforts on establishing continental control, while in the second resources would be spent on Korean assimilation and changes in Korea prior to moving forward. These differences notwithstanding the two approaches shared the same need to annex Korea and as such Korea and Korean issues became deeply embedded in Japan's strategy to develop Korea as a base for national development, while it simultaneously served to restrict the advance of Russia and the West into East Asia.

Andre Schmid's chapter "Japanese Propaganda in the United States from 1905" analyzes Japan's propaganda campaign in the United States from the early nineteenth century until 1930 in terms of its motives, modes of presentation of Korea, the US response, and the short- and long-term consequences of this propaganda for Korea. Japan conducted a propaganda campaign in the United States detailing their colonization of Korea for two reasons. First of all, Japan was an unusual colonizer as it was a non-white nation and had colonized Asian neighbors and members of the same race. Because of this Japan felt a need to justify being an imperialist power. Japanese officials wanted Japan to be recognized as a fully legitimate nation on par with other Western nations as a colonizer and a civilized nation. Second, Japan wanted to make sure that the United States understood its geopolitical ambitions in East Asia.

According to Schmid, Japanese officials judiciously prepared substantive materials that justified its colonization of the Korean peninsula. By profusely providing detailed statistics on the various aspects of the modern changes that had occurred in Korea since annexation in 1910 and contrasting them with precolonial Korean society, Americans were constantly reminded of the benefits the Japanese had brought to the Koreans. The data was presented in the form of annual reports. Prominent colonial administrators participated in this endeavor, including none other than Itō Hirobumi. What was also notable was the fact that Japan was not perceived as actively seeking colonization but rather that the deteriorating situation in Korea forced them to act. Given the paucity of resources on Korea in the United States, the propaganda materials supplied by the Japanese government became important sources for US publications on Korea. This, in turn, reinforced negative images of Korea and thus solidified the justification of colonial rule over Korea among the American public. This then led to a US perception of Korea as being primarily that of an uncivilized nation and thus unworthy of US attention. Even when some Americans were critical of Japan's colonial rule over Korea, they never questioned the colonial rule of Korea.[7] As such Korea never became an "independent variable" for the United States.

Japanese propaganda blinded US society and opinion leaders to the real picture of Korea until the breakout of war between the United States and Japan and the subsequent Cairo Declaration in 1943 when the fog lifted. Relevant discussion on Korean independence was heavily affected by US ignorance. The ignorance of the United States and the absence of detailed and accurate information about the Korean peninsula took its own toll when the US Army Military Government in Korea (USAMGIK) took over governing the peninsula from September 8, 1945 to August 15, 1948.

Schmid's analysis clearly demonstrates that Japanese propaganda was practically the only source of information on Korea available in the United States as Korea had not been prepared to introduce its own history, culture, and version of events to US society. But more importantly Japanese propaganda spread to other parts of the world, causing long-term misunderstandings of Korea. Schmid concludes that this biased understanding and ignorance of Korea had serious implications for US policy toward Korea both during and after Japanese colonial rule.

Yong-Chool Ha and Jung Hwan Lee in chapter 4, "The Impact of the Colonial Situation on International Perspectives in Korea: Active Imaginations, Wishful Strategies, and Passive Action" analyze the distinct international perspectives formed during colonial rule and how the long-term consequences affected both the Korean elites and the Korean masses through to the end of the Colonial Period. They define the distinct international perspectives of colonial rule in terms of active imaginations, wishful strategies, and passive actions. Koreans possessed active imaginations when referring to international development. This came to international politics largely because of the desire on the part of the Koreans to change their colonial situation from the outside. This preoccupation with international politics as a source of change lead Korean intellectuals to assess the international environment unrealistically, and wishful strategies followed from these assessments. One of the examples of this is the Korean anticipation of war in the world, in particular, in the Northeast Asian region. Due to their passive international status and, thus, adherence to passive action, the Korean elites played up a possible war between Japan and Western powers as a way to change the status quo. According to Ha and Lee, the Koreans were also extremely sensitive to any change in the status quo when it came to state policies and ideology.

Fascination with communism was one such example. Koreans' perceptions of the major powers were also frequently influenced by their unrealistic expectations that the powers would consider pro-Korean policies, something that never happened. By comparing the editorials of the *Keijō Nippō*, the official Japanese newspaper of the colonial era, Ha and Lee demonstrate that the colonial situation brought about different perceptions of international affairs among the Korean elites as compared to those of the Japanese officials.

Ha and Lee explore the long-term consequences of these views. They begin by reviewing Koreans' perceptions of the enemy, then discuss the Koreans' perceptions of the major international powers, and finally their deliberations on the importance of a military as a means to conduct international affairs. The Korean intellectuals' frustration and disappointment that stemmed from the gap between perception and the absence of action in international affairs had long-term consequences that, in turn, resulted in simplifying the enemy, acquiring an overzealousness and extreme yearning for military power, and creating an inconsistency between analysis and reality. Ha and Lee argue that colonial rule continued the long tradition in Korea of perceiving the enemy in a simplistic manner. Under the longtime influence of China, Korean elites perceived the world as revolving around China. This naturally gave rise to a curt, black-and-white distinction between friend and enemy. In other words, Korean dynasties had been deprived of developing a complex sense of enemy when regarding how to approach major powers surrounding the Korean peninsula.

Colonial rule inadvertently led to the continuation of this tradition, which was due in large part to the overwhelming preoccupation among Koreans with their liberation from Japan. Koreans viewed Japan as being 100 percent the enemy and this left no room for a strategic partnership. This perception persisted even after Liberation in the context of the Cold War. Another legacy from the Colonial Period has been the Koreas' (both North and South) strong inclination toward military power. The belief that Japan had been able to colonize Korea due to their superior military appears to have led to a perception that a strong military power is essential for independence.

Yumi Moon in her chapter titled "Modern Utopia or "Animal Society"?: The American Imaginaries in Wartime Colonial Korea, 1931–1945" analyzes the extent of convergence and divergence among three ideologically different Korean groups and their perceptions of the United States, and whether and to what extent these groups reflected Japan's claims of a Pan-Asianist order in the 1930s. Based on a comparative analysis of articles in four journals published during the 1930s, Moon concludes that throughout the 1930s, until Japan began to enforce its war narrative in earnest in 1940 and beyond, Korean nationalists and socialists converged and began to come to agreement in their perceptions of the United States. The nationalists perceived the United States to be a beacon for economic wealth and technological progress and a symbol of power. Further, they viewed the United States as being founded on humanitarianism and democracy. In theory, the United States would be the ideal nation and the model for Korea to imitate to modernize itself.

Socialist publications showed ambivalent attitudes toward the United States. On the one hand, they applied the typical Marxian framework in understanding the United States—as seen in their focus on class domination, exploitation, and imperialism—and predicted the fall of US capitalism. However, they simultaneously acknowledged the material and technological progress made in the United States, while recognizing that there were divergent interpretations of the Rooseveltian reforms. One view believed the reforms would fail, and the other predicted the opposite. But overall the tone of the voices was such that they recognized the resilience of the US democracy and its economic system, while expecting a socialist revolution. What was also striking was the fact that even the socialist journals published work by nationalists who held a rosy view of the United States.

The Pan-Asianists basically followed the official war narratives dictated by Japan. They highlighted racial affinity between the Koreans and the Japanese and viewed the US-Japanese confrontation in racial terms; Japan was trying to protect Asia from the white race and Western imperialism. In addition, they urged the Koreans to fully cooperate with Japan and to participate in the war effort.

In the 1930s, apart from the Pan-Asianists, nationalists and socialists maintained different views of the United States and other international situations from those of Japan. First, while Japan recognized the United States' power and progress, it never went so far as to call it the ideal. In contrast, Korean nationalists characterized it as an ideal. Second, both nationalists and socialists highlighted the fact that the United States allowed the independence of the Philippines and predicted a possible military conflict between the United States and Japan during World War II.

These visible differences were put to an end as war between the United States and Japan became imminent in 1941. Korean journals, regardless of their ideological orientations, had to parrot Japan's war narratives in terms of a leftist critique of capitalism and imperialism, and a denunciation of the United States' hypocrisy in not fulfilling its promise of freedom. However, they were different from Japanese war narratives in their marginal attention to the loyalty to the Japanese emperor and the ideology of *naisen ittai* (內鮮一體; Japan and Korea as one body).

Moon's conclusion focuses on the implications of the convergence between nationalists and socialists and how this relates to post-Liberation ideological conflicts in Korea. However, what is more relevant to this volume is the colonial impact on the convergence. The commonly held optimistic, and at times unrealistic, views of the United States can be analyzed as both nationalists' and socialists' wishful thinking that comes from the shared colonial situation. For example, taking up the United States as a model was not only unrealistic for Koreans, but it also became a way of viewing the United States as a possible means for Korea to break out of the colonial situation. Korean intellectuals' understanding was such that they believed the US could bring about changes in the colonial situation even if that meant a possible war with Japan. The ways in which Korean intellectuals perceived the countries surrounding the peninsula were similar to their perception of the United States.

In chapter 6 "The British and American Perceptions of Korea during the Colonial Period," Daeyeol Ku deals with how the US and British perceptions of the Korean peninsula were shaped and how this affected their positions on Korea during the Colonial Period. As such this chapter is distinguished from the other contributions to this volume in that it deals with how actual international politics affected the shaping of the major powers' perceptions of colonial Korea and highlights the international and geopolitical importance of Korea (even though Korea was not independent). Ku contends that although the colonized Korea peninsula could not act on its own in international society, it could play a significant role in the political and economic dynamics that occurred in and around the peninsula and as such shape the perceptions of major powers, which, in turn, determined the future of Korea during the last stage of colonial rule.

Ku observed that the perceptions of Great Britain and the United States (and China and the Soviet Union) fluctuated depending upon developments on the peninsula and their implications on these countries' interests in Northeast Asia. For example, in the early years of colonial rule the major powers did not question the legitimacy of Japan's colonization of Korea based on Korea's "uncivilized" and backward status. However, Ku did find that major power officials questioned the level of violence used by the Japanese colonial authorities, but these critiques never reached the level of denying the legitimacy of Japan's colonial rule.

This kind of thinking was quite clearly manifested in the major powers' reactions to the March First movement of 1919. The Korean Independence movement was seen as nothing more than an expression of a "rancorous hatred of the Japanese" occasioned by a "distorted idea of patriotism."[8] While the major powers recognized the mismanagement of Japanese colonial rule and even went so far as to recommend a more autonomous status for colonial Korea, they never explicitly endorsed liberation or independence. Korean elites who had been encouraged by US President Wilson's self-determination had to swallow frustration when they found that this did not apply to the case of Korea. In response to such international environments, many Korean elites leaned toward new ideas, such as communism.

It was only during the beginning of the 1930s, when Japan started expansionist policies, that the major powers began to reevaluate the strategic values of the Korean peninsula. The realization that Japan intended to use the Korean peninsula as a beachhead for Japan's expansion toward Manchuria and beyond led the major powers to take the Korea issue more seriously. However, each power approached Korea from the perspective of its own unique national interests, and as World War II intensified, the major powers began to consider the future of the colonial situation. A combination of continuing the old perception of Korea as being backward and unfit for independence and the need to consider a new world order at the end of the war led to a vague consensus on trusteeship. Issues related to Korea were quite internationalized and did not leave much leverage to the Korean elites and people to have a say in the leadership of the peninsula.

Sergey Kurbanov (chapter 7) and Kezhi Sun (chapter 8) deal with the perceptions of the Soviet Union and China respectively. These countries' perceptions of colonial Korea constitute a different category in that they focused more closely upon the colonial situation in Korea due to historical, geographical, and geo-political reasons and thus provide unusual observations of colonial Korea as compared to those countries outside of Northeast Asia.

Sergey Kurbanov in his chapter, "Russian Perception of Koreans and the Japanese Colonial Regime in Korea during the First Quarter of the Twentieth Century" states that in the case of the Soviet Union, perceptions of colonial Korea fluctuated along with the different stages of colonial rule and domestic changes in the USSR. During the early stage, prior to and around the establishment of the protectorate, the Soviet Union's perceptions of the developing colonial system in Korea were positive. On the one hand, Russians attributed colonization as necessary to solve the problems with Koreans and Korea as a nation; they regarded Koreans as lacking cultural originality and unity in resisting the Japanese colonial effort due to factionalism. On the other hand, they viewed the defeat of Russia in the Russo-Japanese War as opening the gate for Japan's colonization and the successful early modernization of Japan. They also viewed Japan's superior military power as a factor which facilitated the colonization of Korea.

While Russians focused on some of the positive changes taking place in Korean culture under colonial rule, they later began to assess colonial Korea from a more critical geopolitical and ideological angle. This changed due to the end of the Russian civil war in 1923 and the end of military intervention in the Russian revolution prior to 1923. Of immediate issue for the Soviets was the migration of Korean immigrants to the Russian Far East. Russians began to pay increasing attention to the aggravating colonial situation in Korea and the Japanese government's repression and racial discrimination, which turned Korea from the Land of Morning Calm into a land of grave silence. This change caused the Soviets to pay more attention to the increasing revolutionary potential in colonial Korea after the March First Independence movement because it may result in increased Korean migration.

For the Soviets, Koreans in the Russian Far East posed a thorny issue. On the one hand, the Russians held a very positive view of Koreans as hard working, friendly, and persevering unlike the Japanese characterization of the Korean people as being lazy and uncivilized. On the other hand, Koreans in the Far East posed a potential threat to Russia in that the immigration of Koreans would open up space for more Japanese to migrate to Korea and further their development of Manchuria. To combat this, Soviet officials recommended that the Koreans in the border areas be moved to the inner area of Russia, a precursor to Stalin forcing the relocation of Koreans in the 1930s.

Kezhi Sun's analysis in chapter 8 "Chinese Understandings of Colonial Korea in Modern Times, 1910–1945: Observations and Reflections" specifies the dramatic shift in Chinese perceptions of colonial Korea after China's defeat in the Sino-Japanese War. China no longer perceived Korea as a peripheral barbarian nor did it complain about the fact that Korea became Japan's colony or show any trace of its traditional suzerain-vassal relations. Instead, for the first ten years of annexation (1910–20), China's interest mainly lay in appreciating and learning from the changes that occurred under the new policies of the colonial authorities in Korea in the industries of agriculture and education.9 There were, according to Sun, many official Chinese groups who were invited to visit the Korean peninsula by Japanese colonial authorities, so that they could observe the changes in person. It is striking that the visitors were genuinely impressed with the positive changes in colonial Korea even though most of their visits were carefully programmed by colonial authorities. The Chinese viewed the changes in colonial Korea through their comparisons with precolonial Korea and were preoccupied with what the Chinese could learn from the case of Korea with regards to modernization.

However, these positive perceptions of the changes in colonial Korea began to change with the increasing Japanese threat toward China in the 1920s. The Chinese became quite critical of so-called cultural rule after the March First movement, and policies that sought to co-opt Koreans rather than grant any real freedom for the Korean people. One visible change that was unmistakably clear to the Chinese was Japan's discriminatory system of education in Korea. Contrary to their positive view of education earlier, Chinese observers not only pointed out the discrimination against Koreans in education but also deplored the imposition of the Japanese language. They lamented that Korean culture and identity were being lost under colonial rule. This shift in Chinese perceptions of colonial Korea originated mainly from their need to inculcate awareness of Japan's ambition over China.

Finally, Naoko Shimazu's approach in chapter 9 "Publicizing Colonies: Representations of 'Korea' and 'Koreans' in NIPPON" is different from the previous chapters. Following Shimazu's distinction, there are two different angles: the colonial gaze and the cultural gaze. Most of the chapters in this volume analyze Japan's presentation of Korea from the colonial gaze. Korea and the Korean people are depicted as uncivilized and need to be transformed by Japanese colonial rule; colonial rule would turn Korea into a civilized and modern society. The colonial gaze viewed Korean society as stagnant, underdeveloped, corrupt, and hopeless. This is the image of Korea that Japan used to propagate to the outside world as a way to justify and legitimize Japan's colonial rule over Korea.

Contrary to this prevalent view, Shimazu takes a different position. She does not take the colonial gaze for granted or as fixed throughout the entire Colonial Period. In fact, she views the colonial gaze as evolving and contingent depending on the international, regional, and national contexts. By extension she raises a question as to the consistency in Japan's colonial intention of assimilation. Her interpretation is based on her analysis of the July 1939 special issue of NIPPON, which focused extensively on Korean culture. The magazine was established in 1934 to promote Japanese culture to the outside world. Shimazu views this special issue as a venue to analyze the true intention of Japanese authorities as to why they decided to cover Korean culture in a magazine, which until this point had been committed to promoting Japanese culture.

According to Shimazu, the special issue approached Korean culture through color, clothing, artifacts, and women. NIPPON introduced Korea as a country of two thousand years of history with a distinct penchant for pure colors like white and blue, its own artifacts—pottery—and people who maintained a traditional way of life without much exposure to complex modern society. Shimazu observed that although there was a section in the special issue on the changes that Japanese colonial rule brought to Korea, overall the photographs in this illustrated magazine primarily spotlighted unique Korean tradition and culture, which was quite different from that of Japan. In fact, Shimazu argues that NIPPON's approach to Korean culture was not that different from when it discussed Japanese culture. There was not much binary juxtaposition between Japan and Korea; nor much contrast between the Japanese and Korean peoples. Most significantly Shimazu was impressed with the coverage where virtually no mention was made of *naisen ittai* (assimilation). On the contrary, the issue exposed the differences between the Korean and Japanese cultures. According to Shimazu what is distinctive about the special issue is not its taking the colonial gaze, but rather its being orientalist in its focus on the essentialist and feminist aspects of Korean culture and the implicit juxtaposition between the East and the West.

Shimazu ponders why the magazine took such a purely cultural approach. The fact that the cultural approach was taken is even more striking when the regional and international situations and the general principles of Japanese overseas propaganda present in late 1930s were considered. The regional and international situations were quite tense after the breakout of the Sino-Japanese War. Also, Japanese international propaganda aimed to promote the image of Japan as being equal to the West, while at the same time it attempted to upgrade "uncivilized" colonies into "civilized" ones. Thus, Shimazu concluded that "wartime propaganda needs were not met by the existing structures of cultural propaganda."[10] The case Shimazu analyzed is limited in generalization but raises interesting questions as to whether and to what extent Japan had a consistent strategy on how to present colonies globally, and how Japan would be perceived by the outside world.

Taken as a whole, these essays show the broad influence of Japanese colonialism not simply on the Korean peninsula, but also Japanese colonialism in Korea affected how the world understood Japan, and how Japan understood itself. When initially incorporated into the Japanese Empire Korea seemed lost to Japan's imperial designs, yet Korean resistance to Japanese colonial rule, and fears of Japanese expansion later, led the world to rethink the importance of Korea as a future sovereign nation. The tragedy of a post–World War II Korea that was divided into mutually antagonistic states is prefigured in these essays about the competing colonial discourses within Korea, and about Korea, that lived past the Colonial Period itself to continue to affect Korean development and the international order in Northeast Asia.

NOTES

1. See, for example, Carter J. Eckert, *Offspring of Empire*; Gi-Wook Shin and Michael Robinson, eds., *Colonial Modernity in Korea*, Introduction and chapter 3; Sin Yongha, "Singminji kŭndaehwaron chejŏngnip sidae e taehan pip'an" [A critique of the reformulation to reinterpret colonial modernity]; and An Pyŏngjik, "Han'guk kŭnhyŏndaesa yon'gu ŭi saeroun p'aerŏdim" [New research paradigm for Korean modern history].

2. Ramon Hawley Myers, Mark R. Peattie, and Jingzhi Zhen, *The Japanese Colonial Empire, 1895–1945*; and Peter Duus, *The Abacus and the Sword*.

3. Here I highlight the point that not much has been done on the international impact of colonial rule. An exception to this is Ku Taeyŏl [Ku, Daeyeol; Ku, Dae-Yeol], *Han'guk kŭnhyŏndaesa yŏn'gu* [A study of history of Korean international relations].

4. Hakjoon Kim, "A Devil Appears in a Different Dress," this volume, 42.

5. Mimana is called in Imna in Korean is an alleged colony that Japan established in the Imna kingdom in the latter part of the fourth century.

6. Hakjoon Kim, "A Devil Appears in a Different Dress," this volume, 33.

7. Andre Schmid, "Japanese Propaganda in the United States from 1905," this volume, 73–104.

8. Daeyeol Ku, "The British and American Perceptions of Korea during the Colonial Period," this volume, 187.

9. Kezhi Sun, "Chinese Understandings of the Colonial Korea in the Modern Times, 1910–1945: Observations and Reflections," this volume, 239–258.

10. Naoko Shimazu, "Publicizing Colonies: Representations of 'Korea' and 'Koreans' in *NIPPON*," this volume, 281.

PART I

Colonial Policies for Forging Korea's Image

1

A Devil Appears in a Different Dress: Imperial Japan's Deceptive Propaganda and Rationalization for Making Korea Its Colony

HAKJOON KIM

In order to colonize Korea, commonly referred to as the Yi or Chosŏn Dynasty, imperial Japan resorted to various methods and techniques. These included supporting as well as fostering pro-Japanese Koreans, encouraging the eradication of anti-Japanese Koreans, promising diplomacy between the major powers and Korea, waging war—first against China and then Russia—demonstrating military strength, intervening in Korea's domestic affairs, providing loans—which would make Korea Japan's permanent debtor—and finally buying off and physically threatening Korean bureaucrats. Over several decades many scholars have published work on these methods.[1]

However, from this author's perspective, one method—not mentioned in the above list—was rarely or casually studied. That would be imperial Japan's propaganda, which mobilized psychological warfare techniques and symbolism in an effort to change the international community's thoughts and ideas toward Korea. As one shall see in the following pages of this chapter, Japan's propaganda's basic contents were three-fold: (1) in light of Korea's internal and external conditions, it would be inevitable that Korea would need to receive Japan's protection and control; (2) Japan's protection of Korea in the form of its annexation would be beneficial not only to the Far East but also to Korea; and (3) Korea's participation in an "annexed (or federated) great East" with Japan as its master would be advantageous not only for peace in the Far East but also to the preservation of the Korean nation. Unfortunately, most Western countries and even some Korean leaders swallowed this rhetoric, thereby helping Japan realize its objective. This chapter attempts to examine this important but not as yet systematically studied aspect of imperial

Japan's political propaganda techniques which resulted in Korea becoming Japan's protectorate in November 1905 and ultimately a Japanese colony in August 1910.

JAPAN'S TWIN LOGIC: THE MISSION TO CIVILIZE THE UNCIVILIZED AND TO PROTECT ASIAN NEIGHBORS FROM WESTERN POWERS

The Mission to Civilize the Uncivilized

With the inauguration of the Meiji Restoration regime in March 1868, Japan actively mimicked Western civilization and transformed its political, administrative, and legal systems into Western styles. Boosted by such a seemingly successful transformation, most Japanese intellectuals regarded their country as a civilized nation, while simultaneously referring to other Asian neighbors as half-civilized nations or uncivilized or barbarian nations. With this sense of superiority, Japanese authorities advocated its mission "to civilize Japan's Asian neighbors."[2] One of these officials was well-known Fukujawa Yukichi, who was considered Japan's Voltaire, and who founded today's Keio University in Tokyo.[3]

At this time Japan resembled that of a Western imperialist power—British or American powers for example—which had rationalized their aggression and exploitation of Afro-Asian countries as being a duty and part of the white man's burden. Needless to say, to Western powers and Japan, the noble phrase "to civilize" was a euphemism of the rude phrase "to colonize." Given this background then, how did Japan view Korea? On one hand the Japanese regarded Korea as an uncivilized or barbaric nation, while on the other hand many Japanese regarded Korea to be a half-civilized nation. Irrespective of such a difference, Japanese officials agreed that Japan should make Korea its protectorate or colony. Fukujawa was an exception. Although he regarded Korea to be an uncivilized or half-civilized nation, one that should be civilized by Japan, he wrote in 1869 and 1875 that "Japan's aggression toward Korea at this time would be harmful to Japan." His alternative was his own version of the conventional Asian solidarity thesis, which had been circulated among the Meiji leaders, and read in part that "solidarity among Japan, China, and Korea, for the prevention of the forced civilization or aggression of the Far

East by the Western imperialist nations," was necessary.⁴ This thesis was favorably received by intellectuals from each of the three nations. Chinese, Korean, and Japanese scholars understood that this idea presupposed the independence and equality of the three nations. However, as one shall see later, Fukujawa would come to change his views with regard to the direction of Japan's aggression toward China and Korea.

As for methods to civilize or colonize Korea, two different groups emerged in a broad sense. Hardliners proposed a war against Korea as manifested in the Seikanron debate (the thesis of conquering Korea), which reached its climax in 1870–73. Their ambition went beyond Korea. They proposed that after the conquest of Korea, Japan should also integrate other East Asian nations into Japan, but Japanese scholars who were well-versed in the industrial and military strength of major Western powers through their studies abroad, including Yamagata Aritomo and Itō Hirobumi, opposed it. The two, who would each become prime minister of Japan in the 1880s and 1890s respectively, argued that a Japanese invasion of Korea would arouse wide suspicion from the Western powers in general and invite Russian intervention in particular. Yamagata and Itō offered an alternative suggesting that Japan should foster its national strength first, adopt a gradualist approach, and wait for the appropriate time to colonize Korea. Kido Koin (J. Kido Takayosi), Emperor Meiji's mentor, added, "[l]et us postpone matters for now. We can decide later what to do about Korea. It will not be too late to act when we are properly prepared."⁵ Concerned by the gradualist group, hardliners initiated an insurrection with Saigo Takamori as their leader in 1877, but the short-lived insurrection ended with Saigo's suicide.⁶

The first step of the gradualist approach was to open Korea, a country which had maintained its external policy of isolation or seclusion. Another step toward the opening of Korea included severing Korea's subordinate ties with Qing China. The Japanese leaders thought that as long as Korea remained China's vassal state, a state that refused the establishment of diplomatic relations with all other countries in general and Japan in particular, Japan had no room to advance into the peninsula. With that in mind, Japan resorted to gunboat diplomacy and forced Korea to sign the Japan-Korea Treaty of 1876 (also referred to as the Treaty of Amity or the Treaty of Ganghwa Island) on February 26, 1876. This treaty was the first treaty signed by Korea with a foreign country. Soon after the signing of the treaty Japan opened a legation in Seoul and consulates in major port cities. Under Japanese influence, the Korean court inaugurated a special Japanese-style technical military unit within the existing traditional Korean army.

More important was that the treaty included the clause "an independent state."[7] This meant that Korea was no longer China's dependent state, and Korea should and could develop relations with Japan on its own initiative. Japan began to widely propagate that clause to the international community in its effort to exclude Chinese influence over Korea, while coinciding with the advancement of Japanese influence over Korea. Around the same time, Japanese intellectuals added their stagnated Korea theory to the existing idea of a half-civilized or uncivilized Korea. Fukujawa led this theory. In 1877, he wrote that "Korea has not reformed its old customs since the war between Korea and Japan [initiated with Toyotomi Hideyoshi's invasion of Korea in 1592]. It remains in this stagnated situation without either retrogression or progress."[8] In sum, stagnated Korea was the equivalent to an uncivilized or half-civilized Korea. Fukujawa's stagnated Korea theory would be echoed in Western scholarship, thereby causing some Western leaders to accept, either explicitly or implicitly, the Japanese propaganda that proposed that Korea should accept Japanese "guidance" and even "protection" for its enlightenment and development.[9]

The Mission to "Protect" Asian Neighbors from Western Powers

In 1881, Fukujawa advanced another theory, one that declared that Japan should "protect" Asian nations from Western imperialist powers' common objective to colonize the East. To "protect" its Asian neighbors, Fukujawa argued that Japan may find it necessary to occupy them militarily and to threaten them into adopting reform and progress policies. To illustrate his point, he used a metaphor. Comparing Japan to a stone house and its Asian neighbors to that of wooden houses, he argued that the wooden houses would be vulnerable to the fire ignited by the Western imperialist powers and that the flames may rapidly spread to Japan. In order to check the spread of that fire to Japan, he asserted, it is in Japan and other East Asian countries' best interest for Japan to destroy the wooden houses and reconstruct them into the stone houses.[10] It was clear that his proposition of solidarity among Japan, China, and Korea had been articulated into the notion that Japan may occupy China and Korea for the purpose of the security of Japan. In other words, his theory revealed Japan's imperialistic and aggressive character. In 1889 and 1890, Japanese Prime Minister Yamagata Aritomo declared that to guarantee Japan's national security and prosperity, Japan must safeguard not only its line of sovereignty (i.e., Japan) but also its line of interest (i.e., Korea).[11] One may conclude that Fukujawa's theory of protecting Japan from a fire ignited in Korea developed into Yamagata's theory of safeguarding Japan's interest in Korea.

Within the civilizing the uncivilized theory, the new thesis that proposed protecting Asian nations formed a pair of the twin reasoning to rationalize Japan's aggression. As one shall see later, imperial Japan would extensively propagate these theories to the international community, and many Western intellectuals would later echo it.

THE KOREAN RESPONSE

How did Koreans respond to Japanese reasoning and the signing of the Japan-Korea Treaty of 1876? First of all, the traditional Confucian scholars— who maintained the idea that while China is the center of world civilization, Korea is little China, and Japan belonged to the barbaric nations— rejected the Japanese logic described above and opposed the treaty. Yi Hangno, Kim P'yŏngmuk, and Ch'oe Ikhyŏn represented this view, giving birth to the Wijŏngch'ŏksap'a a conservative group with a mission that intended to "defend righteousness and reject evil."[12] To them Western countries were "animals without basic human morals and ethics," and Japan had become an animal through its reception of the Western value system.[13] In 1881, about 10,000 Confucian scholars presented their joint memorial to King Kojong the contents of which urged the king to take a strong anti-Japanese and anti-Western stance.

In contrast, some young Korean intellectuals—who had read Western books, which had been translated with strong skepticism regarding the existing political order in Korea over which Qing China claims suzerain rights by progressive Chinese scholars—accepted Japanese reasoning and the treaty. Some of these young scholars welcomed the clause in the treaty that declared Korea an independent state in particular. In short, they assumed that Japan was helping Korea to become independent from China.[14]

The number of Korean intellectuals who agreed with the treaty's language increased when opportunities to travel to Japan became more available. After having arrived in Japan, they were impressed by the use of electricity, the printing machine and typography, the telephone and the telegram, and the public waterways, railroads, and modern road construction. In 1880, during his trip to Japan, Yi Tongin, a Buddhist monk, introduced himself to his Japanese counterparts as "a barbarian from Korea," arguing that uncivilized Korea should emulate Japan as early as possible.[15] In 1881, Yu Kiljun, who studied Fukujawa's theories at Keio, repeated his mentor's research of the division of nations into civilized, half-civilized, and uncivilized ones. Yu's analysis determined that most of Japan's laws and systems resembled that of civilized Western countries, and that Korea had better study the path Japan had walked.[16] In 1882, after his first-hand observation of Japan, Kim Okkyun concluded that Korea should emulate Japan as the model for its enlightenment.[17] It appears that these scholars did not read Fukujawa's theory of the spread of a fire. For if they had they might have not disregarded Japan's seriousness. Without a deep understanding of Japan's imperialistic character, these Korean scholars admired the enlightenment or "civilization" of Japan. In response they formed an unofficial "progressive group or party oriented toward [Japanese style] enlightenment or civilization" with Kim Okkyun and Pak Yŏnghyo as their de facto leaders.[18]

There was a third group of Koreans, a group which represented an indigenous religious tenor. Since 1860, some outcast local intellectuals led by Ch'oe Chewu preached the revolutionary message that irrespective of social class, status, sex, age, religion, and region, all Koreans were equal under Heaven. Terming their teaching Tonghak (Eastern learning) opposed to Sŏhak (Western learning), these religious leaders exhibited a strong and nationalistic and anti-foreign inclination. When many commoners and farmers, who had been critical of the existing social systems and ruling class per se, had received this new teaching and acted fervently; the Korean government executed Ch'oe Chewu first and his successor Ch'oe Sihyŏng later. Regardless of the government involvement the number of believers increased steadily.[19]

Even though these three different groups exchanged verbal attacks with each other, in July 1882 a significant number of troops belonging to the traditional Korean army staged a mutiny and began protesting against their miserable working conditions and the newly inaugurated special Japanese technical military unit. In one incident, they stormed the palace and killed some of the high-ranking bureaucrats, thereby threatening the pro-Chinese Korean government itself. In another, they destroyed the Japanese legation in Seoul. The Chinese troops, through its superior military strength, quickly quelled the mutiny and solidified the pro-Chinese Korean government. Fukujawa responded quickly. He urged Japanese officials to send a high-ranking "special inspector" to live with the troops in Korea to "supervise" Korea's domestic affairs.[20] The theory of "supervising" Korea through a Japanese "special inspector" was later translated into action in 1905, when imperial Japan made Korea its protectorate under its resident-general.

JAPAN'S PROMOTION OF THE HERMIT NATION AND RUSSOPHOBIA

Observing a sharp increase in Korean-Japanese contacts since the conclusion of the Japan-Korea Treaty of 1876, China attempted to counter Japanese influence in Korea by widening Korea's external contacts. China advised Korea to sign treaties with Western powers. Through China, Korea concluded the Treaty of Peace, Amity, Commerce, and Navigation (also known as the Shufeldt Treaty) in May 1882. Other Western nations followed suit. By 1886, Korea had signed treaties with Great Britain, Italy, Russia, Germany, and France.

Five months after the conclusion of the Korea–United States Treaty of 1882, William E. Griffis, an American Christian missionary, published *Corea: The Hermit Nation*. Around this time, Korea was unknown to most Americans. When the author raised the question to his American friends as to whether they had ever heard of Korea, one responded that the word meant a "seashell," and another asked "what is Korea?" With the establishment of diplomatic relations with Korea, some US citizens came to have an interest in the country. In response to this new trend, Griffis decided to introduce Korea to the US society.

In order to understand the basic character of this bulky book, one should first consider the author's view on Japan. Since his arrival in Japan in 1870 from the United States, Griffis came to admire Japan's severance of its traditional isolationism and its reception of Western belief systems as well as political institutions. As a firm believer in modernism, Griffis greatly appreciated the modernization or Westernization of Japan. From this vantage point, he regarded any country refusing or slow to adopt Western civilization to be that of a "hermit nation." It is interesting to note however, that Griffis never visited Korea.

Griffis' book proved so popular that by 1911 nine editions had been printed. Griffis himself recognized its popularity. In the preface to the eighth edition (1907), he proudly wrote that for more than two decades his book had enjoyed popular favor and had been used by writers and students in Europe and the United States. Christian missionaries, medical doctors, diplomats, journalists, and even casual travelers read his book before their departure to Korea for a basic understanding of this unknown country. In essence this meant that his book exercised a great deal of influence over many Western intellectuals and their formation of Korea's image.

First of all, *Corea: The Hermit Nation* left the decisive impression on most Westerners that Korea had been a hermit nation for a long time. This impression led to the conclusion that due to Korea's lack of interactions with the West, Korea had failed in its reform and modernization. This supposition was boosted by the author's detailed description of ordinary Korean people and their laziness as well as the Korean court's corruption and misrule. Later some Japanese, as well as Western intellectuals, would argue that Korea's failure to reform and modernize would be the main cause of its loss of sovereignty to imperial Japan. In other words, many would attribute the responsibility of Korea's subjugation to Japan not to Japanese aggression toward Korea but to the Korean failure to modernize due to its "isolationism."[22]

Second, the text stressed that Korea's geopolitical location, that of being surrounded by two fatal rivals: China and Japan, had made Korea an inevitable victim. In stressing Korea's geopolitical location, Griffis went one step further arguing that Korea had, since its inception, always submitted to either China (Han Chinese, Mongols, Manchus) or to Japan to secure its survival.[23] This argument implied that Korea had never been an independent country. Japanese intellectuals used this argument to rationalize Japan's colonization of Korea. Since Korea had never been independent, they wrote, it was not strange to view Korea as a colony of Japan.[24]

Third, *Corea: The Hermit Nation* propagated some Japanese historians' allegations that for about five centuries, since 202 AD, Korea had been "a tributary and dependency [sic] of Japan," and since 369 AD Japan had established the "colony" Mimana (K. Imna) in some of the regions belonging to the southern part of Korea.[25] In addition, Griffis introduced some Japanese historians' allegations that Japan had possessed the port of Pusan in southeastern Korea from the seventeenth century through the conclusion of the Japan-Korea Treaty of 1876. The above-mentioned Japanese scholars' allegations were wholly untrue. Historians of both North and South Korea have commonly asserted that the allegations had been based on distorted and even fabricated records.[26] A significant number of Japanese historians have refused to accept these allegations.[27] In the meantime, the imperial Japanese government used the allegations in its propaganda to rationalize the Japanese colonization of Korea. In short, Japanese propaganda of the time promoted Japanese colonization of Korea by stating that this relationship would not be unnatural in light of the historical fact that Korea had already been a Japanese colony for a long time.[28]

Fourth, Griffis disseminated Russophobia in earnest. Describing imperial Russia as a greedy and rapacious country, the text stressed that since the mid-nineteenth century Russia had continuously expanded its territory into East Asia with the aim of cultivating and preserving its national interest in this region, including Korea. If a war were to occur between Russia and China, Russia predicted it would occupy Korea as a military operations base, and the book concluded that the "possession" of the Korean peninsula would mean the ultimate realization of the "absorption policy," a policy which had been pursued by imperial Russia since Peter the Great (r. 1721–25).[29]

Russophobia had already been introduced to Koreans by 1880 at the latest. When the Korean official delegation visited Tokyo that year, the Chinese legation in Tokyo gave them a book on the direction of Korea's diplomacy. This book, *Ch'aoxian ceLué* (Korean policy), authored by Hwang Zunxian, a Chinese diplomat, pointed out with alarm Russia's advance southward. To curb Russian incursions into Korea, the author recommended a close alignment between Korea and the United States as well as a friendly relationship between Korea and China.[30] Griffis' book having been published in 1882, might have strengthened existing Russophobia. In 1883 and 1885, Yu Kiljun repeated his warning on Russia's "outrageous, atrocious, and greedy" character and its "dark ambition" over Korea.[31]

An incident occurred around this time, which stirred up Russophobia among Koreans. In April 1885, Great Britain occupied Kŏmundo, an island in Korea's southeastern sea which the British navy named Port Hamilton, blaming Russia's advance into the Far East. In order to ensure that the Russians did not advance, the British government alleged, its navy had to occupy the island in advance. Japan fully supported the British stance and began promoting Russophobia. A good number of serious studies have proven that the British and the Japanese allegations were groundless.[32] However, this incident as explained by the British and Japanese governments, contributed to the solidification of exciting Russophobia among Koreans. Japan would use Russophobia to induce many Korean political leaders and intellectuals to believe that they must prevent Russia from entering. After the defeat of China, a long time "protector" of Korea in its war against Japan in 1894–95, this belief would become one pillar of the theoretical basis that Korea had no choice but to accept Japanese "protection."

In sum, Griffis's book was useful and convenient for the imperial Japanese government and helped officials to cultivate and promote their theory which rationalized their aggression and colonization of Korea. A good number of Japanese intellectuals published books on Korea in 1895 and 1901, using Griffis' book as a major source. One book, *Chōsen kaikano kigen* (The origin of Korean civilization [1895]), said in its preface that Griffis' book "contains precious stories we have never heard before."[33] After Japan forced Korea to become its protectorate, Griffis would revise his book and aggressively and publicly praise the Japanese decision while putting the majority of the blame on the Korean court's misrule and corruption.

THE JAPANESE ATTEMPTS TO SEPARATE THE KOREAN GOVERNMENT FROM ITS PEOPLE

While the Japanese leaders clearly showed their imperialistic and aggressive stance on Korea, the progressive Korean leaders did not give up their expectation that Korea could modernize itself through Japanese cooperation and assistance. The Korean leaders might have embraced such an expectation partly due to Fukujawa's recommendation that the Japanese government help the Korean progressive leaders take political power from the pro-Chinese forces and suggested that the Japanese could even use their military strength to accomplish this objective.[34] In December, 1884, the progressive Korean leaders staged a coup d'état under the auspices of the Japanese legation in

Seoul, but the Chinese military forces in Seoul were stronger than the Japanese forces, and the Chinese effectively suppressed the pro-Japanese/anti-Chinese rebellion. Accordingly, the coup failed within three days.

Most of the prime movers in the coup d'état took refuge in Japan. Kim Okkyun and his comrades met Fukujawa Yukichi to discuss the future of Korea and their pro-Japanese activities. They found that Fukujawa had become vehemently angry with the failure of the coup and with the subsequent executions of those who were involved in the coup. Defining Korea as "a savage country which fell backward day by day," he concluded that, "until this country liberates itself from the Chinese yoke and enters into the road of civilization, I cannot feel affection for its people."[35] One should pay special attention to the phrase, "Korea's liberation from the Chinese yoke." As we shall see later, the imperial Japanese government would use this phrase to legitimatize Japan's war against China in 1894–95.

Soon after Fukujawa published a famous article, "Dass-a-ron" (On escaping from Asia [or, On leaving Asia behind]). In this essay, he stressed that Japan should give up the idea of leading other Asian neighbors as their master. His alternative was to deal with them by utilizing "the Western imperialistic methods including the mobilization of military might."[36] With this essay as the new starting point, Fukujawa advanced a good number of ideas on the Korean question. His ideas included proposals that Japan station its troops in Korea, and that Japan induce the collapse of the Korean government for the Korean peoples' safety and welfare.[37] One may take note that he attempted to separate the Korean people from their government. According to him, although most Korean people were living in extreme poverty and suffering from harsh exploitation by corrupt bureaucrats, the incompetent Korean court was merely engaged in the intrigue over political power and disregarded their peoples' miserable living conditions. Under such circumstances, he argued, the fall of the Korean government would be desirable and a benefit to most of the Korean people. The Japanese leaders would repeatedly stress that Japan should "guide and protect" Korea to guarantee the Korean peoples' safety and welfare from their own "inefficient and unjust government, which squeezes its people." Fukujawa died in 1901, nine years before the Japanese annexation of Korea. However even after the annexation, the imperial Japanese government would cite his work as an important theme in its propaganda.[38]

THE JAPANESE PROMOTION OF SOCIAL DARWINISM

At the time when Fukujawa Yukichi openly advocated his thesis to induce the fall of the Korean government, Japan had introduced the theory of Social Darwinism to Korea. At the risk of simplification, one may argue that Social Darwinism represents the principle of "the strong eat the weak." Since the Meiji Restoration, most Japanese intellectuals agonized over the question of how Japan could guarantee its survival in an increasingly competitive world. They found an answer in Social Darwinism, a theory which had been introduced to Japan from the West in the early 1870s. They reasoned on one hand that in order to catch up with the Western countries and to not be "eaten" by them, Japan needed to foster its national strength. On the other hand, they thought that for Japan to win in a strong eat the weak world, it was legitimate for Japan to conquer and exploit its weaker Asian neighbors in general and Korea in particular.[39] With this in mind, Social Darwinism, which to some advocated and justified the strong and its exploitation of and aggression toward the weak, in theory was a weapon Japan could use to "encourage" Koreans to tolerate Japan's governance of Korea. In this sense, it was natural for Japan to introduce and promote Social Darwinism to Korea.

The first person to introduce Social Darwinism to a Korean appears to have been Nakada Takeo, a diplomat at the Japanese legation in Seoul. In his letter to Yi Hŏnyŏng, a Korean bureaucrat who visited Japan in 1881, he wrote that "the present world is the world of force and the world of the strong eat the weak." He elaborated that it was natural for the country with the strong army to conquer the country with the poor army, adding that "the present world is not the world of humanity and justice but the world of might."[40]

Yu Kiljun, Fukujawa's Korean disciple at Keio University, writes of Japanese influence over Korean leaders in his work *Kyŏngjaeng-ron* (On competition) published in 1883. He attributed the main cause of the Korean kingdom's decay to the lack of competition with other foreign countries and Korea's past "isolationism."[41] He recommended that Korea receive Western ideas and systems in earnest. However, he stressed that the Korean reception of Western civilization should not be a Xerox copy of it, but instead that Korea should select aspects of Western civilization based upon human ethics and spirit. Later he would publish a good number of books in order to enlighten his compatriots. Although he did not approve the Japanese annexation of his country, he never participated in the resistance movement or any sort of aggression against Japanese colonial rule.[42]

Yun Ch'iho represented another case of a Korean who was influenced by the theory of Social Darwinism. He had once been a progressive Korean leader who espoused his patriotic spirit and strategy to remake Korea as an independent country. However, after accepting Social Darwinism through his studies in Japan and the United States in the 1880s, he became a pro-Japanese compatriot. In 1892, he wrote in his diary that "'[m]ight is right' in international or interracial dealings? So I have always thought. . . . We find the stronger has been almost always better or less corrupted in morals, religions and politics than the weaker."[43] One year later, he came to praise Japan more ardently. He wrote that "[i]f I had means to choose my home at my pleasure, Japan would be the country." The reason was that Japan was "the Paradise of the East, the Garden of the World!" while China was a country of "its abominable smells," the United States was a country of "racial prejudice and discrimination," and Korea was under its long-lasting "infernal government."[44] It would not be surprising that Yun ultimately became a whole-hearted supporter of Japan's annexation of Korea. His case clearly shows the effect of Social Darwinism upon Koreans.

Pak Ŭnsik and Sin Ch'aeho represented the opposite case. In the 1890s, they accepted Social Darwinism as a universal theory of the present world and recognized the necessity of educating the Korean masses and promoting industry in a traditionally agricultural society. However, they could not approve Japan's colonization of their country. Ultimately they exiled themselves to China and fought against Japan for Korea's independence.[45]

On balance, Social Darwinism contributed only partly to the weakening of the spirit and powers of the Korean resistance against Japan. That is why, after the Japanese annexation of Korea, the Japanese propagated the Social Darwinism theory emphasizing that Koreans had better foster their own individual strengths in order to survive in the long run rather than engage in the anti-Japanese independence movement.

THE JAPANESE DISSEMINATION OF THE ANNEXED (FEDERATED) GREAT EAST THEORY

In 1893, a Japanese intellectual invented a new theory, which would later become one of Japan's theoretical weapons used to justify Japan's annexation of Korea. Since this theory titled the "Annexed (Federated) Great East Theory" significantly influenced not only Korean intellectuals but also Chinese intellectuals, one should begin with an examination of its representative theoretician, Tarui Tokich'i.

Tarui Tokich'i had supported conquering Korea and admired Saigo Takamori. After Saigo's insurrection failed, Tarui visited Korea and China a couple of times to study the various methods Japan could implement to conquer Korea and to advance into China via Manchuria. During this process, he met Kim Okkyun, a Korean political refugee in Tokyo and Toyama Mitsuru, a leader of Japanese "wandering activists in the [Chinese] continent" seeking Japan's mastery over China in Shanghai. In 1885, Tarui Tokich'i finished the first draft of his ambitious book, *Daito gappo ron* (Thesis on the union of the great East) in Japanese. However, when he ultimately published it in 1893, he published it in Chinese in the hope that his book might be more easily read by both the Chinese and the Koreans.

Tarui Tokich'i started with his premise that the Western imperialist powers and Russia were marching into Asia to colonize it. (Note that Russophobia emerged again at this time). In order to curb the Western powers, he proposed that all of Asia unite and integrate as one state with Japan as its master. He went on to suggest the following three stages of integration: (1) the annexation of Korea by Japan as equal partners of the "Great East State"; (2) the establishment of a close alliance between the Great East State and China; and (3) the realization of the "Great Asian Federation" among the Great East State, China, and all other southeastern nations. Although he suggested the three stages, he focused on the first stage. In other words, his main concern was Japan's annexation of Korea.

In his analysis of Korea's internal and external situation, pessimism prevailed. He portrayed Korea as a country, which fell into corruption, disorder, stagnation, and impoverishment internally and lost its autonomy and independence externally. Could Korea depend upon either China or Russia for its survival? He warned that China had already lost its ability to protect Korea and that Russia would make Korea the "Poland of Asia." Under such situations, he stressed, the only option left to the decaying Korean state was its annexation to Japan. According to Tarui, Korea and Japan were "brothers in ethnic terms," and Korea would reestablish its independence and gain the benefit of civilization when Korea received the "protection and guidance" from its fully civilized brother.[46]

Tarui admitted the existence of anti-Japanese sentiment among Koreans due to Toyotomi Hideyoshi's invasion of Korea in 1592. However, he argued that the relationship between Korea and Japan was inseparable because they belonged to "one family" and termed his argument "the thesis of the inseparability of Japan and Korea. . . . The relationship of the two countries may be compared to the relationship of the teeth and the lips, and the relationship of the right wheel and the left wheel in the same carriage. As such, the two countries are brothers and friends."[47]

Although he used all sorts of flowery words to persuade Koreans to accept his thesis, he revealed his real intent with the firm statement that Japan would be able to advance into China, Russia, and the Asian continent through the Korean peninsula after the annexation of Korea into Japan.

This logic was the exact replica of the logic advocators of "the thesis of conquering Korea" had developed. To Tarui, the Korean peninsula was the stepping-stone for Japan to advance into the continent, and his "thesis of an annexed (federated) great East" was the theoretical packaging to justify it. In fact, imperial Japan would take the course suggested in his book. Despite such poisonous elements, some Koreans welcomed it.

Yi Yongku was a representative case. Once a high-ranking cadre of the Tonghak, he became one of the core organizers of the pro-Japanese party, Ilchinhoe (Association for progress), which advocated for the annexation of Korea into Japan.[48] When Japan annexed Korea, it cited, as evidence indicating the Korean peoples' voluntary consent, the "petition" submitted by Ilchinhoe members asking for the Japanese annexation of Korea. Outraged, Son Pyŏnghi, the leader of the Tonghak, expelled Yi and renamed Tonghak to that of Cheondoism (Religion of the heavenly way).

More serious than the whole-hearted support of Ilchinhoe members was the favorable response of the Korean court, including Emperor Kwangmuje (the title given to King Kojong after he declared Chosŏn to be the Korean Empire in 1897). When former Japanese Prime Minister Itō Hirobumi, in the capacity of Japan's "elder," met Korea's emperor and cardinal bureaucrats in Seoul in 1898, he explained his plan of "a close alliance among Japan, Korea, and China" or "a union or federation of the Far East." It was the exactly same version of Tarui's "Great Asian Federation."[49] Emperor Kwangmuje and his senior bureaucrats paid serious attention to this proposal under the premise that it would guarantee Korea's national security from the aggression of the Western imperialist powers. However, others rightly suspected the real intention of Japan and suggested that instead annexation would neutralize Korea. As a result, they could not come to an agreement.[50]

JAPANESE RATIONALIZATION FOR ITS WAR AGAINST CHINA

In February 1894, under the leadership of Chŏn Pongjun, the Tonghak believers rose against the corrupt Korean bureaucrats in the southwestern region. Soon this conflict expanded into a semi-nationwide revolt. When the Korean court in Seoul invited Chinese military intervention to suppress it, the Japanese government responded by sending its troops to Korea. In July 1894, with the Japanese attack of the Chinese troops, the First Sino-Japanese War (August 1, 1894–April 17, 1895) broke out on Korean soil.

Japanese government officials developed theories which rationalized their engagement in the war. First, they attributed the responsibility for the war to China. "Although Japan attempted to solve the Korean question in an honorable way," a US adviser to the Japanese Foreign Ministry and its de facto spokesman Durham White Stevens alleged, "China opposed it, making Japan be dragged [sic] in the war." Moreover, he stressed that Japan's quest for annexation was neither full of dark ambition nor was it a dirty scheme. Instead Stevens posited that it was Japan's bonafide will to help Koreans reform and modernize their country.[51] Inoue Kakukoro, a Japanese adviser to the Korean court's publication department, repeated Stevens. He stated that despite the Japanese government's patience to preserve the "Oriental peace" (peace in the Far East), China provoked the war.[52] One should take note of the phrase, "Oriental peace." The Japanese government and intellectuals used this phrase frequently to explain Japan's foreign policy aims in Korea and China, thereby encouraging some Koreans to embrace the illusion that Korea's cooperation with Japan would contribute to the realization of Oriental peace.

Second, the Japanese government repeatedly claimed that Japan's aim was to liberate Korea from the Chinese yoke. In order to support its own claim, the Japanese government cited the clause included in the Japan-Korea Treaty of 1876, which declared Korea to be an "independent state." Despite this clause, Japanese officials elaborated that China treated Korea harshly as its subject state, thereby violating international law.[53] Trumbull White, a US journalist reporting on the Japanese government, wrote that due to China's opposition to Japan's "sincere" program to make Korea an independent state and "a civilized and enlightened country," the war was inevitable.[54] E. H. Parker, a British diplomat, expressed the same view. He wrote that Japan liberated Korea from Chinese suzerainty through the Japan-Korea Treaty of 1876 first and the First Sino-Japanese War later.[55] William E. Griffis also defended the Japanese government. He wrote that the Japanese victory in the First Sino-Japanese War of 1894–95 provided an opportunity for Korea to make itself an independent country and to modernize and begin reforming all of its political and social systems.[56]

Third, the Japanese government described the First Sino-Japanese War as the war between the civilized and the savage. Japan's other de facto spokesman, Kumpei Matumoto, wrote that Japan, representing the civilized world, attempted to civilize Korea from the bondage of China, which represented the savage world. However, Stevens mistakenly revealed the genuine objective of the Japanese government. Terming Korea a "natural bulwark," he frankly admitted that in order to prevent Korea from being seized by China, Japan had been forced to engage in this war.[57] His logic echoed Yamagata's "safeguarding Japan's interest line."[58]

Fourth, the Japanese government propagated that Japan had taught the art of forestry and agriculture to the Korean people to the Western correspondents reporting on the war from the Korean peninsula. Georges Ferdinand Bigot of *Le Monde illustré* (The illustrated world) wrote on August 30, 1894 that "in Pusan, there is a stretch of forested area with fairly tall pine trees which, I was told, had first been planted by the Japanese when they invaded the peninsula 210 years ago."[59] In the same vein, Griffis wrote that Japan had taught the art of rice culture to Korea in the sixteenth century.[60] These statements were never verified. However, the Japanese government would repeat these same messages in the years after Japanese annexation, implying that the present Japanese colonial administration was following in the footsteps of history.[61]

In the meantime, the Japanese legation in Seoul, with the full support of the victorious Japanese troops in Korea, who had assumed the reins of the Korean court and led former Korean progressive party leaders—who had exiled themselves to Japan—returned home and inaugurated the new cabinet. These pro-Japan Korean leaders carried out reform programs in many fields. In order to widely propagate its position, the Japanese government created a newspaper company under the name of a Japanese civilian in Seoul, Yidach'i Kenjo.[62] The *Khanjosinp'o* (The capital city newspaper), repeated that under Japanese guidance, Korea was entering into the initial stage of modernization. However, most Korean people did not trust the Japanese propaganda and some Koreans resisted the reform programs. At this time, a pro-Chinese Korean by the name of Hong Chongwil assassinated Kim Okkyun, the leader of the progressive party, and Japanese troops executed Chŏn Pongjun, the leader of the Tonghak revolt.

JAPANESE RATIONALIZATION OF ITS WAR AGAINST RUSSIA

With the defeat of China in the summer of 1895 and the subsequent weakening of Chinese influence over Korea, Japan could secure its hegemony over Korea. Since then, a new rivalry and competition began between Japan and Russia in earnest. When some Korean political leaders under the leadership of Queen Min, wife of King Kojong, attempted to "induce Russia in order to resist against Japan," the Japanese legation in Seoul stormed into the palace and assassinated the queen in 1895.[63] Embarrassed, King Kojong took refuge in the Russian legation in Seoul. With the return to his palace in 1897, the king declared the establishment of the Great Korean Empire and renamed himself emperor.

Above all, the Japanese government had to defend the assassination of Queen Min before the international community and Korea. Japan alleged that the Japanese government in Tokyo had not been involved in the assassination but rather the Japanese legation in Seoul had acted without any instruction or even a hint from Tokyo. Japanese government officials emphatically added that Koreans also joined the assassination with the strong belief that the eradication of Queen Min, whom they regarded the obstructionist of reform and modernization of Korea, was necessary. Surprisingly, most Western writers accepted or tolerated this allegation. For example, while explaining the assassination of Queen Min in detail, Isabella Bird, a famous British traveler and writer, never criticized the Japanese government. She merely blamed the Japanese minister in Seoul for his "savage" deed.[64] Griffis followed suit and defined the Queen's incident as the work of "a reckless diplomatic blunderer" in Seoul and defended Koreans—who acted as the Japanese perpetrator—as "patriots" who dreamed of eradicating the obstructionist of Korea's reform and modernization.[65] However, many academic works have agreed that the Japanese legation in Seoul carried out the assassination plan under the instruction of the Japanese government in Tokyo.[66]

While continuing its propaganda that attributed the responsibility of the incident to its local diplomat and Koreans, the Japanese government prepared to wage war with Russia in order to eliminate Russian influence entirely from Korea. In February 1904, two years after the conclusion of the Anglo-Japanese Alliance, Japan declared war against Russia. Immediately after the outbreak of the war, it began publishing two daily newspapers, *Tehan ilbo* (The Korea daily, established March 10, 1904) and *Tedong sinbo* (Great East newspaper, established April 18, 1904) as mouth-pieces in Seoul.[67] At the same time, Japan developed new propaganda. The Japanese government claimed to stand for "the Oriental peace" (i.e., peace in the Far East). Arguing that Russia's continuous advance into Manchuria and Korea endangered peace and security in the Far East, Japan officials concluded they were forced to fight against Russia.[68]

Japanese propaganda also actively advanced the racial rivalry theory. Since Japan and Korea belong to the same yellow race while Russia belongs to the white race, Japan theorized that Korea should join Japan's fight against Russia.[69] Following Tarui Tokich'i, Japanese officials used propaganda that promoted the theory that the Koreans and Japanese were not only of the same yellow race but also originated from the same ancestor. The propaganda elaborated that since the Japanese and the Koreans descended from the same ancestor, their root—in terms of bloodline—was identical. From this they invented the emotional and simple slogan, "the same ancestor and the same root."[70] After the annexation of Korea, the Japanese colonial administration used this slogan extensively and some Korean intellectuals, including Yun Ch'iho and Ch'oe Namsŏn, echoed it.

In addition, the Japanese propaganda stirred up Russophobia and exaggerated Russia's "aggrandizement of neighboring countries" and "atrocity."[71] For example, Inoue Kakukoro warned that if Korea were to lose its spirit and ability to maintain its independence it might be "encroached upon" by Russia.[72] When the war ended with the Japanese victory in May 1905, George Kennan, a US journalist acting as a de facto spokesman of the Japanese government, commented that the war between Japan and Russia was the war between "the civilized and the savage." By defeating Russia, he quibbled, Japan could "protect" Korea from Russia's "dark ambition" to advance into it.[73]

Lastly, it should be pointed out that the Japanese government attempted to lead Western correspondents reporting on the war from Korea toward a direction favorable to Japan. Jack London of the *San Francisco Examiner* was a typical case. He was frequently briefed on the war situation by the Japanese military and treated well with whisky and tobacco. In contrast, he was neither briefed nor treated by the Russian military. As a result, his reports always favorably portrayed the Japanese soldiers and defamed the Russian soldiers.[74]

JAPAN'S EMBELLISHMENT OF ITŌ HIROBUMI AND CRITICISM OF KOREA AND ITS EMPEROR

On September 5, 1905, three months after the end of the Russo-Japanese War, the two belligerents concluded the Treaty of Portsmouth (New Hampshire). This treaty, mediated by the United States president Theodore Roosevelt, reached an agreement that obliged Russia to accept Japan's "paramount political, military, and economic interest" in Korea; Great Britain officially approved it. With these international sanctions, any obstacle in the way to Japan's complete domination over Korea had been removed. Thus, on November 17, 1905, ten weeks after the conclusion of the Treaty of Portsmouth, Itō Hirobumi, who officially represented the Japanese government as its "special ambassador," forced the Korean court to sign the Japan–Korea Protectorate Treaty of 1905 (also known as the Eulsa Treaty). It should be stressed that the Korean emperor and prime minister never signed it.[75]

As some important bureaucrats and intellectuals, including Min Yŏnghwan, Cho Pyŏngse, and Ch'oe Ikhyŏn, committed suicide in protest to the forced treaty, most of the Korean people—with the notable exception of Ilchinhoe members—denounced it severely. Three days after the conclusion of the forced treaty, Chang Chiyŏn, a leading intellectual and critic, published an anti-Japanese article, "Siirya pangsŏng taeyok" (Tonight I weep loudly and bitterly). In this famous article, Chang recalled that when Itō Hirobumi came to Seoul recently, Koreans welcomed him ardently with the expectation that he would suggest a plan for the solidification of Korea's independence based on his idea of Oriental peace. Then, Chang sarcastically asked the Japanese whether this forced treaty meant "Oriental peace" which Itō Hirobumi had propagated. Implicit was that a significant portion of the Korean intellectuals had been belatedly awakened from an illusion of "Oriental peace." Afterward, hot-blooded young Koreans organized the ŭipyŏng (righteous army) and bravely fought against the Japanese Army. Many Koreans exiled themselves to the Maritime Province in the Russian Far East and Manchuria, China, and the United States to engage in the anti-Japanese movement.

In order to placate the Koreans and to induce a favorable response from the international community, the Japanese government carried on its propaganda on a large scale. After the signing of the Japan-Korea Protectorate Treaty, the major tools were the *Keijon ipbo* (The capital city daily) and the *Seoul Press*, an English weekly in Seoul, and the Oriental Information Bureau in Washington DC. In addition, the Japanese government used some Western pastors, professors, diplomats, and journalists as its mouthpieces. However, many Western intellectuals openly denounced them as being bribed by the Japanese authorities.[76]

Japanese propaganda was two-fold in a broad sense. On the one hand was the embellishment of the newly appointed Japanese resident-general in Korea, Itō Hirobumi, under the Japan-Korea Protectorate Treaty. On the other was the criticism of the Korea emperor and Korea itself.

The Embellishment of Itō

First, Japanese propaganda portrayed Itō as a "sincere and honest" statesman. William E. Griffis, who became one of the Japanese mouthpieces in the United States, described Itō as "energetic" and a statesman with "sincere" reform programs for Korea. "As Great Britain is working for Egypt, the United States is working for Cuba, and France is working for Vietnam, Japan is working through Itō for Korea," he quibbled.[77] George Trumbull Ladd, an American philosophy professor, visited Korea in the capacity of Itō's "private guest" and praised him exceedingly. Describing Itō as "Korea's . . . and King Kojong's best friend," he wrote that Itō was the "real statesman" who carried out only peace-oriented policies without considering his own safety and life. Under the Japanese "protection" of Korea with Itō as its "honest and benevolent" chief administrator, the Korean people would be able to manage their lives happily, he said. Ladd even added that he was greatly moved by Itō's "sincere desire" to make Korea "a really prosperous country."[78] In July, 1907, the Korean emperor sent three emissaries to the International Peace Conference held in The Hague in order to appeal for the invalidity of the forced treaty and Korea's independence. Although the Koreans could not participate in the conference due to Japan's obstruction, their press conference stirred up public opinion sympathetic with Korea. Ladd harshly denounced the Korean emperor for his dispatch of emissaries. Arguing that palace intrigue was such that it was extremely corrupt and that this allowed the emperor to misjudge the situation, Ladd wrote that the emperor committed "a fatal error."[79] *The Graphic*, a London-based weekly, followed suit. With pictures showing "reformed" or "modernized" sections of Seoul, the newspaper stated, "Thanks to Resident-General Itō Hirobumi, various reform programs are being carried out peacefully in Korea."[80]

When Itō was assassinated in Harbin in 1909 by An Chunggŭn, who had been serving as general of the Korean Righteous Army, which had been fighting against the Japanese in the Russian Far East, a couple of Americans condemned the act. Ladd compared Ito's assassination to "Lincoln's assassination."[81] Pastor Arthur J. Brown called Itō "the most powerful friend for Koreans" and denounced An as "a fanatic who did the worst thing for his country."[82] William F. Sands, an international relations adviser to the King Kojong, would recollect that "Itō was one of the greatest Japanese statesmen and one of the greatest men in his times" and "[t]he worst thing Koreans ever did for themselves was to assassinate him."[83]

THE DISPARAGEMENT OF KOREA AND ITS EMPEROR

Before Japan made Korea its protectorate, many Western visitors had made their thoughts known about the peninsula's emperor. A retired British officer, Alfred Cavendish, regarded him "a mere puppet" of Queen Min, "a strong minded women."[84] Isabella L. Bird wrote that "[h]e is persuadable by the last person who gets his ear, "[h]e lacks backbone and tenacity," and that "[h]is weakness of character is fatal."[85] William F. Sands suggested the same view:

"[t]he king was a pleasant, good natured man with no will power at all and no understanding of anything that was happening in the world about him."[86]

Other Western observers appreciated him as a monarch. Horace N. Allen, minister of the US legation in Seoul wrote "[h]e is quick of perception and very progressive," however Allen also admitted the king's "feebleness."[87] Owen N. Denny, a US advisor to King Kojong, regarded the king as a "progressive" monarch with the habit of "perfect sobriety and industry." He added that the king did his best in order to civilize his country.[88] Louise J. Miln, a British actress, had written that "[h]e is a man of decided mental strength and of most considerable learning."[89] Still others had glowing reviews of Korea in general. A young French cadet had praised Koreans' love of learning and high rate of literacy.[90] A German ethnologist wrote, "[t]he Koreans as a rule are honest and good-natured, and great crimes, murder, theft, etc., are not frequently committed."[91] An Irish missionary, a US naval surgeon, and a British painter praised Hangŭl, the Korean alphabet.[92] A French folklorist and a German journalist compared some of the Korean mountains to the Alps. Finally, many Western tourists admired Koreans' "kindness," "diligence," "strong filial duty," and "high-level handicraft" as well as "bravery" and Korea's healthy climate as well as natural beauty.[93]

Japanese propaganda stressed the negative side and disregarded the positive reviews completely. After being appointed to the post of international relations adviser to the Japanese resident-general in Korea, Durham Stevens repeated his original comments and reiterated that the Korean monarch was surrounded by "corrupt" bureaucrats and that the king was "incompetent." He added that Koreans would benefit from Japan's "protection" and "wise" policies. He called Korea "an impoverished country abandoned to misrule and corruption" and "a weak and defenseless country." He went one step further and urged Koreans to accept annexation by Japan. These statements did not sit well with Chang Inhwan, a Korean living in the United States, who assassinated Stevens in San Francisco on March 23, 1908.[94]

Japanese propaganda also put emphasis upon the dark side of Korea and Koreans. Before the conclusion of the forced treaty of 1905, Western observers had already described Korea as a "poor, dirty, miserable, disorderly, and uncivilized country which was plagued by various epidemics such as the smallpox and cholera and influenced by superstition and shamanism."[95]

Some described the Korean government as "a gigantic robber" who "squeezed" its people.[96]

Kennan, another Japanese mouthpiece, termed Korea "a degenerate state" and went on to compare Korea to a country whose level was lower than that of Haiti. Kennan ridiculed Korea's culture as not only being stagnant but rotten.[97] Griffis suggested the same view. He wrote that Korea was a country indulged in "fetishism, superstition, and ignorance" and that Koreans fell into the bad habits of telling a lie, theft, gambling, and heavy drinking.[98]

Mobilizing these descriptions and others like them fully, Japan attempted to craft a couple of national images of Korea. In simple terms, they attempted to create an image of Korea as that of a "hopeless country," one which needed Japan's protection and guidance. In particular, the Japanese government propagated the message that "since the probability of Korean independence is nil, to join the Korean independence movement is useless and foolish."[99]

CONCLUSION

In summary, the Japanese government used propaganda in an endeavor to control the Korean people. They began by attempting to implant and solidify an inferiority complex in Koreans. Through the frequent and consistent use of noble terminology and the promise of civilization, the Japanese sought to control the Koreans. Percival Lowell, a US physicist and astronomer, asserted after his visit to Korea that Korea was never an uncivilized country and that most Koreans were enlightened. Nevertheless, under the strong influence of Japanese propaganda, most Koreans lost self-respect and regarded themselves as "uncivilized."[100]

Japan, through its use of propaganda, encouraged Koreans to believe their situation was hopeless. The essence of Japanese propaganda was to imply to Koreans that Korea is unable to regain its independence due to its internal as well as external conditions and not qualified for independence due to their erroneous characters.[101] Koreans' inferiority complex led them to fatalism and nihilism. Such messages significantly impacted many Koreans and many believed this rhetoric and accepted or tolerated the thesis that Korean independence was impossible.[102] Yun Ch'iho represented such a case. On November 2, 1905, he wrote that "[a]fter all, it will be the best possible thing under the circumstances that Japan should take the entire control of Korean affairs and manage them. . . . You can no more expect independence and good government from the present generation of Koreans than Moses could have expected from the generation of slaves whom he led into the wilderness."[103]

In addition, Japanese propaganda attempted to deceive Koreans into embracing an illusion of their future. The grandiose language used in Japanese propaganda was intentionally incising, see for example: "civilization and enlightenment of Korea," "independence of Korea," "liberation of Korea from the Chinese vassalage and the Russian threats to absorb the peninsula," and "Oriental peace through an alliance of Japan, Korea, and China."[104] Only those who understood Japan's hidden agenda, aggressiveness, and ability to commit atrocities were not fooled. Yi Yongku, who had energetically led the campaign in favor of Korean annexation by Japan, represented such a case. Two weeks after Japan annexed Korea on August 29, 1910, the Japanese government disbanded the Ilchinhoe (a pro-Japanese organization) and deserted him. Disappointed, he fell seriously ill. Before his death in 1912, he lamented, "I was deceived since I was foolish."[105]

In closing, it should be stated that with regards to the Korean peninsula and Japanese propaganda, Great Britain was a helpful ally to Japan. Henry James Whigham of the London-based *Morning Post* denounced the emperor of Korea as being "completely devoid of patriotism or of any real solicitude concerning the welfare of the people," and the Korean government as "the worst government in the world." He advised Koreans to accept the "protection and guidance" of Japan who "liberated Korea from the Chinese yoke."[106] Praising Japan highly for its "creation of the new Far East through its victory over Russia," Arthur Diosy of the Japan Association in London defamed Korea as "a truly distressful country" and Koreans as "a dirty race." He added that Korea, "torn by dissensions and misgoverned to an almost incredible degree," should learn from Japan.[107] Joseph H. Longford of King's College, London followed suit calling Korea "a sick man of East Asia." The former British diplomat appreciated Japan's role in "liberating" Korea from Russia's intrigue to annex this poor country and "reforming" Korea. He erroneously predicted that Korea would benefit from annexation.[108] Three other British observers published their joint work, which also justified the annexation. They contended that if Korea were occupied and controlled by Russia there would be a direct threat to Japan and Japan therefore had to annex Korea for the protection of both Korea and Japan.

I refer to the title of this chapter which comes from a German proverb, "A devil appears in a different dress." The imperial Japanese government's use of florid words acted as different "dresses" which were used to cover imperial Japan's devilish character. In this sense, the imperial Japanese government's propaganda represented the art of deception.

NOTES

1. For example, see C. I. Eugene Kim and Hankyo Kim, *Korea and Politics of Imperialism, 1876–1910*, chapter 1. See also, Hilary Conroy, *The Japanese Seizure of Korea, 1868–1910*; and Andrew C. Nahm, ed., *Korea under Japanese Colonial Rule*.

2. Yi Yongju, "Munmyŏngnon ŭl kŏchy'ŏ t'araron e irŭnŭn kil" [A road to the theory of "escaping from Asia" via the theory of civilization: Fukujawa Yukichi's perception of Asia and the "mission to civilize"], 249–68.

3. Yukichi Fukujawa, *The Autobiography of Yukichi Fukujawa*, revised and translated by Eiichi Kiyooka.

4. Fukujawa Yukichi, "Ajia shoku to no wasen to ga eijoku no setsu" [Debates on Japan's war and peace with Asian countries], in *Fukujawa Yukichi zenshu* [The collected works of Fukujawa Yukichi], edited by Keio University 20: 145. Hereafter referred to as *The Collected Works of Fukujawa Yukichi*.

5. Quoted in the introduction of the volume edited by Andrew C. Nahm, *Korea under Japanese Colonial Rule*, 19.

6. Charles L. Yates, *Saigo Takamori: The Man Behind the Myth*.

7. Koryŏ Taehakkyo Asea Munje Yŏn'guso, ed. *Kuhankuk oegyo munsŏ* [Diplomatic documents of late Chosŏn Korea] 1: 48.

8. *The Collected Works of Fukujawa Yukichi* 19: 617.

9. For example, see Augustine Heard, Durham White Stevens, and Howard Martin, "China and Japan in Korea," 308–16.

10. *The Collected Works of Fukujawa Yukichi* 5: 186–87.

11. Quoted in Ch'oe Munhyŏng, *Han'guk kŭndae ŭi sagyesajŏk ihae* [An understanding of modern Korea from the perspective of world history], 104.

12. Ch'oe Ch'anggu, *Kŭndae Han'guk chŏnch'i sasangsa* [A history of modern Korean political thought], part 1.

13. For example, see Kim P'yongmuk, "Ŏyangnon" [On defense of the country from the West], 40–45.

14. Kim Tujin, "Tong-Ajia hwa-iron ŭi pyŏnyong" [A change in the thesis of civilized countries and uncivilized countries among East Asian countries], 15–18.

15. Yi Kwangrin, "Kaehwa sŭng Yi Tongin" [Yi Tongin, an enlightened monk], 461–72.

16. Quoted in Kim T'aejun, "Yu Kiljun ŭi kaehwa sasang kwa minjokjŏk cha-a-insik ŭi hyŏngsŏng" [Yu Kiljun's thoughts on civilization and the formation of national self-identity], 19.

17. Andrew C. Nahm, "Kim Ok-kyun and the Reform Movement of the Progressives," 38–62.

18. For a pioneering book on Kim Okkyun and his progressive comrades, see Harold F. Cook, Korea's 1884 Incident.

19. Benjamin B. Weems, *Reform, Rebellion, and the Heavenly Way*, chapters 1–3.

20. *The Collected Works of Fukujawa Yukichi* 8: 243, and 251–56. For details on Fukujawa's changing views on Korea, see In K. Hwang, *The Korean Reform Movement of the 1880s*, 100.

21. William Elliot Griffis, *Corea: The Hermit Nation*, x.

22. For details and a summary of these views, see William Elliot Griffis, *Corea: The Hermit Nation*, 5–6.

23. Ibid., 8–10.

24. For example, see Honma Kyusuk'ae, *Chōsen zakki* [Miscellaneous notes on Korea], 22–23.

25. William Elliot Griffis, *Corea: The Hermit Nation*, 52–54.

26. For a detailed discussion see Sin Yongha, *Ilche singminji chŏngch'aek kwa singminji kŭndaehwaron pip'an* [A critical study of Japanese colonial policy and colonial modernity], 30.

27. For example, see Oguma Eiji, *Danitzu minjoku sinwano kigen* [The origins of the homogenous nation], chapter 14.

28. Pak Chihyang, *Ilgŭrŏjin kŭndae* [Distorted modern times], 175.

29. William Elliot Griffis, *Corea: The Hermit Nation*, 210–14.

30. Hwang Zunxian, *Chosŏn ch'aengnyak* [Korean policy], translated with annotations by Cho Ilmun.

31. The essays by Yu Kiljun, "Ŏnsaso" [Memorials to the king, (1883)]; and Yu Kiljun, "Chungripron" [On neutrality (1885)] were included in *Yu Kiljun chŏnso* [The collected works of Yu Kiljun], edited by Yu Kiljun Chŏnsŏ P'yŏnch'an Wiwonhoe [Committee for the collection and compilation of works by Yu Kiljun], 63–72 and 319–328 respectively.

32. For example, see Kim Yongku, *Kŏmundo wa Vladivostok* [Kŏmundo and Vladivistok], 5.

33. For a detailed discussion, see Taejin Yi, "Was Korea Really a 'Hermit Nation,'" 13–14.

34. Quoted in Yang Kiwung, "Kim Okkyun kwa Fukujawa Yukichi" [Kim Okkyun and Fukujawa Yukichi], 83–84.

35. Quoted in Ibid., 84.

36. Fukujawa Yukichi, "Dastsu a ron" [On escaping from Asia (or, On leaving Asia behind)].

37. Fukujawa Yukichi, "Chōsen toritono shokei" [The execution of the Korean independence party leaders] 10: 265 and 379.

38. Kang Tongjin, *Ilche ŭi Han'guk ch'imnyak chongch'aeksa yŏn'gu* [A study on the history of imperial Japanese policies for the aggression of Korea], 57.

39. See Hŏ Tonghyŏn, "Ch'ŏnp'al paekp'alsip yŏndae kaehwap'a insadŭl ŭi sahoe chinhwaron suyong yangt'ae pikyo yŏn'gu: Yu Kiljun kwa Yun Ch'iho" [A comparison of the reception of Social Darwinism by Korean progressive leaders in the 1880s: Yu Kiljun and Yun Ch'iho], 173–74.

40. Quoted in Ibid., 174.

41. Yu Kiljun Chŏnsŏ Pyŏnch'an Wiwonhoe, ed., *Yu Kiljun chŏnsŏ* 4: 47–66.

42. For his books and details about this activities, see Yu Tongjun, *Yu Kiljun chŏn* [A biography of Yu Kiljun].

43. Yun Ch'iho's diary entry on November 20, 1892. Kuksa P'yŏnch'an Wiwonhoe, ed., *Yun Ch'iho ilgi* [The diary of Yun Ch'iho] 2: 418–19.

44. Yun Ch'iho's diary entry on November 1, 1893. Ibid. 3: 204.

45. For example, see Sin Yongha, *Pak Ŭnsik ŭi sahoe sasang yŏn'gu* [A study of Pak Ŭnsik's social thoughts]; and Sin Yongha, *Sin Ch'aeho ŭi sahoe sasang yŏn'gu* [A study of Sin Ch'aeho's social thoughts].

46. Tarui Tokich'i, *Daitō gappō ron* [Thesis on the union of the great East].

47. Sven Saaler and Christopher W. A. Szpilman, eds., *Pan-Asianism*. See chapter 7 "Tokich'i's Arguments on Behalf of the Union of the Great East, 1893."

48. For Yi's career and activities see Song Kŏnho, *Han'guk hyŏndae inmulsaron* [Treaties on personalities in Korea's modern history], 411–31.

49. William F. Sands, *Undiplomatic Memories*, 228–29.

50. Hyŏn Kwangho, *Taehan cheguk kwa Rōsia kŭrigo Ilbon* [The great Korean empire, Russia and Japan], 94–95.

51. Augustine Heard, Durham White Stevens, and Howard Martin, "China and Japan in Korea," 313–14.

52. Inoue Kakukoro, "Hanjin kaikaku chiuen" [Essay on the reform of the Korean court (1895)]. This article was translated and included in Sin Yŏnggil, *Chosŏnjo mangkuk chŏnyagi* [On the eve of the fall of the Korean kingdom], 80–82.

53. Julius Kumpei Matumoto, "Preface," in *The War in the East: Japan, China, and Corea* by Trumbull White, vi–vii.

54. Trumbull White, *The War in the East*, part III.

55. E. H. Parker, *China: Her History, Diplomacy, and Commerce*.

56. William E. Griffis, *Corea: The Hermit Nation*, 8th edition (1907), 478.

57. Quoted in Shin Yongsuk, "The Late Chosŏn Dynasty Korea in Contemporary French Newspapers," 54–55.

58. Quoted in Ch'oe Munhyŏng, Han'guk kŭndae ŭi segyesajŏk ihae, 104.

59. Quoted in Shin Yongsuk, "Late Chosŏn Dynasty Korea in Contemporary French Newspapers," 54–55.

60. William E. Griffis, Corea: The Hermit Nation, 8th edition (1907), 444.

61. E. J. Urquhart, Glimpses of Korea, 14–15.

62. Chŏng Chinsŏk, Daehan maeil sinbo wa P'aesŏl [The Korea daily newspaper and (Ernest) Bethell], 239 –40. In February 1895, the Khanjo sinp'o began publishing every other day in both Korean and Japanese. Soon after it began publishing daily papers.

63. Ch'oe Munhyŏng, Myŏngsŏng hwanghu sihae chinsil ŭl palk'inda [I expose the truth about the assassination of Queen Min].

64. Isabella L. Bird Bishop, Korea and Her Neighbours, 333.

65. William E. Griffis, Corea: The Hermit Nation, 8th edition (1907), 481.

66. For example, see Ch'oe Munhyŏng, Myŏngsŏng hwanghu sihae chinsil ŭl palk'inda.

67. Chŏng Chinsŏk, Daehan maeil sinbo wa Paesŏl, 240.

68. Hyŏn Kwangho, Taehan cheguk kwa Rŏsia kŭrigo Ilbon [The great Korean empire, Russia, and Japan], 94–95.

69. Ibid, 224–45.

70. Kang Tongjin, Ilche ŭi Han'guk ch'imnyak chongch'aeksa yŏn'gu, 64.

71. Inoue Kakukoro, "Hanjin kaikaku chiuen," quoted in Sin Yŏnggil, Chosŏnjo mangkuk chŏnyagi.

72. Ibid.

73. George Kennan, "Korea: A Degenerate State," 312–15.

74. Dale L. Walker, "Jack London's War."

75. Yi Taejin, Ilbon ŭi Taehan cheguk kangchŏm [Imperial Japanese forced occupation of the great Korean empire]. Throughout this book the author stressed that the treaty in question was invalid from the beginning.

76. Kang Tongjin, Ilche ŭi Hankuk ch'imnyak chongchaeksa yŏn'gu, 73. The Keijō Nippō was the result of the merger of Tehan ilbo and Tedong sinbo and published its first newspaper on September 1, 1906. See Chŏng Chinsŏk, Daehan maeil sinbo wa Paisŏl, 240.

77. William E. Griffis, Corea: The Hermit Nation, 8th edition (1907), 498–502.

78. George Trumbull Ladd, In Korea with Marquis Ito, 150–52.

79. Ibid., 153–162.

80. See pictures and captions printed in The Graphic, September 26, 1908: 1.

81. Quoted in Chŏng Chinsŏk, Daehan maeil sinbo wa Paesŏl, 257; and Kim Chanch'un, Semirhan illŏsut'ŭ wa huigui sajin ŭro pon kŭndae Chosŏn [Modern Yi Chosŏn Korea seen through rare pictures].

82. Arthur Judson Brown, *The Mastery of the Far East*, 356.
83. William F. Sands, *Undiplomatic Memories*, 227.
84. Alfred Edward John Cavendish, *Korea and the Sacred White Mountain*, 24.
85. Isabella L. Bird Bishop, *Korea and Her Neighbours*, 251–55 and 433.
86. William F. Sands, *Undiplomatic Memories*, 60.
87. Horace Newton Allen, *Korea: Fact and Fancy*, 288–89.
88. Owen N. Denny, *China and Korea*, 45–46.
89. Louise Jordan Miln, *Quaint Korea*, 103–4.
90. Henri Zuber's remarks were quoted in Yi Hyang and Kim Chŏngyŏn, P'uredŭrik Puresuteksŭ ch'akhan migaein tongyang ŭi hyŏnja" [Frederick Boulesteix's "A Good Uncivilized Man and a Wise Oriental Man"], 140.
91. Ernest Jakob Oppert, *A Forbidden Land*, 131.
92. For example, see John Ross, *History of Corea*, 315 and 377.
93. For example, see Percival Lowell, *Chöson: The Land of Morning Calm*, 386–87. See also Fred C. Bhom and Robert R. Swartout, Jr., eds., *Navel Surgeon in Yi Korea*, 14–24.
94. Augustine Heard, Durham White Stevens, and Howard Martin, "China and Japan in Korea," 313.
95. Isabella L. Bird Bishop, *Korea and Her Neighbours*, 21–37.
96. Samuel Hawley, ed., *Inside the Hermit Kingdom*, 162–63.
97. George Kennan, "Korea: A Degenerate State," 307–10.
98. William E. Griffis, *Corea: The Hermit Nation*, 8th edition (1907), 451 and 470.
99. Chōsen Sotokufu [Japanese Governor-General's office], ed., *Chōsen hito no shinsō to seikaku* [Koreans' thoughts and characters], 51.
100. Percival Lowell, *Chöson, The Land of Morning Calm*, 109.
101. For example, see Charles Welsh, "Editor's Note," in Angus Hamilton, Herbert H. Austin, and Masatake Terauchi, *Korea: It's History, Its People, and Its Commerce*, xv–xvi. This book was published under the auspices of the Japanese Government.
102. A study on Korean poets between 1908–11 showed that the most frequently used words were "nothingness," "nihility," and "predestination." See Kim Ch'ŏngkyun, *Chosŏn munyerane nat'anan Hangukŭi yimji* [Korea's image appeared in *Chöson*], 151–61.
103. Kuksa P'yŏnch'an Wiwonhoe, ed., *Yun Ch'iho ilgi* 6: 186.
104. Quoted in Yi Yongju, "Munmyŏngron ŭl kŏchy'ŏ t'alaron e irŭnŭn kil," 249–68.
105. Quoted in Song Kŏnho, *Han'guk hyŏndae inmulsaron* [Treaties on the personalities in Korea's modern history], 429–30.
106. Henry James Whigham, *Manchuria and Korea*, 216–17.
107. Joseph H. Longford, *The Story of Korea*, 351 and chapter 6.
108. Arthur Diosy, *The New Far East*, ix and 84.

2
Establishing Japanese National Identity and the "Chosŏn Issue"

SANG SOOK JEON

This chapter examines the Japanese annexation of Korea in the context of Japan's establishment of a "modern" national identity. East Asian countries opened their doors, overwhelmed by the power of Western countries from the late nineteenth century into the early twentieth century. This led to the transformation from the traditional China-oriented East Asian international system to the Western modern international law system. Japan was at the center of this change. This transformation of the East Asian international system—that Japan initiated—may also be said to have been the process by which the Japanese established their national identity, both regionally and globally, as a modern state. In this context, the annexation of Korea in 1910 spurred Japan's national development and established Japan's national identity as a modern state similar to that of Western powers.

The following pages of this chapter review the changes in the East Asian international system that occurred when Korea was placed in a pivotal position during the pre–Colonial Period from the late nineteenth century into the early twentieth century. It focuses on Japanese views of Korea within the international system and on how Japanese officials tried to manipulate the "Chosŏn issue" for national development. In closing, this chapter highlights the meaning of the "Chosŏn issue" in Japanese foreign policy during national modern transformation and clarifies the meanings and characteristics of the annexation of Korea and Japan's government policies.

Japan acquired exclusive influence over Korea through victories in the Sino-Japanese War of 1894–95 and the Russo-Japanese War of 1904–5 and by excluding China and Russia, which the Japanese government considered to be obstacles to Japan's advance into the continent and to power and influence in Korea. Winning the Sino-Japanese War was the turning point in Japan's rise as a new empire, one that was breaking down the traditional Sino-centric East Asian international order. While victory in the Russo-Japanese War proved that Japan could be a major power like those in the West. Therefore, it may be said that these two wars were instrumental for Japan to become one of the world powers. At the same time, it may be said that those wars were a long "colony acquisition war" through which Japan gained Taiwan and Korea as bases in the "project to become a continental state."[1]

Japan began its national development as an imperial power when the East Asian international order was forced to move toward a Western, modern order caused by the Asia policies of Western powers. Japan's national development has been generally explained in terms of the Japanese continental policies that annexed Taiwan and Korea in the process of becoming an imperial power. In other words, Japan's annexation of Korea and its colonial policies have been explained as a process of either Japanese continental policy or as a series of imperial expansionist policies after the Meiji Restoration that led to Japan becoming a modern power. Thus, the "Chosŏn issue" has been focused upon only when annexation mattered most in the early phases of Japan's northern continental policies. After annexation, the "Chosŏn issue" was rarely recognized as a significant problem. Since the end of the Edo government and after the Meiji Restoration, the Chosŏn issue was of major interest to Japan. However, general interest in Japan regarding Korea decreased dramatically after annexation. This is why modern Japanese political historians do not focus their research on the Chosŏn issue. Why did interest in the Chosŏn issue decline? What caused such a sharp shift in concern regarding Chosŏn after annexation? How is this to be understood?

Japanese rule in colonial Korea has been described as brutal with regards to the manner in which the Japanese Government-General of Chōsen (J. *Chōsen Sōtokufu*) enforced policies and replied to Korean responses. Despite this fact, more questions emerge. What brought about such features? How can colonial rule in Korea be positioned in Japanese colonial policy? Did both the Government-General of Chōsen and the Japanese government have homogeneous policy positions? Can these two governments be treated as equal parties? There may have been some debate regarding policies. If there were differences that could not be reconciled, what caused those differences? What does this mean in the contexts of Japanese rule in Korea and in Korean history? There is not yet enough research to answer these questions.

However, the history of the Colonial Period will be revealed when the mutual dynamics, relations, and realizations between the ruled and the ruler have been examined in greater detail. This study is part of a project examining the overall purpose of the annexation and the peculiarities of the colonial policy of Japan in order to further clarify, and further understand, the general historical context during the Colonial Period in Korea. This project sees the Japanese annexation of Korea as an ongoing process of the "Japanese imperialistic modernization project." Here, the focus is on the reconsideration of the Japanese annexation of Korea, while keeping in mind both the mutual relations between that of the continental policy for Japanese national expansion and Japan's diplomatic policy.

THE OPENING OF EAST ASIA AND THE JAPANESE SEARCH FOR NATIONAL IDENTITY

The three states of China, Japan, and Korea opened their doors and began their modern transformation after encounters with the West. The respective openings to Western powers allowed each state to enter the Western modern international law and order. International law, which organized international relations in the West, was the basic framework for maintaining the balance of power. Simply put, it was a modern way of thinking in the West. The entry of these East Asian states into international law and order meant that Asian civilizations began to be measured by a representative norm that would lead to Western civilization. This was the beginning of the so-called civilization transition.[2]

Western powers armed with advanced modern technology forced "uncivilized" Asian nations to open their doors. The responses of the ruling classes in China and Japan, who had to open their doors after encounters with the West, were similar. They opened their doors politically with closed-door spirits. However, this similarity was superficial and the degree of national unification was significant.[3] The differences led to China becoming a semi-colonial state of the West while Japan overthrew the traditional Sino-centric East Asian international order and pretended to be a leader of the East.[4]

As is well known, China's defeat in the Opium War was the beginning of this subversion. That loss represented the defeat of Chinese civilization by Western civilization, and the impact was significant in East Asia. In 1844, as an intellectual reaction, the book *Haiguo tuzhi* (Illustrated gazetteer of countries beyond the seas) was published in China, where Sino-centrism fascinated people. The publication of this encyclopedia about human geography was epochal, and its author, Wei Yuan, was called "the paradigm converter."[5] Attempts to transform Chinese society into a modern society similar to those in the West had thus begun in a region greatly influenced by Chinese civilization. *Haiguo tuzhi* was an expression of the intellectual desire to overcome the national disgrace. This encyclopedia appeared to detail a strategy against the West, similar to "using barbarians to control barbarians" or "controlling barbarians with barbarian tools." Its publication was a shock especially in Japan, where the Edo government had begun to search for countermeasures to the publication while indirectly experiencing the power of the West through the Opium War. *Haiguo tuzhi* exerted social impact that instigated strategic military concerns and changed the intellectual atmosphere in Japan.[6] It may be said that Japan subjectively opened its doors after encountering the "black ships" of Matthew C. Perry in this time of new international law and order. Perry was a US admiral who led the fleet to pressure Japan to open up in 1863.

During the Edo Period Japan imported from China Western books translated into Chinese through Nagasaki. At first Japan served primarily as an importer of Western knowledge and the Japanese tried to learn of the new world beyond Sino-centrism. They began to use the word "Shina" instead of "China." By using Shina Japan rid itself of Chinese cultural and political superiority and contributed to the fulfillment of Japanese self-satisfaction as the Japanese nation. The concept of Japan's superiority, the country of the emperor, was growing and developing. Japan during the Edo Period had an ideologically self-centered way of thinking when it came to accomplishing economic self-support.[7]

Japan continued to search for self-supporting principles that would separate it from the West, with which strained relations had continued from the late Edo Period. At the same time, Japan had been searching for the means of civilization and modernization that would make real independence possible.[8] Ideological tension between fear on the one hand and realistic recognition on the other formed during this process, and fear stemmed from accepting unequal treaties with Western powers. The latter flowed from the realization that accepting Western superiority meant accepting Western modern civilization. In other words, it meant admitting Japanese inferiority in competing with the West. Therefore, accepting a different civilization's ideological authority for Japanese subjectivity became the core matter of concern. The practical use and execution of ideology for reorganizing the governing system began at the same time.[9] Remarkably, Japan transformed its older world view, based on Chinese and Japanese writings, into a modern world view that accepted Western knowledge.[10]

Importing Western knowledge for practical purposes, Japan developed the idea to enhance wealth and strengthen the military and further objectify the Edo government so as to build a stronger, unified, modern nation that could confront foreign powers.[11] As a result, Japanese realism, cultivated under the old civilizational order, developed in two directions after the Meiji Restoration. One direction included cutting the Meiji state from the old civilizational order. While the other moved to enhance the wealth and military strength of the nation so as to oppose the West.[12]

Basically, during the last years of the Edo Period, government officials had searched for the best manner with which to reverse Japanese inferiority to Western powers, as represented by Perry's black ships. During this time, the Meiji state propelled "modernization from above" by establishing a national educational system. This concept distinguished the Meiji state from the past and unfolded in a way that sought to reconstruct the mythological world with a "god-like emperor," utilizing Japanese ancient mythology alongside Western knowledge such as astronomy and geography to devise a rationalization for absorbing Western civilization.[13] Strengthening the new Japanese government and society sought to establish a modern educational system for training children to become the talented persons needed to construct the new modern state. After abolishing the *han* system and establishing the prefecture system, the Meiji government established power, centralized the national ruling system, and enforced a unified national educational policy through the Ministry of Education.[14] *Han* was an administrative unit under the Japanese feudal system before the Meiji Restoration in 1868, which was semi-autonomous and subject to the Bakufu Central government. It was replaced with *ken* (prefecture), which was a provincial administrative unit under the centralized Meiji government. Immediately after abolishing the *han* system and introducing the prefecture system, the Meiji government dispatched the Iwakura Embassy officials to Europe and the United States to study various Western systems. Japanese society, which was the first to accept the theory of social evolution in East Asia, noted the limitations of international law by stressing the rights of the powerful. Therefore, the Japanese government crafted a new alternative for utilizing the theory of social evolution in foreign relations based upon realism.[15] These efforts converged in the process of establishing the Meiji state system. The result was the firm establishment of an independent and strong Japanese state. That is, the establishment of an absolutist state was the only way to become a "civilized nation" by oneself, like the West, and to revise the unequal treaties with foreign countries.

The Meiji government focused on open-door modernization. The state ambitiously accepted the concept of international law, productively absorbed it into its governing system, and, in a practical manner, utilized it as the driving force of modernization. This modernization project succeeded.[16] It was the result of the interaction between the internal "enlightenment of civilization" and the external "entrance to the West," concepts made possible through the wealth and military strength of the nation since the last years of the Edo government. A wealthy and strong military was the national aim upon which the modern state of Japan had been founded.[17] This stance was also the identity of the modern state that Japan had sought to become.

JAPANESE CRISIS CONSCIOUSNESS AND PERCEPTION OF THE CHOSŎN ISSUE

The occupation of Tsushima Island by the Russian empire in 1861 was a turning point in provoking real change in Korea, Japan, and China. In 1861, Russia anchored its fleet at the port of Tsushima to repair ship damage. However, the Russian occupation stayed longer than the repairs had required, and expressions such as "take Chosŏn" and "protect Tsushima, Chosŏn, and Pusan" were overheard.[18] Continued Russian discussion of the occupation of Chosŏn caused the Edo government to perceive the real possibility of Western aggression against Chosŏn and its threat to Japan.

Japan understood the Russian seizure of Tsushima to be a series of actions through which a Western power would prepare to establish a foothold in Korea. Under the assumption that Western expansion into Chosŏn would impact Japan, diplomatic reasons for controlling Chosŏn first were proposed in Japanese politics. Russian remarks regarding Chosŏn gave Japan an opportunity to realize that a Western power could be a genuine threat to Korea and Japan at any time.[19] Japan was concerned about the interconnections between peninsular Korea and the island country of Japan and how Western influence over the Korean peninsula would affect Japan. Under the Sino-centric order, Japan had enjoyed independence from China through the medium of its good-neighbor policy with Chosŏn. However, great political change would follow in East Asia, especially for Japan, if a Western power forced Japan to open and then set foot in Korea. From the Japanese standpoint, this was inevitable. Japan, therefore, considered the problem that could occur when a Western power occupied Chosŏn as the "Chosŏn issue" and prepared for that contingency. The Japanese perception of the Chosŏn issue was an awareness of a state crisis. From that point on, Japan connected the Chosŏn issue to Japanese international prestige and manipulated the transformation of the traditional Korea-Japan diplomatic relationship into a modernized form in the following series of diplomatic incidents.

After opening China and Japan, Western powers turned their gazes on Korea. In 1866, the French campaign against Korea occurred. The Edo government rapidly gathered information regarding the situation and established countermeasures, including the proposal to invade Korea earlier than the West. The solution was to dispatch a delegation to Korea in order to mediate the conflict between Korea and the West. This was done despite the fact that not only Korea but also the Western powers, including France and the United States, had rejected it.[20] However, due to political changes, Japan could not dispatch a delegation to Korea and the perception toward Korea, the so-called Chosŏn issue, had taken shape. First, Japan had planned to send a delegation from the Edo government instead of a delegation from Tsushima. Second, the delegation had planned to enter through Seoul, not through Pusan, a provincial city. Last, Japan, under the justification of conveying its sincere intentions, had designed to build up a "mighty force" as well as "faith." This meant that the Chosŏn issue had become an important issue for the Japanese government, which was willing to use force.

Three significant factors can be drawn from the Japanese perception of the Chosŏn issue. First, by successfully mediating the conflict between Korea and the West, Japan intended to display its diplomatic ability in both the international and the domestic spheres and sought to gain recognition of its diplomatic capabilities. Second, Japan sought both to revise unequal treaties with the West and to sign a modern diplomatic treaty with Korea as a result of successful mediation. The latter of these, in particular, was intended to cut off the Chinese influence that traditionally had been powerful in Korea and to move forward on diplomatic relations with Korea before the strong Western powers did. Third, Japan officially expressed its will to use extreme measures in negotiations with Korea.

The Meiji government continued this type of diplomatic approach toward Korea. After the Meiji Restoration, the Japanese government dispatched a delegation to Korea to establish modern diplomatic relations. However, these continuous efforts toward a modern treaty reached a standstill. In 1871, at a time of slow progress between Korea and Japan, the United States expedition to Korea occurred. The Meiji government did not miss this opportunity and exploited the incident as a way to take the upper hand in diplomatic relations with Korea. The Meiji government was well aware of the need to change the unequal treaties with Western powers and to enhance its national prosperity and military strength. Therefore, as France had attempted in 1866, Japan sought to display its diplomatic ability by negotiating a treaty between the United States and Korea and thereby secured its interests in Korea before other Western powers did so. That is, Japan would open the Korean door first.

However, a newspaper reported the speculative news that Korea had requested China to be a mediator in resolving the dispute with the United States. Japan considered this a matter of "national dignity" and quickly found a countermeasure. However, diplomatic negotiations with Korea did not go well. As a result, Japan violated international diplomatic custom by suddenly leaving the Japan House (K. Waegwan) in Pusan and unilaterally occupied the area where the Japan House was. This led to the cessation of diplomatic relations between the two countries.[21]

As the diplomatic talks with Korea encountered difficulties, gradually, the concept of *Seikanron*—the argument that Japan should invade Korea before other Western powers did so—appeared. The idea of invading Korea was turned down by a group of figures that included Iwakura Tomomi, Ōkubo Toshimichi, and Itō Hirobumi who insisted that Japan's domestic affairs should come first. They argued that Japan should strengthen its national power first and then expand to the continent, and thus were not directly opposing the *Seikanron* idea. Eventually, the Meiji government dispatched a military expedition to Taiwan in 1874. Then in 1875, the Unyō Incident (also referred to as the Ganghwa Island Incident) occurred on September 20, 1875. This armed conflict between Japan and Chosŏn culminated in the Treaty of Ganghwa that was signed five months later on February 27, 1876. This was Korea's first modern international treaty.

Japan successfully opened the Korean peninsula, through the Treaty of Ganghwa, before Western powers did and obtained exclusive influence over Korean affairs. This was a move to protect Japanese national interests and was based upon the Japanese national crisis of consciousness when facing the Western powers' approaches to Korea. The Japanese opening of Korea was very similar to that of Japan's own experience of having been opened by the United States. Japan projected its experience by insisting that nothing but a forced open door policy would be available to Korea. Compared to Korea, Japan was modernized and when it displayed its modernized military strength Korea surrendered and signed the treaty. Historically, Japan had traded with Chosŏn through Tsushima Island; Tsushima traders had endured their subordinate position before the trade negotiations began and had been taken advantage of by the Chosŏn government.[22] The Treaty of Ganghwa settled the previous, pre-modern relations between Korea and Japan and constructed a new, "modern" relationship between the two "independent" states.

Japan guided the conclusion of the Treaty of Ganghwa, communicating the "Choson issue" instead of its "national crisis consciousness" in the face of the Western entrance into Korea. The Chosŏn issue had been solved by the treaty according to modern diplomatic terms and had the following significant points. (1) According to modern international law, Korea's independence was declared in the first clause. Japan clarified the beginning of new, equal diplomatic relations and announced the end of submissive good-neighbor relations in East Asia through the same clause. This meant forbidding traditional Chinese influence. (2) The treaty placed Japanese national interests before Western advances, thus constricting Western advances into East Asia. (3) The most important aspect of the treaty was that Japan gained stepping stones for an advance into the northern part of the Eurasian continent. Access to these northern areas was needed to resolve the scarcity of resources and overpopulation in Japan and to enable Japan to become a civilized modern state similar to Western powers. Korea was a critical touchstone for Japan in its quest for national modern development and was a bulwark against Western expansion.

THE CHOSŎN ISSUE AND THE "INTEREST LINE"

As shown above, the Treaty of Ganghwa became a challenge to the West. Securing influence over Korea enhanced the power of the modern state of Japan. Korea became a sub-structure for answering overpopulation problems and resolving the scarcity of resources and extended into the continent as a bridge for Japan to become a civilized state similar to that of Western powers. The Treaty of Ganghwa was the catalyst that began the process of replacing the pre-modern, China-centered East Asian order with the new "modern" international order. By signing the treaty, Korea took its first step toward the international law system and modern imperialism. The treaty, designed to be a Japanese demonstration of superior power, allowed Japan to expand its influence. Japan led modern international relations in Korea and East Asia in this way.

Japanese armaments, which would support the Treaty of Ganghwa and the country's national development, began with the modernization of the military system in 1880, following the Seinan War in 1877, and in 1890, the first prime minister of Japan, Yamagata Aritomo (1898–1900), who was the architect of the modern Japanese Army, announced a memorandum that dealt with military problems and Japan's diplomacy. He argued that "the way of self-defense in an independent state" ought to demarcate the "sovereignty line" (J. *shukensen*) and the "interest line" (J. *riekisen*) and protect both.[23] The sovereignty line was the territory of Japan, but the Japanese government linked the sovereignty line closely with the "interest line." Japan would have to protect nearby territory as well in order to secure the country's safety. The principal argument was that Japan should "protect" its interest line by any means necessary. The argument inherited the political genealogy of the *Seikanron* regarding the "Chosŏn issue." Yamagata proposed the interest line so as to hold Russia in check and to postpone its construction of the Trans-Siberian Railway. It was believed that Russian penetration into the Korean peninsula would become more active if the completion of the railroad took place and that Korea's independence was at risk. Were Russia to penetrate Korea, the Japanese sovereignty line at Tsushima would resemble a dagger pointed at the heart of Japan. Therefore, the best strategy to secure the independence of Japan was to protect the interest line, that is, the so-called independence of Korea. The Japanese government adopted the interest line plan and publicized it in the administrative policy speech at the meeting of the first Diet of the Japanese Empire.[24] At the commencement of the Diet, a Japanese memorandum regarding armaments that had been issued in 1893 urged Japanese officials to prepare for the upcoming entry by Russia and other Western powers into East Asia on the eve of the Trans-Siberian Railway's completion.[25]

When Yamagata advocated the interest line in 1890, Japan had been undergoing a broad range of reforms since the Meiji Restoration, including the promulgation of a new constitution, the convening of the Diet, and the adoption of a modernized domestic political system. This was the time when Japan pursued national development in terms of national interest and national power. Yamagata's memorandum was to introduce a new direction toward becoming the strong modern state of Japan and to advocate an aggressive national strategy. Two major historical events in Korea, the Imo Incident in 1882 and the Kapsin Coup in 1884, exerted influence on Japan's interest line, which had established an invasive state strategy and the expansion of the military force.[26] The Imo Incident expressed Korean discontent at the expanding Japanese influence over Korea since the Treaty of Ganghwa. The Kapsin Coup demanded modernization reforms throughout Korean society. These incidents escalated the Japanese crisis of consciousness to secure influence in Korea.

Japan aggressively utilized the interest line to extend into Korea and provoked the Sino-Japanese War and the Russo-Japanese War on the grounds of the interest line by protecting the "independence of Chosŏn." After winning the Sino-Japanese War, Yamagata planned to build two railways, one through Korea from Pusan to Ŭiju and the other through the Liaodong peninsula from Dalian Bay to Lushun. This aggressive expansion scheme would connect long rail lines through Korea and China to reach India.[27] However, Japan experienced humiliating diplomatic setbacks such as the Triple Intervention and the failure to occupy Amoy (Xiamen). After the Triple Intervention in 1895, the Japanese government accepted the Japanese military's goal to expand that same year and sought to become "the leader of East Asia." The Triple Intervention refers to the intervention of Great Britain, France, and Russia to oppose Japan's taking of the Liadong peninsula as part of concession from China as a result of China's defeat in the Sino-Japanese War.[28] The expansion of armaments accelerated. At the same time, Japan paid attention to its diplomatic cooperation with Western powers and succeeded in solidifying the Anglo-Japanese alliance.

As a result, Japan won the war against Russia. By achieving victory in the Russo-Japanese War, though, Japan fanned the flames of the Yellow Peril, an anti-Asian sentiment in the West. The Yellow Peril was a kind of fatalism associated with an image according to which Asians, who had no Western spiritual civilization, would seek to overthrow Western superiority through accepting Western modern technology.[29] The Yellow Peril stimulated another type of Japanese national crisis of consciousness. This crisis focused on Japan's diplomatic cooperation with Great Britain and the United States, which had been quite helpful for the modern development of Japan, in achieving desired goals in negotiations with other powers in East Asia. Through this, Japan strengthened the earlier diplomatic cooperation of Great Britain and United States. On the other hand, Japan accelerated the production of its armaments to accomplish its goal of continental expansion and mediated Japanese continental policy through its cooperative diplomatic relations with Western powers.

Meanwhile, the spread of the Yellow Peril in the West after the Russo-Japanese War served as momentum for Japan to see itself as the "colored" race compared to the "white" race, a barrier built in the West. This was a turning point for Japan in recognizing the need for Asian solidarity against white imperialism and in strengthening its leadership consciousness in Asia. Therefore, it could be said that the Russo-Japanese War was an important crossroad in the idea of Asian solidarity and Asianism. After the war, the insistence that the White Peril, rather than the Yellow Peril, was a more practical scenario was raised and the idea of Asianism—led by Japan—spread widely through Japanese society.[30]

Asianism against the Yellow Peril developed as an aggressive rationalization for justifying Japanese colonialism. In connection with the Chosŏn issue, it strengthened the interest line and articulated, through the *Seikanron*, the logic of the "shared ancestry among the Japanese and Koreans" (J. *Nissen dōsō*) and the view that the "Japanese and Koreans are the same" (J. *Naisen ichiyō*).[31] Racialism was first introduced in the early Meiji Period and developed into

Japanese race studies in the 1880s.[32] The studies of the Japanese race not only insisted that the Japanese race was composed of a mixture of various ethnic groups, it also supported the "shared ancestry among Japanese and Koreans" perspective by stating that the Japanese and Korean ethnic groups had much in common. This meant that Japan had transformed Japanese racial heterogeneity into a reason to invade Korea.[33] While the Yellow Peril was spreading in the West, the view of the "shared ancestry among Japanese and Koreans" and the view that "Japanese and Koreans are the same"—which disregarded the inherent identity of Koreans—were prevalent in Japan.[34] Asianism, according to which Japan considered itself the hegemon, proliferated and at the same time reinforced such views. A social atmosphere, which supported Japan's expansion into the continent, continued to grow in Japan.

Japan's Korea policy, which included in its resolution on the issue of Chosŏn to view Japan as Chosŏn's protectorate, was determined on May 30, 1904, after Japan had gained the upper hand against Russia.[35] Komura Jūtarō, the foreign minister, clarified the government's will to reinforce Japan's military in the war. According to Komura, "[t]his is an opportunity to expand the sphere of influence over Manchuria, Korea, and Yunhaeju (Siberia)." In August 1904, Japan enforced "protectorate politics" in Korea, and Japan made Korea a Japanese protectorate after winning the war with Russia.[36] Eventually, Japan secured exclusive influence over Korea, which had been pursued based upon the justification of "security" and the national goal for "development" since the Russian occupation of Tsushima. In addition, Japan finally carried out the annexation (J. *heigō*) of Korea in 1910 on the grounds that the Korean peninsula was unstable.[37] The official purpose of the annexation was, "regarding the exceptional friendly relations, to enhance mutual happiness and pursue the permanent peace of East Asia."[38]

As mentioned above, the annexation of Chosŏn occurred in the context of the development of the modern state of Japan and was based upon the justification of national self-defense due to the crisis caused by the Russian occupation of Tsushima. The so-called Chosŏn issue was a substitute for the crisis that the approach of the Western powers toward Korea had awakened. Japan began to recognize the traditional East Asian international order in the context of the "modern" imperialistic order. The fact that Japan experienced a crisis when observing the Western approach to Chosŏn meant that Japan considered Chosŏn to be an object of national interest. However, at this time,

Korea still felt a sense of superiority over Japan and treated the country in accordance with their pre-modern, good-neighbor relationship with Japan. In response, Japan took on the doubled tasks of modernizing diplomatic relations of equality with Korea and securing that sphere of influence before Western powers did. Japan's view of international law was affected by the Western powers' advances into East Asia as it began to seek influence in the region. In this context the Korean peninsula was the center of Japan's attention as the peninsula was regarded as the stepping stone to advance into the Asian continent through its annexation.

THE CONTINENTAL STATE PLAN OF JAPAN AND CHOSŎN

The Japanese Army led by Yamagata Aritomo, who had proclaimed the theory of the interest line after the successful modern reformation of the Imperial Army, accomplished the annexation of Korea, which enhanced the power of the modern state of Japan, through following the continental plan. These militarists rose to power and acted as if they had held sway over the destiny of the nation after winning the Sino-Japanese War, which was provoked after making the interest line a policy, from the view of military defense.[39] The Imperial Army of Japan enhanced its political influence through its independence of supreme command from the government and the Ministry of War (J. Gunbu daijin bukansei). In particular, Yamagata, who realized both the need for alliances with Western powers and the northern continental policy after the Triple Intervention, successfully arranged the Anglo-Japanese alliance while arguing against the civilian party represented by Itō Hirobumi. After the Anglo-Japanese Alliance was signed, it became apparent that the faction in the Army that had emerged from the Chōshū Domain (what is now considered Yamaguchi Prefecture) had gained the upper hand against the faction in the civilian party. In short, the continental expansion policy of the Army had been confirmed. The Anglo-Japanese Alliance enabled Japan to actively carry forward the northern continental policy with the support of Great Britain, which, like Japan, opposed the expansion of Russia in East Asia. Yamagata was the mastermind behind the alliance. Further, Prime Minister Katsura Tarō carried out the plan. Both politicians not only played key roles in the alliance with Great Britain, they also determined Japan's army-first continental policy.[40]

Signing the Anglo-Japanese Alliance was the Chōshū faction's proclamation to push forward with the northern continental policy and to establish hegemony over state management. At the same time, it was the foothold for Yamagata's political faction to strengthen its political position.[41] Terauchi Masatake's joining the cabinet as a field marshal in the Imperial Japanese Army following Katsura in 1902, pushed the northern continental policy further ahead when the military and political spheres were united in one governing body. The Russo-Japanese War was led mainly by the Army statesmen from the Chōshū Domain in the Yamagata camp, including the prime minister, the Army chief of staff, Yamagata, and Kodama Gentarō, who was the chief of staff in Manchuria.[42] The Chōshū Army faction around Terauchi strengthened its solidarity and heightened its right to speak in the political realm through its success in the Russo-Japanese War. In reality and in name, the Japanese government combined with the head of the military faction and led by the Prime Minister, who came from the Chōshū Domain, clarified continental policy. This militarily and politically combined leadership led to Japanese success in the Russo-Japanese War, its expanded power, and its sphere of influence. In short, the northern continental policy led by this army group had gained official status.[43]

Following the Russian occupation of Tsushima, Japan considered the Korean peninsula to be the foundation for the development of the "state" of Japan. Securing control over Korea was the priority of the Army after Yamagata's interest line reasoning was adopted by the Diet. In April 1907, the Japanese Diet adopted the Army's northern continental plan as the supreme national project responsible for the military defense policy of the Japanese Empire (J. Nihon teikoku kokubō hōshin).[44] The military defense policy of the empire was created as part of the belief according to which Japan would design a new national developmental direction after it had accomplished the important task of national independence by winning the war with Russia. Therefore, the military defense policy had significant meaning in terms of the course of Japan's state management after the Russo-Japanese War. The leaders of the Army established the military defense policy as a unified plan, which detailed that the Army would act as the main force and the Navy would act as its assistants. In so doing, the Army turned down Navy-inspired courses of action including the logic of a defensive, island empire. In contrast to the Navy, the Army reasoned for an aggressive and continental empire. The military defense policy of the Japanese Empire was a decision made by the Army, which treated Manchuria and Korea as un-detachable components of the empire the government sought to build. In other words, the policy promoted an aggressive course of self-defense.[45] The Army, with firm resolve, proposed that the national goal of Japan should be for it to become a northern continental state, that is, the Korean peninsula would become the continental state of the Japanese empire. This national plan proposed by the Chōshū Domain Army Faction proclaimed the Army's willingness to proceed with the aggressive northern continental policy, which would further strengthen the faction's power when the government signed the treaty with Great Britain in 1902 and also firmly establish the faction institutionally in the government.[46] According to this plan, Korea, which could not be detached from Manchuria and which was the key to the Army's expansion to the north, was the starting point.

Yamagata's idea to expand into the continent, which was directly connected to the Chosŏn interest line, was achieved by annexing Korea. However, two points of view were entwined when it came to the national policy of Japan. One considered the Korean peninsula from the geographic perspective by which Chosŏn would become a bridge between the Japanese islands and the continent. The other perceived the Korean peninsula as a beachhead for expanding further north. The differences were not realized before the annexation of Korea, but the interest line, directly connected with the Japanese sovereignty line, had been achieved.[47]

The different perspectives questioned the real purpose of the annexation of Korea and the direction of colonial policy in Korea, which would both become important for the dynamics of Japanese politics and Korean society in terms of colonial policy and the establishment of the colonial structure. In the same context, the first governor-general, Terauchi Masatake, who was commissioned with full authority for the annexation process, was a key figure. He was one of the central figures among the Army statesmen from the Chōshū Domain who had succeeded Yamagata and Katsura.[48] The primary reason for Terauchi's appointment to Korea was to employ the northern expansion policy by expediting the annexation process. On the other hand, during his remaining time in office, the dynamics of Japanese politics played roles which kept him in check through Katsura's time in office, who had political ambitions to hold the power that Itō had enjoyed. Through the successful campaign in the Russo-Japanese War, Terauchi rose like a meteor in Japanese politics. Katsura felt uneasy seeing this and sent Terauchi to Korea in an attempt to isolate him from Japanese politics.

Katsura and Yamagata favored an aggressive course of action in continental policy, such as supporting the Russo-Japanese War and signing the Anglo-Japanese Alliance. However, Yamagata was careful regarding cooperation with Great Britain and the United States and the economic management of Manchuria (J. Manju keiei). In contrast, Katsura, who paid exceptional attention to the economic benefits of Manchuria, was an aggressive supporter of a pro–continental policy. The difference was realized when Katsura, whose career in the Imperial Army faced downfall in its early stage, began to grow wary of Terauchi's political rise. He formed his own political party, joined hands with Gotō Shinpei—who had successfully reformed the Government-General in Taiwan—and planned to change the governmental system so as to implement an aggressive continental policy. In this way, the northern continental policy of Japan implied differences regarding colonial management. Those differences, which were interconnected with changes in Japanese politics, had created a critical conflict between Yamagata and Terauchi and Katsura and Gotō.[49] In terms of ruling colonial Chosŏn, opinions differed between considering Chosŏn the beachhead for the national security of Japan and seeing Chosŏn as a bridge into the continent and seeking colonial administration centered on Manchuria, which appraised highly the economic value of Manchuria.[50]

Both sides advocated for an active continental expansion policy and for using Korea as a cornerstone in the expansion of Japan, as seen in the Japanese recognition of the Chosŏn issue. According to the imperial course of self-defense, since the interest line had been adopted as national policy, Japan, by annexing Korea, sought a better cause by which to become a continental state. Japan was reluctant to say that Chosŏn had been colonized and instead used the term "annex," which meant, "Korea now faces extinction and the territory has become part of the Japanese empire. The term was carefully selected [so as] not to intimidate others."[51] For Japan, the annexation of Korea not only included a colonization process for expanding imperial benefits overseas, it also was the *sine qua non* of changing from an island state to a continental power. Japan wanted to expand its sphere of influence to the north as a continental state.[52] The major difference between the two would be the direction of foreign policy regarding expansion into the continent and remaining connected to the Chosŏn issue after Korea's annexation.

Regarding the policy for Korean colonial rule, the bridge perspective regarded the annexation of Korea as having been achieved. Japan, now a continental state with a Korean "bridge," had to pivot and focus all of its interests toward Manchuria to maintain the status quo regarding Korea. Japan would also have to be ready to fight Western powers if necessary. On the contrary, Terauchi and his political supporters who backed the beachhead view thought that the stabilization of the unstable Korea domestic situation should be the priority in the development state of Japan. Japan would have to face a similar national threat, such as the Russian occupation of Tsushima, if colonized Korea could not be stabilized. Therefore, to this view, the stabilization of Korea was of prime concern so it was a gradual approach to continental expansion. This stance was under the cooperative foreign relations with Great Britain and the United States.

The Government-General of Korea reflected the beachhead perspective when Terauchi resigned as minister of the Japanese Army and was then appointed as the first governor-general of Chosŏn. In other words, Terauchi was pushed away from the center stage of Japanese politics. At that time, the Army was accused of undermining the relatively stable political system (J. *keien*), and party politics once again emerged while grassroots movements developed during the Taishō democracy period (1912–26) in Japan. Terauchi had established an unprecedented ruling system over colonial Korea by listening to advice from his political friends in Japan, who told him to plan for the future of Korea. The Government-General of Chosŏn's ruling system, designed by Terauchi, was unique in that it gave absolute power to the governor-general of Chosŏn, who was subject only to the Emperor of Japan, so that the colonial government would not be affected by political affairs in Japan. Terauchi, who favored the beachhead concept, designed the colonial ruling system to enhance the stability of both the internal and external affairs of Korea. This became a political foothold for Terauchi and the later governors-general of Chosŏn.

CONCLUSION

Japan abandoned its isolationist policy when the expansion of Western powers into East Asia began and diligently pushed ahead with the modernization process. However, the Western advance into Chosŏn made Japan conscious of a national crisis, and the Korean peninsula was considered linked with the Japanese islands. Russia's occupation of Tsushima Island was a turning point for Japan. Japan saw the occupation as equal to a state of emergency for Japan, having encountered unpleasant experiences when opened by the West after the Opium War and also from that war's lessons. Japan converted its national crisis consciousness, recognized by Western powers, to the "Chosŏn issue." That is, Japan had to protect Korean independence for the sake of the defense of Japan.

That would be done by opening Korea through a treaty with Korea based upon modern international law. The Treaty of Ganghwa considered Korea to be an independent state—not a tributary state to China—and allowed Japan to secure national interests in Korea. Above all, that treaty functioned to eliminate traditional Chinese influences, but the treaty also meant that Japan had to establish its national interests in Korea before the West, and thus restrict the advances toward Korea by Western powers. Japan perceived the expansion of Western powers through the lens of national interest and security. Seeking to become a civilized state like the Western powers, Japan wanted to secure Korea as a base for national development while also restricting the advance of Western powers in East Asia. The *Seikanron* discourse reflected an inherent Japanese sense that Korea could not be detached for Japan to grow and to overcome the limitations of being an island state.

The occupation of Tsushima by the Russian fleet served as an opportunity for Japan to witness the Japanese national development problem and the perceptions of Korea in international contexts. Already having been completely incorporated into the modern world system, the "Chosŏn issue" may be said to have been a pivotal moment for Japan, which sought a means to become a "modern" state like the Western powers. The Treaty of Ganghwa may be said to have been a declaration of Japan's willingness to break down the pre-modern East Asian order and seek its national interest. This national will was reflected in Yamagata's interest line discourse, which became Japan's national policy in 1895. The interest line was the driving force behind the wars against China and Russia and eventually behind the annexation of Korea. By annexing Korea, Japan could resolve its Chosŏn issue. In other words, the annexation of Korea was necessary for Japan to become a continental state.

During this process, when Russia defeated Japan, the Japanese not only recognized Western perceptions of the East but also the perceptions of East versus West, the Japanese identity as Asian, and the development of Japan among other Asian nations witnessing the spread of the Yellow Peril in the West. Asianism became a pretext for the imperial development of the modern state of Japan against the modern of the West. In the same context, the Japan-Korea shared ancestry theory at the base of Japanese racism became a discourse for justifying Japanese rule and the annexation of Korea, which would support the national development of the "modern" state of Japan as a continental power.

Japan established the unique governing system of the Government-General of Chosŏn within the dynamics of its domestic politics. This was a relatively autonomous ruling system in which the governor-general, who was subject only to the emperor of Japan, was assigned full power to control the colony without regard to Japanese domestic politics.[53] The political system of the Government-General of Chosŏn became a foothold for the governor-general, who took a step back from the central political stage in Japan and regained power and prestige during his time in office in Korea. Therefore, the governor sought stability in controlling Korea, which was considered directly related to Japanese security, and pursued the most effective colonial system and policies by taking advantage of the colony's relative autonomy. This is the reason why, in the study of Korean history, the colonial policies of the Government-General of Chosŏn have been characterized as brutal suppression and unprecedented mobilization.

In general, the annexation of Korea was understood in the growing process of Japanese imperialism. On further consideration, however, we can see that it was through the Chosŏn issue that Japan was able to awaken its identity as the modern state of Japan toward Western powers. Japan already had been incorporated into the world system of imperialism and had written modern state laws similar to those of Western powers. The "Chosŏn issue" worked as an accelerator for the development of Japanese identity and national development. Containing and controlling Korea—from recognition of the Chosŏn issue until annexation—was the ultimate purpose of the modern state of Japan.

NOTES

1. Chŏn Sangsuk [Sang Sook Jeon], "Kukkwŏn sangsil kwa Ilbon ŭi Hanbando chŏngch'aek" [Japan's policy toward the Korean peninsula and the deprivation of Korean sovereignty], 8.

2. Chŏn Sangsuk, "Yugyo chisigin ŭi 'kŭndae' insik kwa Sŏgu 'Sahoe Kwahak' ŭi ihae: Kaeguk chŏnhu Kim Yunsik ŭi kaehwa insik kwa sŏyang hangmun suyongnon ŭl chungsim ŭro" [Confucian intellectual's conception of "modernity" and understanding of Western social sciences: Focused on Kim Yunsik's recognition of Kaewha and the reception of Western knowledge], 279–80.

3. Yi Hangi, "Hanguk mit Ilbon ŭi kaeguk kwa kukchebŏp" [International law and the open door of Korea and Japan], 200.

4. Chŏn Sangsuk, "Kŭndae 'Sahoe Kwahak' ŭi Tong Asia suyong kwa Meiji Ilbon 'Sahoe Kwahak' ŭi t'ŭkchil: Bluntschli's kukkahak suyong ŭl chungsim ŭro" [East Asia's acceptance of modern social sciences and modern the characteristics of Japanese social sciences: With priority given to the reception of Bluntschli's political thought], 185.

5. Hihara Toshikuni, *Kandai shisō no kenkyū* [Research on Chinese thought of the Han time], 358–66.

6. Chang Insŏng, *Chang So ŭi kukche chŏngch'i sasang* [Confucianism topics on international relations], 327.

7. Watanabe Hiroshi, *Higashi Ajia no ōken to shisō* [East Asian royal authority and thought], 148–83; and Yosijawa Seich'iro [Yoshizawa Seiichirō], translated by Chŏng Chi-ho, *Aegukchuŭi ŭi hyŏngsŏng* [Formation of Jingoism], 70.

8. Okita Yukuji, *Nihon kindai kyōiku no shisōshi kenkyū: Kokusaika no shisō keifu* [A study on educational history of modern Japan: Genealogy of globalization thought], 96.

9. Ibid., 65–66.

10. Mutō Shūtarō, *Kindai Nihon no shakai kagaku to Higashi Ajia* [Social sciences of modern Japan and East Asia], 7.

11. Isida Tak'esi [Ishida Takeshi], translated by Han Yŏng-hye, *Ilbon ŭi sahoe kwahak* [Japanese social sciences], 45.

12. Okita Yukuji, *Nihon kindai kyōiku no shisōshi kenkyū*, 106–7.

13. Ibid., 79–80.

14. Motoyama Yukihiko, *Meiji kokka no kyōiku shisō* [Educational thought of Meiji Japan], 3–4.

15. Chŏn Pokhŭi, *Sahoe chinhwaron kwa kukka sasang: Ku Hanmal ŭl chungsim ŭro* [The theory of social evolution and a spirit of nationalism], 18–28 and 52.

16. Ichimata Masao, "Nihon no kokusaihō o kizuita hitobito" [Figures who constructed Japanese international law]; and Inoue Isao, "'Kaikoku' to kindai kokka no seiritsu" [Open door and establishment of the modern state], 2.

17. Inoue Isao, "'Kaikoku' to kindai kokka no seiritsu," 34; and Yi Han-gi, "Hanguk mit Ilbon ŭi kaeguk kwa kukchebŏp," 209–10.

18. Pusan Fu, *Pusan fushi genkō* Vol. 6 [Documents of the Pusan official district Vol. 6], 181–85.

19. Pusan Fu, *Pusan fushi genkō* Vol. 6; and Sim Kichae, "Mangmal Myŏngch'i ch'ogi e issŏsŏ ŭi Ilbon ŭi tae-Chosŏn taeŭng" [The early Meiji government's foreign policy toward Korea], 3–4.

20. Sim Kichae, *Bakumatsu ishin Nitchō gaikōshi no kenkyū* [A study on the history of Japan-Chōsen foreign policies from the last period of Japan's feudal government to the Meiji Restoration], 45 and 52.

21. Sim Kichae, "Mangmal Myŏngch'i ch'ogi e issŏsŏ ŭi Ilbon ŭi tae-Chosŏn taeŭng," 9–14.

22. Ibid., 13.

23. Yamagata Aritomo, "Gaikō seiryaku ron" [Political strategy of foreign policies] (March 3, 1890), 196–201.

24. Yamagata Aritomo, "Teikoku no kokuze ni tsuite no enzetsu" [A speech on the empire's national policy] (December 6, 1890), 204–7.

25. Yamagata Aritomo, "Gunbi iken sho" [Opinion on military preparedness] (December 1893), 215–22.

26. Fujiwara Akira, translated by Seo Yungchik, *Ilbon kunsasa* [Japanese military history]; and Dobe Ryoichi, translated by Yi Hyunsoo and Kwon Taehwan, *Kŭndae Ilbon ŭi kundae* [The modern Japanese military].

27. Kobayashi Michihiko, *Nihon no tairiku seisaku, 1895–1914: Katsura Tarō to Gotō Shinpei* [Japanese continental politics 1895–1914: From Katsura Tato to Goto Shinpei], 27.

28. Yamagata Aritomo, "Gunbi iken sho" (December 1893), 230.

29. Iriye Akira, translated by Yi Seonghwan, *Ilbon ŭi woegyo* [Diplomacy of Japan], 56.

30. Sŭben Saarŏ [Sven Saaler], "Kukche kwangye ŭi pyŏnyong kwa naeshŏnŏl aident'iti hyŏngsŏng" [The influence of changes in international relations on the formation of national identity: The creation of Asianism], 139–40; and Chŏn Sangsuk, *Chosŏn Ch'ongdok chŏngch'i yŏngu: Chosŏn Ch'ongdok ŭi "sangdae-jŏk chayulsŏng" kwa Ilbon ŭi Han'guk chibae chŏngch'aek t'ŭkchil* [Japanese "politics of the Korean governor-general," 1910–1936: "Political autonomy" of the Korean governor-general and the "specialty" of Japanese colonial control of Korea], 63.

31. Chŏn Sangsuk, "Kukkwŏn sangsil kwa Ilbon ŭi Hanbando chŏngch'aek," 13.

32. Peter Duus, *The Abacus and the Sword*, 414.

33. Oguma Eiji, *Tan'itsu minzoku shinwa no kigen* [The origin of the myth of a single race nation], 73–79.

34. Nakatsuka Akira, *Kindai Nihon no Chōsen ninshiki* [Modern Japan's perception of Korea], 92.

35. Gaimushō, ed., "Taikan hōshin ni kansuru kette" [Decision on Korean policies], 224–28.

36. Chŏn Sangsuk, "Rŏ-Il chŏnjaeng chŏnhu Ilbon ŭi taeryuk chŏngch'aek kwa Terauch'i" [Terauchi and Japan's continental politics in the Russo-Japanese War], 132.

37. "Kankoku wo teikoku ni heigō no ken" [The matter to annex Korea to the Japanese Empire]; Chōsen Sōtokufu, *Furoku 1* [Appendix 1]; and Shunjō Tokio, *Kankoku heigō shi* [History of Korean annexation], 624–27.

38. Gaimushō, ed., "Kankoku heigō ni kansuru jōyaku" [Treaties on Korean annexation], 340.

39. Inoue Kiyoshi, *Nihon no gunkokushugi III* [Japanese militarism III], 50.

40. Kobayashi Michihiko, *Nihon no tairiku seisaku, 1895–1914*, 55.

41. Chŏn Sangsuk, "Rŏ-Il chŏnjaeng chŏnhu Ilbon ŭi taeryuk chŏngch'aek kwa Terauch'i," 126–27.

42. Kitaoka Shin'ichi, *Nihon rikugun to tairiku seisaku: 1906–1918 nen* [Japanese Army and its continental politics, 1906–1918]; and Matsushita Yoshio, *Nihon gunbatsu no kōbō* Vol. 1 [The rise and fall of Japanese warlords Vol. 1], 353–56.

43. Chŏn Sangsuk, "Rŏ-Il chŏnjaeng chŏnhu Ilbon ŭi taeryuk chŏngch'aek kwa Terauch'i," 129–30.

44. Moriyama Shigenori, *Kindai Nikkan kankeishi kenkyū: Chōsen shokumichika to kokusai kankei* [A study of modern Japan-Korea Relations: Colonization of Korea and international relations], 228–29.

45. Kitaoka Shin'ichi, *Nihon rikugun to tairiku seisaku*, 9–13.

46. Inoue Kiyoshi, "'Kaikoku' to kindai kokka no seiritsu," 74–76; and Chŏn Sangsuk, "Rŏ-Il chŏnjaeng chŏnhu Ilbon ŭi taeryuk chŏngch'aek kwa Terauch'i," 135–36.

47. Chŏn Sangsuk, "Chosŏn Ch'ongdok chŏngch'i cheje wa kwallyoje: 1910-yŏndae rŭl chungsim ŭro, 17.

48. For more details, see Chŏn Sangsuk, "Rŏ-Il chŏnjaeng chŏnhu Ilbon ŭi taeryuk chŏngch'aek kwa Terauch'i," 127–30.

49. Kobayashi Michihiko, *Nihon no tairiku seisaku, 1895–1914*, 43, 139, and 188–216.

50. On the differences and conflict in the Chōshū Domain Army clique, and the conflict between the army clique and the Japanese political parties regarding the power struggle and continental policy, see Chŏn Sangsuk, "'Chosŏn t'ŭksusŏng' ron kwa Chosŏn singmin chibae ŭi silje" [Theory of Korean uniqueness and Chosŏn colonial reality].

51. Kurachi Tetsukichi, *Kurachi Tetsukichi-shi jutsu Kankoku heigō no keii*, 11–12.

52. Chŏn Sangsuk, *Chosŏn Ch'ongdok chŏngch'i yŏn'gu*, 144–45.

53. On the autonomous ruling system of the Government-General of Chosŏn, see Chŏn Sangsuk, "Ilche ŭi singminji Chosŏn haengjŏng ilwŏnhwa wa Chosŏn Ch'ongdok ŭi 'chŏngch'i-jŏk chayulsŏng'" [The colonial administrative unification of Japanese imperialism and the "political autonomy" of the governor-general in Korea], 281–306.

3
Japanese Propaganda in the United States from 1905

ANDRE SCHMID

In 1934, an American observer commented, "[f]ew nations have striven so manfully to create a pleasant impression upon foreigners as have the Japanese."¹ Written shortly after the Japanese invasion of Manchuria, the statement reflected back on the intense propaganda skirmishes that had raged across the Pacific over the last three years. Yet the author's observation, while rooted in the politics of its day, can also be extended back as far as the early Meiji period, when the Japanese government first became concerned with foreign opinion. From its earliest days the Japanese government had sought to influence foreign opinion, combining its diplomatic and military efforts to redefine its position in the international community with what today, in the language of postcolonialism, would be called a commitment to the politics of cultural representation and discourse. Their efforts sought to shape the cultural understandings of Japan that underpinned the diplomatic policies of the powers.

In this long history of propaganda, Korea had a special place. Colonialism as a practice, after all, reflected not just on the colonized but also on the colonizer. To claim the position of a colonizer was to present oneself as possessing all the perquisites purportedly necessary to civilize others. Colonizing Korea, in other words, enabled Japan to present itself as belonging with the Western powers at the highest levels of the hierarchy of civilization—a goal the Meiji government had been seeking ever since notions of civilization had been used by the powers to impose unequal treaties on Japan.

One might expect that there would have been some reluctance, if not outright resistance, among Western commentators to the idea of a new competitor on colonial frontiers. Given the emphasis in postcolonial approaches to the centrality of culture and race to colonial power, it is perhaps somewhat surprising to see Anglo American writers at the outset of the twentieth century so readily acceding to the ascendance of a Japanese empire. After all, as a non-white, non-Western, and non-Christian nation, Japan, according to the dominant colonial logic, fit the criteria for inclusion into the colonized not the colonizing camp. Yet as English-language commentaries on the annexation of Korea show, Japan's rule was almost without exception welcomed by Western pundits.

There are many factors involved in explaining the quick acquiescence of not just the US government but also, more broadly, American public opinion to Korea's subjugation. This chapter explores one aspect: Japanese propaganda. How did the Japanese government solicit support for the colonization of Korea in the United States? In articles published in the mainstream American media—especially magazines—by officials as high as the governor-general, in annual reports distributed free of charge, and in various writings and interviews, Japanese colonial ideology found a prominent place in English-language writings about the colonial conditions in Korea. Using a language and appealing to a wide spectrum of ideologies that were familiar to an American public already enthusiastically engaged in their own colonial enterprise in the Philippines, these propaganda efforts found a sympathetic audience. As I argue, these Japanese voices drowned out the far more marginalized voices of Korean nationalists. Some American critics did nevertheless emerge, but for the most part their criticisms focused on specific excesses without moving to challenge the legitimacy of Japanese colonization itself. It was not until the early 1940s, after the bombing of Pearl Harbor, that articles supporting Korean independence began appearing regularly in US policy journals.

THE MOTIVES FOR PROPAGANDA

The annexation of Korea, as has been well recounted by many historians, involved a number of diplomatic maneuvers by Japan designed to eliminate the potential for international opposition.[2] The Sino-Japanese War in 1895 had eliminated Qing influence in the peninsula. After the continued vulnerability of Japan was exposed by the Triple Intervention, an alliance was concluded with the British in 1902 in preparation for what was seen as an inevitable conflict with Russia. After emerging from the war victorious—much to the surprise of most of the world—Japan approached the United States to settle the question of the Philippines, reaching the Taft-Katsura understanding, which recognized Japanese interests in the peninsula for the acceptance of the newly declared US colony in the Philippines.[3] Although this completed the diplomatic arrangements that enabled Japan to impose a protectorate over Korea, Japan did not rest with this official approval of their growing empire. Its success in establishing itself as a power, not just in Korea but more broadly throughout East Asia, still depended on the continued cooperation of both the British and the Americans, the two global hegemons. Japan had reached its regional position only through their assent and their capital.[4] This dependency, especially given the humiliating experience of the Triple Intervention a decade earlier, made Japanese authorities most sensitive to any criticism emanating from Anglo Americans of their colonizing practices in Korea.

There were also some special concerns about Japanese ties with the United States since this was not a period of smooth relations. Earlier tensions over Hawai'i and the Philippines had, by the early years of the twentieth century, culminated in controversies over the treatment of Japanese immigrants along the West Coast of the United States. The rampant anti-Japanese sentiment in the United States continually threatened to escalate and exacerbate tensions between the two governments. Given these conditions, Japanese leaders were apprehensive that their policies in Korea, if taken up by the American missionary or business community, might become further factors in a tense relationship. One Japanese writer, Adachi Kinnosuke, laid bare these concerns to his English reading audience.

> Why all this solicitude on the part of Japan for the good opinions of the world, especially that of the United States? Simply this: At the present moment the statesmen of Nippon are stalking a large game, a very large game—nothing less than a triple understanding between the United States, Great Britain, and Nippon. In their judgment, this understanding is strong enough to form a despotic tribunal which will be able to dictate the peace of the Far East, whether anybody else wishes it or not.[5]

However important protecting their interests in Korea was to Japan, he elaborated, it was not worth jeopardizing the larger goal of maintaining Japan's relationship with the Americans and the British.

> Now, we want Korea, and want her badly. But, compared with this great game that we are after . . . Korea is nothing. If our action in the Korean peninsula, therefore, is in the least to mar our success in bring [sic] about the triple understanding, we would not hesitate to throw overboard the whole Korean business. . . . If, however, we can obtain both, we shall be glad. This, then, is the reason why we are particularly anxious that the United States should see where we stand, what we are doing, and how we are behaving in Korea.[6]

Propaganda, then, sought to ensure that what had been achieved officially, at the level of inter-governmental understandings, was not undermined by critical reactions among the public. Despite the fact that the Americans and the British signaled their official approval by closing their offices on the peninsula immediately after the announcement of the Protectorate Treaty in 1905, Japanese colonial officials pursued a number of endeavors to pre-empt possible criticism, to garner support for their new colonial role, and to control the damage of any negative publicity.

This propaganda effort in relation to Korea must be seen as part of a long history of attempts to control the international image of Japan in the Meiji period. Since the imposition on Japan of unequal treaties—treaties that rested on an appraisal of Japan's "level of civilization"—the Japanese state had been involved not just in a massive reform effort but also in a wide assortment of endeavors to display their ascension in the international hierarchy. Whether this meant tours of Western countries or the holding of elaborate dance balls in the Tokyo Crystal Palace (Rokumeikan), the intent was to demonstrate that Japan was now civilized and, thus, no longer worthy of unequal treaties.[7] These propaganda efforts reached new heights in the late Meiji period as tensions with Russia became more acute. From 1900 onward Japanese diplomats used connections, influence, and outright bribery to get their views on relations with Russia published in popular newspapers and wire services in Europe and the United States. Eager to assuage the fears that had been stirred up by the Russians about the dangers of the "yellow hordes," the Japanese countered with their own propaganda offensive. Special deals were made with wire services and consideration was even given to buying Western newspapers. High-level cabinet ministers, including Itō Hirobumi, initiated these endeavors, assigning Kaneko Kentaro to the United States and Suematsu Kenchō to Europe on missions to cultivate support for Japan. They were sent with guidelines to present Japan as acting only in self-defense and working for peace and civilization in East Asia. Kaneko vigorously pursued his mission, regularly meeting with journalists, penning his own articles, and giving as many speeches as possible at such places as the Harvard Club. In all, by his own reckoning, he gave more than one hundred speeches, many of which were reproduced in local newspapers.[8]

Whatever the effectiveness of these various efforts, they reached their culmination just prior to Japan's imposition of the Protectorate over Korea in 1905. They were quickly extended to Japan's policy in Korea, as another effort was made to muster support for Japanese policy in the mainstream American press, a policy that was variously pursued into the 1920s. If during the Russo-Japanese War vanquishing a white power required a battle for public opinion so did the usurpation of the sovereignty of a neighbor. In this new effort, colonial officials had it easier, since unlike during the war, Japanese officials had been battling similar efforts launched by the Russians. This was not the case with the colonization of Korea, where, in fact, there was little direct competition. Indeed, with little information available in Western languages about Korea, Japanese officials did not even have to battle many ingrained or established opinions.

In the early years of the twentieth century, far less English-language writing was available about Korea than either Japan or China. Korea had been more isolated than its two neighbors and consequently never attracted as much commercial or cultural interest. Fewer diplomats, fewer missionaries, and even fewer traders led to fewer articles and books about the peninsula. It was not until the end of the nineteenth century that more voluminous and systematic treatments of Korea were published—a time when many writers, following the lead of William Eliot Griffis' use of the appellation "Hermit Kingdom," saw themselves as venturing into unexplored territory on the peninsula. Even George Curzon, visiting Korea in the 1890s, could write about Korea in the vein of a daring buccaneer entering unknown, mysterious lands—a situation that clearly excited a man who was to become the viceroy of British India (1898–1905).⁹ Yet still, with only a small resident community of foreigners, there were few articles, let alone monographs, that were published by people with more than a passing acquaintance with Korea.

The colonization of the peninsula was to alter this state of affairs. The establishment of the Protectorate in 1905 and outright annexation in 1910 attracted greater international attention than ever before. An unprecedented number of articles, editorials, and books emerged discussing peninsular affairs. This heightened interest, however, usually had less to do with Korea itself than an interest in Korea as an unusual site of colonialism. Indeed, the increase in attention to peninsular matters centered as much on Japan as Korea, since most writers focused on the novelty of this parvenu colonizer ruling its neighbor. To one contemporary observer, the colonization of Korea was an "experiment" that was "new in the history of the world. . . . Never before in the history of the world has one oriental nation assumed a protectorate over another."¹⁰ This alone, explained Edwin Maxey in the *Political Science Quarterly* in December 1910, was "worthy of careful study by all interested in political or ethnic science."¹¹ This trope of Korea as an experiment in colonialism became common, usually serving to praise the accomplishments of the Japanese.¹² William Eliot Griffis wrote: "[t]he experiment of Japan in attempting to amalgamate the Korean and the Japanese people . . . is of a sort unique in history and is of world-wide interest."¹³ Deemed an unusual experiment, the colonization of Korea became worthy of observation and evaluation—and it was in this mode of assessing its merits and demerits that much English-language writing was framed for years to come.¹⁴ To this end, most English-language writing focused on the administrative capabilities of the Japanese colonial government, as travelers, journalists, and various styles of pundits sought to judge this new colonial government.

The problem such writers faced was that with such a scanty legacy of English-language works on Korea available, there were few resources to which writers and pundits could turn to provide the context for their evaluations. One option, however, was to turn to Japanese sources of information. With more foreigners residing in Japan than in Korea and with more American newspaper correspondents posted in Japan, the colonization of Korea was often treated as an extension of media treatments of Japan, as a type of foreign policy issue that marked a new stage in the remarkable reform process of the Meiji period.¹⁵ Not surprisingly, coverage of Korea by these writers who were more familiar with the islands than the peninsula, was generally written from the perspective of Japan.

HISTORY AND ANNUAL REPORTS

This reliance on Japanese sources was manifest in English-language treatments of Korean history. Writers who sought to contextualize current events within the past—what were the historical reasons for Korea's fall? —had recourse to few sources. Some missionaries had sought to fill this void with works that today are often hailed as the of origin for Korean studies. Homer Hulbert and James Scarth Gale were two of the most famous.[16]

There were few works written by Koreans available at this time. Inside Korea there had long been calls for a new Korean history among the intellectuals of the Patriotic Enlightenment movement (Aeguk Kyemong Undong), but the likes of Sin Ch'aeho and Pak Ŭnsik were only beginning to offer the first glimpses of what this new history might offer. Although works such as Sin's *Toksa sillon* (A new reading of history) or Pak's *Han'guk tongsa* (Painful history of Korea) offered historical perspectives on Korea, the impact of these historiographical advances was largely restricted to domestic consumption. No foreign language versions of these works appeared and, while works such as Pak's and others were available to Chinese readers, it was not until well after Liberation that a complete version of nationalist Korean historical perspectives reached Western audiences. The timing of colonization was crucial in this regard since it took place before Korean scholars were able to fully explore the potential of nationalist history and before such versions could be disseminated internationally. Editors of the *TaeHan maeil sinbo*, for example, were fully aware of this imbalance and frequently lamented the influence of Japanese representations of Korea on the international stage, yet despite their best efforts, there was little they could do to counter this trend.[17]

In the meantime, it was Japanese versions of the Korean past that dominated. By the first decade of the twentieth century, the Japanese had developed a wide variety of modern versions of the Korean past that served their imperial interests—what Korean historians have long called *singminji sagwan* (colonial historical perspectives). These versions of the Korean past quickly found their way into English-language accounts of Korean history, whether in the case of book length treatments of Korean history or in brief summaries in newspapers. This can be seen in the uncritical use in most English-language writing of Japanese theories of the early state of Mimana—the Japanese pronunciation of the term was always used rather than the Korean pronunciation, *Imna*—and the tendency of some to see Mimana as an early episode of colonialism that foreshadowed contemporary events.[18] Thus, with few early English-language studies of Korea and a still developing Korean nationalist history that had little presence on the international stage, Japanese colonial histories of Korea quickly insinuated themselves into English-language writing on Korea.

The use of Japanese sources of information was not restricted to historical studies alone. Nor was the Japanese colonial government content to let this relationship rest in the hands of private individuals. Indeed, the paucity of information available on current conditions in Korea afforded both a challenge and an opportunity to the colonial government. Stung by the criticism of such individuals such as Homer Hulbert and Frederick McKenzie and worried about the potential of more such broadsides, the colonial government pursued a number of projects to shape public opinion in the United States about the colonization of the peninsula.

This meant the colonial government became involved in publishing English-language materials to publicize its efforts. The most important of these, beginning in 1907, was the publication of a glossy yearbook titled, *Annual Report on the Progress and Reforms in Korea*. During the first decade of publication, the yearbooks' format was a "before and after" presentation offering explanatory, pictorial, and statistical evidence of the changes Japan had made on the peninsula since establishing the Protectorate. This approach could be applied to almost any topic, from hygiene to road systems, with the contrast achieved through the judicious choice of adjectives. Accordingly, the peninsula's financial condition before annexation was in the "wildest confusion," and expenditures "wasted to no purpose," but after Japan's reforms, the foundation of Korea's finances was "firmer," and details of how these achievements had been accomplished were buttressed by reams of statistics.[19] This contrastive effect was also captured in photographs, as in the case of two pictures of the Han River south of Seoul. A photograph of a bridge built under the new Japanese administration was placed next to a second photograph showing a few boats moving back and forth across the river, labeled "before the construction of the Iron Bridge."[20]

The prose of these reports was not always even this subtle. As one historical account opened, "[f]or many centuries . . . her [Korean] people did little towards development as a nation." All the standard reasons were trotted out—reliance on China, corruption, factionalism, and inability to reform. "All culture was lost; industry was at its lowest ebb; and the life and property of the people was in constant danger."²¹ The editor of the 1917–18 annual report wrote an especially enthusiastic description of subsequent changes. "It appears as though the entire Peninsula, for the first time in its modern history, has been blessed with the dawning of prosperity and has recovered from the unspeakable poverty and depression to which its people had been subjected for many a century past." Japanese education policy, it explained, "is making a favorable impression upon the natives and is aiding wonderfully in the promotion of the standard of civilization in both town and country."²² While the emphasis was on material additions—road systems, sanitation facilities, modern buildings, and the like—the editors were careful to make sure that material progress could not be interpreted as leaving moral well-being behind. They may have claimed to be modernizing Korea, but their efforts left no room for the malaise of modernity. "Though the progress of material civilization is apt to induce moral relaxation," one volume stated, "the public morality of the Koreans is in general steadily improving."²³ These volumes were powerful testaments to Japan's purported colonial efforts. Individually, they served to publicize Japanese enterprises on the peninsula during the last fiscal year, and together, they sought to offer a sequential record of—as the titles suggest—progress over time.

These reports presented the public face of colonialism. Written in objective tones and filled with types of statistics that in the early twentieth century symbolized the information of a modern state, the reports were replete with information needed by writers who were unfamiliar with the Korean situation. With few alternatives, writers frequently used these reports and peppered their articles with material gleaned from them. Writers of varied publications such as *The Outlook*, *Scribner's Magazine*, *Unpartisan Review*, and *Political Science Quarterly* used statistics and information from these books.²⁴ One year's edition was praised by the editors of *The Nation* as "a record of enlightening and painstaking endeavor."²⁵ The *Review of Reviews* welcomed the arrival of the 1915 edition, with an approving title, "Korea—A Tribute to Japanese Administration."²⁶ If the Japanese colonization of Korea, for many of these writers, was seen as an experiment to be judged, they came to their positive conclusions on the basis of information provided by colonial officials.

OFFICIAL VOICES

One unusual aspect of Japanese propaganda was the publication by leading colonial officials of articles in the mainstream American media. While there was certainly a type of one-upmanship among rival Western colonial powers, as each sought to prove its administrative superiority to others, no colonizing countries other than Japan had their officials writing to explain the rationale of their colonial policy to the American public. This was a testament to the special circumstances of Japan's rise to the status of colonizer: its lateness in world historical time, its potential for conflict with the United States that was also expanding into the Pacific Ocean, and its continued dependence on the goodwill and capital of the United States. These factors led a wide range of colonial officials, including a number of governor-generals, to publish English-language articles in the mainstream American media. In some cases, these essays sought to elucidate the reasons for recent actions on the part of the colonial government; in other cases, articles were offered as a defense of Japanese actions after negative publicity. Whatever the case, the articles tended to be solicitous in tone as writers sought to convince the readers of the righteousness of Japanese policy.[27]

The first of these articles to appear was published under the name of none other than Itō. Perhaps more than any other action in the colonization of Korea, the appointment of Itō as the resident-general in 1905, helped assuage the concerns of Western powers. Itō was the official best known to Western audiences, the man credited more than any other with leading the reforms that had transformed Japan through the Meiji period or, in the words of one of his English-language obituaries, "the most famous of all the men who have made Japan one of the world's seven great powers."[28] His assassination in 1909 by An Chunggŭn received virtually no favorable mainstream American press and, in the hands of most writers, news of Ito's death was interpreted as an indication of the ungratefulness of Koreans and disgrace to their country.[29]

Itō's article appeared in the widely circulated *Harper's Weekly* on January 11, 1908, titled "Japanese Policy in Korea."[30] The piece sought to explain the need for the seven clause treaty of July 14, 1907 and offered a number of broader rationales for Japanese rule—rationales that with one exception had largely been used in Japan and Korea and now were being reproduced for international consumption. What is most striking about this piece is its passive writing style that gave Japan little agency in the colonization of Korea. Throughout his piece, Itō writes not about Japanese initiatives or desires nor was he interested in offering a boastful account of recent events leading to the Protectorate that would offer credit to Japan. Instead, Japanese policy toward Korea is presented as being foisted onto Japan as a result of events both external and internal to the peninsula. In addressing the Russo-Japanese War, for example, Itō does not address how Korea was central to Japanese security concerns or how Japan's victory offered it an opportunity to establish a protectorate and brushes aside any active Japanese interest with the blandishment, "[t]hroughout the course of the Russo-Nippon War, circumstances brought the two countries together." After the war, he continues, the Japanese did not take advantage of the change in the balance of power, rather "we were compelled to revise our relations with Korea and change our attitude and policies toward her almost entirely."[31] The language of compulsion fills the article. This downplaying of Japanese agency reached the extent of outright prevarication when he denied any Japanese role in the abdication of King Kojong, suggesting falsely that this was the result of those Korean officials "who appreciated the magnitude of the affair" and who "without a single word from Nippon" forced Kojong to abandon his rule.

According to Itō, the problems of Korea were largely the result of Korean incompetence. He explained this in a number of ways, all of which have been widely discussed in historical literature on Japanese colonial ideology. His article especially emphasized Korean reliance on Chinese learning: "beyond that there is nothing," he claimed. As a result, "[t]hey look upon Nippon as a barbarous country, they regard themselves as the civilized and enlightened race. As for the common people and the farmers, they have no education or culture whatsoever." Together with the infighting among officials, this led to no improvement of Korean internal affairs, a situation which Itō asserts Japan could only watch quietly until finally the situation became so bad that it "compelled us to abandon our silent acquiescence." Similarly, the situation "left us in the helpless condition of waiting upon the pleasure and abiding by the judgement of the Koreans." Itō also appealed to internationally held social Darwinian ideas of relations between nations to illustrate how Japan had little choice but to conquer Korea. The Protectorate, for example, "is the natural outcome of the life of the weak that cannot cope against the strong." Put slightly differently, he wrote "the time and the world have compelled the Koreas to walk side by side with Nippon."[32]

Itō's article gained persuasiveness from his confidence to admit the problems facing Japan. He acknowledged that colonization was "not what the Korean prayed for," admitted that mistakes had already been made and would be made again and that there were all sorts of difficulties. For these, Itō took personal responsibility. "I have felt the magnitude of such difficulties at almost every point," and sought to assure the reader that despite these difficulties he was trying his best. In the type of comment that was to become common in Japanese colonial writing for foreign audiences, Itō presented himself as committed not to Japanese interests but to those of Koreans. "Sincerity was the key-note of all that I have tried to accomplish in Korea in behalf of the Korean Imperial family and of the people."[33]

The most unusual thread in the tapestry woven by Itō was his comparisons of Korea to earlier stages in Japanese history, specifically the Meiji period. While such an approach was not uncommon in Japanese-language writing, it took a slightly different twist in English-language pieces. For Itō, these comparisons served to highlight commonalities insofar as he saw the task of reforms in the Korea of today as the same facing Japan in the early days of the Meiji. So, too, was the commitment of the Korean elite to Chinese learning similar to "those young men in the closing days of the Shogunate in Nippon." This comparative tact, in demonstrating similitude, suggested that Japan was best suited to lead Korea on a path of reform. It was Japan that had already undergone the same type of process that now confronted the people of the peninsula and that had the experience to understand just what was needed in Korea. Although in this particular piece, Itō did not frame his article in the style of Pan-Asianism that could be found in Japan and was to increase in the coming years, this notion that Japan shared essential qualities with Korea that made it comprehend its neighbor most fully—in short, as an oriental nation Japan better understood its oriental neighbor and, thus, was best suited to rule the country.

In these many ways, Itō presented himself as a colonial officer devoted to modern reform, a humble bureaucrat earnestly seeking to overcome many difficulties, and a man compelled by historical circumstances to fulfill a mission in Korea. Only in the last line of the article do we get a glimpse of a different Itō. As if unable to maintain his performance for the entire article, he finally discloses his ambitions and desires for Japan in such a way that undermines his attempts to represent Japan as acting without choice. "The one prayer of mine," he reveals in the very last line of the article, "is for the extension of Nippon's power in the Far East." Such sentiments were rarely publicly expressed by the careful Itō, as in other media he extended his usual message about the virtues of Japanese rule.[34]

The content of Itō's message—his emphasis on the lack of modernizing impulses, and the geographical position of Korea—was carried on by many other Japanese officials over succeeding years. These other officials were not, however, always as subtle in their craft. Adachi Kinnosuke, writing in the *Review of Reviews*, was especially blunt.

> We shall be frank about it—we shall say that we are carrying things with a high hand in Korea. We have gone over into the backyard of our neighbor, and we are telling him to kindly move on—simply because we need his home. We are doing this just as the Americans have done to the Indians, the rightful owners of America; just as the British have done to the Hindus; just as the Russians have done to the Tartars and the Chinese . . . Nippon has joined the household of great powers; she has become civilized.[35]

His brazenness stemmed not only from his admission of the highhanded tactics of Japanese colonial rule, but also his linkage of Korea to other colonial settings. What Japan is doing in Korea, he suggested, was little different than what other powers do in their own colonial settings—and such actions are reduced to power and civilization.

Confessional essays about Japanese interests and motives were not welcomed by most of the Japanese charged with soliciting US support for Japanese colonial rule. One of these people, Karl Kiyoshi Kawakami, emerged as a prominent public defender of Japanese policy. Educated in the United States and married to an American, Kawakami was a smooth and articulate writer who, in various media and in published books, wrote more about US-Japanese relations than probably any other English-language author of his age. His concern was not exclusively focused on Korea, as his writing ranged across the full spectrum of US-Japanese relations, but in the years after annexation he devoted a great deal of attention to the peninsula, an indication of just how important annexation was for relations with the United States.[36] In a 1912 book, titled *American-Japanese Relations: An Inside View of Japan's Policies and Purposes*, Kawakami wrote he aimed for "the furtherance of friendship and good-will between my native country and the country which I have virtually adopted—a task to which he devoted 138 pages to what he called the "Korea Question."[37]

He opened his first chapter on Korea, "Why Japan Occupied Korea," by addressing Adachi's essay, without directly naming him. Seeing the piece as one that had "unwittingly added material" that intensified American misconceptions about Japan's role in Korea, Kawakami worked to undermine Adachi's work. He did so largely by giving a brief history of Japanese-Korean relations, one that moved away from Adachi's assertion of a highhanded policy to return to the theme of a Japan that had been compelled by circumstances to take the actions it did.[38] Less willing than Itō to admit to mistakes, Kawakami wrote glowingly of Japanese intentions and deeds. He was also aware that there had been international criticism of certain Japanese policies, and he sought to contain their growth. In so doing, he was open about the relationship between public opinion and US policy. While he was confident of official US support, he worried about criticism in the media.

> As a Japanese, I must add that the prompt recognition by the American government of Japan's claim in Korea, at a time when the Mikado's Empire needed most the moral support of Western powers, will always be remembered with gratitude by the Japanese, and unless those critics, who have their own axes to grind, conspire to misrepresent Japanese activities before the American public, the Korean question will provide no occasion for disturbing the traditional friendship between the two nations.[39]

Preventing such disturbances was certainly an objective that Kawakami shared with the many colonial officials who published in English, but his concerns moved beyond this. As the Japanese writer who was likely most familiar with American opinions about Japan, Kawakami also realized that such disturbances were not likely since Americans appeared to be concerned not so much with the legitimacy of Japanese rule but rather with the consequences of that rule for their own interests. This is why Kawakami's treatment of Japanese policy in Korea devoted considerable attention to commercial interests and the role of missionaries, in both cases attempting to demonstrate that the change in administration in 1910 would not affect US interests in either of these realms. Arguing that Japan was not using tactics that favored its own businesses, Kawakami asserted that the "Open Door" policy was being respected by the colonial authorities—what he called "fair play and a square deal."[40] He described in great detail the achievements that American businesses had already made, sought to show how Japanese laws had made ventures in Korea more profitable and stable, and even went so far as to write that for US trade "there is much room which can be exploited for its further advancement."[41]

Missionaries were a more delicate topic for Kawakami. With some of the most prominent critics such as Homer Hulbert having a missionary background and the fact that missionaries had been one of the most important conduits of information on contemporary events, what negative publicity the Japanese administration had received could be traced back to the mission community.[42] In response, Kawakami sought to smooth over possible tensions. He did this partly by praising the missionaries and their work, asserting that both missionaries and the colonial government served the same civilizing purposes. While there had been some difficulties in the early days, when some missionaries had still hoped the United States would take a stronger stand in Korea, he pointed out that such hopes had been allayed by official US policy. Now most missionaries accepted Japanese rule and worked with the administration, following the policy he credited to Itō of a "harmonious cooperation" of "sound religion and honest government, each working out its own great purposes without interfering with or infringing upon the rights and responsibilities of the others."[43] Kawakami downplayed any conflict—referring to it as an issue of the past and preferring to dwell on the many signs of cooperation—but he could not restrain himself from returning to this theme in his final paragraph. Here he delineated what was a key divide, "[t]here must, however, be a clear line of demarcation between malicious criticism and criticism that springs from genuine sympathy and good wishes for the success of the Japanese administration."[44] He argued in what was tantamount to a warning that it was not that the Japanese did not listen to criticism but that in the past missionary criticism at times had gone over this line and "in many cases (were) far from well-meaning."[45] This style of distinction was not uncommon, yet Japanese perceptions of what constituted "malicious" criticism, were much broader than the depth of these supposed criticisms.

From the Russo-Japanese War to just after the 105-Person Incident, the increase in attention to Korean affairs was reflected in a boom in articles published in mainstream journals. Among these pieces were a large number of pieces written by Japanese officials and supporters, who sought to offer their rationale for Japanese colonization, to prevent any criticism of Japanese rule, and to assure the American public that the annexation of Korea did not threaten US interests. In the end, their messages reached an audience that was already sympathetically disposed.

In contrast to these many Japanese-sponsored articles, there was very little presence of Koreans in the mainstream American press. Articles in magazines did exist, though they were few in number but, unlike the Japanese pieces which elicited much discussion, Korean writing did not seem to attract much attention until the early 1940s.[46] Indeed, prior to the March First movement there was little sympathy for the Korean nationalist movement among the American mainstream press. Some Americans went so far as to dismiss early Korean nationalists outright as, in the words of the editors of *The Outlook*, "picturesque and pathetic."[47] Even after the impressive demonstrations of that year, it was not uncommon to dismiss the movement, as one writer did for *The New Republic*, who described the Korean desire for independence, as "not reasonable perhaps, but they are acting on impulse and not reason."[48] Characterized in this fashion as unreasonable and emotional, American writers seldom represented Korean voices as they did the Japanese—and when American writers did, it was often to undermine a Korean author.

One such example that shows the dilemmas of Koreans trying to get their voices heard can be seen in a piece treating the Korean delegation to the Hague in 1907.[49] Describing the Korean delegation's appeal as "more dramatic" than any of the other small countries that sought to gain admittance, the article began by summarizing the contents of the petition, paying special attention to the assertion that the Protectorate Treaty had been coerced by Japan and, thus, should be void. After this brief account, the article shifted— "it is of special interest to hear the Japanese side of the story" —to an interview with the lead Japanese delegate, Suzuki Keiroku, who proceeded to dismiss every point of the Korean argument.[50] In this conversation-style section, Suzuki impugned the Korean emperor, stressed the peacefulness and legality of Japanese actions, and claimed to understand the situation better than the Korean delegates. The author of the article uncritically repeated Suzuki's statements, presenting them as the disinterested comments of an established statesman, before allowing Suzuki to reflect on the general state of US-Japan relations and his hopes for improved ties. To all these comments, the writer adds a single line to conclude the piece, "[s]urely a sensible and reasonable view!"[51] In a rare piece that represented Korean arguments, the author used Korean arguments to set up Japanese views, which he ultimately affirmed. As this piece showed, Japanese voices carried greater authority, making it most difficult for Koreans to gain an audience for their views.

AMERICAN MAINSTREAM MAGAZINES AND THE LIMITS OF CRITIQUE

Although Japanese colonial viewpoints were being successfully propagated through a variety of means in the United States, it is difficult to assess the impact of these efforts. While Japanese officials themselves expressed their concern about the American public and worried about what Kawakami had called "malicious criticism," in fact, by 1910 the vast majority of Americans who wrote about the colonization of Korea wrote approvingly of the Japanese efforts, if not always each individual policy. Even prior to the Protectorate and certainly thereafter, American reporting on Korea was anything but flattering. Sharing many of the same assumptions as Japanese commentators about the relationship between culture and development, most accounts wrote of Korean traditions and history disparagingly, seeing various internal factors—government repression, lack of commercial spirit, over reliance on Confucianism, and the like—as the main reasons for Korea's decline. It was in the words of one author, "an example of national suicide."[52] One leader of the Presbyterian missionary board, A. J. Brown displayed the full power of racist Orientalism by writing, "[s]o rotten is the entire system that one marvels that the nation has not fallen to pieces before this. Only the stolid apathy of the Asiatic and the rival claims of foreign powers have held it together at all."[53] Together with its geographical position as the "cockpit" of the Orient, as many put it, these had rendered the country unable to resist Japanese pressures.[54] Most of the reports employed the standard repertoire of images and themes characteristic of Orientalist cross-cultural reporting and were based on only the most superficial, if any, engagements with Koreans—much like the Japanese accounts.

One of the few areas that was regularly excepted from this type of pejorative reporting concerned the growing Christian community, which benefited from positive press at the hands of both missionaries and lay reporters. In extolling the new converts and acclaiming them as the future of the country—if not all of East Asia—these reports tended to separate Christians from the rest of their compatriots. If Christians were praised for their vitality and energy, the implicit—and often explicit—corollary was that the non-Christian Koreans were lazy. In this sense, the generous appraisals of Korean Christians came at the expense of reinforcing the hackneyed stereotypes about Korean culture in a maneuver that posed a new Christian Korea against a traditional Korea.

By 1905, with the signing of the Protectorate Treaty, these disparaging accounts tended to be accompanied with rather superficial yet damning comparisons with Japan. From this point on, Korea was regularly viewed in conjunction with its neighbor, and the contrast generally served to legitimize the disparate power relations between the two. One of the most widely read authors of this period and personal friend to President Roosevelt, George Kennan, was a most adept practitioner of this form of analysis. Describing his approach to Korea, when serving as a war correspondent during the Russo-Japanese War, Kennan noted that there were few differences in the look of the land as he approached the shore by ship, but the similarities quickly ended for Kennan, "in all the characteristics that are the outgrowth and flower of human endeavor, the 'Land of the Morning Calm' is ages behind its wide-awake, energetic, and progressive neighbor." He was at least open about his bias, "[m]y first impressions of Korea gave me a prejudice against the Koreans of which I find it extremely difficult to divest myself."[55] He, of course, never did divest himself of this prejudice for his negative view of Koreans always came with positive appraisal of Japan, such that even before the announcement of the Protectorate Kennan sought to point out the mistakes of Japan in Korea, not so much as an end in itself but so as to ease and ameliorate its rule over the peninsula.[56]

This comparative approach moved beyond Japanese-Korean evaluations to encompass US rule over the Philippines. For Americans, who had only recently colonized the Philippines, comparisons between their own nation's actions in the Pacific archipelago made for an easy contrast with those of Japan in the peninsula—and more often than not these comparisons, by equating the two colonial settings, served to legitimize Japanese annexation. What the Japanese are doing in Korea, the logic went, is little different from what the United States is doing in the Philippines. As Kennan wrote, the Japanese role in the peninsula "is a gigantic experiment, and it may or may not succeed; but we, who are trying a similar experiment in the Philippines, must regard it with the deepest interest and sympathy."[57] Perhaps more frequently, writers used the Philippines as a gentle means of castigating certain Japanese policies. Look at the way colonial rule works in the Philippines, the logic of this analysis went, and you will see a more fruitful endeavor.[58] This critical use of comparative analogy became especially common after the March First movement, as Americans sought to show that their superior governance in the Philippines—in particular Japanese reliance on the military and attempts to extinguish Korean national culture—had not resulted in similar types of nationalist demonstrations.[59] Despite these slight variations in the way the example of the Philippines was used, all these arguments served the common purpose of using comparison to show the propriety of Japanese rule over Korea.[60]

In this way, by the time Itō published his article in *Harper's Weekly* in 1907, what little American writing existed about Korea already shared many features with Japanese colonial ideology. This was less the result of Japanese influence, let alone solely the success of Japanese propaganda efforts, but the product of the same set of assumptions underpinning writers committed to what can be called capitalist modernity and the role of colonialization within it.[61] There was a definite convergence of approach to Korea as both Japanese and Americans shared a wide range of cultural representations about Korea. When Japanese efforts to elicit support for their Korean policy among the American public was launched they found an audience already versed in the same colonizing rhetoric, readers sympathetic to the goal of spreading civilization through colonialism, and a public already predisposed to seeing the Korean people as unfit to carry out the burden of self-rule. Japanese colonial ideology readily translated into dominant perceptions of Korea that had been disseminated widely in American magazines. Given this situation, it is not surprising to find that annexation was widely accepted and even heralded in the American mainstream press. In the words of many of an observer, annexation was "inevitable."[62] It was "more and more apparent that the independence of Korea was a moral impossibility."[63] Koreans, wrote the Reverend Arthur T. Pierson, "should very cheerfully accept the new relations and profit from them to the very highest extent."[64] It was, in the oft-reproduced words of G. T. Ladd, a "benevolent assimilation," one that would, according to an editorial in *The Independent* "be a great blessing to the country."[65] Or, in the more sweeping conclusion of W. E. Griffis: "[t]he rise of a great double star on the political firmament will be the source of good influences for the blessing of mankind."[66]

This general welcoming of annexation did not mean that there was no criticism. Judging by Japanese officials' frequent complaints about the misrepresentations of foreigners—"malicious" reports, in the words of Kawakami—it would appear that criticisms were widespread. This was hardly the case. Japanese sensitivities should not be taken as a measure of this criticism, whether in terms of its quantity or nature. In fact, with the exception of the former missionary and well-known essayist Homer Hulbert, there was no prominent, public call by an American for a return to Korean independence in the first years of colonial rule. The negative evaluations of the potential for a sustained Korean sovereignty coupled with the enthusiasm for a reforming Japan made such a position rare.

At a time when there was a great deal of anxiety about Japan in the mainstream American media, it is somewhat unexpected that there were not more voices willing to take up the Korean cause. The immigration issue had long been sparking anti-Japanese sentiment. Rivalry over expansion into the Pacific Ocean set the imperial interests of the two countries in conflict with one another. As a result of this tension, the daily presses regularly raised the specter of a future conflict with Japan. Even staid publications such as *The Outlook* asked in an editorial title, "Will there be War in East Asia?"[67] In perhaps the best illustration of the lack of interest in the Korean cause among Americans, these many anti-Japanese critics did not take up the issue of Korea as potential ammunition in their salvos against Japan.[68] Korea was simply not brought into the debate on US-Japan relations, despite the many points of ill-ease. The ready acceptance of annexation in 1910 on the part of American observers reflected tension: although many writers deemed Japan sufficiently civilized to colonize Korea, they did not see this level of civilization as adequate for allowing Japanese migrants onto US shores.

Immigration and colonialism were, for the most part, two separate subjects for American commentators.

In the few cases when a linkage between immigration issues and annexation was made, it served not as a criticism of Japan but to offer further support for colonization of Korea. In publications such as *The Outlook*, it was suggested that Japan—by colonizing Korea—would obtain a new outlet for Japanese population pressures, possibly diverting Japanese emigrants toward Korea. This might, in turn, relieve the United States of the controversial Japanese immigration issue in what *The Nation* called "an indirect solution of our Pacific Coast problem."[69] Indeed, while such linkages were still relatively rare and generally not the main point of articles, such suggestions still outnumbered the calls for outright opposition to Korea's colonization.

Given this general lack of sympathy, occasional linkages to American self-interest, and the decision of the US government to support Korea's colonization, what criticism did exist was always raised within certain bounds. In effect, critiques came to be restricted to discrete aspects of colonial rule without questioning colonial rule itself. The president of Stanford University, David Starr Jordan, reflected this attitude, when after a brief trip through Korea, he wrote,

> Whether the blotting out of Korea be right or wrong, an inevitable step of manifest destiny or a needless suppression of unique national life, it is not necessary for us now to decide. The occupation of Chōsen is an accomplished fact. It is part of the future of Japan.[70]

That Jordan even raises the moral question of the rightfulness of Japanese rule was rare, yet he quickly brushed aside this line of reasoning as unworthy of further contemplation. Instead, accepting the status quo as a fait accompli, the task he set was one of judging the appropriateness, not of Japanese colonialism itself but of its individual policies. "It is worthwhile to know that the Japanese are taking their new responsibilities seriously." He continued, "Japan has undertaken to carry Western civilization into this stronghold of the 'Unmitigated East.'"[71]

Jordan's inclination that attention should be given to individual policies rather than the legitimacy of Japanese colonialism itself was nothing new. From the years immediately after the establishment of the Protectorate through the annexation and even after the March First movement, much American commentary took precisely this tack. Especially after the March First movement many disgruntled articles appeared in the American media. Much attention was given to the involvement of the Christian community in these events, especially by missionary writers, but other authors expanded beyond this issue. Contributing in *Atlantic Monthly* one of the more detailed explorations of Japanese policy after the March First movement, E. Alexander Powell offered a trenchant piece about Japanese mistakes in Korea. In an argument that after the March First movement gained wide currency, he focused primarily on the assimilation policy,

> They made the mistake of attempting to extirpate the language and the literature of the Koreans, to destroy their national ideals, to root out their ancient manners and customs. . . . I am tempted to believe that they dreamed of eventually bringing the Koreans to a status not far removed from that of the American negro, thereby giving to the Empire twenty millions of patient, uncomplaining and submissive subjects, hewers of wood and drawers of water, who would accept without remonstrance the role of social, political, and economic inferiority.[72]

Tellingly, Powell did not question this depiction of African Americans but did go on to show that Japanese policies were misguided. He wrote of "discrimination of the most flagrant character," continuing that "instead of putting Korean interests first, Japan made the mistake of ruling the peninsula primarily for her own glory and the benefit of her own people."[73] Even still, for airing these problems, Powell felt a need to apologize.

> To minimize, or apologize for, or ignore the deplorable blunders which marred Japan's administrative record in Korea during the decade immediately following the annexation, as certain American champions of Japan have done, would only impair the value of this paper . . . without rendering any corresponding service to the Japanese or Koreans.[74]

For Powell, such "service" meant not an end to colonial rule but reform such that colonialism would become more effective. Powell understood that this was not the "service" that Koreans envisioned, since he prominently noted that the March First movement represented a genuine nationalist movement that showed Koreans "were hungry for freedom."[75] But he was unwilling to call for Korean sovereignty. Instead, proposing that more autonomy, even home rule, be given Koreans, Powell essentially took up the line of reasoning used by so many of his compatriots that Japanese colonialism could be improved by following the precedents established by British and US colonialisms.

In this way, Powell assumed a hierarchy of colonialisms, with Japan below that of the more able US administrators in the Philippines and the British throughout their empire. Criticisms about the harshness of Japanese rule served to promote the virtues of US colonialism without taking the more radical step of calling for Korean independence. After devoting much of the article to a wide-ranging and harsh criticism of Japanese rule, Powell reversed himself to conclude, "I believe that the balance inclines heavily in favor of Japan. I will go further than that and assert that 'Korea could suffer no greater calamity than to have Japan go.'"[76] With this one sentence, Powell reigned in all of his earlier criticism, in effect urging his readers not to take his negative evaluations of Japanese colonial rule as an indication that Korea should be freed from that rule. In short, his criticisms—which, in the estimation of someone like Kawakami would likely merit rating as "malicious"—ultimately offered as a set of proposals on how to better Japanese rule by bringing it up to standards achieved in other colonial settings. This was the "service" of his criticism.

Powell's approach was quite common in the years after the March First movement, when for a brief period there was a surge in the number of articles published about Korea. Like Powell's piece, these articles tended to lament and target certain policies of Japanese rule, almost always remaining within circumscribed limits. Whether an author criticized the persecution of Christians, the over-reliance on the military, the effort to obliterate Korean national culture, or the lack of roles granted Koreans within the administration, these critiques could be harsh without taking the extra step of calling for Korean liberation.[77] Many Japanese officials were incensed by these foreign criticisms, yet, ironically, for the most part these criticisms did not go beyond the logic of reform that the colonial government itself began to promote in response to the March First movement.[78]

That there were certain similarities and shared assumptions between colonial notions of "cultural rule" and these American critiques can be seen in an article contributed to The Independent by Baron Saitō Makoto, the new governor-general appointed with the task of reasserting Japanese control over the peninsula.[79] Directly addressed to the American people, Saitō sought to show that what he called the "unfortunate occurrences" of March 1919 needed to be addressed by a better colonial policy. Such a position required him to accept on behalf of the colonial government a certain responsibility for the less than ideal approach of his predecessors, who while "committed to improve the conditions of the Korean people," sometimes carried out their policies in a "tactless manner," usually because of the actions of "petty officials."[80] In a comment that both affirmed the successes of colonial rule while accepting some blame, Saitō wrote that previous officials had failed to adjust policies "to keep pace with the intellectual and economic advancement made in the meantime by the Korean people."[81] He then tried to dismiss the role of the uprisings in forcing a change to cultural rule by stating that the colonial government had already been in the midst of planning reforms, only they had been too slow, "unfortunately this was not made known promptly enough."[82] Saitō's argument presented the demonstrators as discontent with the ways of administration rather than the nature of the administration itself, suggesting that if news of the imminent reforms had been more widely disseminated, it might have been "in time to prevent the outbreak of those demonstrations" as though the March First movement struggled for nothing more than administrative reform.[83] Consequently, he was able to claim that the reforms currently being implemented and planned for future use adequately addressed the demands expressed by the demonstrators. The remainder of the article outlined the changes: Japanese and Koreans placed on equal footing, greater attention to the opinions of Korean people, autonomy in the affairs of localities, the issuance of Korean-language newspapers among others—all were presented as policies of a more enlightened colonial rule, which would better suit Koreans as imperial subjects. In this way, Saitō sought to present a new face for the much criticized Japanese rule of Korea, attending to both the so-called demands of the demonstrators and the criticisms of outside observers.

The logic displayed in Saitō's explanation of this new style of colonial rule shared much in common with the American critics, such as Powell. To be sure, there were differences in tone and scope—sufficiently so that Saitō could lament that Japan had been "grossly and unjustly misrepresented" by foreigners.[84] Resting beneath these differences were a number of shared assumptions. Both framed their evaluations around the dilemma of how to establish and carry out effective colonial rule. Both positions emphasized administration and governance—what was the best policy in these particular circumstances? Neither, however, moved beyond the question of administrative implementation. Moreover, both assumed Koreans were unable to rule themselves and, consequently, that Japanese colonial rule was best for Koreans. On these assumptions they may have differed about the emphases on education, the degree of autonomy that could be offered, the repressiveness of the police—all questions of policy—but the assumptions underlying these policy concerns were virtually never raised, let alone challenged. Criticism was indeed widespread but even that which embarrassed and angered Japanese colonial officials was articulated within circumscribed bounds that did not go so far as to question the legitimacy of Japanese rule.

As Japanese policy was reformed and no new demonstrations on the scale of the March First movement arose, interest in Korea as indicated by the number of articles published in American magazines faded. The changes wrought by Saitō—the man credited by many a writer as the Japanese naval officer who had not interfered with Dewey's triumphant 1898 entrance into the Manila Harbor—were seen as attempts, successful or not, to deal with the weaknesses of its colonial administration.[85] Thereafter, occasional articles appeared, usually in relation to a specific incident, and the missionary community maintained a watchful eye over the activities of its charges. As interest in Korea declined, Japanese colonial officers rarely felt the need to publish in American magazines.[86] Their earlier concerns about the possibility that American public opinion might turn against them had never materialized. The colonization of Korea had come to be widely accepted in the United States, and even the demerits of Japan's policies were no longer worthy of extended consideration, as other issues in US-Japan relations, especially China, rose to the forefront.[87]

CONCLUSION: THE POST-1941 TURN

The relative dearth of articles concerning Korea in the late 1920s and the 1930s was to reverse itself in the early 1940s after the Japanese attack on Pearl

Harbor. So, too, did American attitudes reflect a deep shift once interest in Korea revived. Now with Japan as its enemy, Americans tended to write, in both foreign policy journals and popular magazines, of Korea as a potential ally, as a site that revealed the deep contradictions in Japan's Pan-Asian ideology, and as a potential weak point in Japan's Empire.[88] Now for the first time, Korean nationalist arguments received a sympathetic hearing, and the Korean struggle against Japanese rule was not dismissed but praised.[89] The admiration for the achievement of Japanese rule disappeared as commentators emphasized its oppressive nature—"Japan's record is one of unredeemed failure," wrote one author.[90] Less concerned with the past and the reasons for Korea's subjugation, writers wrote of the future, speaking more positively than ever before about the possibilities of Korean sovereignty.[91] For the first time mainstream American reportage on Korea separated itself from Japanese colonial ideology, which itself had changed since the earlier period. By the end of World War II, some authors were even willing to write of US culpability in Japan's colonization of the peninsula.[92]

Yet these articles were also playing catch-up. For almost two decades there had been little attention directed toward Korea and now that the Cairo Declaration had raised the possibility of independence, however limited, Americans sought to overcome their lack of knowledge of Korea. As US soldiers moved into the peninsula to set up a military government over Koreans in September of 1945, this ignorance about Korea—one of the many legacies of Japanese colonialism—was to repeatedly haunt US relations with the Korean people and their administrations.[93]

NOTES

This chapter was partly supported by a research grant from the Taesan Foundation. I would like to thank my research assistant, Jane Kim, for finding some of the articles used for this chapter.

1. Harry Emerson Wilde, *Japan in Crisis*, 201.
2. Peter Duus, *The Abacus and the Sword*.
3. Kirk Larsen and Joseph Seely, "Simple Conversation or Secret Treaty."
4. Bruce Cumings, "Archaeology, Descent, Emergence," 79–111.
5. Adachi Kinnosuke, "The Japanese in Korea," 472–75.
6. Ibid.
7. Carol Gluck, *Japan's Modern Myths*.

8. Robert B. Valliant, "The Selling of Japan," 415–38.

9. George H. Curzon, *Problems of the Far East*. For one study of Curzon's Korea writings see Jihang Park, "Land of the Morning Calm, Land of the Rising Sun, 513–34. There were many pieces that described trips to Korea in this mode. See also, Gordon Casserly, "From Chemulpo to Seoul," 613–21.

10. Edwin Maxey, "The Reconstruction of Korea," 673.

11. Ibid., 673–87.

12. This was also used by George Kennan. See his "The Korean People," 409–16.

13. William Elliot Griffis, "Japan's Absorption of Korea," 516–26.

14. This approach had a history that extended beyond the colonial era. For one example see David Brudnoy, "Japan's Experiment in Korea," 155–95.

15. For a survey of some American media coverage of Meiji Japan, see Joseph Henning, *Outposts of Civilization*.

16. Andre Schmid, "Two Americans in Seoul."

17. For a few examples see the following *TaeHan maeil sinbo* editorials: "Ilbon sinmuji" [Newspapers in Japan], August 14, 1906; "Kinaenssi jiron Nanjŏng" [The situation of Korea by Keenan], October 23, 1906; "Oein ŭi nune yonghanŭn Chosŏn "[Korea in the eyes of foreigners], March 10, 1910; and "Kumigaek kwa Han'gugin" [Western visitors and Koreans], April 5, 1910.

18. I deal with this issue in my book *Korea Between Empires, 1895–1919*, 167–70.

19. Government-General of Chōsen, *Annual Report on Reforms and Progress in Chōsen (Korea)*, 1918–21, 32–36.

20. Government-General of Chōsen, *Annual Report on Reforms and Progress in Chōsen (Korea)*, 1917–18, 60–61.

21. Government-General of Chōsen, *Annual Report on Reforms and Progress in Chōsen (Korea)*, 1918–21, 1–3.

22. Government-General of Chōsen, *Annual Report on Reforms and Progress in Chōsen (Korea)*, 1917–18, xi–xiii.

23. Government-General of Chōsen, *Annual Report on Reforms and Progress in Chōsen (Korea)*, 1916–17, xii–xiii.

24. George Kennan, "Is Japan Persecuting Christians in Korea?" 804–10; Charles H. Sherrill, "Korean and Shantung versus the White Peril," 24–42; W.W. Willoughby, "Japan and Korea," 370–71; and Edwin Maxey, "The Reconstruction of Korea," 673–87.

25. "Japan as Colonial Administrator" (editorial), 702.

26. "Korea: A Tribute to Japanese Administration" (editorial), 232–33.

27. Some English-language articles published by Japanese authors but not treated in this chapter include I. Yamagata, "The Korean Annexation," 185–88; Count Okuma, "Japan's Policy in Korea," 571–80; K. Asakawa, "Korea and Manchuria under the New Treaty," 699–711; Kuma Oishi, "The Causes Which Led to the War in the East," 721–35;

also see the chapter contributed by Terauchi Masatake, "Reforms and Progress in Korea," 215–390.

28. Edward Wheeler, "The Assassination of Itō," 613–14.

29. The idea that assassination was a tradition in Korea was first promoted in a letter to the *New York Times* by George Trumbull Ladd, "Letter to the Editor: America and Japan, March 22, 1907 and then taken up by George Kennan. See George Kennan, "Prince Itō and Korea."

30. Itō Hirobumi, "Japanese Policy in Korea," 27.

31. Ibid.

32. Ibid.

33. Ibid.

34. There were no other articles published in the American mainstream press under Itō's name, however through interviews and meeting of prominent visitors his views were often reported. For the most notorious example of this, see George Trumbull Ladd, *In Korea with Marquis Itō*; and F. T. Piggot, "The Itō Legend," 173–88. For a summary of one of Itō's manifestos, see William Thomas Stead, ed., "'The Honest Broker' between East and West," 66; William T. Ellis, "An Interview with Prince Itō," 1068–70; and George Kennan, "Prince Itō and Korea."

35. Adachi Kinnosuke, "The Japanese in Korea," 472.

36. See Karl Kiyoshi Kawakami, *Japan and World Peace*; Karl Kiyoshi Kawakami, *What Japan Thinks*; Karl Kiyoshi Kawakami, *The Real Japanese Question*; and Karl Kiyoshi Kawakami, *Japan Speaks on the Sino-Japanese Question*, among others.

37. Karl Kiyoshi Kawakami, *American-Japanese Relations*, 17.

38. Ibid., 143–56.

39. Ibid., 171.

40. Ibid., 250.

41. Ibid., 264.

42. For one overview see Donald N. Clark, *Living Dangerously in Korea*.

43. Ibid., 280.

44. Ibid., 281.

45. Ibid.

46. The Korean National Association's appeal was published under An's name in *The Nation*. See Ch'ang-ho An, "A Korean Appeal to America," 228–29. Rhee's most significant work was his more influential Syngman Rhee, *Japan Inside Out*. See also Henry Chung, "Korea Today," 467–74; Henry Chung, *The Oriental Policy of the United States*; and Henry Chung, *The Case of Korea*. Some others include, P. K. Yoon, "The Present and Future of Korea"; and Prince Ye We Chong, "A Plea for Korea," 423–26, among others.

47. This was specifically in relation to the delegation to The Hague; the editorial also ridicules the ŭibyŏng. See the editorial in *The Outlook*, April 4, 1908.

48. Nathaniel Peffer, "Korea." For a more sympathetic yet still critical view, see E. Alexander Powell, "Japan's Policy in Korea," 395–412.
49. Elbert F. Baldwin, "Korea and Japan at The Hague," 26–28.
50. Ibid., 27.
51. Ibid., 28.
52. Edwin Maxey, "Korea: An Example of National Suicide," 281–90.
53. Arthur Judson Brown, "Unhappy Korea," 147–50.
54. A. Tendon, "Korea, the Cockpit of the East," 176–81; and Gordon Casserly, "From Chemulpo to Seoul," 613–21.
55. George Kennan, "The Land of the Morning Calm," 363–69.
56. George Kennan, "The Korean People," 409–16; George Kennan, "The Japanese in Korea," 609–16; George Kennan, "Prince Itō and Korea," 665–69; George Kennan, "Is Japan Persecuting Christians in Korea?" 804–10; and George Kennan, "Are the Japanese Honest?" 1011–16.
57. George Kennan, "The Korean People," 409–16. For other articles of this type, see Arthur Judson Brown, "The Japanese in Korea," 591–95; and Albertus Pieters, "The Korean Conspiracy Case: A Review," 120–24.
58. There were countless articles of this type see W.E. Griffis, "Japan's Absorption of Korea," 516–26; and W. E. Griffis, "An American View," 830–31; and Walter E. Weyl, "Korea: An Experiment in Denationalization," 392–401.
59. Rae D. Henkle, "The Benevolent Assimilation of Korea," 505–6.
60. One of the difficulties for critics of Japanese rule was to avoid having their criticisms of Japanese colonialism being interpreted as criticisms of US rule. For one example see Henry Chung, "Korea Today."
61. This argument is further developed in Andre Schmid, *Korea Between Empire*, especially chapters 3 and 4.
62. Arthur Judson Brown, "The Japanese in Korea," 591–95.
63. H. H. De Forest, "The Moral Purpose of Japan in Korea," 13–17.
64. Arthur T. Pierson, "First Impressions of Korea," 183–90.
65. George Trumbell Ladd, "The Annexation of Korea," 639–56; and Albertus Pieters, "Editorial: The Korean Conspiracy Case."
66. W. E. Griffis, "Japan's Absorption of Korea," 516–26.
67. "Will there be War in East Asia?" (editorial), 258–60.
68. One exception to this was the Canadian writer F. A. MacKenzie, who made this link in his work *The Unveiled East*.
69. "Japan as Colonial Administrator" (editorial), *The Nation*, June 24, 1915; and "Editorial," *Outlook*, April 4, 1908.
70. David Starr Jordan, "Japan's Task in Korea," 82. For a similar work by the president of Harvard University, see Charles William Eliot, *Some Roads Towards Peace*, 45–46.

71. David Starr Jordan, "Japan's Task in Korea," 81–82.
72. E. Alexander Powell, "Japan's Policy in Korea," 397–98.
73. Ibid., 400 and 401.
74. Ibid., 398.
75. Ibid., 404.
76. Ibid., 406.
77. A few other examples include W.W. Willoughby, "Japan and Korea"; Nathaniel Peffer, "Korea"; and Rae D. Henkle, "The Benevolent Assimilation of Korea."
78. For some exceptions to this after the March First movement, see the little known piece by Marjorie Barstow and Sydney Greenbie that challenges many Japanese assertions, "Korea Asserts Herself." See also the periodical *Literary Digest*, which offered a number of more deeply critical pieces on Japanese colonialism itself.
79. Baron Saitō Makoto, "A Message from the Imperial Japanese Government to the American People," 167–69 and 191.
80. Ibid., 167.
81. Ibid., 168.
82. Ibid.
83. Ibid.
84. Ibid.
85. For an entire article on this theme, see Geo. Bronson Rea, "Saito."
86. I. Yamagata, "The Korean Annexation."
87. One of the main exceptions to this, of course, was the implementation of Shinto Shrine Worship policy.
88. Selden C. Menefee, "Our Korean Allies," 509; George Kent, "Korea: Exhibit 'A' in Japan's New Order"; and George W. Keeton, "Korea and the Future," 354–58.
89. The attention given to Syngman Rhee's book is the best example. Syngman Rhee, *Japan Inside Out*. See "Rhee's Revival," 60.
90. George W. Keeton, "Korea and the Future," 354–58; and George W. Keeton, "Background for War: The White Man of the Orient," 34.
91. Andrew Grajdanzev, "Korea in the Postwar World"; and Andrew Grajdanzev, "Problems of Korean Independence," 416–19.
92. This was in a review of M. Frederick Nelson, *Korea and the Old Orders of Eastern Asia*. See also John Goette, "One Roosevelt Proposes, Another Disposes," 26–27.
93. This is a key assumption in Bruce Cumings, *The Origins of the Korean War Volume 1*.

PART II
Colonial Korea's Perception of Foreign Societies

PART II

4

The Impact of the Colonial Situation on International Perspectives in Korea: Active Imaginations, Wishful Strategies, and Passive Action

YONG-CHOOL HA and JUNG HWAN LEE

This chapter aims to make observations and to raise critical questions regarding the impact of colonial rule by mapping perceptions on international relations in Korea from 1920–30 through media analysis. It may sound empty to talk about the international dimension when Korea ceased to exist legally on the international scene and thus could play no active role in international affairs. Indeed, the fact that sovereignty was lost must have affected the low level of interest in research on colonial international relations. Seldom have the studies of colonialism focused on its international aspects. Most studies deal with domestic issues and, more specifically, domestic economic issues. Even when international aspects are addressed, most of the time they are comprised of research related to Japanese imperialism and international rivalries surrounding the Korean peninsula and Northeast Asia. Seldom has the focus of research been on the world as seen from the eyes of the colonized.

This chapter attempts to address this neglected aspect of Japanese colonial rule in Korea. It purports to portray the world filtered through the colonial situation. Arguably one may ask why it is important and relevant to understand the world through the colored lens of the colonial situation. Other than just for the sake of maintaining a balance in studies between the international and domestic sides of colonial rule and of satisfying intellectual curiosity, this chapter argues that the world, the region, and the ideologies and strategies as perceived by Koreans under colonial rule have had a long-lasting impact in shaping distinct, if not unique, international perspectives which go beyond the Colonial Period.

More specifically, as analyzed in the following pages, colonial rule had unintended consequences—beyond that of creating a mere passive existence and an actor without a state—or the international perspectives of Korean elites and the common Korean people in terms of their perceptions of the enemy, the world around them, and their conduct of international relations. This chapter will try to demonstrate how and why the colonial situation gave rise to such distinctive international perspectives.

Colonial rule, at the international level deprives a nation of state status as a legal entity. Thus a colony could not conduct normal diplomatic activities in terms of daily diplomatic interactions, such as setting short- and mid-term foreign policy goals and preparing long-term strategies. In other words, a colony could be neither a nation nor a state or a nation without a state. Korea belonged to the latter case. This chapter analyzes the international world through the eyes of a nation without a state, the implications of these international perspectives, and how these perspectives have affected post-colonial conduct toward international relations in Korea.

This chapter will demonstrate that colonial rule inevitably led Korean elites and the masses to acquire an unusually high degree of interest in international affairs. The irony of the colonial situation is that domestic powerlessness forced people to look outside for possible sources of change. The high level of attentiveness to international affairs contrasts with the unrealistic and sometimes contradictory expectations of colonial attitudes based on wishful thinking, unrealizable strategies, and powerless action. The frustration and disappointment—from the gap between free perception and the absence of action on international affairs—left unintended long-term consequences including simplifying the enemy, encouraging an overzealous and, at times, extreme yearning for military power, and creating an inconsistency between analysis and reality.

The colonized Koreans can be summarized as having active imaginations and wishful strategies, while being passive in action when it came to international affairs. The perspectives of the colonized contrasted greatly with the realistic and pragmatic actions of the Japanese colonizers. The Koreans, who did not have an internationally recognized state on the global stage, therefore vigorously dreamed of obtaining confirmation of state status. The Japanese colonizers, on the other hand, who already had a state fully confirmed in the international arena, focused their attention on how to fortify Japan's interests in international affairs.

ACTIVE IMAGINATIONS, WISHFUL STRATEGIES, AND PASSIVE ACTIONS IN THE 1920S

As Arlene Tickner points out, the discipline of international relations has neglected to discuss colonized nations.[1] If the colonized nations did not resist the colonizers—United States, Britain, or France for example—international relations scholars did not carefully examine the colonized. In the late twentieth century during the post–Cold War period, newly independent former colonized nations mainly in Africa and Asia began to form a group known as the Third World. In so doing, they made their voices known, and international relations scholars started to pay attention.[2] However, these scholars never grasped the nuances of the colonized and their differences and preferences with regards to international politics. Instead they were more likely to fit the colonized's actions into traditional international theories which originated from the experiences of Western countries. Although some research has speculated on the weak or middle-power countries' actions, most international relations research has assumed that all countries have the same preferences, that is, to increase their own interests.[3] This assumption has extended to the study of the colonized nations' actions in international politics. Like powerful countries, all colonial nations are assumed to be actors behaving according to realist calculations.

However, colonial nations are unique. They are nations without state status. As a political community without internal or external sovereignty, they cannot determine their own destiny in international politics. This unique situation makes the colonized's preferences and behaviors different from other government entities. As Homi Bhabha argues, colonial situations make for unique identities.[4] Their unique identities make it difficult to apply realistic understanding to the colonized perception over international politics. We would like to suggest that the concepts of active imaginations, wishful strategies, and passive actions are means to understand the colonized's perceptions toward international affairs. The unique character of colonial nations originates from the absence of state status. In essence, this situation does not allow room for effective actions in international politics on the part of the colonized.

International political passivity sets colonial nations apart from other powers. Since colonized nations do not have opportunities to exercise practical autonomous actions, their ideas on future developments in international politics are more likely to be adventurous. If the colonizers' control is concrete and stable, the colonized's strategies within the international realm are more likely to become even more ambitious and detached from reality.

Although they do not have the ability to interfere with or change international politics, the colonized are acutely aware of and actively dream about changing the colonial situation. We argue that "active imaginations," "wishful strategies," and "passive actions" can be theoretical terms for understanding the colonized's international perspectives beyond that of more traditional calculations.

This chapter attempts, through an investigation of the Korean people's perceptions on international politics during Japan's colonial rule, to understand how active imaginations, wishful strategies, and passive actions shaped the colonized's perspectives on international issues. This chapter will concentrate on examining international perspectives of the Korean colony during the 1920s. Unlike the 1910s, when Japanese colonizers censored Koreans and did not allow the colonized to express their views, in the 1920s the Japanese loosened their control, so it can be assumed that more revealing opinions were expressed during this decade.

During the 1920s there were a lot of opportunities for different paths for expression. Unlike the 1930s, when Japan chose to go to war and thus terminated the Korean colonized dream of being involved on the global stage, in the 1920s colonized Koreans had room to discuss their survival and their chances in the international arena. After World War I, the world in general and East Asia in particular began to search for a new balance of power. The United States came on stage as one of the most powerful countries in the world. However, the rise of the United States increased tension with Japan. The tension between these two countries intensified when it came down to their different approaches to China. While Japan claimed its vested interests, the United States urged an open door policy. The United States and Japan were also keenly aware of each other's military reinforcement. This situation encouraged Koreans to imagine a scenario wherein a change in the balance of power occurred in East Asia. On the other hand, the Soviet Revolution in Russia became a crucial factor that influenced Koreans to dream of change. In the fluid international environment of the 1920s, Koreans actively envisaged the change of their international situation regardless of its feasibility. We can see the self-desiring perception of colonized Koreans on international politics when we compare their perceptions with the perceptions of their Japanese colonizers.

NEWSPAPERS OF THE COLONIZED: SOURCES FOR THEIR INTERNATIONAL PERSPECTIVES

The purpose of this section is to analyze the international perspectives of the Korean elites and the masses under Japanese colonial rule.[5] The best manner with which to accomplish this goal is to locate sources which may shed light on Koreans' perceptions of international politics. This chapter uses the *Chosŏn ilbo* as an indirect way to understand Koreans in terms of their international perceptions.

As always it is not easy to define what the masses are or how to get access to their perspectives, especially when it regards something that happened in the past. This is difficult because they do not tend to leave written records. This is especially true of the masses under colonial rule in Korea. In this case, as Christine Sylvester points out, "world traveling," a post-colonial research methodology would be the better way to find the perception of the masses.[7] Rather than world traveling, however, if we look at the perspectives of the elite, this can be an indirect way of finding ordinary discourses circulating in both elite circles and the masses. The rationale here is that there had been vigorous interactions between the elites and the masses in colonial societies. Newspapers were read, at least at the level of the local elites, and in turn, the local elites influenced the masses with whom they interacted. We cannot ignore the following observations of one contemporary observer of the time on how enthusiastic average people were about worldly affairs. "If you go down to the countryside, people gather around a lantern light at night and read the newspaper by rotation."[8]

It is safe to say that the average Korean had limited access to newspapers on a daily basis. Only intellectuals and the well-to-do enjoyed readership. However, rumors about international situations trickled down from the elite especially at village levels. It can be safely said that average people had indirect access to information on international situations. Considering that communicating the state of international affairs in venues other than newspapers did not reach average people, it is safe to say that the newspaper was the best means available to comprehend the general level of understanding of international conditions in colonial Korea.

This chapter analyzes the editorials on international affairs published in both the Chosŏn ilbo and the Keijō Nippō from 1920 to 1930. The Chosŏn ilbo was chosen primarily for technical reasons in that it has been digitized and is available for free access. The Keijō Nippō was the official governmental newspaper produced by the Government-General of Chōsen and represents the view of the Japanese colonizers. Therefore, by comparing the editorials of Chosŏn ilbo with those of the Keijō Nippō, we can search for consistency and for the differences of international perspectives between the Korean colonized and the Japanese colonizers.

Tables 4.1–4.4 detail the number of editorials related to international topics in both the Chosŏn ilbo and the Keijō Nippō. Several observations can be made by reviewing these statistics. First, in the 1920s, both newspapers paid increasing attention to international affairs. In the 1920s, both the Chosŏn ilbo and the Keijō Nippō dedicated almost 20 percent of their editorials to international affairs (19.7 percent in the Chosŏn ilbo; 18.8 percent in the Keijō Nippō).

Table 4.1 Distribution of editorials on international affairs, Chosŏn ilbo (1920–30)

Year	1920	1921	1922	1923	1924	1925	1926	1927	1928	1929	1930	Total
Number of Editorials on International Affairs[a]	6	33	2	51	61	57	62	61	28	62	37	460
Total Number of Editorials[b]	94	184	27	312	221	266	274	242	137	283	293	2,333
Percent (%)[a/b]	6.3	17.9	7.4	16.3	27.6	21.4	22.6	25.2	20.4	21.9	12.6	19.7

Source: Chosŏn ilbo, 1920–30.

[a] Censored and seized articles have been excluded.

[b] Censored and seized editorials have been included.

[a/b] Serialized editorials have been counted once.

This indicates that both the Japanese colonizers and the colonized Koreans had considered international changes—including the postwar international system after World War I, the Soviet Revolution, and Chinese relations—as significant factors to consider when determining their future.

Second, the *Chosŏn ilbo* and the *Keijō Nippō* differ in their timing of their interest in international affairs. The *Chosŏn ilbo* began its representation of international affairs the year it was founded in 1920. The proportion of edito-

Table 4.2 Number of editorials related to international affairs in the *Chosŏn ilbo* (1920–30)

Category/Year		1920	1921	1922	1923	1924	1925	1926	1927	1928	1929	1930	Total (%)
International Situations	General (international order and peace)	3	5	0	4	6	3	8	2	2	1	3	37 (8)
	Military issues (arms reduction)	0	3	0	1	2	1	0	2	0	3	3	15 (3.2)
	International economy	0	0	0	0	0	1	0	1	1	1	3	7 (1.5)
	Ideology	0	2	0	1	1	1	5	1	0	1	0	12 (2.6)
	Int'l organizations (trans-regional & multilateral)	0	3	1	3	3	2	2	0	0	4	0	18 (3.9)
European Situations	Europe (general)	0	1	0	3	0	3	1	2	0	0	1	11 (2.3)
	Bilateral & Multilateral	0	2	0	5	4	3	1	4	1	1	0	21 (4.5)
	Europe (domestic)	1	1	0	3	6	8	15	3	2	7	2	48 (10.4)
	Russia (domestic)	0	1	1	2	0	3	4	1	1	1	1	15 (3.2)
North America	US (domestic)	0	2	0	0	5	2	0	1	2	3	1	16 (3.4)
East Asia	East Asia (general)	1	3	0	1	1	2	1	1	0	0	0	10 (2.1)
	Bilateral & Multilateral*	0	2	0	13	12	6	4	8	5	10	4	64 (13.9)
	Chinese (domestic)	0	5	0	9	13	13	8	25	13	19	12	117 (25.4)
	Japan-foreign policy	0	1	0	2	4	2	3	3	0	3	0	18 (3.9)
Korean Problems	Status of Korea & Koreans	0	0	0	0	1	1	2	6	0	4	1	15 (3.2)
Other Colonies	Oppressed peoples (India, Middle East, & Ireland)	1	2	0	4	2	5	6	1	1	3	5	30 (6.5)
Other**		0	0	0	0	1	1	2	0	0	1	1	6 (1.3)
Total Number of Editorials		6	33	2	51	61	57	62	61	28	62	37	460 (100)

Source: *Chosŏn ilbo*, 1920–30.

*Bilateral and multilateral issues between the West and East Asian countries are counted as East Asia.

**Other refers to international coverage which does not belong to the above categories, such as non-political issues.

rials on international affairs increased significantly from 6.3 percent in 1920 to 27.6 percent in 1924 when it stabilized and maintained this level. On the other hand, the *Keijō Nippō* published more editorials related to international affairs in the early years of the 1920s than in the later years of the decade. We can extrapolate that this is because the Japanese colonizers were more interested in the postwar international system than the Korean colonized. The *Keijō Nippō* paid their highest attention to international affairs in 1922—the same year the Washington Navel Conference and the great countries of the world discussed the postwar balance of power. The *Chosŏn ilbo* was never neglectful in covering international affairs during this decade. Even though there were only a few editorials published in 1922, it covered the postwar balance of power several times in the mid-1920s. In retrospect, the *Chosŏn ilbo* was much more focused on China over the postwar balance of power than the *Keijō Nippō*.

Third, the most frequently mentioned areas in both the *Chosŏn ilbo* and the *Keijō Nippō* editorials were located in East Asia. Although the *Chosŏn ilbo* expressed more interest in the Chinese domestic situation than the *Keijō Nippō*, both newspapers maintained sustained focus on China.

These tables show similarities and differences in editorials of the *Chosŏn ilbo* and the *Keijō Nippō* in quantitative comparison. With regard to the numbers of editorials published on international affairs, both newspapers had a

Table 4.3 Percentage of *Keijō Nippō* editorials related to international affairs (1920–30)

Year	1920	1921	1922	1923	1924	1925	1926	1927	1928	1929	1930	Total
Number of Editorials on International Affairs[a]	54	27	21	13	16	24	19	38	38	49	-	299
Total Number of Editorials[b]	152	131	51	64	82	210	223	245	213	214	-	1,585
Percent (%)[a/b]	35.5	17.7	41.1	20.3	19.5	11.4	8.5	15.5	17.8	22.8	-	18.8

Source: *Keijō Nippō*, 1920–30.

[a] Censored and seized articles and Japanese domestic issue have been excluded.

[b] Seized editorials have been included.

[a/b] Serialized editorials have been counted once.

The Impact of the Colonial Situation on International Perspectives in Korea 113

similar level of awareness on international affairs. However, both newspapers acquired different attitudes when dealing with international affairs. The following section discusses how the *Chosŏn ilbo* and the *Keijō Nippō* had different stances on international affairs.

Table 4.4 Number of editorials related to international affairs in the *Keijō Nippō* (1920–30)

Category/Year		1920	1921	1922	1923	1924	1925	1926	1927	1928	1929	1930	Total (%)
International Situations	General (international order and peace)	1	0	0	0	0	1	0	0	0	0	-	2 (0.6)
	Military issues (arms reduction)	2	4	3	0	1	0	0	7	1	8	-	26 (8.6)
	International economy	1	1	2	0	0	0	0	0	0	0	-	4 (1.3)
	Ideology	0	0	0	0	0	0	0	0	0	0	-	0 (0)
	Int'l organizations (trans-regional & multilateral)	0	0	0	0	1	2	0	2	0	5	-	10 (3.3)
European Situations	Europe (general)	2	0	2	1	1	1	0	1	0	0	-	8 (2.3)
	Bilateral & Multilateral	3	0	2	2	1	0	0	0	1	0	-	9 (2.6)
	Europe (domestic)	5	0	1	3	2	3	6	1	0	2	-	23 (7.6)
	Russia (domestic)	2	2	1	0	0	1	2	1	0	0	-	9 (3.0)
North America	US (domestic)	6	2	2	0	2	1	0	1	5	3	-	22 (7.3)
East Asia	East Asia (general)	0	0	1	0	0	0	1	0	0	1	-	3 (1.0)
	Bilateral & Multilateral*	14	8	3	3	7	5	4	12	10	16	-	82 (27.4)
	Chinese (domestic)	6	1	2	3	0	5	6	5	7	11	-	46 (15.3)
	Japan-foreign policy	10	5	1	0	1	4	0	7	6	2	-	36 (12.0)
Korean Problems	Status of Korea & Koreans	0	3	0	1	0	0	0	1	2	0	-	7 (2.3)
Other Colonies	Oppressed peoples (India, Middle East, & Ireland)	1	0	0	0	0	0	0	0	0	1	-	2 (0.6)
Other**		1	1	1	0	0	1	0	0	6	0	-	10 (3.3)
Total Number of Editorials		54	27	21	13	16	24	19	38	38	49	-	299 (100)

Source: *Keijō Nippō*, 1920–30.

*Bilateral and multilateral issues between the West and East Asian countries are counted as East Asia.

**Other refers to international coverage which does not belong to the above categories, such as non-political issues.

IMAGINED PERCEPTION OF INTERNATIONAL ORDER: FROM INTERNATIONAL COOPERATION TO WARFARE

International Cooperation

One manifestation of the active imagination of the colonial Korean intellectuals can be seen in the early 1920s in terms of the high expectation of international cooperation. Of course, the colonial situation gave rise to multiple forms of inconsistency and contradiction. Korea's status as a nation without a state was the international manifestation of this inconsistency; Korea existed as a nation without the capacity to exercise state power. This inconsistency, in turn, led to active imaginations and wishful thinking about international politics. Under such a passive international status what intellectuals could do was to project their wishful thinking through imagination, which could be actively and freely done without interference, but such active imagination was bound to be affected by the ever fluctuating international environment of the time.

The international environment after World War I looked as though there would be new room for the Korean colonized. The self-determination principle suggested by Woodrow Wilson and the Soviet Revolution caused Koreans to pursue imaginative strategies for Korea's independence. The Korean colonized considered how they could prepare for the changes that would come in international politics, so that they could come back as a state to the world scene. In other words, history became a waiting game which would bring new opportunities for Korean people. Both nationalists and class-based Marxists began to share common views. Nationalists argued that the Chosŏn people were capable of independence, citing Korea's 5,000 years of state existence and 23 million people.[9] To class-based Marxists, the rise of the Communist Soviet Union was a beacon for colonial Korea; it set directions and strategies (although in a twisted form). Communism's class-based view of the world transformed in such a way as to accommodate the oppressed Korean people. Communism was appealing to the colonized because it was transformative and suggested specific strategies and stages of development.

However, the colonized Koreans found that their dreams would not be realized. *Chosŏn ilbo*'s editorials lamented that the world where the power of ideas and ideals ruled supreme did not play much of a role in the lives of

Koreans and appealed for human grand unity (*daedong*).¹⁰ The real world of the 1920s, however, did not allow any room for passively waiting for a better future. Instead, this decade was characterized by postwar rivalry, competition, and jockeying for new positions among major powers. While *Chosŏn ilbo*'s editorials captured the real politick in detail, there was not much to be done by colonial Korea and the Korean people except for passively watching the development of the world and Northeast Asia. Efforts were made to imagine international politics based on nations without states. However, in reality international relations were based on national competition with states (not nations that held no true status):

> The spirit of the League of Nations is based on a progress from the conventional balance of power idea. The principle is from power is law to law is power, and the basis of power should be righteousness and legitimacy. But relations among the victorious countries still are based on the old notion of balance of power. The five-year-old League of Nations, the London Conference, and the Geneva Convention, what did they accomplish? . . . All were under the total control of the big powers like Great Britain and France. This applies not only the inter-state relations but also to international relations; the rights of weak states and weak nations are violated by strong nations.¹¹

When Koreans became aware that international cooperation would not help their colonial status, they lamented their fate as being a nation without a state. *Chosŏn ilbo*'s editorials acutely described the sorry state of affairs on numerous occasions. The following excerpts are typical examples:

> Although in the past we achieved a lot in the way of inventions and scholarship, in the changed world under Western civilization, we do not have much to contribute to the world in the way of economics, culture, invention and ideas, and literature. If we do our best to educate the masses and better the economy and thus expand our general level of knowledge, we can contribute to the world culture . . . but under the present circumstances it is unrealistic to realize these goals, and thus it may sound hollow and idealistic. We only appeal to individual reflection and a determination for the future.¹²

> It is true that we are part of the world human community and that Chosŏn, with its long history, is a part of the world. It is not that we do not have the courage to claim these realities, but rather that we are excluded from coexisting with the world and thus do not have the same existence as others and are deprived of the right to express ourselves. We have not been engaged with the ever complex world and are not party to the opportunities of this world so as to be a part of the fierce struggle for life is an international society.[13]

The Rise of Destructive Dreams

Koreans soon found that their idealistic visions of international politics, based on cooperation and humanity, did not fit with reality. In response, they focused more attention on the possibility of change based on the conflicts and warfare among the major world powers and started to expect status quo ante from conflicts that would change their colonial status in the future. This was not the transformation from an idealist vision to a realist vision. Their international perception remained wishful and their strategies were imaginative and lofty. The actual content of their imagination, vis-à-vis editorials discussed in this chapter, transformed from expectations of international cooperation to a desire for warfare. Therefore, we can propose that colonized Koreans had acquired a more chaotic vision on international politics.

This destructive vision of international politics originated from Koreans' awareness of shifts in the balance of international power. According to the *Chosŏn ilbo* editorials analyzed for this chapter, Koreans felt two shifts in the balance of international power. One was geographical in nature and the other was related to the center of power. The former referred to the shift, geographically, from Europe or the Mediterranean to the Pacific and the latter to the shift of power from Great Britain to the United States.

> With the progress in civilization and the development of transportation means, the focus of international competition has moved from the Mediterranean to the Pacific Sea. The Mediterranean has lost its value as an important battleground for national competition in the world.[14]

The Pacific age was viewed as being no less volatile than the Atlantic age, and it was predicted that the country that emerged as a dominant power in the Pacific would gain world hegemony. The two major countries in contention were the United States and Japan. The United States was a country that did not want to overturn the present international order, which was challenging Japan in the region.

> The dominance of the Pacific means the securement of hegemony of the world and the center of international competition has shifted from the Atlantic to the Pacific. The United States is beefing up its Army and Navy in the backwater of the Pacific and challenging the "island empire" behind which lies the resource-rich Asian continent.[15]

> Nowadays, starting with China's national revolution and the anti-imperial and anti-capitalist struggles between the strong and the weak peoples, has added a new development in the Far East. The present Pacific problems are different from the past ones. Ideological clashes between strong nations on the one hand and weak nations on the other will collide someday, which will develop into a large conflict.[16]

It is interesting to note that *Chosŏn ilbo*'s editorials depicted the United States as an imperialistic country with conflicting principles. For instance, it was criticized for maintaining the Monroe doctrine in its own sphere while taking the opposite "open door" policy toward China and Asia.[17] Perhaps criticism of US foreign policy was a smoke screen for highlighting the inevitable clash between Japan and the United States in the Pacific. In fact, the core of the Pacific problem was viewed as coming from the rivalry between the United States and Japan. In fact, one editorial endorsed the prediction by a Frenchman who said something to the effect that without the cooperation among the countries in the Pacific region, an unprecedented scale of war could break out in the area, the most terrifying of all the wars so far.[18]

This conviction about the inevitability of war was closely related to the perception of the post–World War I international situation. The newspaper editorials never failed to point out the grim prospect for and ineffectiveness of the League of Nations in terms of arms reduction and security guarantees. One editorial warned that "we should not be confused between ideals and reality. Even if all the people want peace, the reality is that neither arms reduction nor peace are guaranteed."[19]

In addition, editorials more specifically predicted that the Washington Naval Conference on naval force reduction was another sign of the arms race, and that reductions, paradoxically, would only expand the naval influence of the major powers such as the United States, Japan, and Great Britain.[20] In fact, *Chosŏn ilbo* editorials argued that arms reduction talks were not the ultimate cure-all to prevent war because arms reduction is nothing more than the mutual cancellation of military power rather than its elimination. The real source of war, according to the editorials, lied in economic competition.[21] Thus, the Non-Aggression Pact was simply regarded as hypocrisy. The real source of conflict was arising and surrounding China where Great Britain and Japan held vested interests while the United States did not.[22]

One is curious as to why the editorials allocated an inordinate amount of space and time to the issues of international security, the arms reduction talks, and the inevitability of war in the Pacific. This is particularly intriguing considering the fact that the Korean nation had been deprived of any military force, not to mention that it was not a participant in any of the international discussions on peace, war, or arms talks. One natural and obvious reason for this interest in international affairs is that it was in response to the culmination of the frustration of Korean intellectuals together with the masses when their appeals to the international community and the League of Nations for autonomy and independence went unheeded.

One can also speculate that it is the result of active imaginations, wishful thinking, and passive actions. For a nation without state status or military power—with a geographical location squeezed between China, Russia, and Japan—Korea became a totally powerless nation. Meanwhile Koreans yearned for a peaceful coexistence in a friendly, international, and regional environment while they simultaneously envisioned that the only way out of their shackled conditions would be a war between the major powers that surrounded the Korean peninsula. This possibility appears to have been viewed as more feasible given the chaotic nature of the newly emerging international and regional relations. By constantly and passionately condemning the ever rising military build-up and possible military conflicts, Koreans might have also wanted to see some kind of military conflict between Japan and other powers, especially the United States, as a means to exit from the colonial situation. In the twisted logic present in colonial peoples' psychology, one both condemns war while anticipating military conflict. Similarly, behind the constant appeal for international moral standards and the liberation of oppressed nations lurked the desire to see actual action from the places beyond the colonized nation's control, a typical example of passive action. Given what happened in reality, namely the actual war in 1941 between Japan and the United States, one may concur that Korean editorials' view of the world was prophetic, but we would argue it was more wishful thinking than visionary.

Another point to make about the high degree of attention given to the military aspects of international relations was that Koreans' intentional condemnation of military forces brought home the precious lesson that Korea was militarily weak. The military competition among the major powers in and around the region must have been a belated reminder to the Korean people—the elite and the masses alike—regarding how backward Korea was, especially when it came to its inability to protect itself.

JAPANESE REALITY AND HOW IT DIFFERED FROM THE COLONIZED KOREANS' PERSPECTIVE

While the Koreans dreamed of change, the Japanese colonizers preferred that the East Asian international politics of the 1920s stay the same. However, the Japanese colonizers were well aware that there were many transformative factors present at this time. Unlike the Koreans, who did not have formal state status nor material powers, the Japanese held a very realistic stance for maintaining their national and economic interests.

The expanding US influence in Asia had serious negative implications for Japan. Besides, the Communist revolution in Russia also acted as a negative factor to Japan's future interests. Therefore, Japan was a country under pressure to not act as one in favor of the status quo; it had strong interests in Manchuria and Mongolia. Also, it was constantly expanding its base in mainland China, causing various military and political confrontations and incidents. Its interests were increasingly in conflict with those of the United States and even with those of England. The political and military emergence of Chiang Kai-Shek was also a big challenge for Japan to handle, while the newly emerged Communist Russia was influencing Japanese domestic political and social changes by focusing on workers and peasants.

Japanese officials took a realistic approach. They calculated Japan's powers and that of other international actors. In the 1920s, if Japan seemed to be more powerful than its rival major powers like Russia and China, it took on a hostile attitude toward them. However, Japan tried to coordinate with more powerful countries like the United States, when they calculated this action would be more in line with the interests of Japan.

Similar to the Koreans, the Japanese had active imaginations in the early twentieth century.[23] However, their dreams were never realized because the Japanese colonizers knew well the importance of calculated thinking before taking an action. Since Japan had vested interests in East Asia, as one of the Great Powers in the 1920s, they took a position as that of one of the status quo countries. Although Japan transformed itself into one of the status ante countries of the 1930s, it took conciliatory approaches to other Great Powers in the 1920s in order to maintain the balance of power.

Japan's realistic stance in the 1920s can be seen in its agreeing to and coordinating with the reduction of its naval arsenal with the United States and the United Kingdom at the Washington Naval Conference, even though Japan considered the United States to be a future enemy. Since the end of World War I, Japan viewed the United States, the newly ascending power, as increasingly challenging Japan's interest in East Asia. As we can see in the following section, Japan was worried about the United States' hostile attitude toward Japan. As the official newspaper of the Government-General of Chōsen, *Keijō Nippō*, discussed in its editorial on the possible danger of a US-Japan war in the future:

> Now we can see America's hidden ambition. In the perspective of economic imperialism, America has the ambition of maximizing American interests in East Asia. This will be a crucial factor of a military collision in the Pacific. If there will be a war between Japan and the United States, it will be the largest-scale warfare in modern history. If there will be a war, Japan should face this war with the firm determination to reserve the state's dignity.[24]

However, Japan understood that it should avoid a war with the United States as much as possible. Therefore, Japan agreed to reduce its naval military resources at the Washington Naval Conference held from November 12, 1921 to February 6, 1922. Although there was a significant backlash in Japan, the Japanese government made a deal with the United States and other Western countries to shrink their naval forces. The *Keijō Nippō* welcomed the agreement.

> If the Japanese government and the American government can reduce the possible sources of hostile clashes between them, this will be a chance to diminish mutual understanding. The Japanese government and the Japanese people are fearful because of the American plan to maximize its naval forces. On the other hand, the United States is suspicious that the UK-Japan alliance will be against the United States. Therefore, the United States considers Japan to be a potential enemy. . . . This conference is a chance to clean the slate of mutual misunderstanding and suspicion.[25]

Japan feared that it would lose a lot of the vested interests in East Asia if there were to be a war with the United States. Therefore, Japan preferred international coordination with the United States instead of warfare in the early 1920s. Japan's practical approach differed greatly from the Korean colonized's preference to warfare through active imagination.

INTERNATIONAL CONCERNS AND MAJOR GLOBAL POWERS: THE SIMILARITIES AND DIFFERENCES BETWEEN THE JAPANESE AND THE KOREAN RESPONSES IN THE 1920s

In the 1920s, both the Japanese colonizers and the Korean colonized had been highly sensitive to international affairs, which, in turn, had a tremendous influence on them. In the 1920s, there were three key international concerns for both the Japanese and the Koreans that went beyond the Washington Naval Conference: (1) the Yellow Peril; (2) the Communist revolution in Russia; and (3) China's future. Each of these concerns was related to the relationships among the major global powers (the United States, Russia, and China) with Japan and colonized Korea. The Yellow Peril was a racially motivated issue between the United States and Japan in the 1920s. The Yellow Peril broadly refers to the idea that East Asian peoples are a threat to Western civilizations. In the context of this article it refers to anti-Japanese attitudes and the laws of the United States, one of which was the Immigration Act of 1924, which banned immigration from Japan. As an Asian nation, the Korean people held an identical position with their Japanese colonizers. However, when these two Asian nations faced the Communist revolution in Russia they held different views. While the Japanese considered the Communist revolution a threat to Japan's influence over the Korean peninsula and Manchuria, the Koreans expressed feelings of anticipation. With regards to China's future, the Japanese emphasized Japan's interests in East Asia, while Koreans expected more changes in the balance of power in East Asia with China's stabilization. Overall, the Japanese wanted to maintain the status quo while the Korean colonized dreamed of change. While the Japanese colonizers' preference to stay the course originated from their practical vision, the Koreans actively imagined warfare as a means to change the balance of international power.

The Yellow Peril and the United States

The Koreans agreed with the Japanese on the Yellow Peril in the United States. Both nations considered the Yellow Peril to be a sign of racial tension between the Western white race and the Asian race and also between the whites and the African Americans. The *Keijō Nippō* indicated numerous times that the implementation of the Emergency Quota Act of 1921 (also known as the Emergency Immigration Act), the Cable Act of 1921 (often referred to as the Married Women's Independent Nationality Act), and the Immigration Act of 1924 (Johnson-Reed Act) was a sign of racial discrimination.

> Although the population of the white race does not cover a third of the whole population in the world, the white race dominates over nine-tenths of the world.... Among the Asian races, the Japanese is the only one not dominated by the white race.... The white race is facing resistance against their domination in Asia from a young Japan.[26]

> The United States reveals its own true nasty color with discriminatory acts against the Japanese. The United States continued to disguise its identity as a country of liberty, peace, justice, and equality. Now, however, the United States throws off its mask and shows its real identity. The United States is the biggest hypocrite.[27]

> It is an inconsistency that the United States limits immigration from Japan but continues to accept immigration from other Western countries. . . . The new Immigration Act is not only to discriminate Japanese. The United States has maintained its discrimination against all Asian peoples including the Chinese. Therefore, this situation is a huge concern to all Asian peoples as well as the Japanese.[28]

Even though the Japanese were upset about the US's discrimination against Japanese immigration and thought these policies constituted racial discrimination, they took very pragmatic means when it came to compromising with the United States with regards to the reduction of arms at the Washington Naval Conference. In the 1920s, the Japanese anger against the Yellow Peril phenomenon in the United States did not transfer into hostile foreign policy.

Korea shared Japan's view of the US's unfairness toward Asian races. One of the *Chosŏn ilbo*'s editorials declared that the twentieth century would be one of inter-racial competition in contrast to the competition of culture of the nineteenth century.

> The world is full of insecurity in spite of the superficial talks about peace or war. In the center of the insecurity lies the resistance of colored races by the white race, friction among the colored races and conflicts between workers and capitalists. The world has been viewed as existing solely for the white race but now there is, here and there, a resistance of the colored races against the white race, causing fear for the white race.[29]

The Japanese and the Korean perception of the United States made a sharp and negative turn right after the United States failed to join the League of Nations and did not heed the Korean people's appeals. In fact, the US image as an ideal liberal country quickly changed. The Koreans agreed with the Japanese that the true intention of the United States in World War I was seen to be to protect the interests of Anglo-Saxons against those of the Aryans.

However, while urging Asian races to unify against the Western white race, the *Chosŏn ilbo*'s editorials made it clear that the Asian peoples had not fully overcome the obstacles among themselves. Editorials never failed to mention that ethnic conflicts between the Koreans and the Japanese were a serious issue in the Pacific. In the editorial below there would be an inevitable clash between Japan and the United States and that such conflict might bring about change for colonial Korea.

> Nowadays, starting with China's national revolution, the anti-imperial struggles, and anti-capitalist struggles between strong and weak peoples is added a new development in the Far East. The present Pacific problems are different from the past ones. Ideological clashes between strong nations on the one hand and between strong and weak nations on the other will coincide someday, which will develop into a large conflict.[30]

Although the Korean colonized criticized the Yellow Peril, the United States was viewed as the country leading the shift of international attention from the Atlantic to the Pacific. According to one editorial, the United States appeared to be trying to carve out its own areas of interest in China by rendering support to the Kuomintang government (KMT; Nationalist Party of China), an action which caused serious concerns in England and Japan. By doing so, the United States was bringing about changes in the region; the US approach to China and its support of the KMT was working in such a way as to break down the Anglo-Japanese alliance, for Japan had a range of interests that differed significantly from those of England when it came to China.[31]

The *Chosŏn ilbo*'s editorials pointed out the importance of the United States to the future of Korea. The United States, with its supreme naval force and its increasingly expanding network of financial capitalism in China and the rest of the world, was bringing a new wind to the region. Considering the fact that colonial Korea could not do much in changing its international status on its own, the editorials held the view that Koreans would only benefit from changes in the international situation which the United States might be able to bring through its engagement in China, and as such urged that more attention should be paid to shifts in US policies in East Asia.

This was particularly true for Korea, according to editorials, which held high hopes that Korea would benefit from any change in the colonial status (domestic political stability or regional changes) through US engagement in China and stressed that more attention should be paid to the United States.[32]

Unlike the Japanese, who worried about changes in the East Asian international order—with the increasing influence of the United States within this region and wanted to diminish the US influence—the Koreans considered the United States to be a welcome factor, if it could initiate change.

Communism and Soviet Russia

The Chosŏn ilbo's editorials expected that the Communist revolution in Russia would change the international balance of power. First, Koreans perceived Russia to be a motor for historical change in Asia and the world. Russia's defeat in the war with Japan (Russo-Japanese War, 1904–5) brought about dramatic change in and around the Korean peninsula. Many expected that Communist Russia would play a similar role and thus urged that close attention be paid to Russia's development.[33] Of particular importance was Russia's relations with China. As Russian military confrontation with China and the Eastern China Railway showed, Moscow's traditional geopolitical interests in the region would not only affect China's future but also the Korean peninsula.

More importantly, Koreans saw Communist Russia as exercising a different kind of influence through its revolutionary ideology, one that set limitations on the extent of its cooperation with China and Japan in the region. What is noteworthy in this regard is that the editorials recognized the ever increasing political force of workers and formulated a theoretically possible, but unrealistic, scenario about the impact of the emergence of socialism as a main power source in Japan and China.

> The world is experiencing a reactionary trend, but the instability and insecurity of East Asia attracts our attention. It is possible to see some positive development in Japan and China for us [Korea]. The emergence of the force of the proletariat in Japan cannot be ignored. The center of the labor movement has been shifting from England to Germany to Japan where the movement is picking up activism. . . . When the new force comes to dominate Japan and the same thing happens in China, for the first time we can speak of peace in the Far East. It is not simply wishful thinking to consider that the Korean people can play an important role at that time. The three forces in the Far East will demand a buffer zone among themselves, and then it will be necessary to separate Korea and Manchuria from them [China, Japan, and Russia]. Manchuria is a region with long historical ties with Korea, and millions of Korean people have emigrated there. We can imagine Manchuria and Korea existing as a unit.[34]

Not only in hindsight but also from the perspective of contemporary development, this line of thinking was clearly a manifestation of active imaginations and wishful strategic thinking. Koreans perceived Russia and its new ideology as a different theoretical tool whereby they could conjure future hopes under colonial deadlock. Clearly Russia was viewed as a country that does not change.

Unlike the Koreans, the Japanese worried about Soviet Russia's negative impact on the existing state of affairs in East Asia. The *Keijō Nippō*'s editorials highlighted several times that Soviet Russia's control of Siberia would be a future danger to Japan's interests in Korea and Manchuria. Therefore, the *Keijō Nippō* suggested that the Japanese dispatch military forces in Siberia to reinforce the forces there in the early 1920s, when other Western countries started to withdraw their military forces.

> If radical Bolshevik groups controlled Siberia, the northern three provinces of China will be the biggest threat. This will be the future development which we want to avoid most. We are worried whether the radical Bolshevik groups will attack our small military bases or a supply complex in the future.... Therefore, we argue that we should refuse to withdraw the army from Siberia.[35]

> Now there is no durable political authority in the northern three provinces of China.... If Japan withdraws the Japanese military forces from Siberia, this will be the abandonment of overall security in Manchuria and Siberia. Therefore, we should be very careful withdrawing our army from Siberia. Another solution is to make a buffer zone between the regions belong to the Soviet government and Manchuria.[36]

Since Japan dispatched its army to Siberia to hold back the Communist revolution in Russia, the successful establishment of the Communist regime in Russia became a negative factor to the future of Japan in East Asia. The reason for the Korean anticipation of a Communist revolution in Russia mirrored that of the Japanese: a rise of a country that did not change the rules.

China and the Future of East Asia

As table 4.2 shows, China received the most attention from the *Chosŏn ilbo*. The reasons are clear. Koreans viewed China as being the focal point of the new Pacific era. Thus, the present and future development of Chinese domestic politics and international relations would have serious impacts on colonial Korea. The most consistently mentioned themes regarding China by editorials were related to domestic stability and China's autonomy. Particularly fierce contention for supremacy among the different military factions was a serious concern to Koreans. The following editorial excerpt is an example.

> Northern and southern China are divided and struggling against each other. Warlordism is running rampant, so that the people do not know what will happen, and the financial situation is so bad that China relies on foreign debts. Even at the Geneva Convention the representatives from both the south and the north denounced each other. How can foreign powers trust China?[37]

The immediate future of China's domestic political situation was not viewed positively. The wish and strive for a stable China forced editorials to express their desire for civil upheavals in China to finally put an end to the domestic political chaos.

> We, 20 million Koreans, do not spend a day without tears born out of foreign pressure, however we feel sympathetic and concerned about domestic warlordism present in our neighbor. Rather than criticizing the rampant warlordism, we wish that 400 million people rise with fierce resistance can lay a permanent foundation for world peace and humanity and/or friendship with us.[38]

Another example of this wish for a stable China is the belief in the invincibility of China in spite of constant foreign intervention. One editorial noted, "any country which starts a war with China will have to provide endless military manpower."[39] And another, that even when China loses one million people a year, it will take fifty years to destroy China.[40]

This view slowly began to change as the grip of Chiang Kai Shek was reinforced by the defeat of rival military factions in 1928. Several editorials noted Chiang's military victory, although they quickly added that the victory was not complete. After Chaing created a coalition with the bourgeois class, Koreans viewed China as having become more stable. At the same time, editors noted the increasing signs of Chiang's dictatorship, which caused a new surge in resistance and the rise of military factions and even the mobilization of workers and peasants.[41]

The stability of China is important as it affects the future of Korea, the East Asia region, and the world. As mentioned earlier, social revolution in China, when it is followed by revolution in Japan and in coordination with Russia, will bring about a new power balance in and around the Korean peninsula. On the other hand, when China becomes a battleground among major powers, it will not change a thing.

> The Chinese domestic situation concerns us. If China enters into a social revolution, it will greatly affect our life, and this is not likely to happen. If China turns into the battlefield of the world, it will also tremendously affect our political life. In recent years after changing the president five times and reshuffling the cabinet tens of times, China has not gained any stability, which greatly concerns us.[42]

If China had stood on fragile stability and coalition, what was expected was continuous meddling of foreign powers in China's economy and politics. Here China becomes a new battleground between Japan and England on the one hand and the United States on the other. The United States was viewed as trailing Japan and England in trade with China.[43] Editorials noted US support for the KMT and China's national revolution, while Japan and England were trying to maintain their previous influence and ties with old military factions in Guangdong and Manchuria.[44] England made, however, a quick move to support the KMT away from the Kwangseo faction. Japan was a different case from England in that it had strongly vested interest in Manchuria and Mongolia. England and Japan now came to diverge in terms of their strategies in China. The former's low level of interest made it easier to negotiate with the KMT, while the latter still had to deal with remaining issues in Manchuria and Mongolia.[45]

Given the uncertainty of China's domestic political stability, the emergence of the Pacific as a new arena of competition, with the United States becoming a new hegemonic power and Russia's entry into East Asia, editors predicted that "East Asia will be swirled into an international conflict due to US-Japanese rivalry."[46] In fact, Koreans viewed this tension as a potential means to develop into a catalyst for regional peace and stability.

The Impact of the Colonial Situation on International Perspectives in Korea 129

> The anti-Japanese phenomenon in California is only a precursor to what will be a major clash between the United States and Japan on the rich plains of China. As attention of the powers shift from Europe to Asia, we predict that an unavoidable power clash will be repeated in the coastal areas of the Pacific as a way to come to terms with the remaining bloody tragedy.[47]

China was perceived by Koreans as an important regional power. In fact, China loomed so large in the strategic imagination of Korean intellectuals and the masses that the future of the Pacific region appeared to be determined by what would happen in China. There were basically three ways in which the Chinese were thought to affect Korea and the Korean people. First, the emergence of any stable regime in China would be better than chaos. A stable China could work as a possible check on Japanese influence in Manchuria and Korea. At the same time, the pattern and degree of the success of China's domestic political, social, and economic changes could affect Korea. If a workers and peasants revolution broke out and especially if a similar situation developed in Japan, it would do away with militaristic regimes, not only in China but also in Japan. A changed Russia would bring about a new balance of power in the region, which, in turn, would enable Koreans to enhance their own level of autonomy.

Not unlike the *Chosŏn ilbo*, the *Keijō Nippō* paid a significant amount of attention to China in its editorials. Many of the *Keijō Nippō*'s editorials on China discussed warlordism and domestic warfare. The *Keijō Nippō* also pointed out the importance of a stabilized China, and it highlighted Japanese security and interests in mainland China and Manchuria. To this point, the *Keijō Nippō* mobilized a debate on Japan's role in helping liberate China from Western powers.

> China is dominated by Western powers. The United Kingdom controls the northeast areas of China, and the United States has been increasing its influence in China's southwest areas. . . . In this situation, the Chinese people can become eternal slaves of Western peoples. Since the Chinese people do not have enough capability to drive out Western powers, we, the Japanese, should help the Chinese.[48]

As we can expect, the *Keijō Nippō* viewed China's domestic political instability as a threat to Japan's control over Korea. In emphasizing the side effects of China's instability to the Korean people, the Japanese argued that they (the Japanese) should also expand their control into Manchuria. The *Keijō Nippō* provided numerous views of the interconnecting stability of Korea and Manchuria.

> If Manchuria is unstable, this will be a negative factor in our rule in Korea. . . . In order to protect ordinary citizens, we should prepare to send troops to Manchuria. . . . Although Manchuria is a territory of China, the Chinese will accept our military forces, which will focus on the maintenance of public security.[49]

Even when Chiang Kai-shek accomplished the unification of China, Japan expanded its military into China under the motto of protecting the interests of Japan and the Japanese people. Following this, the *Keijō Nippō* emphasized that China's stability could be enhanced with the existence of Japanese military bases in China. To the Japanese, China's stabilization was only necessary to maintain when it was in the best interest of Japan.

> The Japanese government decided to send military forces into China's northern areas. The *North China Daily News*, a Shanghai English newspaper welcomed Japan's expanding military. . . . This military dispatch is inevitable to protect the lives and property of Japanese residents. . . . We do not have any intention to become involved in warfare between warlords. We intend only to stay the spread of warfare.[50]

The stabilization of China had different meanings to the Japanese and the Koreans. While the Koreans expected change in East Asia, the Japanese considered China's stabilization a necessary condition for guaranteeing and protecting the interests of Japan and Japanese citizens in mainland China and Manchuria.

CONCLUSION

Based on the above analysis, several observations are in order by way of addressing the question originally posed as to how the colonial situation affected and was mirrored by the international perspectives of the Koreans.

First, in terms of coverage, we see the impact of the colonial situation. The high level of attention focused on the international situation indicated the importance of international affairs in the understanding of the future of colonial Korea. More proactively, coverage of these issues demonstrated an effort of the Koreans to seek possible scenarios and strategies. The colonial situation itself is a condition that warranted high-level attention to international affairs. Naturally, attention was heavily skewed toward ideology, the military, and political affairs with far less attention on economics. This came from Koreans' active attention on international sources of change in response to their passive colonial situation. Even if the number of editorials on Japan was small, Japan, in fact, loomed largest (larger than China); every editorial ended up with direct or indirect implications for Japan and their colonial situation. In fact, it is safe to say every editorial in the *Chosŏn ilbo* was about Japan and the colonial situation. Next to Japan, China receives the frequent attention of editorials because China was viewed as a country which could bring possible change in colonial Korea either through China's new political order or by the consequences of international competition among the major powers centering around China.

Second, idealism based on cooperation and humanity quickly disappeared as a possible source of change for colonial Korea. It was replaced with a destructive vision which looked for change based on warfare among the major powers. Editorials were quick to recognize the utility of connecting Soviet communism to the colonial situation. Communism had a strong influence on colonial Korea with its transnational boundary nature. It carved out some room for nations without a state. Truly revealing Koreans' wishful thinking, editorials expressed an unrealistic view of the impact of Soviet communism around the world and in Asia. The active search for change under passive colonial conditions led to an unintended penchant for possible conflicts in and around the Korean peninsula. Constant references to grim prospects when it came to arms reduction, the recognition of class and the liberation war as being legitimate, and specific references to possible changes in the colonial situation from the socialist revolution in Asian countries—and from the rivalry among major powers in China—all testify to the mental status and the active search for alternatives under the passive behavioral conditions of Koreans subjected to colonial rule. Perhaps peace under the colonial situation was less preferable to the possibility of change through military conflicts which were beyond Koreans' control. A realistic logic of the weak is to prefer conflict rather than peace. Japan and China loomed large when we analyze Koreans' major power perceptions, but more importantly it seems that the colonial situation led Koreans to have skewed and biased views of them. Intentions and realities of the major countries in and around the region were frequently interpreted to suit the wishful thinking and strategies of that time. The penchant for stability in China, the sheer grim picture of Japan, and the role of Russian ideology are a few examples.

Third, international perception during the colonial era appears to have simplified Koreans' view on who was an enemy or friend in the post–Colonial Period. It is striking to observe that in spite of extensive attention to international affairs, practically all of the editorials were devoted to the possible impact of global affairs on the colonial situation in Korea. Such a response by the media appears to resemble narrowing tunnel vision. This meant that the focus was on Japan as the primary enemy. In a strange way, after all the attention to world affairs colonial Korea had not much room to think about the diversification of its enemies or friends. With China being the next target for attention, intended or not, this manner of thinking reinforced Koreans' tradition of having an under-differentiated or simplified understanding of the enemy.

The tradition of dealing with a single power continued during the Cold War under US hegemony and the bifurcated ideological confrontation. The historical background of the black-and-white view of the world can be traced to the far distant history of the Chosŏn Dynasty, but the current analysis shows that the colonial international experiences are a more immediate cause for the simplification of the enemy on the present-day Korean peninsula. The legacy that Korean intellectuals could not but imagine international politics without actual practice during the 1920s and the 1930s and that they were bequeathed with the simplistic understanding of the enemy was hard to shed when faced with a dominant power like the United States during the Cold War.

Perhaps it is high time for Koreans to look back at their own intellectualization effort of the 1920s as a possible source of strategic inspiration for the present-day Korean peninsula. For example, North Korea's equidistance policy has been attributed to Sino-Soviet conflicts.[51] However, it can be argued that without prior thinking, learning, and preparation opportunities such as the Sino-Soviet conflicts cannot be taken advantage of. In this regard one may speculate that Kim Il-Sung might have learned complex international politics from those being played in Manchuria among the major powers, and he was thereby able to apply it to Sino-Soviet conflicts. Kim Il-Sung learned a precious lesson from the complex international politics in Manchuria during the 1930s and 1940s, which he applied to the Sino-Soviet conflict in the 1950s and 1960s to secure maximum autonomy.

Fourth, the infatuation with the military during the colonial years is interesting. Since the forced opening of Korea, an unfounded sense of military supremacy quickly evaporated in front of the superior firepower of Japan, but the pervasive perception of Koreans was that the difference between the Koreans and the Japanese military arsenal was minimal. During the colonial years, especially the 1920s and 1930s, there were constant reminders of the need for strong military power. Military competition and practice among the major powers during the colonial years alone must have been a sufficient enough reminder for the need of a strong military force among Koreans. If this is a plausible argument, the historical source of the militarization of the Korean peninsula in the latter twentieth century must go farther back than the Cold War period.

Finally, when we compare the *Chosŏn ilbo* with the *Keijō Nippō*, Koreans' active imaginations and wishful strategies become clearer. Japan did not want large-scale change of the international environment in the 1920s. As a rising powerful state in East Asia and the Pacific, Japan already had a lot of vested interests. Therefore, Japan chose international cooperation or aggressive military actions based on realistic calculations. The cooperative negotiation at the Washington Naval Conference in 1922, when the Japanese expressed anger about American racial discrimination on immigration, is the result of Japan's calculation about the United States' increasing power. In the 1920s, Japan preferred the status quo. When, however, Japan considered that neighboring countries like Russia and China were weak, it exercised military actions insisting upon the appropriateness of those behaviors. This was also a result of realistic calculations about Japan's superior capabilities to Russia or China. In contrast, the Koreans preferred to imagine solutions that were distant from realistic calculations. We should carefully consider what kinds of impacts the colonial situation and international relations had on the Koreans' imagination rather than assume that all nations behave realistically.

NOTES

1. Arlene Tickner, "Seeing IR Differently."
2. For example, see Stephanie G. Neuman ed., *International Relations Theory and the Third World*.
3. Regarding criticism on the dogmatic assumption over state action in the IR discipline, see Stanley Hoffmann, "An American Social Science"; and Steve Smith, "The Six Wishes for a More Relevant Discipline of International Relations."
4. Homi Bhabba, *The Location of Culture*.
5. Past studies of the international perspective of intellectuals include Yi Hojae, Han'guk ŭi kukche chŏngch'i gwan: Kaehang hu 100-yŏn ŭi oegyo nonjaeng kwa pansŏng [International political views of Korean people: Diplomatic disputes and self-examinations over one hundred years after the opening of a port]; Ko Pongjun, "1920-yŏndae chisigin ŭi kukche chŏngch'i insik e kwanhan yŏn'gu" [A study on the intellectuals' recognition of international relations in Korea in the 1920s]; and Chŏn Sangsuk, "Che 1-ch'a Segye tajŏn Ihu kukche chilsŏ ŭi chaep'yon kwa minjok chidojadŭl ŭi Taeoe insik" [Reorganization of international relations after World War I and the understanding of Korean national leaders].
6. For information on past studies using mass media of international situations during the Colonial Period see, Kim Hyŏndae, "Ilcheha *Tonga ilbo* ŭi minjok undongsajŏk koch'al: Munhwa chŏngch'i kigan (1920–1928) ŭi sasŏl punsŏk ŭl chungsim ŭro" [A study of the nationalistic movement of the *Tonga ilbo* under Japanese imperialism]; Yu Chaech'ŏn, "Ilche ha Han'guk chapchi ŭi kongsanjuŭi suyong e kwanhan yŏn'gu" [The study of the accommodation of communism in Korean magazines during the Japanese Colonial Period]; Im Kyŏngsŏk and Cha Hyeyŏng, Kaebyŏk e pich'in singminji Chosŏn ŭi ŏlgul [The colonial Korea's face in the journal *Kaebyŏk*]; Son Chunsik, "Singminji Chosŏn ŭi taeman insik: *Chosŏn ilbo* (1920–1940) kisa rŭl chungsim ŭro" [The perception of colonial Chosŏn on Taiwan: Focusing on *Choson ilbo*'s articles, 1920–1940].
7. Christine Sylvester, "African and Western Feminisms," 946–47.
8. Kim Younghee. "Ilche chibae sigi Han'gugin ŭi sinmun chŏpch'ok kyŏnghyang" [The trends in newspapers exposure of Koreans under Japanese imperialism], 63.
9. "Kukka, minjok, keyegŭp" [The state, nation, and class], editorial, *Chosŏn ilbo*, June 19, 1926.

10. "Hyŏnha sasang ŭi aidia choryu" [The two ideological currents in the contemporary world], editorial, *Chosŏn ilbo*, May 17, 1924; and "Taedong isang ŭi yoksajok tongŭ" [Historical consensus on grand jury], editorial, *Chosŏn ilbo*, December 8, 1929.

11. "Segye chongse ŭi hyŏnse i" [The current trend in world politics], editorial, *Chosŏn ilbo*, March 22, 1925.

12. "Segye wa Chosŏn" [The world and the Chosŏn nation], *Chosŏn ilbo*, January 21, 1924.

13. "Segyejŏk minjok" [The nation in the world], *Chosŏn ilbo*, December 12, 1921.

14. "Taep'yŏngyang ŭi hyonjae wa changnae" [The here and the hereafter of the Pacific], *Chosŏn ilbo*, May 15, 1921.

15. "Soyang kwa tongyang (sang)" [The West and the East (I)], *Chosŏn ilbo*, August 22, 1920.

16. "Taep'yŏngyang ŭi yangmyŏnjŏk ch'undol" [Double-sided clashes of the Pacific], *Chosŏn ilbo*, January 7, 1927.

17. "Miguk ŭi kyŏngjejok chinch'ul: Chungguk e taehan kihoe ŭi kyundŭng undong" [Economic entry of the United States: The movement of equal opportunity for China], *Chosŏn ilbo*, May 20, 1929.

18. "P'yŏnghwa wa chŏnjaeng: Puchŏn choyak kwa kunbi ch'ukso" [Peace and War: Antiwar treaty and arms reduction], *Chosŏn ilbo*, September 23, 1928.

19. "Segye p'yŏnghwa nŭn ŏnje toel kŏtin'ga" [When will world peace be coming?], *Chosŏn ilbo*, January 2, 1929.

20. "T'aep'yŏngyang hoeui wa Il-Yŏng Mi haegun ryŏk [The Pan-Pacific conference and naval power of Japan, Britain, and the United States], *Chosŏn ilbo*, August 3, 1921.

21. "Kunbi ch'ukso wa Ilbon yoron" [Arms reduction and Japanese public opinion], *Chŏson ilbo*, November 29, 1921; and "Kyongje palchŏn ŭi sin sigi wa sinbangmyŏn" [New era and the way of economic development], *Chosŏn ilbo*, December 16, 1921.

22. "Pujŏn choyak ŭi mosun" [Contradictions of the antiwar treaty], *Chosŏn ilbo*, April 19, 1928; and "Pujŏn choyak pijun" [Ratification of antiwar treaty], *Chosŏn ilbo*, January 19, 1929.

23. Sven Saaler and Christopher W. A. Szpilman, *Pan-Asianism*.

24. "Nichi beisensō" [Japan-US war], *Keijō Nippō*, March 10, 1922.

25. "Gunshuku kaigi no kōka" [The outcome of the disarmament conference], *Keijō Nippō*, March 7, 1922.

26. "Nichi beisensō."

27. "Jōyaku ihan o kōgi seyo" [Protest the violation of the treaty], *Keijō Nippō*, May 7, 1924.

28. "Hainichi hōan shikō [The enforcement of the anti-Japanese bill], *Keijō Nippō*, May 8, 1924.

29. "Segye p'yŏnghwa nŭn hŏ-sik ŭi mungu" [World peace is the ostentatious slogan], *Chosŏn ilbo*, June 28, 1921.

30. T'aep'yŏngyang ŭi yangmyŏnjŏk ch'ungdol."

31. "Yŏng-Mi ŭi 250ŏk t'uja kyehoek: Chungguk kŏnsŏl saŏp ŭl wihayŏ" [Twenty-five-billion-dollar investment plan of Britain and the United States], *Chosŏn ilbo*, October 24, 1928.

32. "Miguk ŭi kyŏngjejok chinch'ul: Chungguk e taehan kihoe ŭi kyundŭng undong" [Economic entry of the United States: The movement of equal opportunity for China], *Chosŏn ilbo*, May 20, 1929.

33. "Miguk ŭi kŭktong" [US policy toward the Far East], *Chosŏn ilbo*, July 5, 1925. For previous studies on the perspectives of Korean communists during the Colonial Period see Chŏng Yonguk, "1920-yŏndae kongsanjuŭi undong yŏn'gu" [A study of Communist movement in the 1920s]; and Sŏ Chungsŏk, "Ilche sidae sahoejuŭjadŭl ŭi minjokkwan kwa kyegŭp kwan" [Socialists' perception on the nation and class under the rule of Japanese imperialism].

34. "Chumokhal nonongro sŏa ŭi tae chung ch'aek" [The Russian Soviet Federative Socialist Republics' noteworthy policy toward China], *Chosŏn ilbo*, January 4, 1927.

35. "Dankotaru socihi o yōsu" [Require strong measures], *Keijō Nippō*, May 21, 1921.

36. "Shiberia taisku no shōrai" [The future of the Siberia policy], *Keijō Nippō*, May 21, 1921.

37. "Chungguk kukche kwalliron ŭi ch'ulch'ŏ" [The origin of the Chinese international management theory], *Chosŏn ilbo*, August 18, 1921.

38. "Chungguk ŭi p'ungun (sang)" [Chinese storm (1)], *Chosŏn ilbo*, August 30, 1924.

39. "Gisil ihae ŭi pangyŏk 1" [Prevention of actual profits and losses], *Chosŏn ilbo*, August 20, 1920.

40. "Chunghwain sŏn'gakcha chekun ege yŏham."

41. "Kungmin chŏngbu ŭi oegyo chŏngch'aek"; "Tongyo rŭl chŏnhanŭn chungguk chŏngse" [The chaotic news from Chinese circumstances], *Chosŏn ilbo*, September 24, 1929; and "Suraksŏkch'ul ŭi chungguk chŏngse" [Chinese circumstances become clear], *Chosŏn ilbo*, October 1, 1929.

42. "Chungguk ŭi p'ungun (sang)."

43. "Miguk ŭi Kyŏngjejŏk jinch'ul" [US policy toward the Far East], *Chosŏn ilbo*, July 15, 1925.

44. "Chŏngsin Haptong ŭi sirhyŏn" [Realization of combining political affairs with new things], *Chosŏn ilbo*, July 7, 1929.

45. "Miguk ŭi Kyŏngjejŏk jinch'ul."

46. Ryu Ki Du, "Kwagŏ illyŏn ŭi taep'yŏngyang chungsim ŭi kukche chŏngso" [Past one year's international situation in the Pacific], *Chosŏn ilbo*, January 1, 1929; and "Kyŏngsiji mothal Il-Mi kwang'gye" [Deteriorating US-Japanese relations], Editorial, *Chosŏn ilbo*, July 5, 1925.

47. "Hwainul pojanghan chungguk ui tongnan" [Disaster containing Chinese civil war], Chosŏn ilbo, October 7, 1924.

48. "Nisshi kyōei-ron" [The co-existence of Japan and China], Keijō Nippō, January 28, 1920.

49. "Tai Manshū konpon taisku no juritsu?" [The establishment of the fundamental countermeasures against Manchuria], Keijō Nippō, February 9, 1921.

50. "Shuppei no igi o mattou seyo" [Let's fulfill the original meanings of military dispatch], Keijō Nippō, May 31, 1927.

51. Byung Chul Koh, The Foreign Policy of North Korea; Chin O. Chung, Pyongyang Between Peking and Moscow; Helen-Louise Hunter, "North Korea and the Myth of Equidistance"; and Tae-Hwan Kwak, Wayne Patterson, and Edward E. Olsen eds, The Two Koreas in World Politics, 195–210.

5

Modern Utopia or "Animal Society"? The American Imaginaries in Wartime Colonial Korea, 1931–1945

YUMI MOON

Historian Akira Iriye wrote that a "cold war" took place for several years between the United States and Japan before the eruption of the Pacific War on December 7, 1941. According to Iriye, this cold war did not originate in a fundamental disparity of ideology and interests, as in the postwar Cold War between the United States and the Union of Soviet Socialist Republics (USSR). Rather, the belligerent discourse and antagonism between Japan and the United States belied the deeper "undercurrents" of compatible interests and international visions observed in their relations before 1929.[1] Iriye highlights the inconsistency within wartime Japan's rhetoric and diplomacy for a Pan-Asianist order and its ambivalence toward US power, culture, and foreign policy. This emphasis on ambivalence provides a context in which to understand Japan's swift reconciliation with the United States in the postwar era, but it discounts the intensity of the wartime confrontations in East Asia and their historical legacy beyond the postwar US-Japan rapprochement.

During the wartime period, Japan's perceptions of a desirable society and world sharply diverged from US ones, and Japan's mobilization to enforce this vision altered the ideological and political landscape of the region under Japanese rule. Harry Harootunian wrote that the anxiety of Japanese intellectuals toward Anglo American culture made them acknowledge the war as an occasion to criticize "the meaning of modernity" entrenched in Japan since the Meiji era. They assigned Japan a "civilizational mission" to overcome the problems of modernity, attached prominently to the "negativity of American materialism and its superficiality" that was collapsing Japanese culture into "mediocrity and triviality."[2] Cemil Aydin calls Japan's alternative worldview

"Pan-Asianist internationalism" and argues that Japanese intellectuals and public figures became receptive to this vision after Japan's conflicts with the League of Nations.[3]

How, then, did Koreans under the Japanese conceive of this new civilizational mission, and of Japan's wartime narrative seeking "new moral principles different from those that had governed Europe"?[4] How did Koreans respond to the ongoing imperialization—or the Japanization of Korea—so as to change its colony according to this Pan-Asianist order? This chapter explores the Korean imaginaries of the United States in wartime colonial Korea and examines their implications in terms of answering these questions. In defining the term "imaginary," I use Charles Taylor's concept of the social imaginary. Taylor differentiates social imaginary from philosophy or social theory because (1) "imaginary" refers to "the way ordinary people imagine their surroundings," which is "often not expressed in theoretical terms" but "carried in images, stories, legends, and other media"; (2) "theory is often the possession of a small minority, but the social imaginary is shared by larger group of people"; and (3) "the social imaginary is a common understanding" that makes people engage with common practices invoking a shared sense of normal expectations.[5]

The Korean wartime discourse on the United States included diverse types of writing such as stories, reports on events, columns, statistics, miscellaneous essays of tourists, and imaginary claims about the United States' characteristics. Mass consumption of US films during colonial rule might have influenced the broader Korean population in imagining the United States and Americans. Although Korean authors were mostly educated élites, they seldom supplied sophisticated analyses of the United States and lacked the theoretical coherence to be a subject for intellectual history. Nevertheless, these writings still conveyed the positions of the authors "interwoven with an idea of how [Korean society] ought to go."[6] The United States, in this sense, was the topic via which these Korean authors discussed their ideas and desires about a model society for Korea, or their criticism of the country's ongoing imperialization without ever mentioning Japan—a realistic approach, given the harsh colonial censorship.

As mentioned earlier, Japan's Pan-Asianist discourse in the 1930s advocated an alternative civilization, or "utopia," as opposed to Anglo American imperialism at a time when Japan still wanted to avoid the war with the United States.[7] The Korean wartime narratives on the United States did not endorse this Pan-Asianist turn. On the contrary, some authors depicted the United States as an "ideal place" and sought a solution for Korea's problems in US experiments. Such Korean narratives made a sudden transition in 1941 when Japan, expecting the Pacific War, closed down the major Korean newspapers and filled the remaining magazines with Japan's wartime messages.[8] This shift became acute when the famous Korean journalist and Columbia University PhD Chang Tŏksu (1895–1947) called the United States "an animal society" (tongmul sahoe) in his speeches mobilizing Koreans for the Pacific War.[9]

This chapter is a preliminary attempt to identify the areas of ideological contention and convergence among different élite groups in wartime colonial Korea. The wartime discourse on the United States in Korea contains elements that revisit the thesis of an ideological schism between nationalists and socialists—or between cultural nationalists and revolutionaries—that Michael Robinson analyzed in his work on Korean nationalism in the 1920s.[10] Bruce Cumings, the eminent author of *The Origins of the Korean War*, also defines the Korean situation at Liberation in 1945 as "revolutionary." He understands that preexisting schisms in colonial Korea were released into a civil war situation when the formidable colonial administration abruptly disappeared from Korea.[11]

The research provided in the following pages will suggest that such an ideological schism changed its characteristics during the wartime period. In the wartime discourse on the United States, Korean nationalists and socialists indicated not as much contention as agreement, especially in their positive appraisal of the United States under President Franklin D. Roosevelt (1882–1945). This implies mutual penetration rather than a path to an irreconcilable split. The sharpest ideological divide actually appears between the Japanese Pan-Asianist discourse and some Korean Christian narratives on the United States printed before the attack on Pearl Harbor. The sources used in this chapter are from the essays in Korean-language magazines published between 1931 and 1945. The majority of these Korean-language writings are literary pieces, but they also include some political essays as well. I selected four major magazines: *Chogwang* (The morning light), *Chungang* (The central post), *Pip'an* (Criticism), and *Samch'ŏlli* (The Korean peninsula), since they voiced the relatively distinctive positions of the cultural nationalists (*Chogwang*), socialists (*Chungang* and *Pip'an*), and Pan-Asianists (*Samch'ŏlli*). The magazines were not strictly divided along distinctive political lines, but their general editorial directions are distinguishable from one another. Some essays from other magazines, including *Sijo* (Trends) and *Sahae kongnon* (Cosmopolitans), are occasionally used as points of reference.

CULTURAL NATIONALISTS: US CIVILIZATION AS THE FUTURE OF THE HUMAN RACE

Not the Americas but rather Europe was central in the Japanese intellectual discourse before World War II, according to Peter Duus and Kenji Hasegawa, the editors of *Rediscovering America: Japanese Perspectives on the American Century*. Fascinated with European debates on Marxism in the 1920s and National Socialism in the 1930s, Japanese magazines remained indifferent to the United States' New Deal in coping with the crisis of capitalism.[12] The Japanese essays collected in *Rediscovering America* include some positive observations on the United States' and its modern lifestyle and global influence but never designate the country as an ideal land. In contrast, the Korean essays on the United States published in the 1930s and early 1940s increasingly acclaim US development. Both Korean nationalists and socialists paid close attention to President Roosevelt's reforms and to the US congress' acts to grant independence to the Philippines.[13]

Korean Christians and cultural nationalists provided the most idealized portraits of the United States. The Christian magazine *Sijo* considered the United States a model society that agreed with the magazine's conservative ethics. American missionaries of the Seventh-Day Adventist Church created the magazine in 1910, and it was widely read by non-Christians due to its broad coverage of nonreligious subjects.[14] *Sijo*'s July 1937 edition reprints an article from a magazine called *Segye chisik* (World knowledge). Titled "Silchae haeyŏ innŭn yut'op'ia: Miguk teksasŭ kin [Keene] ch'on ŭi ip'unggyŏng" (On utopia in this world: Keene Village, Texas, United States), the article insists that this village has brought into reality all the elements that Thomas More imagined in his book *Utopia*. All the residents in Keene, the article says, had occupations and carried on "peaceful, idealistic, angelic" lives, with no prison, police, mayor, or court, and virtually no crime in the past forty-two years, except for a young boy's theft of snacks from a store. The Keene villagers neither joined labor movements nor received relief from others.

Sijo ascribed this utopia to the ethics of the village residents, who curtailed their secular desires and suspended the consumption of alcohol, cigarettes, meat, lipstick and manicures for women, and so forth. If the villagers violated these suspensions, they were called to the church council to receive reproach, but the regulations were not forceful, the article claims, because villagers were free to leave if they disliked such rules. The article celebrated the fact that the village had no houses for gambling, movies, dancing, and no film posters encouraging the "objectionable" desire for romance between men and women or drinking alcohol.[15]

While this Sijo article presented the Christian sect's conservative vision and its criticism of the modern lifestyle, the timing of the article in 1937 and the location of the ideal village in Texas represented increasing Korean interests in the United States and its material and cultural capacities. Many Korean intellectuals, especially cultural nationalists, considered the United States a sensible and non-Soviet example to emulate in modernizing Korea and even recognized a glimpse of utopia in the United States' development. Before the attack on Pearl Harbor, the magazine Chogwang exhibited such an orientation. The Chosŏn ilbo Company published Chogwang as a monthly magazine between November 1935 and December 1944 and continued the magazine even after the colonial government banned its daily newspaper, the Chosŏn ilbo, in December 1940.

Chogwang covered the United States' technological and economic advancements, the US decisions on the independence of the Philippines, the labor movements under the Roosevelt administration, US women, US foreign relations and its conflicts with Japan, and more. Many authors of Chogwang articles on the United States were meticulous in delivering objective details on the subjects concerned but cautious in giving their explicit opinions. Nevertheless, those articles associated the United States with images of enormous wealth, progress, and power. One of the magazine's most opinionated authors depicted the country as representing a future civilization for the human race. After the attack on Pearl Harbor on December 7, 1941, Chogwang's articles changed tone, calling the United States the enemy, the imperialists, and the racists. This betrayed the magazine's main contentions between 1935 and 1940, which esteemed the United States' system and practices as a standard or a destination in reforming the present circumstances of colonial Korea. Several writers who had studied in the United States set the tone of the *Chogwang*'s coverage of the United States in the late 1930s. Han Poyong (1901–?) was a key US studies expert. He was originally from Chŏngp'yŏng, South Hamgyŏng Province. After majoring in politics at Japan's Meiji University and graduating from New York University, Han worked as the chief editor of the *Chosŏn ilbo*'s politics section for seven years. In 1946, after Liberation, Han became the mayor of Taegu City, under the US Army Military Government in Korea (USAMGIK).[16] Another contributor, Chŏng Irhyŏng (1904–82), published an essay on US civilization based on his firsthand experience in the United States. Originally from P'yŏngan Province, Chŏng had graduated from Yonsei College, studied theology and sociology in the United States for seven years, and earned a PhD in 1935 from Drew University in New Jersey.[17] After returning from the United States, he taught at the Seoul Methodist Church Seminary (Kyŏngsŏng Kamni Kyohoe Sinhakbu). Chŏng joined the US Military Government in 1945 as a high-level administrator and then became a leading politician in South Korea.[18]

A third author, Han Ch'ijin, contributed two articles on the foundation of "American civilization," rendering the country's pragmatic and humanitarian characteristics. His family lived in Yonggang, South P'yŏngan Province. Han studied at a middle school affiliated with Jinling (Kŭmgnŭng) University, established by US missionaries in Nanjing, China, and received a PhD from the University of Southern California. After his return to Korea, Han taught at Ehwa Womans University but resigned in 1936 due to Japanese objections to his professorship. The Japanese colonial government had recorded Han's profile on a list of suspicious Koreans (*yongŭi chosŏnin*) and jailed him in 1944 due to the tenor of a speech he gave at a school on Japan's (probable) defeat in the Pacific War.[19]

In the later issues of *Chogwang*, between 1937 and 1942, Ham Sanghun, the editor-in-chief of the *Chosŏn ilbo*, covered the wars in Europe and the Pacific and articulated the significance of US moves for the Japanese Empire. Born in Songhwa, Hwanghae Province, Ham graduated from the College of Politics and Economy at Waseda University and served as the politics section chief at the *Tonga ilbo* before becoming editor-in-chief of the *Chosŏn ilbo*. During the final years of the war, Ham joined various pro-Japanese collaborative organizations as a well-known journalist. After Liberation, he chaired the Kongbobu

(Public Relations Bureau) of the Han'guk Minjudang (Korean Democratic Party).²⁰ It merits notice that these authors on the United States were all from Korea's northern region, that Chŏng Irhyŏng and Han Ch'ijin were Christians, and that all of them cooperated with the US Military Government in Korea after 1945.

When the *Chogwang* published its first issue in November 1935, the independence of the Philippines prompted strong interest among Korean journalists. The US negotiation with the Filipinos added to the United States an image of a *benign* power, which preempted the Japanese wartime messages reiterating the colonial Philippines as evidence of US imperialism. When the United States passed the Philippine Independence Act (Tydings-McDuffie Act; Public Law 73–127) on March 24, 1934, both Korean nationalists and socialists treated this subject attentively. The leftist Pae Sŏngnyong published an article in the *Sahae kongnon* when the Philippines passed its new constitution by popular vote following the Tydings-McDuffie Act. Pae spelled out the conflicts of interest that the plan for independence could entail for Filipinos and Americans alike. He suspected that the United States wanted to liberate the Philippines for economic reasons but could not yet do so from a military viewpoint, given the numerous US military bases there. Pae aspired that the newly elected President Manuel Quezón would manage the situation well during the ten years assigned before independence and would revise the country's economic terms with the United States more to the Filipinos' advantage. Nevertheless, Pae sincerely celebrated the agreement, calling it "a historic event at the corner of the West Pacific," and hoped that all Filipinos would unite and cooperate for their independence.²¹

Han Poyong also covered this subject in the *Chogwang* in December 1935. His article provided a fuller history of the Philippines: the years under Spanish colonial rule; the country's independence movements led by the patriots Jose Rizal and Emilio Aginaldo in the mid-1890s; the US occupation of the islands during the Spanish-American War; the failure of the Filipino guerrilla movements against the US occupation; and the subsequent "Yankee imperialism" in the Philippines for thirty years. Despite this US aggression, Han argued that US rule was more "generous" than that of the Spaniards, "achieving much more for the islands in thirty years than Spain accomplished in its three-hundred-year rule."²² Han continues that, right after the occupation, US President William McKinley, Jr. (1843–1901) had promised the future independence of the Philippines. Filipinos could discuss their independence in public because the United States had already implemented the self-rule (*chach'i*) of the islands and established the Congress of the Philippines in 1907.

Han then noted that US politicians had discussed Philippine independence, including President Woodrow Wilson in his 1912 inaugural speech and the US Congress approval of the Philippine Autonomy Act of 1916. This discussion was suspended under the Republican administration between 1921 and 1929 but resumed during the Great Depression, when the Americans resented the entrance of agricultural products from the Philippines, as well as the immigration of Filipinos to the United States.[23] President Franklin Roosevelt completed the US procedure with his signature on the Philippine Independence Act. The Filipinos approved the act by plebiscite in May, elected the nationalist Quezón president in September, and declared the foundation of the Republic of the Philippines in November 1935. Han introduced the specific contents of the Philippine Independence Act, other acts and bills, and the way the United States transferred sovereignty to the Philippines.[24] These details informed Korean readers of the procedure through which the two countries reached agreement and of the exact terms of the conditions that both sides considered significant.

While Philippine independence distinguished the United States from other powers, the *Chogwang*'s language remained careful in calculating the United States' position on the Sino-Japanese conflict. In 1936, a year before Japan's full-scale war against China, the *Chogwang* published several articles on this subject. The journalist Sŏ Ch'un, for example, called attention to President Roosevelt's address on November 11, 1935, quoting Roosevelt's statement, "[w]e are acting to simplify the definitions and facts by calling war 'war' when an armed invasion and a resulting killing of human beings take place."[25] Sŏ commented that this speech offered a new reference point in applying the Kellogg-Briand Pact (Pact of Paris) of 1928, which objected to the use of a war as a means of solving international conflicts. Sŏ interpreted the Roosevelt speech as the US objection to military acts by anti–status-quo countries, predicting the possibility of a second world war between the United Kingdom, the United States, and the Soviet Union on one side, and Germany and Japan on the other side.[26]

In the same January 1936 issue of the *Chogwang*, Han Poyong discussed "The Crisis of 1936," which at the time had strong currency in Japan.

Criticizing Japanese rationale, Han identified the crisis not as one that was internationally provoked but as a crisis created by Japan. According to Han, Japanese journalists assumed potential international retaliation in 1936 in response both to Japan's occupation of Manchuria and to its withdrawal from the League of Nations. This might cause Japan to lose its mandate on the South Pacific islands and the transfer of the mandate to the United States, the Japanese journalists estimated, and that would be a great threat to Japan.[27] They also suspected that the British and the Americans were assisting China's anti-Japanese struggles behind the scenes.[28] Han criticized such arguments for the following reasons: Japan's withdrawal from the Naval Conference in 1935 had occurred without serious international conflict; Japan's South Pacific Mandate was not revoked; and China's anti-Japanese struggles were meager. Han estimated that the emergence of Nazi Germany and Fascist Italy had further reduced the possibility of international retaliation against Japan. The Western powers were less interested in solving the problems of the Far East than in dealing with Hitler's violation of the Treaty of Versailles and Italy's military actions.

However, Han wrote, the international focus had again moved to Northern China in October 1935 because "so-and-so" country (*moguk*) had established a "self-rule" government in Northern China. Due to censorship, Han did not name this country, though from the context he was apparently referring to Japan.[29] Han thus identified Japan's actions in Northern China since October 1935 as the true cause of the "Crisis of 1936." While Han recognized that Japan's actions had aroused concern in the United Kingdom, the United States, and the USSR, he doubted that these countries would take immediate military action against Japan's move in Northern China. Han concluded that a major international military conflict would not occur in 1936, and that the Northern China incident would, for the time being, result in what Japan intended. He nevertheless expected that a "self-rule government" in Manchuria controlled by Japan would cause, rather than solve, a lot of problems in China.[30]

After the outbreak of the Second Sino-Japanese War in July 1937, Han published an article updating the potential choices of the British and the Americans in the Far East. Han still did not think they would intervene immediately but pinpointed the signs of the United States' more active engagement with China.[31] The British feared that their repression of Japan in North China would force Japan's expansion in the South Pacific. Thus, Han argued, the British would stand still as long as they were concerned about both the South Pacific and China and were restrained by more urgent problems in Europe. The US interests in China were not more substantial than those of the British, but the United States had become China's number-one trading partner, and its Open Door policy had helped China preserve its territory. American missionaries also wanted to expand their Christian mission in China. Under such conditions, Han argued, both the US government and US citizens were willing to help China, as long as such commitment did not come at a great cost to the United States. Upon the outbreak of the Second Sino-Japanese War, the United States should have put into effect the Neutrality Act (Chungnippŏp) between China and Japan but did not do so on the pretext that the law could harm the weaker party in favor of the country with a strong navy. Han estimated that the United States claimed neutrality in word but denied it in action. If a country (the United States) had such a mindset, Han insisted, it was just waiting for an opportunity (to act against Japan).[32] After this article, for whatever reason, Han's columns did not appear in the *Chogwang* until the end of World War II.

While speculating potential US-Japan military conflicts, the *Chogwang* also published a series of essays on the nature of US civilization. Chŏng Irhyŏng's essay after his recent return from the United States voiced his amazement and dismay about the "grandiosity," "modernity," "brilliance," and "decadence" of that civilization. Chŏng diagnoses that the "tide of material civilization" is moving from London and Paris to New York. At the sunset of those European cities, New York had emerged as the capital of the "Yankee Empire" and the "Holy Grail (Kŭmjat'ap) of twentieth-century material civilization." It is impossible, Chŏng asserted, to describe in words the magnitude, luxury, and flamboyance of New York, the "Golden Castle of the Twentieth Century" equipped with so many cultural facilities, concrete buildings, iron walls, and web-like transportation networks.[33]

Chŏng counted modernism, democracy, and pragmatic philosophy as essential characteristics of US civilization, repeating modernity as the thrust of the US lifestyle. Just as the Empire State Building symbolized the essence of modern scientific knowledge, so the United States was a barometer of modernism and the center of modernity, leading the world by the invention of new ideas and values. Chŏng acknowledged that this modernity had also brought anxiety and tragedy to the US lifestyle. People in New York, for instance, carry on lives that are acutely diversified and intense enough to "numb" human nerves.[34] Chŏng attributed this lifestyle to the United States' economy of prosperity founded upon mass production, standardization, and mechanization. This economy produced wealth but generated social problems as it forced people into an artificially restrained lifestyle, beset as they are by machines and standardization.

Chŏng appreciated US democracy, as articulated in the Declaration of Independence and President Abraham Lincoln's 1863 Emancipation Proclamation, as the "most remarkable ideological achievement in modern liberal thought."[35] He considered this idea of democracy the "highest form of American nationalist thought" and "the essence of Americanism," guiding the country's education, the arts, intellectual thought, and religion. Chŏng also viewed this democracy as a source of US expansionism undergirding the Monroe Doctrine and its transition to Pan-Americanism. At the stage of Pan-Americanism, Chŏng argued, US democracy had lost its authentic characteristics as a manifestation of the Puritans' liberalism and had been transformed into a "liberal expansionism" in pursuit of external freedom. Concurrently, this liberal expansionism had directed the United States to propose the League of Nations and the Permanent Court of International Justice, not to speak of relieving the Philippines of its colonial rule.[36]

Chŏng praised some specific features of everyday life in the United States: its wealth, the hygienic lifestyle and convenient housing, the transportation networks with their speed and size, and the excellent educational system. He particularly admires US public education, its "perfect" institutions and tremendous scale, and the quality of higher education that he observed at Columbia University and other colleges in New York. Chŏng found an "unbridgeable gap" between this US education system and the Korean situation, describing US college campuses as "euphoric spaces where young men and women enjoy their beautiful youth, obtain learning and discipline for their future, and experience a cradle for romance and love marriage."[37]

Chŏng foresaw that there would be a "revival of the Roman Empire" in the future of US civilization as its materialism created a luxurious life side by side sexual disorders and moral decadence. Nevertheless, he anticipated the arrival of an "American era" and placed great hope in Roosevelt's reforms. The "frantic individualism and worship of gold" in US civilization, he wrote, would be corrected with the "birth of a new social system," initiated by the leadership of President Roosevelt and his "fight against big business." Whether Roosevelt succeeded or failed, Chŏng considered that his efforts would lead Americans to acknowledge the urgency of reforming the country's economic system and encourage cooperation among them. Once this US reform succeeded, Chŏng insisted, the world would see a "morning" when this "Holy Grail of the beaming material civilization will renew its face and dominate the coasts of the Pacific."[38]

This affection toward the Rooseveltian reforms was also found in other *Chogwang* essays. The aforementioned Han Poyong evaluated the United States' labor movements in the Roosevelt era as a non-Communist road to solve working-class problems and contrasted the Rooseveltian "promise" with the "dark prospect" of Europe under the Fascists.[39] In his June 1937 article published in *Chogwang*, Han cited the Inter-American Conference for the Maintenance of Peace in Buenos Aires—initiated by Roosevelt—and called this Pan-American assembly of the North and South American republics a "ridicule" of the militaristic regimes in Europe, which constantly invaded each other. Han wrote that labor movements were constrained where the "spiritual movements couched in statism and nationalism" prevailed and antagonized foreigners.[40]

Because of such Fascist oppression, Han continued, the working class in Europe, suffering from high inflation and no wage increases, never dared to conduct labor movements for fear of being labeled "anti-statist" or "anti-nationalistic." Han witnessed a very different development in the Rooseveltian United States. The US president was still making efforts to find a compromise, since the US business class opposed his policies and the US Supreme Court judged some laws unconstitutional. Despite such obstacles, Han reported, the leftist Committee for Industrial Organization (CIO) and its leader John Llewellyn Lewis had achieved concessions from the business arena on the rights of the working class to collective action, a minimum wage rate, and minimum working-hours. The US Supreme Court also ruled that these labor laws were constitutional.[41]

Han seemed to suggest that the United States' labor movement was an alternative to Communist movements. Given the United States' freedom of the press, he argued, the US Communists could circulate their official newspaper, *The Daily Worker*, and other publications for the working class. However, he posited, their radical position was unpopular in the United States because the lives of US laborers were not as miserable as that of the European working class. Although the Third Communist International had opened a branch in the United States, Han continued, US citizens tended to regard them as "alien" or "anti-American." Han introduced in detail the reform proposals of the United Automobile Workers (UAW) union, including a six-hour work day, a minimum wage system, and the articles of the National Labor Relations Act (Wagner Act) of 1935, referred to as the *Magna Carta* of the working class.[42]

A systematic presentation of the United States as a "model" country was articulated in Han Ch'ijin's two articles published in 1940 in the *Chogwang*. In his May 1940 essay on US sociology, Han defined sociology as the knowledge for constructing the "happiest human society on earth."[43] Distinguishing this knowledge from socialism, Han calls US sociology a philosophy for praxis, combining "the utopian ideals of the human race" with the Comtian methodology of positivism. According to Han, US sociology made a transition from Herbert Spencer's social Darwinism to the theory of Lester Frank Ward (1841–1913), who revised sociology from a psychological perspective. Han summarized Ward's theory as arguing that culture was produced by willful activities of human beings, and that it was constructed not just from individual efforts but from social control and cooperation.[44]

Han related this psychological theory of culture to US idealism and values. According to Han, Americans were idealists (*yusimnonja*) rather than materialists who considered the mental power of human beings critical to their domination of nature and their organization of society. He maintained that this "idealism or subjectivism" makes independence a unique aspect of the American spirit and the foundation for US social life. The spirit of independence in turn promoted democracy and individualism, and this idealism encouraged positive activism and made the United States the space where ideas can be most easily transformed into actions and politics.[45]

Repeatedly, Han identified American social philosophy with humanism, which he defined as the ideas that "men (human beings) are the masters of all creatures and the standards of all values" and that "men are autonomous and independent, in that they voluntarily reform and control their environment."[46] This humanism leads Americans to think that people can do whatever they want and should never surrender to obstacles rising from the environment. Han called the Americans the most idealistic of people, who believe in achieving tasks that have been considered impossible in the past. He did not fail to relate this "humanism" to Americans' religious belief that men do not belong to any man-made state and should revere not the state but God, the sovereign of the world.[47]

Han Ch'ijin published a second article in July 1940, making a sweeping argument on "American civilization."[48] In it he maintained that American humanitarianism is a "savior" of civilization in the then-current international crisis and that "no country but America" could stop the surreal reality that the people of the world were all facing. Readers should understand, Han asserted, that there was more than materialism to the United States' leadership and power, and that pragmatism constituted the "deeper base" of materialism in US civilization. Han associated the characteristics of US civilization with the culture of immigrants. The first US citizens, as exiles from foreign countries, did not fear borrowing foreign ideas and systems nor did they hesitate to test the merits of those systems and evaluate their truth or falsity. Han argued that this tradition has made the United States a "laboratory of the world" and that it has imbued US history, culture, religion, and ideologies with the conviction that "if you have will to do so, you can achieve anything."[49]

Han thus designated pragmatism as the US philosophy, as synthesized by the philosopher William James (1842–1910). According to Han, this pragmatism preferred experiences to abstract theories, domination to being dominated, an open and public world to an exclusive and closed society, and practicing imperfect knowledge to holding out for its faultlessness. This philosophy values outcomes, nurtures "epicurean" attitudes on life, and considered humanism to be its key feature and democracy its political expression.[50] Han tried to defend the contradictions that Korean intellectuals found in the United States between its humanism and its racial discrimination, between the country's wealth and the great poverty of the weak, between its isolationism and interventionism in foreign relations, and between the utilitarianism and the vulgarity in US popular culture. Han attributed these contradictions to pragmatism itself, the overarching American ideology, which accepted the conflicts in things and in the world. From this viewpoint, such contradictions in American culture were correctible problems and even sources of progress.[51]

Justifying United States' contradictions as a source of progress, Han was very optimistic about its future. Since Americans have been experimenting with all sorts of human ideas and practices, their current culture was a "product of what men achieved with their free will in a free land." He was very generous when writing about the United States' problems, "if American culture has a defect, it is because human nature has a defect. If there is strength in the country's culture, it proves that human nature has such a character."[52] Han was eager to see how this United States would exert its leadership in the future world. Regarding Pan-Asianist claims about the relief of Eastern civilization, Han added that American ideals are not simply Christian but consistent with the Confucian theorem in *The Analects*, "[d]o not do to others what you do not desire [for yourself]."[53] Han concluded that Americans had not yet achieved this ideal, and that their global destiny would change depending on whether or not they, in fact, accomplish this vision.[54]

It is surprising that some *Chogwang* authors defended the United States in such bold and optimistic terms while Japan intensified its Pan-Asianist propaganda and rapidly mobilized Korea for the war in China and, potentially, in the Pacific. Approaching the Pacific War, the *Chogwang* began printing anti-American essays.[55] It is striking how these new essays contravened the magazine's earlier recognition of the United States and, indeed, admiration of its civilization. The new anti-American authors criticized the history of US imperialism in East Asia by suddenly recalling the memory of the Korean-American War in 1871. They emphasized the United States' "hypocrisy" on the grounds that US imperialist history in Asia and Latin America violated the country's idealistic rhetoric. These anti-American articles also appropriated leftist critiques of capitalism and imperialism in projecting an evil image of the United States as the most threatening enemy of East Asian Co-Prosperity.

Ham Sanghun, who had generally reported on international relations in an empirical attitude, was among those who transmitted Japan's justification for war to his readers. In the *Chogwang*'s December 1941 issue, published right before the attack on Pearl Harbor, Ham wrote that war with the United States was imminent, given the tense situation in the Pacific and the United States' unyielding position toward Japan. After the Second World War broke out in Europe, Ham argued that Japan, as a "hegemon of East Asia," "naturally" demanded the areas under the domination of France, Holland, and the United Kingdom and tried to establish the East Asian Co-Prosperity Sphere. Referring to the US-British "ambition for world domination," Ham contested that the Americans wanted to connect the British, Dutch, the Chinese, and the Soviets in a ring and confine the Japanese Empire. Ham maintained that only "power" could solve this US-Japan conflict, and that Japan should avoid being (uselessly) induced to follow the appeasement measures of the United States.[56] His article thus advocated Japan's rationale for war with the United States even though Ham's wording remained less enthusiastic than that found in other Pan-Asianist articles.

Anti-American essays in the *Chogwang* after 1941 were stereotyped replications of Japan's wartime messages. Mogya Hongil (Yi Hongjo), a Tokyo University graduate and official of the Yi Royal House Library, published an article on US imperialist history in Asia after the attack on Pearl Harbor. Mogya argued that the United States dropped its Monroe Doctrine after completing the development of the West Coast and became a modern imperialist country. The United States colonized the Philippines and ultimately wanted to transform China into a semi-colony. Depending upon its military bases in the Philippines and China's hostility toward other powers, the United States had aimed its Open Door Policy at preventing other powers (Japan) from obtaining exclusive privileges in China, so as to better wield the United States' own power there. Mogya blamed the US for not "understanding" Japan's aims in the "Holy War" and for trying to monopolize China for US profit. Because the United States fostered its "sinister ambition" in the East and the Pacific, Mogya asserted, the Japanese Empire attacked Pearl Harbor on December 8, 1941 (December 7 in the United States). Mogya agitated that it was time to "eliminate the invasive footprints of Western imperialists in East Asia," and that Japan would, in the near future, expel whites from the region and establish the "Great East Asian Co-Prosperity Sphere."[57]

The *Chogwang* also printed the public speeches organized by war support organizations. The language of these speeches was repetitive, reciting the "evil ambitions of American imperialism and its hypocrisy."[58] For example, Chu Yohan said that the United States' slogans "Open Door," "Equal Opportunity," and "Preservation of China's Territory" were all good lies for its plan to invade Asia. Chu declaimed that Japan's war is a "just war" to save Asians from Western exploitation, and that Japan alone was fighting the war that all Asians should fight altogether.[59] The journalist Yu Kwangyŏl also attacked the United States' Open Door Policy as a selfish excuse for "sucking China's blood and flesh, while other Western powers wanted to butcher China into pieces."[60] Quoting the United States' "New Immigration Act" against Asian immigrants, Yu argued that the United States wanted to keep the Monroe Doctrine within the United States but demanded the Open Door Policy in China. He called this

American contradiction a *Nolbu simppo*, referring to the heart of the greedy older brother in the traditional Korean tale who says, "[w]hat is mine is mine, and what is yours is mine, too."[61]

The *Chogwang*'s articles after the attack on Pearl Harbor thus blatantly demonized Americans, calling them "modern barbarians" and "schizophrenic Yankees."[62] One author of such articles, Han Hŭkku, used leftist logic in demeaning the United States' "greed." He argued that only a small number of Yankee millionaires possessed the United States' wealth and exploited the proletarian class; more than 85 percent of Americans were living in serious poverty without any security measures. As evidence of this inequality in the United States, he quoted excerpts from the literature of American leftists, such as Upton Sinclair's *The Jungle* and Carl Sandburg's *Chicago Poems*. Han argued that the United States' democracy and freedom were established on a "system coercing the subordination of powerless people" and on the United States' free media and journalism functioning as an "instrument of the powerful."[63] Han had once lived in the United States, and his article contained a strong racist tenor, describing the "disgraceful" physical appearance of Americans, such as their "lax" noses, "flippant" lips, and "licentious" eyes.[64] This hatred sharply countered the pre-1941 *Chogwang* discourse on the United States as a modern utopia signaling the "future of the human race."[65]

SOCIALISTS: AMBIVALENCE TOWARD ROOSEVELTIAN AMERICA

Two tendencies are found in the Korean socialist writings on the United States published during World War II. On the one hand, the leftists applied a Marxian analysis of imperialism and predicted the inevitable fall of US capitalism. On the other hand, like some authors in the *Chogwang*, the leftists cautiously yet sympathetically observed the New Deal of the Roosevelt administration and its impact on the working class. While some authors in the early 1930s, in parallel with the Great Depression, carried out typical Marxian criticism of US society, the articles published in the mid- and late-1930s were more ambivalent.

The magazine *Chungang* (The central post) existed between 1933 and 1936. The leftist leader Yŏ Unhyŏng (1886–1947) launched this magazine as the chairman of the Chosŏn Chungang Ilbo Company. Reflecting Yŏ's own nationalism and his broad social relations, *Chungang* did not strongly advocate a communist ideology but manifested a moderate position in its coverage of the United States. During the magazine's short life, *Chungang* frequently reported the progress of the Rooseveltian reform and its prospects. For example, Hong Sŏngha's article on the National Recovery Administration began with a Marxist take on the destiny of US capitalism, yet also introduced the basic concepts and details of the National Recovery Administration and their implications for the working class.[66] Hong reported that the government reduced the average work week from fifty to sixty hours to forty hours, increased the minimum wage, and legalized workers' collective action. He also explained that the Roosevelt administration set out to organize advisory committees of industries, consumers, and laborers in order to represent their interests and opinions in the National Recovery Administration. In his conclusion, Hong expressed skepticism as to whether these committees could collectively manage the concerned agendas and effectively moderate the different interest groups despite the increased presidential power granted by the National Recovery Administration.[67]

In 1933, an author using the pen name Chaha Sanin deemed the New Deal the "Fascistization" of the US economy. The article put forth a bizarre conceptualization yet revealed the mindset of a Korean socialist who applied the analogy of the Socialist revolution in understanding the New Deal. Recalling Mussolini's Fascist statement in October 1932, the author associated this European event with the election of Roosevelt, calling him a "dictator" chosen by the "leftist majority." According to the author, this event indicated the "transformation of American democracy into a dictatorship" and became one of the most interesting subjects in world politics. The author distinguished Roosevelt's "dictatorship" from other forms because it did not involve a coup d'état nor receive the legal authorization of the US Congress or observe the four-year limit of incumbency.[68]

Chaha Sanin thus seemed to use the term "dictatorship" in order to compare Roosevelt's social control to the USSR's planned economy. He or she introduced the major legal acts of the Roosevelt administration and called the "Blue Eagle Revolution" (referring to the National Recovery Administration) a crucial experiment of world economy comparable to the Soviets' development plans. The author defined the Blue Eagle Revolution as a dictatorship because it took the form of free choice but involved "psychological violence" in reality. The Roosevelt administration allocated a Blue Eagle symbol to companies that participated in the government program and organized patriotic campaigns urging citizens to buy products with this label. According to the author, such measures embodied the essence of a dictatorship because they force citizens to comply via moral and psychological threats. The author identified three types of dictatorship, one in the Soviet Union, one in Italy, and one in the United States. In comparison to the Soviet one, the author evaluated the performance of the US dictatorship as "imperfect" because it mainly depended on moral persuasion. Given the strength of the opposition party, the author argued, the Blue Eagle symbol would be insufficient to solve the United States' "fundamental" social problems.[69]

The *Chungang* neither depicted the United States as a model society nor provided unrelenting socialist critiques of the country as a capitalist or imperialist country. The magazine's distinctive position might be found in its recognition of social progress under the Roosevelt administration and of the US development as a useful reference for reform in Korea. The magazine even published the essays of some nationalist authors who were more positive about the US model. For instance, Sŏ Chaep'il, the famous leader of the Independence Club, published an article in the *Chungang* on the United States' transformation over the fifty years he had lived in the United States.[70] Sŏ deemed the United States' change as an "incredible evolution" and a "massive social experiment for developing an equal and fair society and economy" without a bloody revolution.[71] In the past twenty-five years, he wrote, the United States had transformed itself from an agricultural to an industrial society, and its wealth had reached the highest level in human history. While this wealth was concentrated among a small number of people, Sŏ still saw that the growth had provided "good opportunities to most Americans in seeking prosperity and happiness for their families." If the people are to a degree satisfied with such evolution, Sŏ argues, communism and fascism will not be able to take root in such soil.[72]

Another *Chungang* article in 1935 reported on the victory of Roosevelt in the general election when Democrats occupied two-thirds of the seats in both the US Senate and the US House of Representatives. Chin Uhyŏn wrote that the New Deal failed to garner enthusiastic support among the business or working classes, but that this lukewarm attitude from both sides functioned as a factor in favor of Roosevelt's victory. The author argued that this victory would secure Roosevelt's reelection as president and continue Democratic rule until 1940 because the Republican Party had failed to propose any constructive alternative to the New Deal. The author criticized the idea that Roosevelt established Fascism like Hitler and Mussolini because he found Roosevelt exercised only partial control in order to maintain the "laissez faire" of the entire society, the general character of his country.[73]

The *Chungang*'s reports on Roosevelt's experiment turned pessimistic when the US Supreme Court decided in January 1936 that the Agricultural Adjustment Act (AAA) of 1933 was unconstitutional. Pae Sŏngnyong commented that the US Supreme Court decision frustrated Roosevelt by eliminating one of the two pivotal measures of the New Deal following the Court's 1935 decision that the National Recovery Administration violated the US Constitution. After introducing the logic behind the Court's decision, Pae argued that the decision revealed the serious contradiction between Roosevelt's "control economy" and the United States' liberal institutions. Although the Roosevelt administration might have devised new policy measures to compensate for the loss of the AAA, Pae speculated, it would encounter other accusations of being unconstitutional as long as the United States maintained its current institutions and political system.[74]

Pae criticized the people who called the New Deal "a bloodless revolution" and considered it a model for reforming capitalism. He argued that the US monetary and industrial capitalists facilitated anti–New Deal opinions among the public, and that the US judiciary reflected such voices. He handed down a socialist verdict on the National Recovery Administration, saying that it was impossible to revise capitalism with the methods of the middle class or to accomplish the new economy with incomplete control.[75]

Another socialist magazine *Pip'an* (Criticism) was published between 1931 and 1940. In comparison to the *Chungang*, *Pip'an* gave less attention to the United States and offered a general leftist critique of capitalism. The article in *Pip'an* that was most critical of the United States was published in October 1932. Titled "Hwanggŭmŭi nara migugŭi imyŏnsang" (The other side of the gold country, the United States), it described the poverty of US workers in the shadow of the Great Depression.[76] The author, Kim Hoch'ŏl, sent his article to the magazine from the United States, briefing Koreans on the communist movements in the Chicago area, the misery of an unemployed worker in New York and his death by starvation, and the then-current labor strikes and racism in the United States. Kim wrote that the workers faced such misery because they were kicked out of factories, which had "sucked up" their blood.[77] Kim quoted the newspaper of the US Communist Party, writing that 12 million workers were then unemployed, homeless, and surviving on food offered by philanthropists.

Another article in an early issue of *Pip'an* (January 1932) criticized US missionaries and their management of mission schools. The author, Yi Ch'ŏn, appreciated the historical contribution of US missionaries to Korea's cultural and medical developments, but he estimated that the missionaries had become more *reactionary* since the ideological climate of Korean society had changed in the past several years and youth with anti-religious attitudes had emerged. According to Yi, in the past the missionaries considered education a self-sacrificing task for God, but now they were using schools to increase the numbers of Christians, attaching material strings to students. Yi wrote that one college in Seoul expelled ninety students for a trivial reason and kicked out others who made comments against Christianity. He called on missionaries and their Korean staff to manage their schools better by understanding Korea's reality and the ideological sentiments of Korean youth.[78]

Despite such sharp criticism in the early 1930s, *Pip'an* overall did not publish many articles about the United States. Rather, the *Chungang*'s coverage of the Rooseveltian United States shaped the agenda for *Pip'an* editors and their readers. For example, the article in *Pip'an* by An Pyŏngju, titled "Miguk ŭn ŏdi ro kana: Rujŭbelt'ŭ ron (Where is the United States headed?: A debate on Roosevelt), revealed that the leftists were affected not only by *Chungang*'s ambivalence toward the New Deal but also by the *Chogwang*'s discourse on a democratic United States.[79] An wrote this article in the form of a debate between two critics of US politics. Critic B in the article appeared to have represented the author's position.[80] An Pyŏngju scripted the debate under four topics: (1) the United States and Fascism; (2) the evaluation of New Deal; (3) the personality of Roosevelt; and (4) the future of the United States.

An's first topic questioned whether or not the Rooseveltian reform could be called Fascistization. Critic A argued that Roosevelt established a "presidential dictatorship," disturbing the United States' unique balance of power between the executive, legislative, and judiciary branches of government. Critic B disagreed because the United States had no social embryo that could breed Fascism; its strong democratic tradition was irreconcilable with Fascism; and a few presidential documents could not change the whole system. In any case,

Critic B insisted, "American Fascism" could be a temporary political regime to survive the Great Depression but had no background for establishing a strong and stable dictatorship. Critic B diagnosed that Roosevelt's reform could not cure the "fatal disease" of its "dying capitalist economy."[81]

Critic A rejected this diagnosis, estimating that the United States might prosper more than before, given its abundant natural resources and Roosevelt's "luck" as a leader. Critic B refuted A's evaluation, referring to the violent strikes at General Motors and other labor struggles in the United States. Critic B accused Critic A of being confused by phenomena on the surface without understanding the fundamental logic (of the US economy). Critic A did not give in, asserting that Roosevelt had improved the lives of Americans; workers and farmers supported Roosevelt and reelected him as president; and Roosevelt had a very promising future. Citing the negative data of the New Deal, Critic B commented that the New Deal had only benefitted the big capitalists, increased the number of unemployed workers, and added to the burdens of small- and middle-sized companies.

Critic A partially admitted this but still defended Roosevelt and his promising future, acknowledging him as a "man on the side of workers."[82] Critic B responded with long quotes from Joseph Stalin's interview with a British reporter. The article did not name Stalin but referred to him as the secretary of the Soviet Communist Party. It was unclear whether this interview with Stalin actually occurred or whether the author of the article crafted it for his argument. A British interviewer asked the question posed earlier as to a convergence between the New Deal's economic control and the USSR's socialist system. The Soviet secretary replied that the New Deal attempted to alleviate the Great Depression without changing the liberal economy, whereas the USSR had a fundamentally different objective. Critic B finally discouraged Critic A by borrowing from Stalin's authority and Stalin's denial that Roosevelt could save capitalism. Thereupon Critic A asked when the Roosevelt administration would perish.[83]

From there, the debate takes an interesting turn. Critic B answered uncertainly that another depression or an international war may cause a moment for great transformation in the United States, but Critic B also predicted that, due to its advanced capitalism, the United States could manage the disorder of the interim period well and quickly. Alluding to the Spanish Civil War, Critic A questioned the possibility that a protracted civil war might occur among different social, class, and racial groups within the United States or that the US military (chŏngbugun) might establish a Fascist regime after subduing them. Critic B casted doubt on this scenario, arguing that an advanced United States differs from a feudalistic Spain. Even if Americans experienced a temporary dictatorship for a transition, they will quickly terminate this process. Critic B's narrative from here on resonates with the notion of a democratic United States expressed in the Chogwang. Critic B argued that US tradition would not allow Americans to bear a political dictatorship for long. Americans are deeply rooted in their passion for freedom and equality and their convictions about democracy. Therefore, they would quickly eliminate the dictatorship and open the final road (for a socialist utopia) for themselves.

Critic B was optimistic about a socialist revolution in United States. He doubted that Americans could survive another Great Depression without creating a "new New Deal," and wished that this "new New Deal" would be an ideal one (i.e., a socialist revolution).[84] Critic B thus represented the Marxist conviction about socialist revolution, but the overall debate disclosed that the Korean leftists valued the Rooseveltian measures for the working class and discussed whether or not the US model could replace a socialist revolution. While the leftists were pessimistic about the future of the New Deal, they still shared assumptions about a democratic United States with some of the authors of the Chogwang articles published before the attack on Pearl Harbor. The socialists counted the United States' democracy, its active citizens, and its technological advancement as good resources for building democratic socialism for a utopian future.

THE KOREAN PAN-ASIANISTS: ANTI-IMPERIALISM, ANTI-RACISM, AND PRO-DEMOCRACY?

It is not an exact science to characterize the magazine Samch'ŏlli (The Korean peninsula) as Pan-Asianist.[85] The Samch'ŏlli is also a limited source when it comes to comprehensively studying the wartime Pan-Asianists.[86] After the Second Sino-Japanese War began, however, the Samch'ŏlli boosted Japan's Pan-Asianist messages and accommodated its wartime mobilization. As seen above, at least before 1941, the authors published in the Chogwang or Pip'an remained reserved in their reporting on the war. With less caution, the Samch'ŏlli allocated many pages to the colonial government's statements on the war and to the wartime speeches of pro-Japanese Koreans, but the *Samch'ŏlli* also printed many essays for casual pleasure, including gossip about elite society. Merging its pro-Japanese tone with carefree entertainment, the *Samch'ŏlli* covered Japan's battles in China, Chiang Kai-shek's whereabouts, and even the accounts of Kim Il Sung's guerillas. In comparison to the *Chogwang*'s "international" perspective, the *Samch'ŏlli* focused more on what was going on in the Sino-Japanese conflicts on the continent. In this sense, the magazine had a Pan-Asianist voice.

The *Samch'ŏlli*'s Pan-Asianism did not establish a clear enemy before 1940. The United States was genuinely obscure in the magazine between 1937 and 1940. The wartime Pan-Asianist speeches in the *Samch'ŏlli* sound as though they were insulated from the Korean discourse on the United States of the same period. The speakers were talking to their audience about Asia, Japan, and the West without conversing with the contemporary discourse of other Koreans on the subject. This disjuncture in communication was unlike the dialogue between the authors published in the *Chogwang*, the *Chungang*, or the *Pip'an*, who cross-referenced and debated one another despite their different ideological positions. Yet a few ideological threads penetrated the two disjointed narratives: the official Pan-Asianist discourse and the Korean narratives of an advanced United States. Anti-imperialism, anti-racism, and pro-democracy were underlying themes even in the highly stereotyped language of wartime Korean speeches. Some speakers supported Japan's "moral" mission to rejuvenate East Asia, but more speakers centered on universal values in condemning Japan's enemies. The wartime Pan-Asianist discourse lacked a stable logic to rationalize the Japanese Empire when pro-Japanese speakers criticized the British or the Americans in terms of their imperialism, racism, and hypocrisy in violation of freedom and equality.

One *Samch'ŏlli* article, published in January 1937, revealed a cynical Korean response to this ideological poverty of the wartime Pan-Asianist discourse.[87] It presented a debate between the eminent Chinese intellectual Hu Shih (1891–1962) and the *Nihon hyōron* (Japan commentary) editor Murahuse Kōshin (1892–1970). The author Wŏn Sehun, who reportedly studied Russian literature at Beijing University, translated and edited this debate.[88] Wŏn wrote that he simply wanted to introduce the debate, rather than criticize Hu or Murahuse's positions or submit his own viewpoint. However, Wŏn's clever edition rendered this debate a critique of Japanese Pan-Asianism. The contents of the debate were sharp in the context of early 1937, right before Japan's full-scale war with China.

According to Wŏn's introduction, Hu and Murahuse had met in Beijing in the summer of 1936 and agreed to exchange their thoughts on Japan-China relations. Hu's article and Murahuse's counterargument were published in the *Nihon hyōron* in November and December 1936, respectively, and were also printed in several Chinese magazines. In this exchange, Hu asked, first of all, that the Japanese stop talking about Japan-China friendship (*ilchung ch'insŏn*). He could not bear to hear this term used when the relationship between the two countries for the past four years had been something (the original word is censored) other than amity. Second, he requested that the Japanese recognize Chinese psychology. The Chinese people were excited by the Ethiopian resistance against Italy and also ashamed (of their own inaction). Mentioning the Japanese slogan of "Scorched-Earth Diplomacy" (*Ch'ot'o oegyo*), Hu warned Japan not to drive China onto a narrow road. If they did so, the Chinese would fight against Japan like besieged animals and with their own strategy of annihilation. Praising the Meiji Restoration as Japan's glory and a miracle for the human race, Hu recommended that Japan consider Germany's rise and fall during World War I as a cautionary tale, commenting that Japan's current move helped neither China nor the world.[89]

To Hu's first request (not to mention the friendship between Japan and China), Murahuse replied that Japan and China should recover trust for each other despite the unpleasant events in Manchuria. He claimed that Japan truly intends to save East Asia and its cultural heritage. Chinese intellectuals, including Hu, received the influence of Western civilization and accepted the idea of enlightenment. Meiji intellectuals took the same road and buried the heritage of East Asian civilization in the name of eliminating reactionaries. Murahuse considered this trajectory limited because men (human beings) are not free from their geographical environment and historical legacy. East Asians ultimately originated from the East Asian region's history and tradition. Although materialism, Judaism, German militarism, and British imperialism had left strong influences (in Japan or in the region), Murahuse argued, Japan now faced a moment for deep self-reflection and self-criticism. He called this moment "the time for a verdict."[90]

Murahuse insisted that Japan was taking on the "burden" or "responsibility" for this self-reflection because the Japanese nation was now pressing a "most advanced step" toward a "golden age unprecedented in human history." He bragged that "those who curse Japan will be cursed, and those who oppose Japan will be crushed to pieces." Why? Because Japan had such power, and the Japanese recognized their mission. Murahuse blamed China for treating Japan with the tactic "constrain barbarians with other barbarians" (yi yi che yi)—that is, by allying with the United States, the "evil" British, and the Soviet Union. He asked that the Chinese remember their suffering by Westerners and never fall for this British seduction.[91]

Hu sharply repudiated Murahuse's contention that Eastern civilization had been buried under Western influences. Hu argued that great and valuable cultures never disappear easily. The recent Japanese visitors to Beijing worried too much about the loss of Eastern heritage. To Hu's eyes, they wanted Eastern youth to read Buddhist or Confucian texts but never become fascinated with historical materialism or believe in liberalism. Hu never worried that the East Asian heritage would collapse but grieved that Eastern nations had barely begun connecting with the new cultures of human civilization before they quickly withdrew to protect their old customs or rushed to exaggerate about themselves. Most urgently, Hu anguished as to whether or not the Eastern nations would create the ugly scene of killing each other and elicit the ridicule of the world.

Regarding yi yi che yi which, translated into a modern world, means "borrow one friendly country's assistance and restrain one enemy country," Hu called this a common practice of nations and noted that Japan had been successfully practicing this in its alliance with the British and the Americans.[92] Hu stated that China was not prepared to be a friend of others and even less so to be a friend to an enemy of others. With respect to China's forgetfulness of British deeds, Hu quoted the Chinese old proverb, "[d]on't be anxious about old evils" (pulgŭp kuak). "Beauty and sly seduction" can easily make people forget old pains, whereas "armed fists" are the most magical antidote to this "amnesia." If you (Japan) were to fire a cannon today, send bombers, and dispatch trains of soldiers, Hu asks, wouldn't this threat wake China from its "amnesia?"[93] Wŏn cut the debate here at Hu's reply and did not add any comments. It was obvious that he translated this debate from Hu's viewpoint.

Wŏn's clever criticism of Pan-Asianism did not dominate the Samch'ŏlli's articles. It was juxtaposed with the wartime speeches cheering the Japanese Army in Northern China and Shanghai. The Samch'ŏlli's October 1937 issue published the speeches delivered at the Youth Hall (Ch'ŏngnyŏn hoegwan) in Chongno, Seoul. Yun Ch'iho gave the opening remarks, and Yi Tonhwa, the Chŏndogyo leader, recapped in his speech the Chŏndogyo religion's earlier Pan-Asianist rhetoric.[94] According to Yi, Japan shed blood not only for its own interests but for the peace of East Asia. Japan punished China for its self-aggrandizement in the First Sino-Japanese War and established a balance of power between the West and the East in the Russo-Japanese War. Yi identified the "greedy forces of the white race" and Red Russia as the enemies who are creating "chaos" in the East Asia. He argued that without the Japanese Empire, China would be reduced to being a market for Westerners because China's state formation was "not yet complete." Yi went further and denounced the Chinese for rejecting Japan's leadership and demanded that Koreans support the cause of "Japan and Korea as one" and the Japanese Empire.[95]

An Insik, another speaker, claimed a "Monroe Doctrine for Asia," since Europeans governed Europe and Americans ruled the United States. Unlike other wartime speakers, An identified himself as a Japanese subject, saying that in Asia, only "our Japan" has a long history and a strong national body and preserves the "samurai spirit," crystallized in the values of loyalty and filial piety. An glorified Japan's withdrawal from the League of Nations as an act to protect "the independence of Manchuria" and a "great resolution" according to the "new East Asianism," saving Asian comrades (tongji) from the "evil hands of Europeans." At this early stage of the Second Sino-Japanese War, An's Asianism antagonized communism, castigating it as "the enemy of the human race and a reckless robber." He warned that the Chinese anti-Japanese struggles, "poisoned by communism," have disrupted the progress of this East Asian solidarity. He demanded that Japan punish the Chinese so as to awaken them from such "dismay," and that Koreans not separate Korea from Japan but exert genuine efforts for this "ideal."[96]

Although it printed such war-promoting speeches, the Samch'ŏlli did not call the United States the enemy before 1941.[97] Expecting a war with the United States, however, such ambiguity disappeared. In March 1941, Mitarai Tatsuo (1895–1975), the owner of the Japanese settler newspaper Keijō Nippō (Seoul daily), published the Samch'ŏlli column titled "Kinjanghan t'aep'yŏngnyang hyŏngse: Miguk ŭi chŏksŏng ŭl pora (Tense political situation in the Pacific, recognize the enemy state America)!"[98] Mitarai argued that the war in Europe had transformed world politics and had nearly overthrown Anglo-Saxon global domination. Despite the Japanese Army's "progress" in China, Mitarai resented the fact that Japan had not yet destroyed Chiang Kai-shek's government. He attributed the tenacity of China's resistance to the military assistance of the United Kingdom, the United States, and the USSR, calling Chiang a "robot of the three Western powers." Mitarai argued that Germany, Italy, and Japan had become allies in order to modify the "exploitative regime of the British and [the] Americans" and to construct a "fair and new world order." Mitarai called on the "nation" to make up their minds to fight to the death against the United States' "arrogance, arbitrary and greedy ambition, and its hypocritical humanitarianism."[99]

After the attack on Pearl Harbor, the Samch'ŏlli's January 1942 issue printed a set of several speeches made at war-mobilizing assemblies. Famous Korean figures had appeared at those assemblies and assailed the United States with aggressive words. The report under the title, "Tongyang ŭi ch'imnyakcha yŏngmi t'ado ŭi taesajahu!" (Invasion of the Orient and the brave roars for overthrowing the United Kingdom and the United States!) included speeches by Yŏ Unhong, Yi Kwangsu, Chu Yohan, and others.[100] Yŏ scorned US racism and imperialism. Yi criticized US individualism, commercialism, and democracy narrowly centered on their own rights and happiness. While Chu ridiculed Roosevelt and US hypocrisy, Ch'ae P'ilgŭn, the principal of P'yŏngyang Presbyterian Seminary, called the war a mission for "the Great East Asian Restoration" and for rescuing Asians from the Anglo-Saxon racism and imperialism they had suffered since the Opium War.[101]

The same January 1942 issue of the Samch'ŏlli published another set of speeches under the title "Taedonga chŏnjaeng kwa pando ŭi mujang: Kyŏlchŏn taeyŏnsŏl kirok ŭi t'ŭkchip" (The Great East Asian War and the armament of the Korean peninsula).[102] At this assembly, the speakers included Yun Ch'iho, Chang Tŏksu, and Sin Hŭngu, famous Korean leaders who had once studied in the United States. Yun Ch'iho sounded genuinely excited about this war against the United States and framed the attack on Pearl Harbor as a racial war.[103] He recalled the humiliation of his first visit to Shanghai fifty-five years before. When he entered the city's British district, he saw the sign on the gate of a park reading, "[d]ogs and Chinese, do not enter here." Yun excoriated the British, who came to China as guests yet degraded the Chinese people to the level of dogs. He also mentions that arrogant Anglo-Saxons in Canada erected such signs as "[d]o not enter, yellow race." In the Pearl Harbor attack, Yun exclaims that the yellow race finally had a chance to wreak vengeance. With enthusiasm, he called the Pacific War the "holy war of holy wars" and demanded that everyone join this effort. He expressed his joy at this "retaliation," saying that he felt ten year younger than before.[104]

Chang Tŏksu gave a speech titled "The Real Face of the Enemy State." Chang was the former editor of the *Tonga ilbo*, and a leader of the Korean Democratic Party after Liberation. He was assassinated in 1947 by a member of the South Korean police.[105] Chang's speech, at least in its printed version, did not transmit the enthusiasm of Yun Ch'iho but rather focused on criticizing the British and the Americans for the inconsistency between their liberal values and their actual conduct. Chang described the United Kingdom and the United States as two of the wealthiest countries in the world and in possession of the strongest navies. Chang's criticism first targeted the identity of the United Kingdom and the United States as "Christian states" which did not follow the "love of Christ" but regulated their conduct according to the needs of a secular power state.[106]

Chang then criticized the history of slavery and racism in the two countries, introducing his own experience of racial discrimination at a barbershop in Oregon, where the barber refused to cut an Oriental's hair. He continued to question whether countries with a history of slave trading could truly establish individualism, which cherished the value of each human being, or practice liberalism, with its respect for individual freedom. Chang then told his audience, "[i]f you deny the value of the human being, you cannot create a foundation of morality," and "[w]here morality is destroyed, you cannot build a house for individualism or liberalism."[107] Chang thus argued that individualism and liberalism in the United Kingdom and the United States were none other than selfishness and self-indulgence.

Chang also problematized British and US industrialism, where workers were seen primarily as the means of production rather than as human beings, and capitalists functioned primarily as businessmen rather than as citizens. In this circumstance, capitalists and workers fought each other over profits and their own interests with no sympathy toward the other side; the stronger survived while the weaker collapsed. Chang asked, in this "animal society of the survival of the fittest," how one could discover liberalism or individualism. He concluded that this "utilitarian civilization" did not extend virtuous or benevolent hands (to others), and that its exploitation and violence had dried the blood of the Eastern nations and bent their bones.[108]

Regardless of its harsh rhetoric, Chang's speech was nevertheless moderate and intelligent, combining historical evidence with his reflections on British and US society. It was difficult to tell whether Chang had been forced to support the war or whether he had personally begun to accept the Japanese Pan-Asianist messages. Be that as it may, this was a speech in which Chang criticized the United Kingdom and the United States not because he rejected their values of Christianity, individualism, and liberalism but because their own history had betrayed such values. Another speaker, Sin Hŭngu, also spoke along these lines, berating the Anglo Saxons for their racism and colonialism. Sin argued that "global chaos" had been instigated by those who had colonized the world over the past several hundred years. They invaded and exploited other races and countries with wicked means and brutal violence, yet fancied they were benefitting others. Sin depicted Rudyard Kipling (1865–1936) and his term the "white man's burden" as symbolizing Anglo-Saxons' "delusion" about being "burdened" with "guiding colored races." Due to this arrogant perception, Sin argued, the Anglo-Saxons propagated humanitarianism or democracy but actually rejected racial equality. Sin criticized that this hypocrisy endangered not just East Asians but all colored races.[109]

CONCLUSION

John Lewis Gaddis emphasized "peripheral origins" and "inadvertence" in the development of the Cold War in Asia. He argued that the United States and USSR had "barely" started the Cold War in the region before the Chinese Communist Revolution in 1949.[110] He identified the Korean War as a case in which the local civil war, "which would have existed in any event," drew the United States and USSR into their "unintended confrontations."[111] Bruce Cumings, in contrast, found an earlier symptom of the Cold War in the postwar US intervention in the Far East and its reversal of the "Korean revolution," which he regarded as imminent at the time of Korea's Liberation in August 1945. The characteristics of this civil war or revolution were still unclear because historians had insufficiently examined the transition from wartime colonial Korea to this postcolonial civil war. To clarify the nature of this revolution, this chapter has made an initial attempt to map out the ideological landscape of late colonial Korea, reviewing the wartime discourse on the United States.

Several observations from this investigation modify the notion of severe ideological splits in colonial Korea and their extension into the postwar era. The Koreans who wrote on the United States during the wartime period maintained different ideological positions, but their disagreements were more complicated and ambivalent than the antagonism of the 1920s between nationalists and socialists. To my own surprise, the wartime Korean imaginaries of the United States strongly countered the Japanese Pan-Asianist discourse. While the Japanese expressed the urgent need to overcome modernity and the superficiality of Americanism, some provocative Korean authors called US civilization the future of the human race. Not all leftists gave up their socialist criticism of capitalism, but many of them were impressed by the progress for the working class in Rooseveltian America.

On the eve of the attack on Pearl Harbor, a sharp ideological split was indeed established between this Korean sympathy for Rooseveltian America and the wartime Pan-Asianist narratives criticizing the British and the Americans and their exploitation of colored races. The Korean speeches for Japan's war effort delivered a mixture of several ideological elements, including a Pan-Asianist history framed in terms of the strife of East against West, a leftist critique of Western capitalism and imperialism, and a denunciation of United States' hypocrisy in not fulfilling its promise of freedom. Loyalty to the Japanese emperor and the ideology of "Japan and Korea as one body" (naesŏn ilch'e) remained marginal in the Korean wartime speeches printed in the magazines analyzed here. The Koreans who gave these speeches drove their points home to their Korean audience primarily by invoking the history of US imperialism in Asia, and the ways in which US racism and exploitation contradicted the notion of a humanitarian United States. In this sense, the wartime Korean speeches reflected the ideological climate of late colonial Korea, rather than simply imitating the official Japanese Pan-Asianist discourse.

Finally, many authors analyzed in this chapter continued their political careers after Liberation. The most outspoken writers on the United States in the *Chogwang* cooperated with the US military occupation. Although Ham Sanghun had a record of collaborating with the Japanese, Han Poyong and Chŏng Irhyŏng were silent during the peak of wartime mobilization, and Han

Ch'ijin was jailed at the end of the Pacific War. As mentioned earlier, Han Poyong served as the mayor of Taegu, and Chŏng Irhyŏng held a significant position in the administration of personnel and resource distribution under the US Military Government in Korea. Han Ch'ijin, an admirer of US pragmatism, also worked with the US Military Government as a staff member of the public relations bureau, edited the bureau's official journal Minju Chosŏn (Democratic Korea), and published his theory of democracy there. The North Korean government kidnapped Han and brought him to North Korea during the Korean War. Chang Tŏksu and Ham Sanghun became leading figures of the Korean Democratic Party and could not avoid responsibility for their collaborative acts. Yet, they had been more reserved in the language they used to promote the war than more enthusiastic Pan-Asianist speakers such as Yun Ch'iho, Yi Kwangsu, and Chu Yohan.

I have yet to consolidate the postcolonial trajectories of the socialist authors covered in this chapter. Hong Sŏngha, the economist who wrote on the National Recovery Administration in the Chungang, participated in the Korean Democratic Party. I have been unable to establish the identity of the author who used the pen name "Chaha Sanin" in 1933 or in the records of the socialists Pae Sŏngnyong and An Pyŏngju in the 1940s and 1950s.[112] While these leftists showed ambivalent sympathy toward the Rooseveltian United States, many other Korean socialists faced charges of collaboration, given the massive wartime thought conversion directed by the Japanese colonial authority. This suggests that the splits of the 1920s and early 1930s between nationalists and socialists changed their forms during the wartime period and did not straightforwardly transfer into the confrontation (or "civil war") between collaborative nationalists and leftist revolutionaries after 1945.

The wartime discourse on the imaginary United States did not convey the entire range of ideological, political, and socio-economic agendas in wartime colonial Korea. The magazines reviewed here omitted the voices of underground revolutionaries within Korea and anti-Japanese guerrillas abroad. However, this wartime discourse on the United States leads me to question whether Korean nationalists and socialists were indeed on the verge of war with each other before 1945. Their discourse on the United States sounds not so much like a call to armed conflict as a sign of dialogue. I hypothesize that wartime colonial Korea was different from Greece, the Balkans, or mainland China during World War II, where rightists and leftists were already waging armed conflicts against or in alliance with foreign powers. Kim Il Sung's anti-Japanese guerrillas had only limited connections with the political groups within Korea and reflected the civil war situation in China more than such a split in Korea itself at the time. If the temper of the times, as reflected in the magazines reviewed here, was less one of civil war than of an ideological rearrangement within wartime colonial Korea, then it is important to reexamine the characteristics of postcolonial Korean revolution and the sources of the violence, rebellions, and armed conflicts that swept South Korea under the US military occupation.

NOTES

1. Akira Iriye, *Power and Culture*, 1.
2. Harry Harootunian, *Overcome by Modernity*, chapter 2, 34–94.
3. Cemil Aydin, *The Politics of Anti-Westernism in Asia*, 161–66.
4. Harry Harootunian, *Overcome by Modernity*, 43.
5. Charles Taylor, "Modern Social Imaginaries," 106–7.
6. Ibid., 106.
7. Akira Iriye, *Power and Culture*, 8–35; and Cemil Aydin, *The Politics of Anti-Westernism in Asia*, 171–72.
8. See for example "Siljae haeyŏ innŭn yut'op'ia: Miguk teksasŭ kin (Keene) ch'on ŭi ip'unggyŏng " [On utopia in this world: Keene Village, Texas, United States].
9. Chang Tŏksu, "Chŏksŏng kukka ŭi chŏngch'e" [The true identity of the enemy states], in "Taedonga chŏnjaeng kwa pando ŭi mujang, kyŏlchŏn taeyŏnsŏl sokkirok ŭi tŭkchip" [The Great East Asian War and arming the Korean Peninsula: The special issue of recording the great speeches for the decisive war], 27.
10. Michael Robinson, *Cultural Nationalism in Colonial Korea, 1920–1925*; and Michael Robinson, "Ideological Schism in the Korean Nationalist Movement, 1920–1930," 241–68.
11. Bruce Cumings, *The Origins of the Korean War*, xvii–xxix and 3–38.
12. Peter Duus and Kenji Hasegawa eds., *Rediscovering America*, 4–5.
13. Pae Sŏngnyong, "T'aep'yŏngyang sang e saero tongnip han piyulbin konghwauk ŭi changnae: Miguk ŭi kŭktong chŏngch'ak e yŏn'gwan haya" [The future of the Philippines emerging as a new independent republic in the Pacific].
14. "Sijo," in *Han'guk Minjok munhwa taebaekkwa sajŏn* [Encyclopedia of Korean culture].
15. "Silchae haeyŏ innŭn yut'op'ia: Miguk teksasŭ kin [Keene] ch'on ŭi ip'unggyŏng," 11–13.
16. "Han Ch'ijin," in *Han'guk kŭnhyŏndae inmul charyo* [The biographical database of Koreans in the modern and contemporary period].

17. "Chŏng Irhyŏng," in Han'guk minjok munhwa taebaekkwa sajŏn [Encyclopedia of Korean culture].

18. "Chŏng Irhyŏng," in Han'guk kŭnhyŏndae inmul [The biographical database of Koreans in the modern and contemporary period].

19. "Han Ch'ijin," in Han'guk kŭnhyŏndae inmul charyo; "Han Ch'ijin p'an'gyŏl" [The verdict on Han Ch'ijin] (1945); and Hong Chŏngwan, "Ilche ha haebang hu Han Ch'ijin ŭi hangmun ch'egye chŏngnip kwa minjujuŭiron" [Han Ch'ijin's scholarly development and his theory of democracy during the Colonial Period and after Liberation], 159–60.

20. "Ham Sanghun," in Han'guk kŭnhyŏndae inmul charyo; and Ch'inil Panminjok Haengwi Chinsang Kyumyŏng Wiwŏnhoe, ed., Ch'inil panminjok haengwi kwan'gye saryojip [Compilation of historical sources on pro-Japanese acts of traitors].

21. Pae Sŏngnyong, "T'aep'yŏngyang sang e saero tongnip han piyulbin konghwaguk ŭi changnae: Miguk ŭi kŭktong chŏngch'aege yŏn'gwan haya."

22. Han Poyong, "Sin tongnip piyulbin taegwan" [An overview of the new independent Philippines], 142.

23. Ibid., 139–46.

24. Ibid., 142–44.

25. The original excerpt is quoted from the US Department of State, *Peace and War: United States Foreign Policy 1931–1941*, 289.

26. Sŏ Ch'un, "Che ich'a segye taejŏnnon" [A theory of World War II], 94–98.

27. These islands now make up Palau, the Northern Mariana Islands, Micronesia, and the Marshall Islands.

28. Han Poyong, "Sinch'un kukche chŏngguk ŭi tonghyang: Sisa munje" [The trends of international politics in this spring: Current affairs], 306–19.

29. Ibid., 319.

30. Ibid., 317–19.

31. Han Poyong, "Ilchi punjaeng kwa yŏngmi ŭi tonghyang" [The China-Japan dispute and the trends in the United Kingdom and the United States], 52–59.

32. Ibid., 57–59.

33. Chŏng Irhyŏng, "Amerik'a munmyŏng ŭi chonghoenggwan" [A comprehensive overview of the American civilization], 136–49.

34. Ibid., 139–40.

35. Ibid., 140.

36. Ibid., 140–41.

37. Ibid., 143.

38. Ibid., 148–49.

39. Han Poyong, "Sŭngsehan miguk ŭi nodong undong: CIO ŭi yakchin'gwa AFL ŭi mollak" [The US labor movement on the winning side: The great advancement of CIO and the fall of AFL], 163–75.

40. Ibid., 163.

41. Ibid., 164–65.

42. Han Poyong, "Sŭngsehan miguk ŭi nodong undong," 173. Other short articles in the *Chogwang* published in 1937 and 1940 also reveal this Korean "amazement" at the United States' progress. An essay titled "Wŏsingt'ongŭi ch'uŏk" [The memory of Washington days] indicates that this admiration for American life existed among Korean students. The author of this essay wrote that Americans live in a peaceful, secure, and orderly society, create the conveniences of life from scientific knowledge, and enjoy their freedom in the land of liberty. Simdang Hagin, "Wŏsingt'ong ŭi ch'uŏk" [Remembering my days in Washington DC], 60–65.

43. Han Ch'ijin, "Miguk sahoejŏk sasang ŭi hyŏndan'gye" [The current stage of US sociological thoughts], 122–29.

44. Ibid., 123–26.

45. Ibid., 126.

46. Ibid., 129.

47. Ibid., 128.

48. Han Ch'ijin, "Amerik'a munmyŏngnon" [A perspective on American civilization], 146–55.

49. Ibid., 147–48.

50. Ibid., 148–50.

51. Ibid., 150–51.

52. Ibid., 155.

53. Ibid.

54. Ibid., 159.

55. On the Korean-American War of 1871, see Ch'a Sangch'an, "Sinmi tae yangyoran: Yuwŏl sahwa" [What was the great Korean-American War of 1971?], 66–71; and Ch'a Sangch'an, "Sasang ŭro pon Chosŏn'gwa miguk ŭi kwan'gye" [Korea-US relations from a perspective of ideas], 98–107. A more critical history of the United States also appeared, see Yi Myomuk, "Miguk ŭi ŏje wa onŭl" [The past and present of the United States], 64–71.

56. Ham Sanghun, "T'aep'yŏngnyang t'ŭkchip: Miguk ŭi t'aep'yŏngnyang chŏngch'aek" [A special issue on the Pacific: The US policies on the Pacific].

57. Mogya Hongil [Yi Hongjo], "Ilmi oegyo p'alsimnyŏnsa" [The eighty years of Japan and the US relations], 58–67.

58. Chu Yohan et al., "Tae miyŏngjŏng kwa uriŭi kago" [The Great War against the United States and the United Kingdom and our resolution], 72–74. The names of the speakers are written in a Japanese style following the name change policy.

59. Ibid., 72.

60. Yu Kwangnyŏl, "Wae miyŏng ŭl ch'ina" [Why do we strike the United States and the United Kingdom?], 37.

61. Ibid., 37–42.

62. Han Hŭkku, "Munhaksang ŭro pon migugin ŭi sŏnggyŏk" [The characters of Americans in their literature], 142–47.

63. Ibid., 147.

64. Han Hŭkku wrote his memory of his years in the United States in "Chaemi yungnyŏn ch'uŏk p'yŏnp'yŏn" [Remembering my six-year stay in the United States] published in the Sinin munhak in March 1936. Han's recollection of his years in the United States is not negative in this essay. Han Hŭkku, "Munhaksang ŭro pon miguk ŭi sŏnggyŏk," 142.

65. Han Ch'ijin, "Amerik'a munmyŏngnon," 146–55.

66. Hong Sŏngha graduated from Chuo University in Japan and taught at Posŏng College (current Korea University) for eighteen years. After Liberation in 1945, he joined the Korean Democratic Party and was elected as a member of the first National Assembly for drafting the South Korean constitution. "Hong Sŏngha," in *Han'guk kŭnhyŏndae inmul charyo*.

67. Hong Sŏngha, "Sanŏp puhŭngbŏp kwa miguk kyŏngjeŭi changnae" [The National Industrial Recovery Act and the future of the US economy], 23–24.

68. Chaha Sanin, "Miguk kyŏngjech'aegŭi p'asyohwa: Ch'ŏngch'i hyŏngmyŏngŭi naeyong kŏmt'o" [Fascitization of the US Economic Policies: Reviewing the contents of the political revolution], 19–21.

69. Ibid., 21.

70. Sŏ Chaep'il, "Chaeryu osimnyŏn: Miguk sahoeŭi tongt'ae" [Living abroad for fifty years: The dynamics of the US society], 12–14.

71. Ibid., 13.

72. Sŏ Chaep'il, "Chaeryu osimnyŏn," 14.

73. Chin Uhyŏn, "Nyu ttŭil miguk ŭi tonghyang" [The situation of the New Deal America], 21–25.

74. Pae Sŏngnyong, "Miguk nongjobŏp p'ajŏnggwa nyu ttŭirŭi unmyŏng" [The breakdown of the Agricultural Adjustment Act and the destiny of New Deal in the United States], 38–41. Pae's negative view is comparable to Han Poyong's article, "Sŭngsehan miguk ŭi nodong undong: CIO ŭ yakchin'gwa AFL ŭi mollak."

75. Pae Sŏngnyong, "Miguk nongjobŏp p'ajŏnggwa nyu ttŭirŭi unmyŏng," 41.

76. Kim Hoch'ŏl, "Hwanggŭmŭi nara miguk ŭi imyŏnsang" [The other side of the golden country the United States], 74–76.

77. Ibid., 74.

78. Yi Ch'ŏng, "Miguk sŏn'gyohoeŭi Chosŏn kyoyuk pangch'ime taehaya" [The policy of US missionaries on Korean education], 66–70.

79. An Pyŏngju, "Miguk ŭn ŏdiro kana: Rujŭbelt'ŭ ron" [Where is the United States heading?: A theory on Roosevelt], 18–24.

80. According to Japanese records, An Pyŏngju was accused of having contacted the USSR Consulate General, as detected by the Seoul Chongno Police Station in January 1938. "Soyŏnbang ch'ongyŏngsagwan ch'ulipcha kŏmgŏŭi kŏn [On arresting the visitors of the USSR Consulate-General in Seoul].

81. An Pyŏngju, "Miguk ŭn ŏdiro kana: Rujŭbelt'ŭ ron," 19.

82. Ibid. 20.

83. Ibid., 21–23.

84. Ibid., 24.

85. *Samch'ŏlli* (The Korean peninsula) changed its name to *Taedonga* (The great East Asia) and was published in Japanese between 1943 and 1945.

86. A separate essay would be required to do a comprehensive study of wartime Pan-Asianism.

87. Wŏn Sehun, "Ilchung yangguk aegukchaŭi nonjŏn" [A debate between a Chinese patriot and a Japanese patriot], 82–94.

88. Wŏn Sehun, "Ilchung yangguk aegukchaŭi nonjŏn," 82–83. If Wŏn really earned a diploma from Beijing University, his years on campus may have overlapped with Hu's tenure at the university. Wŏn spent his youth in China and Russia and reportedly joined in the Korean Provisional Government. After the liberation of Korea in 1945, he participated in the construction of the Korean Democratic Party. "Wŏn Sehun" in *Han'guk kŭnhyŭndae inmul charyo*.

89. Wŏn Sehun, "Ilchung yangguk aegukchaŭi nonjŏn," 84–86.

90. Ibid., 88–80.

91. Ibid., 90.

92. Ibid., 91–94.

93. Ibid., 94.

94. "Chŏnsihaŭi siguk yŏnsŏl" [Wartime political speeches], 6–9.

95. Yi Tonhwa, "Tongyang p'yŏnghwaŭi kŭnbonch'aek" [A fundamental solution for peace], 6.

96. An Insik, "Sigukkwa oinŭi kago," from "Chŏnsihaŭi siguk yŏnsŏl," 8.

97. For example, Pak Indŏk, a female leader who had studied in the United States, published an essay on two black American women educators and their school for black students. Pak Indŏk, "Miju kangyŏn'gi: hŭgin hakkyowa widaehan yŏin kyoyukka" [My lecture travel in the United States: A black school and a great woman educator], 59–62.

98. Mitarai Tatsuo, "Kinjanghan t'aep'yŏngnyang hyŏngse: Miguk ŭi chŏksŏngŭl pora" [Tense situation in the Pacific: Watch the hostility of the United States].

99. Ibid., 8–15.

100. Yŏ Unhong was Yŏ Unhyŏng's younger brother. Yŏ Unhong joined the Independence movement in the 1920s but, as shown in this speech, joined various collaborative acts in the wartime Colonial Period. He graduated from Wooster College in Ohio and taught at Posŏng College (Korea University). After Liberation, he helped organize a moderate socialist party, the Social Democratic Party (Sahoe Minjudang) and was elected a national assemblyman in South Korea. "Yŏ Unhong," in Han'guk kŭnhyundae inmul charyo [The biographical database of Koreans in the modern and contemporary period].

101. Chu Yohan, "Tongyangŭi ch'imnyakcha yŏngmi t'adoŭi taesajahu!" [Invasion of the Orient and the brave roars for overthrowing the United Kingdom and the United States!], 44–59; and Ch'ae P'ilgŭn, "Tongaŭi yusin, miyŏng kyŏngmyŏrŭi p'yŏngyang taeyŏnsŏlhoe sokki" [The record of the great speech assembly in P'yŏngyang for the restoration of the Orient and the extermination of the United States and the United Kingdom], 38–43.

102. Yun Ch'iho et al., "Taedonga chŏnjaenggwa pandoŭi mujang: Kyŏlchŏn taeyŏnsŏl kirogŭi t'ŭkchip" [The great East Asian War and the armament of the Korean peninsula], 18–36.

103. Sin Hŭngu was Christian and studied at the University of Southern California. After Liberation in 1945, he worked as a diplomat in the South Korean government. "Sin Hŭngu," in Han'guk kŭnhyundae inmul charyo.

104. Yun Ch'iho et al., "Taedonga chŏnjaenggwa pandoŭi mujang."

105. "Chang Tŏksu," in Han'guk minjok munhwa taebaekkwa sajŏn [Encyclopedia of Korean culture].

106. Yun Ch'iho et al., "Taedonga chŏnjaenggwa pandoŭi mujang," 24–27.

107. Chang Tŏksu, "Chŏksŏng kukka ŭi chŏngch'e," 27.

108. Yun Ch'iho et al., "Taedonga chŏnjaenggwa pandoŭi mujang," 24–27.

109. Ibid., 28–29.

110. John Lewis Gaddis, We Now Know, 55.

111. Ibid., 71.

112. Pae Sŏngnyong wrote an article in the first issue of Minju Chosŏn that Han Ch'ijin edited and published. See Pae Sŏngnyong, "Sinjŏngch'i chŏngse ŭi kusang, t'ŭkchip: Sinjŏngch'i chŏngse ŭi yŏksasŏng [A visions of the new political situation, the special report: The history of the new political situation].

PART III
Foreign Societies' Perceptions of Colonial Korea

6

The British and American Perceptions of Korea during the Colonial Period

DAEYEOL KU

This chapter discusses how the perceptions of Korea—held by two major Western powers, Great Britain and the United States—changed during the Colonial Period, and how their perceptions ultimately influenced their decisions over the future of Korea when the country was liberated from Japan's yoke in 1945. To begin with, this chapter will briefly discuss, as a backdrop, how the United States and Great Britain formed their impressions of Korea and how they maintained or changed these views thirty years prior to the Japan-Korea Protectorate Treaty in 1905 and later when Japan's annexation of the country in 1910 absorbed Korea.

Then, the chapter moves on to the Colonial Period (1910–45). We must note that "Korean international relations," according to the strict definition of the term, did not exist during the Colonial Period. A nation-state is traditionally the formal actor in international politics, and Korea had lost that qualification and could not play a part in the international arena as a result of the 1905 Protectorate Treaty (a treaty in which Japan deprived Korea of its right to conduct its own foreign affairs) and the subsequent 1910 annexation of the Korean peninsula. Korean international relations, then, entered what we might call a forty-year "blank space" due to Korea's status as a Japanese protectorate and colony. With Liberation in 1945, the Korean peninsula revived and the subsequent establishment of the Republic of Korea (ROK, South Korea) and the Democratic People's Republic of Korea (DPRK, North Korea) occurred in 1948.

Korea's status during this time (1880–1945) inevitably led to questions of what forms the proper subjects of inquiry for a discussion of international relations on the Korean peninsula, and what is the significance of an exploration of these relations? Apart from the work to fill in the Korean Colonial Period blank space, which has not been treated in the historiography on Korean diplomacy, research on the international relations of this period can shed light on Liberation and Korean independence, the two elements which comprised "the Korean question" in the eyes of the United Kingdom and the United States as well in the eyes of the Korean people. The Korean situation during the Colonial Period was, of course, determined in large part by the opposition of the Japanese exploitation/oppression of versus the resistance of the Korean people. This framework, however, does not provide us with an adequate approach to question Liberation and the independence of Korea. This becomes all too evident when we recall that international factors exerted influences on the deliberations concerning Korea at the end of World War II.

During the Colonial Period the United Kingdom and the United States did not support Liberation nor the independence of Korea. What, then, constitutes the Korean question, the question the powers were so concerned with? In what ways is the Korean question linked to Liberation and independence? We begin to answer these questions by pointing to the fact that even after the loss of the Korean nation-state due to annexation, both the society collectivity known as the Korean people and the geopolitical, strategic, economic, and cultural value of their place of residence—the Korean peninsula—continued, as before, to be of considerable global importance. Indeed, because the powerful Japanese Empire held sway over the peninsula and was using it as a stepping-stone to pursue an expansionist policy toward the continent, the significance of Korea in the international political arena of East Asia was all the more heightened.

A second aspect of the Korean question stems from the Japanese rule over the peninsula, that is, the governance of Koreans by a foreign nation. For centuries Western powers had confronted questions associated with colonial governance. Was it a legitimate endeavor to rule the local Korean people? What was the role of fairness in the practical application of this rule? Over this long period of time, considerable changes occurred in the way Western powers administered colonial rule. We see this quite clearly in the system of mandatory rule and trusteeship established after World War I and World War II respectively. The Western powers left records of their observations of various aspects of Japanese rule on the peninsula, including the relationships between themselves and Japan and the Government-General of Korea; the relationship

The British and American Perceptions of Korea during the Colonial Period 181

between Japan as the foreign—alien— ruler of Korea and the Korean people; and the nature of the changes which occurred in Korean society. The conclusions drawn by the Western powers regarding these issues were to carry tremendous weight in their condemnation of Japanese rule over Korea when, as a result of World War II, the liberation of Korea was brought up for concrete discussion.

We see, then that during the Colonial Period, Korea was precluded from carrying out an autonomous role in international relations. The Colonial Period, however, functions as an important backdrop for our understanding of the issue of liberation and the independence of Korea by allowing us to observe the perceptions and reactions of the Western powers vis-à-vis the Korea question.

Next, we will discuss the leading elements that prodded the Western powers to change their attitudes toward the Korean question in the early days of annexation. Did this occur because of Japan's relations with the two Western powers—the United States and the United Kingdom—were getting worse or was this change due to any specific Japanese colonial policy in Korea? And how did the 1919 March First movement, the largest mass demonstration against Japanese colonial rule, contribute to the two Western powers changing their attitude toward Korea? When these powers observed the Korean uprising, how did they approach the Tokyo government and the Government-General of Korea to ameliorate the Korean situation? How did the two Western powers perceive the geopolitical role of Korea in Japan's expansionist strategy into Manchuria and China in the 1920s and 1930s? After twenty or thirty years of Japanese colonial rule, did the United States and the United Kingdom really believe that Korea or the Korean people had changed—or transformed in a positive direction—enough to run its own government in the modern age, and if so, on what grounds? Lastly and as a conclusion, did the accumulated perception of Korea through contacts and the personal experiences of Western diplomats and missionaries—through their bilateral relations with Japan and by observing Japan's colonial policies over Korea and their consequent outcomes—lead the two Western powers to change their minds when they began to discuss the Korean question during World War II?[1]

THE WESTERN PERCEPTION OF KOREA BEFORE 1910

It must be noted that in the social sciences, the notion of perception originates from the idea that knowledge is a social product. Human beings do not, on an abstract mental level as an isolated individual, observe or reflect on objects. The basic idea behind the sociology of knowledge is that not only are ideologies, myths, moral prescriptions, and value systems influenced by society and history, but scientific knowledge and objective "truths" are also related to and under the same influence. In short, all knowledge is social in nature and this social relationship is a perceived relationship.[2] As far as this chapter is concerned, this implies that the Western powers' perceptions of Korea were not always correct. Notwithstanding such limitations, the question of perception is very important in the study of Korean international relations especially during the entirety of the Colonial Period preceding World War II, largely because Korea was not a formal actor in international society, while after the war the two powers would control the path the Korean peninsula would follow after 1945.

Among the perceptions of Korea, historically created and accumulated amid complex interactions since the 1880s, the most critical criterion was the developmental stage of "civilization." In short, the Western powers considered the Korean sociopolitical situation backward in terms of the evolutionary stages of civilization. From the earliest official relations with Korea during the 1880s onward, the United States and Britain witnessed corrupt and incompetent political leadership, the lack of a drive to reform to become a modern state, as well as the inability to be independent. All of this contrasted distinctively with Japan's Meiji reform measures. The powers compared the Korean government and its monarch to the Sultans in the Islamic world—in radical contrast to the modern European states—and deemed Korea as being incapable of managing a modern state. In so doing, Korea lost the sociopolitical competition in the international arena.[3] Although a similar situation would have been observed in any pre-modern society, including China and Turkey, with the collapse of the existing order and the penetration of foreign influences, this negative perception of the Chosŏn Dynasty consistently appeared in Western records, which detailed Korean relations and thus powerfully influenced Western policies toward Korea.

The British and American Perceptions of Korea during the Colonial Period   183

The Western perception of Korea was largely due to social Darwinism, a doctrine that prevailed in the late nineteenth century. Evolutionary ideas such as *Machtpolitik* (power politics) or the survival of the fittest had existed to explain human history, even before the publication of Charles Darwin's influential text *The Origins of Species* (1858). Regardless of Darwin's original intentions, which is to explain the process of organic evolution, the survival of the fittest theory began to be applied to social groups, a consequence of which was, as far as this chapter is concerned, used to justify the policies and attitudes of the Western powers toward Korea. A typical comment in this case came from US President Theodore Roosevelt who supported the expansion policies even at the cost of the weaker nation. He stated, "Korea was powerless to strike a blow in her own defense" and acknowledged Japan's protective rights in 1905. Great Britain also did not hesitate to predict that the "timid and inoffensive" Korean people and their declining nation would be subjected to a foreign nation, whether it be Japan or Russia.[4]

This negative view of Korea, in contrast to the positive one of Japan, put the latter in a strategically advantageous position in its advances toward the Korean peninsula. The Western powers highly praised the Japanese efforts toward political and institutional reform and its propagation of a civilized culture to Korea. When Japan took control of the Korean government and announced diverse reform measures at an early stage of the Russo-Japanese War, the British considered this action to be modeling the British rule of Egypt and commended it as a "step in the right direction."[5] This perception of Japan, along with the United States and Britain's political and strategic interests in the region, formed the basis of support for the Japanese expansion into the Korean peninsula from the moral perspective. For Japan, this international support became the foundation of an alliance with Great Britain, a friendly relationship with the United States, and a war with Russia. After the Russo-Japanese War, Japan used its winning circumstances to persuade the Western powers of the inevitability of their rule over Korea, either with a protectorate treaty or with annexation.

THE ISSUES OF THE 1910S

By obtaining concessions on the peninsula, the 1910 annexation of Korea by Japan brought about the temporary cessation of the struggle among the powers to seize regional hegemony. Based on the strategic position of the Korean peninsula and the advantage of the power vacuum, opened up by the withdrawal of European powers from East Asia due to the outbreak of World War I in 1914, Japan pursued a new round of expansionist policies, thereby altering the configuration of international relations in the region. These policies infringed upon the interests of Great Britain and the United States, both allies of Japan. Rivalries between Japan and these countries emerged later as factors of overwhelming importance in determining the course of international politics in the region.

Thus, even though the Western powers regarded Korea to be a part of the past, they inclined to link the regional conflict in East Asia to Korea by approaching Japanese expansionism from the vantage point of what they termed "experiences in Korea." John N. Jordan, who had actively supported Japanese policies in Korea, when he served as the British minister in Seoul during the closing days of the Chosŏn Dynasty, and who became the British minister in Beijing from 1906 to 1920, now warned that the "shadow of Korea is spreading over Manchuria." According to Jordan, those who had observed Japanese methods in Korea and Manchuria were aware that the way Japan "owned, policed, and controlled" the railroads in Manchuria was an "old familiar device" employed by Japan for the purpose of territorial expansion.[6] The United States also recalled that Japan had employed an "inching-along diplomacy" prior to the annexation of Korea as a means of securing economic interests which were then later converted into political hegemony.[7] The United States cautioned that if China accepted the Twenty-One Demands by Japan in 1915 it would suffer a loss of sovereignty in the political and economic realms and be placed along with Korea "in a position of vassalage" to Japan.[8] Indeed the powers now regretted their allowing Japan to annex Korea in the first place.

Following annexation, Japan adopted a strategic policy, which called for an increase of two army divisions on the Korean peninsula. With the resignation of the Katsura cabinet (which had overseen the third revision of the Anglo-Japanese Alliance on July 13, 1911), the Saioniji Kinmochi cabinet assumed power in 1912 and attempted to restore the sociopolitical system of Japanese society to its former peacetime status.[9] The Japanese army and navy, however, demanded the appropriation of budget expenditures to strengthen the military. At first, the army, placing particular emphasis on the 1907 Imperial National

Defense Policy, designated Russia as the most likely threat to national security and submitted a plan calling for an increase of all four divisions. However, the army later reserved two of these divisions to be allocated to the Korean peninsula. The United States and Britain viewed the continued insistence of Japanese military authorities—in face of strong public disapproval—as formulated "for obvious strategic reasons," with interests in both an advance on the continent and a relationship with Western powers in mind.[10] With intellectuals and the business community joining in the public outcry against an increase in military expenditures, the army delayed, at the end of 1912, the implementation of the plan for one to two years. The Japanese government finally approved the plan in 1915, however, and in 1916 they deployed the 19th Division at Nanam near the Russian border, with the 20th Division taking up position at Yongsan on the outskirts of Seoul in April of 1919.

The second strategic policy formulated by Japan was to extend the Seoul-Ŭiju railway into Manchuria by constructing a railway bridge across the Yalu River and linking it to a new line from Andong (today's Dandong) to Shenyang, a major city in Manchuria. The Japanese embarked upon the Yalu River railway bridge project in 1909, completing it in the short span of two years. They then built the Andong-Shenyang line and connected it to the Seoul-Ŭiju line. In the age of imperialism, the political, strategic, and economic function of railroads enabled them to serve as the spearheads of expansion, and it was due to the significance of this role that they were raised as an issue of central importance in the diplomacy of the Colonial Period. The Western powers, worried that Japanese bridge and railroad construction would infringe upon their interests more directly than the increase of troops stationed in Korea, mobilized their diplomatic corps in East Asia to observe the pervasive effect of railway construction.

A symbolic but hardly known aspect of the reaction of the powers to Japanese strategic policies on the Korean peninsula can be found in the provision concerning Korea brought up for discussion during the third renewal of the Anglo-Japanese Alliance in 1911. The second Anglo-Japanese Alliance, concluded when Japanese victory in the Russo-Japanese War was assured in 1905, had been scheduled for renewal in 1915. However, in response to the altered political circumstances in East Asia arising from the Japanese annexation of Korea, and, in particular, to the British concern over the possibility of conflict between Japan and the United States, treaty negotiations were moved up four years, resulting in the signing of the third Anglo-Japanese Treaty in 1911.

By means of this treaty, the British placed a check on unilateral Japanese activities in China, particularly on those activities which could possibly harm British interests. The British position on curbing Japanese expansionism was well reflected in the provision concerning Korea and in the process of negotiating how to revise the treaty. The second alliance had allowed the British "a special interest" in maintaining stability "in the proximity of the Indian frontiers," extending to the British the right to take appropriate measures to protect these interests.[11] The Japanese now insisted that the British allow them the same rights on the Korean peninsula, which formed a new frontier for Japan. However, the British possession of special rights over the Indian frontiers (Afghanistan, Bangladesh, and Pakistan—in particular the Afghan border with Russia) was purely defensive. On the contrary, the Japanese considered British special rights over the Indian frontiers to represent British expansionist desires upon Manchuria. The British, in return, interpreted the Japanese position on the provision concerning Korea as an attempt to transform established Japanese interests in Manchuria—such as the South Manchurian Railway—a new political interest in the Korea-Manchuria border region. The British rejected the Japanese demand, deleting in its entirety the provision proposed by the Japanese in the draft agreement.[12]

The period of 1910–20 covers the first ten years of Japanese rule in Korea. Establishing a Government-General invested with supreme authority by the emperor and therefore unhindered by the Japanese constitution, the Japanese pursued, on the one hand, a simple and effective modernization policy, while on the other hand they installed an assimilation policy bent upon eradicating the national identity of the Korean people. While the Western powers did not agree with this program in its entirety, they expressed a supportive attitude, especially when they compared the Japanese policies with the corruption and inefficiency of the former Korean government. While the United States and Great Britain characterized the projects pursued by Japan as "costly and burdensome," and Japan as "having bitten off more than she can chew," they also portrayed them as "decidedly progressive" and as programs that would result in an increase of material wealth for Koreans. They, therefore, emphasized "it is patience and help, not criticism, that are required."[13] At the same time, Korean resistance against the Terauchi administration was roundly condemned: "still the voice of calumny is raised against the authorities by good-for-nothing fellows whose ambitions are thwarted."[14] In other words, as long as Japanese policies were viewed positively, the Korean Independence movement was seen as nothing more than the expression of a "rancorous hatred of the Japanese" occasioned by a "distorted idea of patriotism."[15]

The United Kingdom and the United States' positive appraisal of Japanese colonial policies in Korea, however, did not last for long. When Terauchi became the Japanese prime minister in 1916, the British described him as a strong personality who had "ruled the country with an iron hand" and "with German discipline."[16] Hasegawa Yoshimichi, appointed as Terauchi's successor, was described as possessing the ability to strike fear in the hearts of Koreans, one who was "essentially a soldier, a bluff, straightforward man, free from secretiveness."[17] By 1919, the conclusion was that the governor-general of Korea was "no doubt despotic and at times reactionary."[18]

The Western powers did not leave memoranda or other comprehensive records which would explain this shift in attitude vis-à-vis Japanese policies toward the peninsula during this time period. However, a review of various records from the eight- to nine-year period leading up to 1919, allows us to infer which events in Korea caused the powers to alter their stance. First of all, from 1910–19, the position of the Western powers concerning material prosperity achieved under the auspices of the Government-General of Korea did not change. In contrast, Western powers viewed Japanese colonial rule as having failed its moral obligations to provide legal protection to Koreans and to treat them in an equitable manner. This problem was of importance to the great powers because it was not confined merely to the legal protection of Koreans; the Western powers had a direct stake in the application of an equitable set of laws because their own rights and privileges—such as missionary activity and educational projects—were affected. Moreover, this side of Japanese colonial rule invoked loud condemnation of Japan's rule over the peninsula after 1945.

Along these lines, the decisive event which altered the perception of the powers was the 105-Person Incident in 1911 by which Korean nationalists were accused of allegedly trying to assassinate Governor-General Terauchi.[19] The powers' expression of interest in this event was due not to what constituted its essence—the Japanese suppression of Korean nationalism—but to the following: (1) international opinion insisted that Christians were being oppressed because the Japanese were propagating rumors that missionaries had been involved, and the majority of those rounded up were Christians; (2) inhuman acts such as torture were being used to force confessions from the accused; and (3) the court had disallowed accused defendants to testify on their own behalf or to provide legal defense for themselves. The final issue of legal defense contradicted with the public pledge the Government-General of Korea had made to establish an equitable legal system and stood "as a commentary on Japanese methods in Corea [sic] and the Japanese judicial system in general."[20]

The British ambassador to Japan, Sir Claude MacDonald, expressed criticism of the kind rarely heard in diplomatic exchanges with the Japanese foreign minister, Uchida Yasuya, stating that the trial in Seoul was a "travesty of justice." MacDonald reminded Uchida that at the time of the annexation he had on several occasions advised the Japanese government that fairness and justice were absolutely necessary in administering colonial rule in Korea.[21] MacDonald's successor in Tokyo, Sir William Conyngham Greene, castigated the proceedings as "the most gigantic miscarriage of justice in history," pointing both to the release upon retrial of ninety-nine of the original 105 defendants on lack of evidence and to the 600 years of prison time in the retrial from sentences totaling 630 years in the first trial "as the best evidence of the grotesque irregularity of the earlier trial."[22] For the Western powers the incident revealed the falsity of the claim that Japan was the bearer of civilization to Korea. The United Kingdom and the United States also considered the incident to be a further attempt—in addition to the Education Ordinance of 1911—to restrict missionary activity and to ultimately eliminate their rights and privileges on the peninsula.

In addition to the intensifying regional conflict between Japan and the Western powers and the skepticism evinced by the latter regarding Japanese policies in respect to colonial governance, the factor which slowly but decisively altered the stance of the powers vis-à-vis the Korean peninsula proved to be the various economic policies carried out by the Japanese following annexation. As a general rule, the Western powers supported the policies of the new Government-General of Korea aimed at reforming the system which had existed under the former Korean government. Determining that development of the Korean economy made trade with Korea "just now distinctly favourable" and that mining in Korea possessed "infinite possibilities,"

Western diplomats advised companies in their home countries to invest in Korea.[23] These expectations, however, were soon dashed as a result of the promulgation by the Government-General of Korea of a variety of laws dealing with economic matters. The first of these laws was the Company Law, put into effect in early 1911. The Company Law made it necessary to obtain government approval to set up new companies, to locate branch offices, and to conduct business in Korea. In its practical application, this law was used in a variety of ways to discourage and prevent foreign firms from establishing a base of operations in Korea.[24] As a result, the Western powers lost nearly all of their rights and privileges on the peninsula within a few years of annexation. In brief, from the Western perspective, Japan had lost almost all of its legitimacy and moral justification to rule the peninsula after just ten years of colonial rule.

THE MARCH FIRST MOVEMENT AND THE POLICIES OF THE WESTERN POWERS

The March First movement stands out as the largest scale Korean national resistance movement of the entire Colonial Period. It was also extremely important in terms of the contemporaneous international relations swirling around and on the Korean peninsula. The complete absence of research on international relations during the Colonial Period, however, has resulted in a lack of awareness in both academic circles and in Korean society in general of its importance in the March First movement. Once we recognize that foreign relations are the extension of the domestic situation and that in the Colonial Period the "Korean question" signaled nothing more than the issue of Korean independence, we can understand the meaning of the March First movement in terms of international politics. The outbreak of the March First movement in 1919 caused the Western powers to reexamine the issue of Korea, which had been forgotten in the arena of international relations of East Asia, since annexation in 1910. In addition, when the Western powers discussed the question of Korean liberation and independence at the close of World War II, they would not only recall the organizational ability, capacity for independence, and spirit of sacrifice Koreans had demonstrated in the March First movement, but also the subsequent establishment in 1919 of the Provisional Government of the Republic of Korea in Shanghai.[25]

The March First movement occurred in the midst of worsening relations between the Western powers and Japan following the end of World War I. During the war, Japan had occupied both the German-held Qingdao on the Shandong peninsula and the South Sea Islands (modern day Palau, Northern Mariana Islands, Federated States of Micronesia, and Marshall Islands), and was given the rights to these territories through the South Pacific Mandate at the Paris Peace Conference in 1919. Following the war, however, the United States and Great Britain once again became active in East Asia and demanded that Japan return these possessions. President Woodrow Wilson advised Japan to assume a "liberal spirit" unfettered by past agreements and to return to China the rights to the Shandong peninsula it had gained by covert diplomacy during the war.[26] As payback for Japanese support of the Allies in the war, Great Britain could not help but back the Japanese position at the Paris Peace Conference. Following the war, however, relying on the global superiority of its naval power, the British sought to implement an "adverse verdict."[27] In the course, then, of the post–World War I reshuffling of the pecking order in East Asia, Japan and the Western powers were placed at bitter odds with each other. As a result, anti-American and anti-British sentiments heightened in Japan, and in the midst of this climate the March First movement took place.

While the reaction of the powers to the March First movement was antagonistic toward the Japanese, it was not, in the final analysis, pro-Korean. The British, for their part, responded in an ambivalent fashion. Itself in possession of the greatest colonial empire in the world, Great Britain expressed absolutely no sympathy whatsoever for the Korean Independence movement, viewing the "uprising" as a Japanese domestic affair, one which would be easily suppressed.[28] At the same time, however, William M. Royds, the acting British consul general in Seoul, joined several other diplomats in accurately identifying the Japanese assimilation policy as the underlying cause of the Korean uprising. Emphasizing the extent to which the level of public order and organizational prowess demonstrated by Koreans on March 1, 1919, indicated a capacity for independence unseen in the past, Royds recommended that Koreans be offered "an extension of local self-government instead of gradual diminution."[29] The British Foreign Office in London, however, expressed no particular interest in the Korean movement, except to note that it provided the "perfect answer" to the inflammatory behavior and criticism of the Japanese vis-à-vis British rule in India and other colonies.

When news of the massacre carried out by the Japanese military at Cheam-ri near Suwŏn on April 15, 1919, reached London in early May, the British began to exhibit an interest in the Korean situation. The acting British ambassador to Japan, Beilby Alston, protested to the Japanese foreign undersecretary, Shidehara Kijuo, that the Japanese were "out-Hunning the Huns" in committing atrocities and were "out-rivaling the Germans in War." Alston requested that the British Foreign Office pursue an active course in informing the Japanese ambassador in London of the "utter horror felt by the civilized world towards the barbarity of the Japanese."[30] Given this situation, the British Foreign Office initiated a broad-based investigation of the Korean question. In a memorandum titled "On the Japanese Policy in Corea," the head of the Far Eastern Department, G. W. Max Muller, found that the "underlying cause" of the current situation is "the Japanese policy of 'Japanizing' Corea completely." While making it clear that Great Britain should avoid becoming involved in the question of Korean independence, Muller requested that as the final solution to the issue Japan adopt measures such as "some form of self-government" for Korea—the cessation of the assimilation policy, and the encouragement of Korean-language education.[31] The British deputy foreign secretary, Lord George N. Curzon, who met with the Japanese ambassador, Chinda Sutemi, twice in July, criticized "in very frank and unequivocal terms" the Japanese policy of suppression and recommended that Japan institute the reforms mentioned in Max Muller's memorandum.[32]

Policies aimed at improving the situation were announced in August when Admiral Saitō Makoto was appointed governor-general, but these measures stopped far short of instituting substantial reforms. The British expressed particular indignation at continued instances of flogging, insisting that the Government-General, if it so desired, could put a stop to the barbaric practice "by a stroke of the pen."[33] British diplomats continued to raise this problem as a central issue in their contacts with Japanese authorities. When the Japanese introduced a bill banning flogging in early 1920, the British concluded that their protestations "had not been without good result" and discontinued their intervention in the matter.[34] We see, then, that the British had retreated from their earlier approach of raising political issues such as the expansion of self-government and the elimination of the assimilation policy and now addressed the Korean question through a diplomacy purely concerned with human rights.

The response of the United States to the Korean uprising was much more noncommittal than that of Great Britain. With the outbreak of World War I, international politics in East Asia had begun to revolve around the deepening confrontation between Japan and the United States, while Britain was retreating. The fact that relations between Japan and the United States were extremely strained at the close of the war gave the United States no room to intervene in Korean affairs, which had fallen under the rubric of Japanese domestic problems. Intervention under government auspices, then, was completely out of the question. The United States, in fact, was concerned that Japan would make the most of the involvement of missionaries or other US civilians in the Korean movement, and that this alone would be enough to effect an even further deterioration of the US-Japan relationship across the board. For their part, Koreans in the Independence movement viewed the United States, due to its backing of the doctrine of the self-determination of nations (in contrast to Japan's ally, Great Britain) as the only power which could support Korean independence. Korean leaders working at home and overseas for independence pursued their activities, therefore, both directly and indirectly in relation to the United States. The upshot of this, however, was that the United States government assumed an even more passive stance toward the Korean question.

Immediately following President Woodrow Wilson's declaration of the Fourteen Points (included among which was the doctrine of the self-determination of nations) in January 1918, Korean overseas nationalists determined to send the following representatives to Paris: from Shanghai, Kim Kyushik; from Jiandao in Korea and Nikolsk in Siberia, Yun Hae and Ko Changil; and from the United States, Syngman Rhee and Henry Chung (Chŏng Hangyŏng). The move by the Korean National Association in the United States to dispatch Rhee and Chung, however, was blocked by the refusal of the United States to issue Rhee and Chung passports on the grounds that the Korean question was "not a war-related issue" and therefore Koreans would not be allowed a hearing at the peace conference.[35] Wilson's devotion to the doctrine of the self-determination of nations notwithstanding, he realized the difficulty of finding a solution to the colonial question in the midst of the postwar settlement. The other victorious powers—Great Britain, France, and Japan—were unwilling to place colonial issues (with the exception of the dispensation of the former German colonies) on the table in Paris. The United

States, moreover, was concerned that the indiscriminate application of the self-determination of nations doctrine would alter the borders of over fifty countries and thereby become a threat to world peace rather than a stabilizing factor. Accordingly, the United States abandoned its espousal of uniform adherence to the doctrine.[36]

The situation in Korea, however, did not develop in accordance with US desires. Around the end of 1918, US authorities in Seoul and Tokyo became aware of a flurry of activity among Koreans inspired by Wilson's declaration of the Fourteen Points, in particular to the self-determination of nations doctrine. The US consul general in Seoul, Leo A. Bergholz, noting that the Korean anti-Japanese movement was gathering strength from a renewed sense of loyalty to the monarchy among Koreans following the death of King Kojong, the last monarch of the Chosŏn Dynasty, expressed his concern that the movement, in the midst of the anti-American sentiment permeating Japanese society, contained the possibility of bringing about tremendous discord. Bergholz felt the need to take the precautionary measure to reminding US missionaries suspected of inciting Koreans from behind the scenes that they were not to interfere in Korean political affairs. This official notice issued on January 18, 1897 by the US minister in Seoul, John M. B. Sill, directed missionaries to adhere to a policy of "scrupulously abstaining from participating in the domestic affairs of the country."[37] Following the outbreak of the Korean uprising and the rising tensions between missionaries and the Government-General of Korea, the US State Department issued a directive to US authorities in Seoul requesting that they "exercise the greatest precaution and restraint" in dealing with the situation in Korea and matters related to the Americans. In so doing the US State Department clarified their position and did not give the Japanese reason to harbor suspicion that the US government sympathized with the Korean nationalist movement.[38]

This was the sum total of US policy toward the Korean nationalist movement. As was the case with Great Britain (Japan's ally), the United States also demonstrated that it was in no position to interfere in Korea. Once, in a meeting between US and Japanese authorities in Washington, the issue of Korea was raised but this was in the context of a consultation with officials from the Division of Far Eastern Affairs requested by the Japanese chargé d'affaires, who was troubled by the increase in anti-Japanese sentiment in the US society arising from the situation on the Shandong peninsula. The Japanese merely conveyed their concerns over the fact that the issue of Korea had been brought up in the US Senate.[39]

In spite of the passive stance of the United States government, leaders of the Korean Independence movement had considerable success in promoting their cause by appealing to US public opinion. Sŏ Chaep'il (Philip Jaisohn), Syngman Rhee, Henry Chung, and other leaders held the first Korean Congress from April 14–16, 1919, in Philadelphia, inviting Americans from the business, education, and religious communities, as well as the press. They took the opportunity at this meeting to explain the actual situation of the Independence movement in Korea and to denounce its suppression by the Japanese. On the final day of the Congress, Syngman Rhee led a march of demonstrators to Independence Hall and read the Declaration of Independence.[40] Sŏ Chaep'il and other leaders organized the Friends of Korea, a group that worked hard to steer public opinion in the United States toward a more sympathetic view of Korea. The outcome of this was the formation of seventeen branches of the organization across the United States. As a result of all these efforts, the Korean question received continuous coverage by important US newspapers and wire services.[41]

The Korean Independence movement leaders living in the United States experienced success publicizing their cause due to rising opposition to the formation of the League of Nations and the Treaty of Versailles and also to the existence of anti-Japanese sentiment in the United States brought on by the situation playing out on the Shandong peninsula. Korean leaders, in this environment, emphasized that Japanese expansionism would not cease at the Asian continent but could eventually target the United States. This strategy, however, presented the Koreans with a dilemma. Theoretically, concluding the Paris Peace Conference in June 1919 without discussion of the Korean situation meant that the opportunity for Korean independence to be raised as an international issue would have to come through the League of Nations. For this to be accomplished, it was the support of the United States—a country which was favorably disposed toward the independence of weaker peoples—which was absolutely necessary, not that of European imperialistic powers such as Great Britain. According to this logic, then, Korean leaders should have supported the ratification of the Treaty of Versailles and the entry of the United States into the League of Nations. On the other hand, opposing the Treaty of Versailles and the League of Nations had acquired an anti-imperialist character and was, therefore, receiving the support of the Irish and other oppressed peoples. Faced with this dilemma, Korean leaders immersed themselves in an anti-Japanese movement, which, in keeping with the general trend of the times, eschewed their long-term goal of achieving independence through the League of Nations.

INTERNATIONAL RELATIONS OF THE KOREAN PENINSULA IN THE 1920S

In the 1920s, through the Washington Naval Conference formulated under the leadership of the United States, East Asia entered a period of stability. In its practical application, however, this conference had limits. For example, other than issuing warnings based on moral grounds, it allowed for no specific checks on the Japanese should they choose to pursue expansionist policies. Given this kind of international environment, the Western powers chose to respond to Japanese colonial policies on the peninsula in a different manner. The decade of the 1920s corresponded to Saitō Makoto's first term as governor-general (1919–27) and his adoption of what is known as Japan's "cultural policy" toward Korea, which stood in contrast to the military rule of his predecessors, Terauchi Masatake (1910–16) and Hasegawa Yoshimichi (1916–19). Saitō stabilized the political situation in Korea by means of somewhat mild, liberal policies and improved relations between the Government-General of Korea and Westerners (including missionaries). This made Saitō, from the point of view of Japan and the Western powers, the most successful governor-general to date. A British report from 1929, published after Saitō had been appointed governor-general for the second time, commented sardonically that Koreans were unhappy with the appointment. According to the report Koreans had no reason to complain about Saitō, because Saitō was giving the Koreans what they wanted.[42] The United States credited the fact that the June 10 movement, which occurred on the same day as King Sunjong's funeral in 1926, had not developed into a situation as serious as the March First movement due to Saitō's liberal policies and his having received trust and respect from all classes.[43]

Whether the Koreans themselves bestowed praise upon this foreign ruler, however, was quite another question. The US consul general in Seoul, Ransford Miller, reported in 1929 that Koreans were indifferent toward Saitō's second appointment because they stood to gain nothing no matter who became governor-general.⁴⁴ The truth of the matter was that in spite of appearances the relationship between ruler and ruled on the peninsula had not undergone any changes by the time of Saitō's second appointment and the hope of independence through struggle had by no means faded away. Koreans were aware that no matter what pretexts Saitō manufactured to justify his policies, he would never move in the direction of weakening Japanese rule over Korea.⁴⁵

The spread of communist ideology was a new problem introduced into the Korean political scene in the 1920s. Lenin had succeeded after 1919 in producing an anti-imperialist atmosphere in China by engaging in projects such as the promotion of the liberation movement of colonies and the formation of an alliance with the nationalist Guomindang. The failure of the March First movement, the disappointment of the Western powers resulting from the fact that the issue of Korean independence was not raised at either of the conferences in Paris and Washington, and the expectations Koreans held for the newly formed Soviet Union combined to induce Koreans to seek deliverance from the Soviet Union which professed itself to be the savior of the East.⁴⁶ Simultaneously, the Soviet Union took a considerably aggressive stance in its propaganda campaign and its offer of support toward Korea. The Soviet propaganda campaign to incite revolution in Korea began with the June 1919 publication of a pamphlet under the name of Foreign Minister Lev Karakhan titled, "The Koreans Who Are Being Trampled Under Foot by the Imperialist Party of Japan."⁴⁷ Soviet propaganda asserted that Koreans had received no assistance from the United States and other Western nations and that their only hope was revolution along Bolshevist lines; the Soviet Union promised to work together with Koreans to plan and carry out this revolution on the peninsula.⁴⁸ In 1923, Korean organizations in the Soviet Union—including its Russian Maritime province—agreed to create an autonomous Korean state in the province and to provide mutual assistance in the event of any military provocation.⁴⁹

Soviet support for Korea, along with the propaganda effort, faded with the announcement in January 1925, one year after Lenin's death, of a treaty normalizing relations between the Soviet Union and Japan. In exchange for the Soviet Union's promise to block the establishment of anti-Japanese organizations working for independence in its territory (organizations, for example,

The British and American Perceptions of Korea during the Colonial Period   197

that might resemble the Provisional Government of Korea in Shanghai), Japan agreed to put a stop to the activities of the White Russian movement's political organizations.[50] The Soviet Union sought to regain its position in East Asia by putting an end to the instability brought on by civil war and the interference of Japan and the United States (both countries had dispatched troops to Siberia). All of this bore significance for the future outcome of the Korean question. This incident shows that the fact that the possibility—in reality quite dim—of establishing an autonomous entity, creating an independent state with its own military and concluding treaties of mutual assistance was inextricably linked to fluctuations in relationships among powers. These were the same goals that leaders of the Independence movement in the 1940s worked to achieve as a means of bringing about Korean independence. They were the goals subjected to lively discussion between Koreans and the Soviet Union in the 1920s, only to be sacrificed when relations were normalized between the Soviet Union and Japan.

INTERNATIONAL RELATIONS OF THE KOREAN PENINSULA IN THE 1930s

During the 1930s, international relations in East Asia underwent rapid change and entered a period of instability. The primary reason for this shift lay in the increasingly sharp odds at which the powers found themselves in terms of their vested interests in the outcome of regional issues, and therefore the policies of each country began to develop more along the lines of confrontation than compromise. Japan abandoned its policy of maximizing national interest within the framework of the Washington Naval Conference system in favor of the pursuit of an overtly expansionist project, which resulted in the manufacturing of the Manchurian Incident in 1931 and entering into war with China in 1937. The resulting confrontation with the powers engendered the opportunity for the latter to reexamine the role played by the Korean peninsula in the execution of Japan's expansionist policies, that is, to reassess and recognize the geopolitical value of the peninsula. The Western powers' guarantee of Korean independence following World War II was grounded in precisely this reassessment.

The United States and the United Kingdom laid great emphasis on the political and strategic issues confronting the peninsula in the 1930s. One concern was the way the peninsula, due to its geographical proximity to Manchuria, served as a beachhead providing human and material resources for the invasion of Manchuria by Japan. A related strategic concern of even more importance was the absolutely indispensable role the peninsula could act as a bridge connecting the Japanese islands to Manchuria, allowing for the development of the latter into a Japanese strategic base and economic sphere. A third concern revolved around the question of the Korean residents in Manchuria—Japan was using these Koreans as instruments to carry out its policy of invasion.

The Mobaoshan Incident in 1931 formed the prelude for the development of these concerns. On July 2, 1931, approximately two months prior to the Manchurian Incident, a dispute over irrigation canals broke out between Korean and Chinese farmers in Mt. Mobaoshan, Jilin Province, China. The subsequent persecution of Chinese residents in Korea and the intervention by the Japanese consulate in Manchuria under the pretext of providing protection for Koreans transformed this incident into a diplomatic dispute between China and Japan.[51] At the heart of the controversy was the question of the "Manchurian-Koreans." The Japanese Foreign Ministry, estimating that a total of one million Koreans resided in Manchuria by 1930, viewed them as a factor which could no longer be ignored in resolving political, social, and racial problems in Manchuria.[52] Japan, moreover, encouraged Korean immigration to Manchuria. In a 1939 speech, Governor-General Minami Jiro announced a long-term plan with the goal of placing one million Korean households (five million people) in Manchuria.[53] China, on the other hand, in keeping with an anti-Japanese atmosphere, had begun to clamp down on Korean residents in Manchuria beginning around 1927. These developments demonstrate the validity of the view expressed in one United States report that the Koreans had become a "pawn" in the international game being played out in East Asia between Japan, China, and the Soviet Union.[54] The Mobaoshan Incident, then, pointed to the international upheaval, which was to come in the form of the Manchurian Incident.[55]

With the political situation in East Asia undergoing rapid change, the strategic value of the Korean peninsula was becoming readily apparent. If Japanese military forces were urgently needed in Manchuria, it would be much easier to dispatch troops from the peninsula than from the homeland. Indeed, Japanese troops stationed in Korea had already played an important role in the

Manchurian Incident, demonstrating an additional advantage by attracting little attention from the powers.[56] The real strategic value of the peninsula, however, lay in the fact that it formed the heart of the Japanese conception of transforming Manchuria, Korea, and Japan into a single economic and military sphere. Governor-General Ugaki Kazushige (July 1931–July 1936) and his successor, Minami Jiro (August 1936–May 1942) began in earnest the attempt to realize this conception.

The distance between Dailian (Dairen: in terms of location, the most important port in Manchuria) and Shimonoseki is 615 miles, and the distance between Dailian and Nagasaki is 563 miles. Following the East Sea (formerly known as the Sea of Japan), however, it is only 469 miles from Tsuruga to Ch'ŏngjin; the fact, moreover, that Ch'ŏngjin is a warm water port made it Japan's future "front door to northern Manchuria and Mongolia."[57] The development of the port city of Najin and railway linkage to China would shorten transport routes between Japan and both Manchuria and the northern part of Korea, leading to an increase in trade and exerting tremendous influence over a variety of areas. In addition, while the route between Dailian and Japan would be exposed externally during the war, the Najin-Japan route, running through the East Sea, would be easy to defend. The US State Department noted that the latter was the shortest route from Japan's industrial center to the Manchurian capital of Xinjing (Hsingking, now Changchun).[58]

Appointed governor-general in 1936, Minami, in the manner typical of a "protagonist of the 'forward' movement," completed the project of combining Japan and Manchuria via northern Korea in an atmosphere of national emergency arising from the outbreak of war with China.[59] Minami insisted that although Manchuria was certainly an independent country, in reality the national border of Japan had expanded from the Yalu and Tumen rivers to the Heilong and Ussuri rivers and, particularly in terms of national defense, Japan (including the Korean peninsula) and Manchuria had coalesced into one. The role of the peninsula and the manner in which it was to be governed, therefore, could no longer be the same as in the past. While Minami's predecessors had claimed to promote the welfare and prosperity of Koreans as basic policies, Minami's policies of assimilation and industrial development of the peninsula were now necessarily formulated with their positive contribution to the Japanese imperialist project in mind. Great Britain was concerned that if progress was made in the industrialization of the peninsula, Japan would accelerate its economic invasion of Manchuria and into the Northern part of China with the result that the interests in the region of Great Britain and other powers would be threatened.[60]

Saitō's limited liberal policy, then, was eliminated, and Koreans entered a final "dark period" of militaristic colonial rule. The Government-General, warning its colonial subjects that the domestic and international political situation was developing into a crisis, strengthened organizations used for the mobilization of the population. This mobilization movement took place on different levels, all with the aim of completely militarizing Korean society. It took on the character of a social movement, engaging activities such as the repair of sanitary facilities and the paying of respect to the elderly. In the name of national defense, it solicited patriotic contributions for the purchase of fighter planes and anti-aircraft artillery. Under the rubric of emergency measures, it advocated frugality in the consumption of food and clothing, the elimination of extravagant rituals and ceremonies, the ban on smoking and drinking, and a "moral rearmament" to secure a proper East Asian sense of morality.[61]

Given this situation, however, the powers' appraisal of the Korean question was ambivalent. They continued as before to view positively the economic development carried out under the auspices of the Government-General. In other words, while admitting that Japanese policies were formulated to serve Japan by exploiting Koreans, the powers considered quantitative growth an incontrovertible fact, one that pointed to a radical departure from the corruption and decadence marking the last years of the Chosŏn Dynasty. In their eyes, the Korea of 1935 (the twenty-fifth anniversary of the inauguration of the "administration") had been transformed from a pre-modern hermit kingdom into a new society enjoying the benefits of modern civilization such as roads, rail lines, electricity, hospitals, and schools.[62] The view was that in spite of the strong political orientation of the educational system, the fact that 700,000 Koreans had received the benefits of education represented "remarkable progress."[63] Even William Royds, the British consul general who had served for more than twenty years in East Asia and had authored numerous reports critical of the Government-General policies at the time of the March First movement, wrote that the entire Korean peninsula had experienced incredible progress in an orderly fashion.[64]

This positive assessment, however, was limited to the material aspects of the situation; the perception remained that rule by the Government-General represented an "unbridled despotism."[65] In the view of the powers, absolutist rule in colonized Korea had not given rise to a crisis because the masses had not experienced political freedom from the time of the Chosŏn Dynasty. In addition, Korean resistance had been effectively suppressed and driven underground with the result that the majority of Koreans "accepted their fate with apathy."[66] The Japanese suppression of the Korean resistance, however, had by no means eased the tensions existing between the two peoples; no compromise had been reached between the Japanese policy of assimilation and the agenda of the Korean resistance in the 1930s.

From the time of Saitō's tenure as governor-general in the 1920s, the question of self-rule for Korea had been intermittently raised as one means of resolving the sharp conflict between Japan's assimilation policy and the goals of the Independence movement. Both the United States and Great Britain—particularly the latter, as a great imperialist power—did not consider Korean independence to be feasible. Nevertheless, they did view self-rule for Korea as a necessity in that it would allow Japan to demonstrate a receptiveness to the Korean desire for independence and to provide an outlet for that desire without weakening Japan's grip on the peninsula. The relatively stable political situation in East Asia following World War I, coinciding with a general increase in political consciousness in the colonized regions, was related to an international atmosphere in which a fairly wide-ranging discussion could take place concerning issues raised by colonial rule such as the political participation of colonial subjects and the improvement of their political status. Also coming into play regarding self-rule for Korea was the negative view of the powers that Korea was "quite unfit in its present stage of development to govern itself."[67] Admitting that Japanese colonial rule in Korea was at times "harsh," in general, they believed that the Koreans were "quite incapable of producing orderly government and political stability by their own efforts" and that Japan was bringing them great material benefits.[68] Korean self-rule, then, was viewed by Great Britain and the United States as one of the important reforms they hoped to see enacted during Saitō's tenure. As for the Japanese, Korean self-rule was put under consideration following the Manchurian Incident and the expansion of the conflict with China into its northern region because Japan recognized the need, now that it was engaged in war, to stabilize the rear by providing more of an outlet for Koreans' political aspirations.[69]

From the Korean perspective, however, self-rule was nothing more than a fiasco, an idea brought up for consideration a number of times in the history of Japanese rule on the peninsula only to be discarded as an option with the installation of military government in the mid-1930s. In any event, self-rule would function merely as a containment mechanism designed to regulate the conflict between the Japanese assimilation policy and the desire to complete independence. Theoretically, the notion of self-rule stood in direct opposition to the assimilation policy, which formed the cornerstone of Japanese colonial rule. The view of the United States, Great Britain, and also Japanese intellectuals, of course, was that the assimilation of an alien people was an impossibility. Indeed, even if Japan did succeed in assimilating the Korean people, it had not explored the question of treating Koreans as equals, of offering them the same political rights possessed by Japanese, nor did it have any intention whatsoever of doing so. The fact, however, that Korean self-rule was never implemented proved unfortunate. When the powers during World War II brought up the question of Korean independence for formal discussion, Koreans lack of political experience was interpreted as indicative of an insufficient ability on the part of Koreans for independence. This interpretation, in turn, was used as a pretext to legitimize trusteeship.

Minami, however, vigorously pursued the assimilation policy. According to Minami, Japanese colonial rule in Korea necessarily differed from Western-style colonial methods. He insisted that the Western powers treated their colonies as little more than milk cows, engaging in self-interested exploitation with the aim of accumulating wealth for the mother country. He also boasted that while the Western powers impeded industrial development and advances in education, fostering a system of racial discrimination, Japan had eliminated discrimination against Koreans by pursuing its policy of "Japan and Korea as one body" (*naisen ittai*).[70] Minami evoked the notion of the Greater East Asian Co-Prosperity Sphere (a conception which had already begun to manifest itself in Japanese foreign policy), asserting that the countries of East Asia must harmonize with each other and coexist in mutual prosperity, relying on the moral and spirit embodied in the phrase "East Asia as one family" (*toyo ikka*).[71] Minami declared the assimilation policy successfully completed in 1938.

In contrast, the British conception of the true assimilatory process was one that occurs within the individual, not as a result of external change that for the Korea of 1938, as one British official remarked in 1938 "the process has hardly begun."[72] United States Consul General William Langdon, however, pointed out that following the Manchurian Incident Koreans had begun to achieve a measure of economic success, with some receiving appointments to high-level posts in Manchuria. In addition, pro-Japanese sentiment was on the rise, with Japanese victories in the war with China and in the 1939 Nomonhan Incident with the Soviet Union near the Mongolian-Manchurian border.[73]

The Korean anti-Japanese Independence movement developed in new directions under these complex circumstances. While public opposition to Japanese rule declined, passive resistance seeking to maintain national identity in the face of the assimilation policy emerged. Koreans possessed deeply rooted nationalist sentiments which precluded their abandoning the struggle for the ideal of complete independence even if the use of military force was impossible.[74] This was particularly worrisome to Japanese military authorities, who undertook a survey of Korean dignitaries in an attempt to determine how many Koreans would be loyal to Japan in the event Japan found itself in a truly critical situation. Survey results indicated that provided Japan's power was in ascendance, many among the younger generation would continue to cooperate with the Japanese as they had in the past; if, however, signs emerged that Japanese fortunes were taking a turn for the worse, or that Japan had suffered defeat, they would turn their backs on Japan without hesitation.[75]

Resistance to Japanese rule in the early 1930s also took the form of terrorist attacks and assassination attempts, particularly following the successful Yun Pong-gil Incident in which Yun killed several high-ranking Japanese officials and officers by bombing a celebration event in April 1932 in Shanghai. On the international front, a petition for independence was submitted to the League of Nations; inside Korea, an underground communist movement, comprised mainly of intellectuals, had formed. Influenced by these forms of resistance, students boycotted classes and violated school regulations, causing considerable trouble for the authorities, who attempted to prevent these frequent acts of disobedience. In addition, Syngman Rhee and other leaders continued to pursue independence by diplomatic means. Making the claim that he represented Koreans residing on the peninsula, Manchuria, and in all other parts of the world, Rhee succeeded in April 1934, in submitting a petition for Korean independence to the secretariat of the League of Nations by way of the Chinese delegation. Rhee also predicted to the US consul in Geneva that Korea would be liberated as the result of a war between a powerful country and Japan.[76]

During this period, the communist movement stood at the forefront of the Independence movement in Korea. According to a survey conducted by an American missionary deeply involved at the time in the Korean situation, next to acquiring an education, young people were most interested in socialism. The political attitudes of young people at one high school expressed their political attitudes, at the end of 1932, as follows: 67 percent supported socialism, 4 percent supported communism, 4 percent supported capitalism, 25 percent were undecided. Royds viewed these results as corresponding exactly with his own observations.[77]

Engulfed in World War II, Japan was unable to complete its project of transforming the Korean peninsula into a strategic base of operation. The powers, however, now approached the question of Korean independence differently than they had in the past, with the intention, that is, of defeating Japan and reducing its strength as an insular nation.

CONCLUSION: KOREAN LIBERATION AND INDEPENDENCE

The outbreak of World War II placed the Korean question in a completely different light. While the states combating each other in the war did not of course consider the Korean peninsula to be the direct objective of the struggle, the defeat of Japan would present the opportunity for the liberation and independence of Korea. The issue of Korea was no longer one concerned solely with the peninsula itself, but was not inextricably linked to the postwar realignment of the world order. The post-Liberation division of the peninsula however was not the satisfactory solution of the "Korean question" which Koreans had been yearning for since the annexation. The Allies had heartily supported Koreans in their desire for liberation but hesitated to establish Korea as an independent nation. We see, then, that the "Korean question" of the Japanese Colonial Period cannot be explained simply by recourse to the formulaic evocation of Japan-Korea conflict.

With the war in the Pacific between Japan and the United States becoming linked to the general conflict of World War II, Korea emerged as one of the issues placed under the Allies' consideration. It was the United States, however, which became the party most concerned with the Korean question due to the fact that it was engaging in the war with Japan virtually by itself. Particularly in contrast to the policies of other allies such as Great Britain, China, and the Soviet Union—each in pursuit of its own national interest—US wartime policies assumed a universalistic nature, focusing on such issues as the realignment of the world order and the establishment of a lasting peace settlement. US President Franklin D. Roosevelt's wartime diplomacy provides an example of this, based as it was on the vigorous attempt to establish the United Nations, create multilateral trusteeships, institute collective security arrangements, and achieve cooperation between the four powers: China, Great Britain, the United States, and the Soviet Union. This policy had crucial implications for the handling of the Korean question. The United States adopted such measures as the "Allies common policy" vis-à-vis the issue of Korea; that is, it consulted with and obtained the approval of Great Britain and China (both of which had participated in the war against Japan) before concretizing the policy. At the same time, recognizing that China and the Soviet Union had vital interests at stake in the disposition of the Korean questions, the United States sought to maintain its leadership role in the handling of the matter by involving both of these countries in the process while simultaneously blocking their attempts to achieve hegemony on the peninsula. The participation of China and the Soviet Union allowed the United States to avoid bearing sole responsibility for the settlement of the Korean question. The underlying framework of this policy manifested itself clearly in the notion of a four-power trusteeship.

British and Chinese policies toward Korea are important for the influence they exerted on the formulation of US policy. The policies of these two nations, however, were completely centered on the achievement of their own national interests. Chinese policy represented an attempt to regain the status it had held in the past when it exerted overwhelming and unquestioned influence over the affairs of the peninsula. In order to accomplish this, it was necessary to exclude the Soviet Union from involvement in Korean affairs; should this prove untenable, the Chinese aim was to minimize the role of the Soviet Union to the greatest extent possible by cooperating with the United States. However, at the same time as the United States welcomed Chinese cooperation, it was clear that the Chinese policy itself failed to coincide not only with US plans for the postwar order but also with those of Great Britain and the Soviet Union. The central postwar objective of Great Britain was to maintain control of the British Empire. This stood directly at odds both with the US notion of trusteeship and, unavoidably, with Chinese aspirations. It was important for Great Britain that the dispensation of the Korean question not become an impediment to the management of their own colonial affairs. The British, in other words, did not believe that an early discussion of Korean independence would be favorable to their interests, as they dealt with the situation in India and other British colonies. Due to its treaty of neutrality with Japan, the Soviet Union entered the Pacific War only at its very end and therefore was not invited by the United States to join in discussions regarding the Korean question. The United States, however, acknowledging that the Soviet Union possessed a vital interest in the Korean peninsula, had attempted to include the Soviet Union in the process of formulating policy by sounding out the Soviet view on the peninsula at both Tehran and Yalta. Participation in the war with Japan at the last hour, of course, placed the Soviet Union at center stage in the dispensation of affairs regarding Korea.

The outbreak of war in the Pacific forced the United States to confront the Korean question (even though the issue of Korea was not of central concern in the conflict). The United States had been requested to recognize the Provisional Government of Korea in Chongqing and also had to make a quick decision regarding participation of Koreans in the war against Japan.[78] The State Department, however, approached the matter with care not only due to the inherent complexity of the Korean question but also because making a determination regarding Korea represented a "significant step" involving the simultaneous consideration of other extremely important matters such as the formulation of a strategy for the war in the Pacific and the future arrangement of a postwar peace settlement.[79] At this time, the United States adopted a policy grounded in a multilateral approach to the issue of Korea, one which entailed discussion of the problem with wartime allies such as Great Britain and China. In August 1941, prior to the outbreak of the Pacific War, the US Division of Far Eastern Affairs had directed the US ambassador to China, Clarence E. Gauss, to make "very discreet inquiries" of the Chinese government regarding the Korean organization in Chongqing, the Korean restoration army, and the relations between these entities and the Guomindang.[80] In February of the following year, the United States, informed Great Britain that it felt the need to make "some general statement to the press" regarding US interest in bringing Japanese oppression on the peninsula to an end and requested the British provide an opinion on the matter.[81]

The response of the British and Chinese, however, was negative from the beginning. Gauss reported from Chongqing that less than 200 people were affiliated with or supported the Provisional Government of Korea and that China was "not enthusiastic" about the organization.[82] The British Foreign Office sent the United States a list of nine points outlining the position of the British government on the matter. Among them were the following: (1) factional infighting between Korean independence organizations was severe; (2) the Chinese, emphasizing this factionalism, had determined not to proffer any form of recognition to these organizations unless they resolved their differences; (3) it was impossible for Koreans to conduct anti-Japanese activities in either Korea or Japan; (4) at the present time, general statements regarding Korean independence or recognition of the latter were meaningless because of continuing Japanese military victories, and it was, therefore, (5) better to wait until the war developed in a positive direction; and (6) concerted action was necessary and Chinese concerns regarding the Korean question should be considered.[83]

The US State Department determined that in general the British view of the situation coincided with its own and decided to make no further comments regarding eventual Korean independence until the time came to raise the question of Korea in the context of the general dispensation of colonies in Asia or if and when the Korean Independence movement demonstrated "significant, concrete development." At this time, the US State Department also reaffirmed its position of refusing to recognize a particular organization such as the Provisional Government of Korea on the grounds that it must treat all Korean independence organizations equally.[84] In spite of steady pressure from domestic and international forces, this US policy underwent no alteration until the Cairo Declaration at the close of 1943.

The visit of the British foreign secretary, Anthony Eden, to Washington in March 1943, provided an opportunity for the United States and Great Britain to exchange views regarding the concept of trusteeship and its practical application. Roosevelt proposed to Eden that Korea be placed under a multilateral trusteeship which would include the United States, China, and one or more other countries. Eden responded positively, indicating that the United States and Great Britain were in agreement regarding the Korean question. The United States then explained the joint position it was taking with Great Britain on the matter with China on the occasion of Deputy Foreign Minister Song Ziwen's visit to Washington for the Pacific War Council. The Chinese and the Americans came to a tentative understanding that Korea would be placed in a trusteeship following the war, with both sides agreeing not to comment on the matter for the time being (until the Cairo Conference in November 1943).[85]

In the final analysis, focusing on issues which had been raised time and again in connection with the international relations of the peninsula following the annexation (and, indeed, preceding the annexation) such as Korean's lack of experience in both democratic self-governance and in the administration of a modern nation-state, the powers agreed too readily on trusteeship for Korea. Trusteeship, of course, was a measure to be applied universally in resolving the postwar dispensation of liberated colonies, Korea among them. The evocation of a principle of universal application of trusteeships, however, does not seem to provide in itself an adequate explanation for the United States' attempt to implement the concept of trusteeship in Korea, particularly when we consider that in the process of actually implementing trusteeships worldwide, the following factors came into play: conflict occurred between the United States and Great Britain; the strategic demands of US military planners came to the fore; and regions emerged in which trusteeship was precluded as a viable option due to the onset of the Cold War.

The position of the United States, Great Britain, and China regarding the Korean question was made public at the close of 1943 in the form of the Cairo Declaration. The stance taken by the United States (along with Great Britain and China) concerning Korea in the declaration, however, represented no departure whatsoever from previously existing policy. The US Division of Far Eastern Affairs (which had not been consulted by Roosevelt during the composition of the declaration) interpreted the declaration as indicating that no revision had been made of US State Department policy, including that which had been formulated regarding the Provisional Government of Korea.[86] At this time, of course, US inquiries into the Korean question had led to the conclusion that Korea's lack of experience in self-government, coupled with the likelihood of interference in Korean affairs by powerful nations with conflicting interests in the strategic location of the peninsula, would make the maintenance of independence by Koreans an extremely difficult task without international support. As a means of resolving this situation, the United States proposed that the United Nations guarantee the independence of Korea and that a multinational trusteeship, followed by an interim government, be installed. The United States made it clear that it had no intention of bearing sole responsibility for the settlement of the Korean matter.[87]

The disposition of the Korean question, however, was not announced through a proclamation of the United Nations (which did not yet exist), but by means of a joint Allies declaration signed by the powers invested with de facto authority, the United States, Great Britain, and China. In the Cairo Declaration of December 1, 1943, which followed both the Cairo Conference (November 22–26, 1943) between the United States, Great Britain, and China and the Tehran Conference (November 28–December 1, 1943) between the United States, Great Britain, and the Soviet Union, allied leaders formally proclaimed their wide-ranging postwar objectives, one of which was the granting of independence to Korea "in due course." Prior to the publication of the Cairo Declaration, Stalin (at the Tehran Conference) had affirmed the results of the Cairo Conference (in which he had not participated) by stating that "Korean independence is just and proper."[88] At a meeting of the Pacific War Council on January 12, 1944, Roosevelt stated that he was satisfied that cooperation with the Soviets in the matter was possible because Stalin had given his complete approval of the contents of the Cairo Declaration and had agreed that "the Koreans are not yet capable of exercising and maintaining independent government and that they should be placed under a 40-year tutelage."[89]

The United States made no further attempt to clarify its policy on Korea. While postwar disposition of East Asian affairs was placed on the table at the Yalta conference (February 1945), Roosevelt, excluding Churchill from the discussion, merely reconfirmed with Stalin, through an "oral understanding," the previous agreement concerning Korea. From this point on until the end of the war, US planners generated considerably detailed research reports for internal use concerning approaches to the postwar administration of Korea and the follow-up measures necessary to implement trusteeship. While discussion of these issues continued between the United States, Great Britain, and China, the United States did not confer with its most important counterpart, the Soviet Union, concerning the formulation of specific measures. In both form and content, therefore, the Korean question was able to advance no nearer to a resolution than it had at the time of the Cairo Declaration. It is possible, then, to view the Cairo Conference itself as having had significance for the future of the Korean peninsula as well as for the question of Korean independence. The allies' agreement in Cairo to act in concert regarding Korea prevented China from engaging in unilateral action on the peninsula (the possibility of which had troubled the United States). In addition, when later confronted with Soviet expansionism, the United States was able to invoke Stalin's support of the Cairo Declaration in Tehran as a means of blocking unilateral Soviet domination of Korea.[90]

Regarding the claim of Korean leaders in the Independence movement that the expression "in due course" pointed to the possibility of trusteeship, the US State Department asserted that the phrase was "reasonable when taking into consideration both the Korean situation of the past thirty-five years and the fact that we are in the midst of war."[91] In other words, the expression "in due course" referred to the fact that it would take an indefinite amount of time to defeat the Japanese in war, liberate Korea, and establish a civilian government. In the midst of carrying out the overwhelming task of defeating the Japanese in war, only the broad outlines had been sketched of what amounted to the most pressing and crucial issue of all—the formulation of postwar security arrangements. Given these circumstances, then, the US position was that it was impossible to provide a blueprint delineating the aspects of each issue in perfect detail.[92]

Following these events, the US State Department conducted interdivisional research regarding the Korean question, resulting in the creation of a number of important memoranda. At the same time, the State Department began to confer in earnest with Great Britain, each side responding to the questionnaire of the other in order to formulate a joint approach to the Korean question. In the course of this discussion, both sides generated a considerable number of reports on the postwar political and military aspects of the Korean situation and even on a hypothetical joint military operation in Korea should the war with Japan spill over onto the peninsula. In addition, the United States initiated talks in early 1945 with China regarding the Korean question. The problem, however, was that all of these reports on Korea were written under the supposition that trusteeship was a foregone conclusion. What appears here, then, is first a discussion of Koreans capacity for independence followed by a consideration of what factors would be used to determine the length of time inferred by the phrase "in due course."[93]

The British Foreign Office, delegating the matter to the Korea Committee headed by Professor Arnold Toynbee, responded to the US questionnaire in March 1945, with four reports outlining the British position.[94] With this basic understanding, the United States and Great Britain then approached China on the matter. China, considering the formulation of an agreement between the three countries as constituting a joint position vis-à-vis Soviet policy, quickly accepted the offer of participation and dispatched two experts to Washington in early 1945 to join with the United States and Great Britain in conducting full-scale research into the matter.[95] The British, however, considered the Chinese position that the exchange of opinions between the three countries regarding the Korean question would result in a "common understanding of the three countries to be presented to the Soviet Union" (the so-called A-B-C [America, Britain, China] entente) as "the most dangerous" way of dealing with the Soviets and expressed the view that for its part, the wisest course would be to give up participating in the entente.[96] Following this, informal talks between the United States and China were held in Washington, with representatives from the two countries meeting eleven times between January 24 and February 14, 1945; the Chinese, however, merely sounded out US intentions without presenting any plans of their own.[97] In spite of considerable effort, the attempt of the three countries to formulate a joint approach to the problem failed both because of the structural limitations inherent in working-level research (which are not invested with the power to make policy decisions) and the unexpectedly rapid conclusion of the war. At the close of the war, therefore, the "oral understanding" made between Roosevelt and Stalin at Yalta represented the most recent allied agreement on a guideline of how to proceed in Korea.[98]

In the end, the US State Department assessed its Korea policy as standing "in the best American tradition."[99] In other words, it was a joint policy, one which, in essence, defined itself as attempting to achieve a balance of power between the parties concerned. The United States acknowledged without hesitation the precedence of China (a powerless nation) in the Korean question and included Great Britain (which had no particular interests at stake on the peninsula) in discussions on the matter, since at the time a traditional framework of international relations was established in which the United States was just one of many powerful countries.

The postwar position of the United States in the world order, however, bears no comparison whatsoever with its prewar status. Organizations, which now play a vital role in the formulation of US foreign policy such as the Central Intelligence Agency, the National Security Council, and the Department of Defense, did not exist prior to the war—even the number of personnel working in the US State Department had quadrupled by the end of the war. As the United States redefined its postwar role to meet the polarization brought on by the Cold War, revision of policies formulated in the prewar period was unavoidable. This manifested itself in the division of Korea. We end here with one question: Was "the capacity of Koreans for independence" really at the center of US consideration when it discussed Korean question with the Allies or was it merely an excuse for the imposition of the US postwar plan of trusteeship?

NOTE ON SOURCES

All the sources used in this chapter come from their original sources. British documents on foreign policy are cited as follows: recipient to sender, date / FO (Foreign Office) / classification number/ file number / document number. Foreign Office (FO) materials are kept in Public Record Office (National Archives), Kew Garden, London. US documents are cited as follows: sender to recipient (or document title), date, classification number, volume, document number (or page number). Documents on microfilm are cited as follows: sender to recipient (or document title), date, microfilm classification number/roll number (page range). US materials are kept at the National Archives and Records Administration (NARA), in Washington, DC. The designations M and ML refer to microfilm series in NARA.

NOTES

Parts of this chapter have been reprinted with permission from the *Korea Journal*. See Daeyeol Ku, "Korean International Relations in the Colonial Period and the Question of Independence," *Korea Journal* 38, no. 4 (Winter, 1998): 90–129.

1. The term "great powers" (*yŏlgang*) is normally used to refer to powerful nations involved in issues of central importance affecting a region. In this chapter however, I

The British and American Perceptions of Korea during the Colonial Period 213

use the expression to refer to the United States and Great Britain, the two nations outside the Asian region possessing the capability of exerting significant influence on East Asian politics during the Colonial Period. Other powerful nations such as Germany, France, and the Soviet Union were preoccupied with European matters and had little at stake in East Asia at the time.

2. For an overview on the question of knowledge in social sciences, see "Maurice Duverger, *An Introduction to the Social Sciences*; William A. Dairty, *International Encyclopedia of the Social Sciences*, 64; and Peter T. Manicas, *A History and Philosophy of the Social Sciences*, 261–65. In this chapter, the words "perception" and "cognition" are not strictly distinguished nor qualified but are generally addressed as perception.

3. For the British view of Korea during this period, see Dae-Yeol Ku [Daeyeol Ku; Dae Yeol Ku], *Korea under Colonialism*, 77–80. For the United States view, see Raymond A. Esthus, *Theodore Roosevelt and Japan*, 7, 39, 96–100, and 110–11; and Fred H. Harrington, *God, Mammon, and the Japanese*, 96–98 and 326. For the comparison of the Korean monarch and those of other oriental empires, see Dae Yeol Ku, *Korea under Colonialism*, 25; and Ian H. Nish, "Korea between Japan and Russia, 1900–1904," 186.

4. Raymond A. Esthus, *Theodore Roosevelt and Japan*, 110; James E. Dougherty and Robert L. Pfaltzgraff, *American Foreign Policy: FDR to Reagan*, 9–10. For the British appraisal, see "Jordan to Lansdowne," January 20, 1904, FO/17/1659 (17) and its enclosure.

5. "Minutes on Cockburn to Grey," May 15, 1906, FO/371/179 (22706/306); and "Lansdowne to MacDonald," September 26, 1905, FO/46/590 (151).

6. "Jordan to Grey," November 16, 1914, FO/371/2018 (83412/35445). Jordan repeated this warning in 1919. See "Jordan to Cuzon," September 5, 1919, *Documents on British Foreign Policy* (DBFP), First Series, Vol. 6: 731.

7. Harley Farnesworth MacNair and Donald F. Lach, *Modern Eastern International Relations*, 151.

8. "Reinsch to SS," January 23, 1915, *Foreign Relations of the United States* (FRUS), 79–80 and 85–86.

9. "Rumbold to Grey," December 5, 1912, FO/371/1390 (55167/37637).

10. "Sommerville to MacDonald," September 11, 1911, FO/371/1140 (42466/2370).

11. "Draft Agreement proposed by the Japanese Government," July 28, 1911, FO/371/1140 (29759/1827).

12. Ibid.

13. "Lay to Grey," February 7, 1911, FO/371/1142 (9244/9244); and February 22, 1911, FO/371/1136 (10188/138). For the US report, see "Conditions in Chosen, Scidmore to SS," May 1, 1913, M426, R.2, 895.00/555.

14. "Lay to Grey," February 22, 1911, FO/371/1136 (10188/138).

15. "Lay to Rumbold," July 24, 1911, FO/371/1144 (33591/33591).

16. "Greene to Grey," October 10, 1916, FO/371/2694 (234308/185538).

17. "Wheeler to SS," October 21, 1916, M426, R.3, 895.001/2; and "Greene to Grey," October 17, 1916, FO/371/2694 (234314/234324).

18. "Memorandum on Korea's relations with China, Russia, and Japan," May 20, 1919, FO/371/4379 (PID, 435).

19. For a discussion of this incident, see Kuksap'yŏnch'an Wiwŏnhoe ed., *Hanminjok tongnip undonsa charyojip I–105 in sagŏn kongp'an simalso* [One hundred and five persons incident trials: Materials of the history of the Korean Independence movement]. For a contemporaneous perspective, see *The Conspiracy Case in Chosen*.

20. "Japan, Annual Report, 1912," January 1, 1913, FO/371/1666 (7834/7535).

21. "Japan Annual Report, 1912," FO/371/1666 (7834/7835); and "MacDonald to Grey," August 2, 1912, FO/371/1388 (135539/10684).

22. "Green to Grey," April 25, 1913, FO/371/1168 (21904/21904).

23. "Bonar to MacDonald," February 2, 1912, FO/371/1388 (10689/10689); "MacDonald to Grey," February 2, 1912; and "FO to Board of Trade," April 15, 1912, FO/371/1388 (10689/10689).

24. "Green to Grey," January 16, 1917, FO/371/2952 (40718/40718) and minutes.

25. The American historian William Langer, head of the Research and Analysis Branch, Office of Strategic Services, that "organized resistance in Korea began in 1919 with the March First movement." See "The Korean Independence movement" April 25, 1942, LM79, R.1, 895.01/60–21/26. Arnold Toynbee, chairman of the Korean Committee in the British Foreign Office, emphasized the significance of the March First movement and the subsequent establishment of the Korean Provisional Government in several memoranda discussing the future of Korea, September 2, 1944, FO/371/41813 (990/443/23); and "Korea's Capacity for Independence," February 14, 1945, FO/371/46468 (2330/1394/23).

26. "Memo by SS of a Conversation with the Japanese Ambassador," August 18, 1921, FRUS, 1921, Vol. 1: 616; and "SS to Schurman," September 19, 1921, FRUS, 1921, Vol. 1: 619–21.

27. "Curzon to Alston," July 22, 1919, DBFP, First series, Vol. 6: 634.

28. "Minutes on Earl K. Paik to Lloyd George," April 4, 1919, FO/371/3817 (54904/7293).

29. "Royds to Greene," March 29, 1919, FO/371/3817 (68041/7293).

30. "Alston to Curzon," May 5, 1919, FO/371/3817 (71169/7293).

31. "Memorandum on Japanese policy in Corea," July 5, 1919, FO/371/3818 (10671/7293).

32. "Curzon to Alston," July 22, 1919, FO/371/3818 (100885/7293).

33. "Alston to Curzon," November 27, 1919, FO/371/3818 (166709/7293).

34. "FO to Buxton," August 12, 1920, FO/371/5252 (1753/56/23).

35. Frank Baldwin, "The March First Movement," 128.

36. Ibid.,132.
37. "Bergholz to SS," 1919.1.29, FRUS, 1919, Vol 2: 458–59.
38. "SS to Morris," April 12, 1919, M426, R. 2, 895.00/595; and FRUS, 1919, Vol 2: 462.
39. "Memorandum of conversation with the Japanese chargé d'affaires," July 3, 1919, M426, R. 2, 895.00/film page 406–407.
40. See "First Korean Congress, held in the Little Theatre, Philadelphia, 1919," M426, R. 3, 895.000/647.
41. See Tonga ilbosa ed., *3.1 undong 50 chunyŏn kinyŏm nonjip* [Collection of articles in commemoration of the fiftieth anniversary of the March First movement], 544–45.
42. "Korea, Annual Report, 1929," FO/371/14755 (1538/1534/23).
43. "Miller to SS," June 12, 1926, M426, R.6, 895.44Yi/1.
44. "Miller to SS," August 20, 1929, M426, R.3, 895.001/15.
45. "Korea, Annual Report, 1928," FO/371/13967 (6787/994/23); and "White to Domer," April 27, 1928, FO/371/13247 (3019/189/23).
46. "Korea Annual Report, 1924," January 6, 1925, FO/371/10065 (1873/1873/23).
47. Pamphlet enclosed in "FO to Lampson," March 12, 1920, FO/371/5351 (138/56/23).
48. "FO to Lampson," March 12, 1920, FO/371/5351 (138/56/23).
49. "G.C. Hanson to SS," April 5, 1923, M.426, R.5, 895.20293.
50. "Eliot to Chamberlain," January 29, 1925, FO/371/10963 (775/273/23).
51. For a discussion of this incident, see Pak Yongsŏk, *Manbosan sagŏn yŏn'gu* [Study of the Manbosan incident].
52. "Lindley to Simon," May 21, 1932, FO/371/16248 (4914/2931/23).
53. "Kermode to Craigie," May 23, 1939, FO/371/23566 (7895/817/23).
54. "Davis to SS," February 9, 1931, LM78, R.2, 895.56/org.
55. "Linsay to Henderson," June 16, 1931, DBFP, Second Series, Vol. 8: 635; "Memorandum Respecting Sino-Japanese Relations," September 19, 1931, DBFP, Second Series, Vol. 8: 662.
56. Davis Bergamini, *Japan's Imperial Conspiracy*, 426.
57. "David to SS," July 7, 1932, LM78, R.1, 895.156/1.
58. "Davis to SS," September 2, 1932, LM78, R. 1, 895.156/3.
59. "Phipps to Clive," November 5, 1936, FO/371/20264 (7833/616/10).
60. "Phipps to Clive," November 5, 1936, FO/371/20264/ (7883/616/10). The British Foreign Office concluded that Minami's policies emphasized "'strategic' rather than 'colonial' considerations." See "Annual Report, Korea, 1936," FO/371/21042 (1241/1241/23); and "Minutes of Annual Report, Korea, 1936," FO/371/21042 (1241/1241/23).
61. "Cowley to Clive," November 13,1934, FO/371/18185 (7554/640/23); "March to SS," May 6, 1938, LM78, R.1, 895.00/724; and August 25, 1938, LM78, R.2, 895.5017/1.

62. "Annual Report, Korea, 1935," FO/371/20289 (900/900/23).

63. "Minutes of the Division of Far Eastern Affairs," December 26, 1935, LM78, R.1, 895.42/37.

64. "Annual Report, Korea, 1931," FO/371/16245 (739/202/23).

65. "Phipps to Clive," January 1, 1936, FO/371/20289 (900/900/23).

66. "Cowley to Clive," November 10, 1934, FO/371/19349 (35/35/23).

67. "Ward to FO," November 16, 1921, FO/371/6706 (4215/2905/23) and minutes.

68. Malcom D. Kennedy, *The Estrangement of Great Britain and Japan 1917–35*, 37.

69. "Davis to SS," July 31, 1935, LM78, R.1, 895.01/41.

70. "Kermode to Craigie," December 7, 1938, FO/371/23566 (817/817/23); and May 17, 1939, FO/371/23566 (7895/817/23).

71. "Marsh to SS," May 6, 1938, LM78, R.1, 895.00/724.

72. "Kermode to Craigie," December 7, 1938, FO/371/23566 (817/817/23).

73. "Memorandum by Langdon," February 20, 1942, LM79, R.1, 895.01/79.

74. "Annual Report, Korea, 1931," FO/371/16245 (739/202/23).

75. "Annual Report, Korea, 1934," FO/371/19361 (1110/1110/23).

76. "Gilbert to SS," April 28, 1933, LM78, R.1, 895.00/718. See also February 9, 1933, 895.01/36.

77. "Annual Report, Korea, 1932," FO/371/171758 (764/744/23).

78. "Cromwell to Hull," May 5, 1942, LM79, R. 1, 895.01/123.

79. "Memo for the President," April 23, 1942, LM79, R. 1, 895.01/96.

80. "SS to Gauss," August 18, 1941, LM79, R. 1, 895.01/54.

81. "SS to Winant," February 12, 1942, LM79, R. 1, 895.01/68a.

82. "Gauss to SS," January 3, 1942, LM79, R. 1, 895.01/56.

83. "Mathews to SS," February 28, 1942, LM79, R.1, 895.01/73.

84. "DFEA Memo," April 1, 1942 LM79, R.1, 895.01/88.

85. "Memo of Conversation by SS," March 27, 1943, FRUS, 1943, Vol. 3: 37.

86. "DFEA Memo," December 2, 1943, LM79, R.2, 895.01/301.

87. "Problems of Korean independence," PG–32, October 2, 1943, RG59, Box 119; "Possible Soviet attitudes toward far eastern questions," PG–28, October 2, 1943, RG59, Box 119; and "Sino-Russian problems in the post-war settlement," October 4, 1943, PG–34, RG59, Box 119.

88. "Memo of luncheon conversation among Roosevelt, Churchill and Stalin," November 30, 1943, FRUS, Conferences at Cairo and Tehran, 1943, 566.

89. "Memo of luncheon conversation among Roosevelt, Churchill, and Stalin," November 30, 1943, FRUS, Conferences at Cairo and Tehran, 1943; and "Minutes on Pacific War Council," January 12, 1944, FRUS, Conferences at Cairo and Tehran, 1943, 869.

90. "Soviet support of the Cairo Declaration," June 29, 1945, FRUS, Conferences at Berlin, 1945, Vol 1: 926–28 and 310–11.

91. "Salisbury to Show," December 27, 1943, LM79, R.2, 895.01/304.
92. "Gauss to SS," May 19, 1944, LM79, R.2, 895.01/338.
93. "Questionnaire on Korea," April 18, 1944, FO/371/40798 (4320/4320/70).
94. The four reports were: (1) "The Achievements and Failures of the Japanese Administration in Korea"; (2) "Korea's Capacity for Independence"; (3) "Economic Conditions in Korea and Future Problems"; and (4) "Korean Committees Abroad." See "Toynbee to Gore-Booth," April 19, 1945, FO/371/46471 (2670/1653/23).
95. "Gauss Memo of Conversation with T.V. Soong," September 26, 1944, LM79, R.2, 895.01/8–1644; and "Memo of Conversation," November 29, 1944, 895.01/12–1344 supplement.
96. "Seymour to Eden," January 20, 1945, FO/371/50806 (482/189/70).
97. "Memo of conversation by Ballentine," February 17, 1945, 1022; and "James C. Dunn (Acting SS) to Hurley," February 20, 1945, FRUS, 1945, Vol 6: 1022–23.
98. SWNCC-176, "Draft Memo to the Joint Chiefs of Staff," (undated: 1945. 8.22?), FRUS, 1945, Vol. 6: 1038 and 1040.
99. Division of Historical Policy Research US Department of State, *United States Policy Regarding Korea 1834–1950*, 87.

7
Russian Perception of Koreans and the Japanese Colonial Regime in Korea during the First Quarter of the Twentieth Century

SERGEY O. KURBANOV

Russia possesses a unique geo-cultural position, situated directly between Europe and Asia. Since the second half of the nineteenth century, the Russian Far East has attracted attention from the populations of its three neighboring countries—China, Korea, and Japan. At the turn of the twentieth century, many migrants from these three countries settled in the Russian Far Eastern Primorye Province. Koreans were the most numerous among them. Migration of East Asians to the Russian Far East became an urgent problem for local authorities. At the beginning of the twentieth century, after Japanese colonization of Korea, Russian Empire authorities undertook several investigations in the Russian Far East to learn more about the problems presented by Korean immigration to Russia.[1] These investigations compared Korean immigrants with those from China and Japan. At the heart of the researchers' interests was how Japanese colonization particularly urged Korean immigration to Russia.

THE RUSSIAN VIEW OF KOREA DURING THE JAPANESE PROTECTORATE PERIOD

Korea Just Before the Japanese Protectorate Treaty

The two or three years before Korea began to lose her independence in 1905 had a significant effect on Koreans' attitudes toward the Japanese. It is important to note that these attitudes were not always negative, especially among educated Koreans.

Immediately after signing the Kanghwa Treaty in 1876, many groups of Korean officials and intellectuals visited Japan to study Japanese modernization.² Kim Okkyun established the Kaehwadang (Party of reforms) and planned a coup d'état in close connection with the Japanese political elite. Russian records describing the situation in Korea just before and after the Japanese Protectorate Treaty indicate the partial support of the Japanese protectorate by Koreans. The last director of the Russian Orthodox Church Mission in Seoul wrote in his book, published in 1926 in Harbin,

> [After the Russo-Japanese War] Korea as a state lost her independence; the Korean government was close to being nonexistent, though from the formal point of view it was still in power, headed by its emperor. Life in the country had changed greatly and began "to flow as another river-bed." Koreans, though it may seem quite strange, *sympathized at that time with the Japanese and hoped that their leadership would bring changes leading to a better life.* [Italics added]. This attitude lasted for at least three or four years after the newcomers [Japanese] had appeared [in Korea]. But later came disillusionment regarding the Japanese, and [this attitude] transformed into hostility, which was displayed in the form of open uprisings in 1919–20 and in other anti-Japanese protests.³

It is clear that just before and after the Japanese proclaimed their protectorate over Korea, there were some Koreans who sincerely believed Japan to be a nation friendly to Korea.

Russian military researcher Piotr (Peter) Rossov discovered that many Korean organizations, which later became patriotic and anti-Japanese, were founded in the early 1900s as organizations that wished to learn about the Japanese experience of modernization and to follow the Japanese example in Korea. Thus, P. Rossov writes that in 1904, Koreans founded the Poanhoe (Society for keeping tranquility). At first, the Japanese thought this society had been founded to keep Koreans quiet and to suppress their displeasure about the "law by Nagamori," a law that stated that all free land and forests in Korea should be transferred to the Japanese, but the Japanese soon discovered that the Poanhoe encouraged anti-Japanese activities, and Government-General officials closed it within its first year of operation.

In February of 1904, a few Koreans founded the Hŏnpŏp Yŏn'guhoe (Society for research constitution). The society officially proclaimed that its aim was to study the Japanese constitution and to introduce the Japanese administration system to Korea, but in reality the society studied Japanese laws in order to use them as a means to resist growing Japanese influence. At the same time, history has revealed that the Hŏnpŏp Yŏn'guhoe had some two-faced members. After signing the Protectorate Treaty on November 17, 1905, the former head of the society, Kim Jonkan, left his post and moved to pro-Japanese organizations.[5]

The Kei Kyo Saenmyeonhoe (Society of self-education and personal inviolability) was established in May of 1905. It was an open society and had been originally formed to protect Koreans from social arbitraries, including arbitraries coming from the Japanese. Eventually society members separated into three groups: (1) opponents to the Japanese, (2) those only searching for personal benefits, and (3) pro-Japanese agents.[6]

Even the pro-Japanese society most hated by Koreans, Ilchinhoe, was not able to avoid duality. The Ilchinhoe was formed in August of 1904 by Jo Heeyoon, a former Korean military minister who escaped to Japan in 1894, accepted Japanese citizenship, and remained in Japan until 1904.[7] In 1905, the society had around 50,000 members, among whom were some who belonged to the Tonghak movement. After signing the Protectorate Treaty on November 17, 1905, some of the members of the Ilchinhoe issued proclamations of protest against the Protectorate Treaty.[8] This act of defiance is where Japanese displeasure and conflicts with the Ilchinhoe began.

According to Russian records, in the early 1900s, the Korean reaction to the strengthening of Japanese colonial policy toward the Korean peninsula was very complicated. Some strata of Korean society supported it, believing it may help Korean modernization. Others protested the changes, while some maintained dual and contradictory positions.

Korea during the Early Protectorate Period

Korean attitudes toward the Japanese began to change soon after the signing of the Protectorate Treaty on November 17, 1905, which was followed by the enactment of Japanese policies over Korea. In the beginning, Koreans continued to camouflage their anti-Japanese activities so they could look as neutral—or even as pro-Japanese—as possible.

According to Rossov, at the end of 1906, a Canadian missionary opened a branch of the Young Men's Christian Association (YMCA) in Seoul.[9] Bit by bit, young Koreans who visited this association began to discuss some political issues. Later, this group of politically active young people established their own organization, which they named the Ch'ŏngnyŏnhoe (Young Men's Association, YMA). The YMA membership in the early 1900s was 80,000 strong, according to YMA records.[10] As a result, Japanese authorities were quite confused at first and could not distinguish between the YMA and the YMCA; they could not determine which one was the original group, and which one needed to be terminated. According to Russian military research records, in the first few years after the signing of the Protectorate Treaty, Koreans appeared to be calm and peaceful. Instead, under masks of calmness, they harbored hatred for the Japanese.[11] Russian officer P. Rossov noticed this prior to 1905, when Koreans had twice attempted to kill Itō Hirobumi (who later became the first Japanese resident-general of Korea). The first attempt was when Itō was riding a train and someone threw a stone at the window of his car. The second attempt took place during talks at the Korean emperor's palace. In this second attempt, one of the guards shot at Itō. The soldier was arrested and claimed to be insane. In prison, the soldier refused to eat and died on his sixth day in captivity.[12]

Another interesting observation made by Rossov is related to Korean anti-Japanese activists who called themselves the ŭipyŏng (righteous army). He wrote that educated Koreans regarded these activists in a negative way; they considered them a "product of the ignorant and fanatic masses of the population" and did not believe them capable of becoming a serious resistance power for a national movement.[13]

We can see that according to the Russian view of the first years of the Protectorate Period, Koreans did not share a united perception of Japanese policy with regards to the Korean peninsula and therefore had no common idea as to what to do. They could either struggle against the Japanese or partially support Japanese policies. This is why it was not easy for Koreans to fashion a united anti-Japanese front that could have been able to effectively resist Japanese colonial policy over Korea.

P. Rossov wrote that according to the opinion of educated Japanese, Korea would lose her independence after twenty years, but Korea lost her independence within just five years.[14] Due to lack of unity, Koreans were unable to fight against the Japanese. According to the reports by Russian diplomats, it was only Emperor Kojong who tried to fight against Japanese attempts to annex Korea. Russian Consulate General G. A. Planson, stationed in Seoul, stated in 1906 that "while all former friends have turned aside from [the] Korean Emperor, he continues his fight [for independence] all alone,"[15] but even Kojong, after having been dismissed by the Japanese in 1907, lost all hope for keeping Korea independent and planned his escape from Korea to Russia.[16]

In 1910, former Emperor Kojong wrote to Russian Emperor Nicholas II that "Japanese treatment toward Korea is not that of a country as being part of a protectorate, not as to that of a conquered colony but as to that of an enslaved country . . . so my people and I, we hope that someday you will liberate us from this hateful yoke."[17] Seeing no hope for his future in Korea, Kojong planned to escape to Russia. "He [Kojong] hopes to cross the Russian border and to be safe in Vladivostok."[18] In the middle of 1910, Russian diplomat Goyer wrote that "in Korea nobody doubts that annexation of Korea is a matter of the nearest future, or that this will cause new uprisings all throughout the country."[19]

THE RUSSIAN VIEW OF THE JAPANESE COLONIZATION OF KOREA

Reasons for Japanese Colonization

The first decade of the twentieth century is usually viewed as a time of Japanese aggression and Korean resistance toward Japanese colonial policy, but this is a modern evaluation of the process of Japan's colonization of Korea, from the hindsight point of view of a liberated Korea and a Japan that was defeated during World War II.[20] The Korean perception of Japanese influence on Korea at the time of colonization, however, was significantly different from the modern view and quite complicated.

In the early 1910s, Russian specialists in Korea studies performed their own evaluations of Japanese colonial rule. First, let us look at how Russians explained Japanese colonization of Korea in the early 1910s. The famous Russian Koreanologist of the early twentieth century, N. V. Kuehner, witnessed several reasons for Japanese colonization of Korea. First of all, Korea's geographical position would be a powerful resource—situated between two rival nations, China and Japan. In addition, for several centuries Korea had served as a bridge over which Chinese culture had been channeled to Japan. And in the nineteenth and twentieth centuries, European culture was transferred to Korea via Japan. Historically, Korea seemed to lack her own cultural originality, which must be why, Kuehner supposes, it appeared to have always been under another country's domination.[21] Kuehner goes on to state that in addition to the circumstances above, there were other reasons for Korea being dominated by Japan. For example, Japan had recently adopted European methods of colonial policy. There had been a surplus from the rapidly growing industry in Japan, and Japan had the means (increasing military power) necessary for colonizing Korea.[22]

According to N. V. Kuehner, the aforementioned colonial intentions of Japan were restrained for a period of time by Russia and some European countries, but Russian activities—that had resulted in the defeat of Russia in the Russo-Japanese War—simultaneously restrained Japan from her colonial activities while it sped up the colonization of Korea.[23]

TRANSFORMATION OF THE RUSSIAN VIEW ON THE CHARACTER OF JAPANESE COLONIZATION

In this section we look at the following questions: How did Russians evaluate the Japanese colonization of Korea? And how did Russian views on colonization change after the annexation of Korea in 1910 and the continuation of colonial rule during the 1920s and the 1930s?

The Russian View of the Japanese Colonization of Korea in the Early 1910s

The Vladivostok-based Russian Koreanologist professor N. V. Kuehner saw Japanese colonization of Korea in a dualistic way and evaluated both the negative and positive aspects. At times, it appeared that Kuehner's positive perception of Japanese colonization predominated over the negative.

Kuehner believed that if it were possible to smooth the friction and conflicts between the Japanese and the Korean people the "benefits of the new political situation of the country [meaning the benefits from colonization] would fall on the Korean population too, not only on the Japanese."[24] Kuehner continued, stating that the "interests of the Koreans themselves" are not in question because, even before colonization, no neighboring country of

Korea, including Japan, ever took into account Korean interests. He concluded that for Japan, Korea is the best of her colonies, because Korea is rich in natural resources and possesses high cultural value.[25]

Professor Kuehner noted that in Russian and European literature one can find discussion and contradictory opinions concerning the facts of the Japanese colonization of Korea, but all of these discussions originated from limited knowledge about the real situation in Korea and from a lack of information about Korean geographical and economic positions.[26] Describing the population of Korea, Kuehner informs readers of the Japanese theory of common roots shared by the Japanese and Korean languages, a theory advanced by Japanese scientist Kanazawa Shosaburo. Kuehner does not criticize this theory but rather silently accepts the idea of Korean and Japanese people sharing common roots.

When introducing the economic situation in Korea in the early 1910s, Kuehner described only the country's agriculture, as though in Korea there was no industrial production. It is interesting to look at how Kuehner evaluated the Japanese agricultural colonization policy. On June 17, 1904, when Japanese authorities proposed to the Korean government that they give all uncultivated lands in Korea to Japan, this proposal resulted in a storm of Korean protests. Nevertheless on August 27, 1908, Japan established the Oriental Colonization Company, whose aim was "to develop natural resources" and "to improve agriculture in Korea."[27] The Japanese began to build their "clean, white" houses, and relations between the Japanese and the Koreans in the countryside were much friendlier than in the cities.[28] In regards to Koreans losing their lands to the Japanese, Kuehner writes that "Koreans are fully responsible for that because they sold their land to the Japanese not thinking about tomorrow."[29]

Furthermore, Kuehner found another positive result of the first few years of Japanese colonization of Korea. He wrote that the peasants of Northern Cholla Province learned new modes of intensive labor and accepted innovative agricultural methods and instruments from the Japanese. It was the Japanese who repaired and even built new irrigation facilities in Korea. The Japanese established a special organization responsible for developing Korean agriculture—the Chōsen Nokaiho (Chōsen agricultural association). Soon Koreans, following this pattern, began to establish their own Korean agricultural organizations throughout the countryside.

In 1911, a correspondent of the Russian newspaper *Dalyokaya okraina* (Distant outskirts)–a Russian Korean, Kim Man Gyem–described the newly colonized Korea in a way very similar to professor Kuehner:

> Koreans themselves voluntarily have sold to the Japanese their real estate property, and now they have to live on the streets. . . . Wherever Japanese appear, one always can see cleanliness, tidiness, and work in full swing. . . . Only representatives of the old government . . . live good . . . even better than before. . . . Poor, long-suffering Korean people have lost all of their property . . . and die out under the suppression of fresh foreign energy.[30]

This relatively positive (but nearly neutral) perception of Japanese colonial rule in Korea can only be found in Russian works published in the first years after the merge of Korea and Japan. Later, when the character of Japanese colonial rule in Korea began to transform, and the Koreans themselves realized their situation under Japanese rule, the Russian view on Japanese colonial policy over Korea began to change.

THE RUSSIAN VIEW OF JAPANESE COLONIZATION OF KOREA FROM THE MID-1910s TO THE EARLY 1920s

After two or three years of Japanese colonial rule, Russians began to describe the situation in colonial Korea more and more critically. A Russian reporter, Ermolenko, who worked for the *Kharbinskiĭ vestnik* (Harbin bulletin), wrote the following about colonial Korea in 1913,

> [t]he railway system in Korea [built by the Japanese] is very good. And the degree of freedom for a foreigner in Korea in 1913, if you compare with 1911, became much higher. Northern lands of Korea look much more deserted than they were before. [Ermolenko explains this fact by Korean emigration from the North]. It is very difficult to predict the results of the Japanese policy in Korea because in the districts populated with foreigners, Japanese authorities try to make the impression that their attitude toward Koreans is good. But this impression is false. It is impossible to say anything about the future assimilation of the Koreans and the Japanese, because the Japanese

think themselves to be higher than Koreans. And Koreans hate the Japanese and there will be no "mixed" marriages, which are necessary for real assimilation. It is absolutely impossible to see a Korean peacefully speaking with a Japanese person. Even on trains Koreans and Japanese take seats on opposite sides.[31]

Koreans hated the Japanese not only because the Japanese government system suppressed Korea but also because of the way Koreans were treated by the Japanese. The Korean nation was beaten not only by the Japanese but also by the Europeans and the Russians. During this period in Korea, the Korean people appeared to be lazy, but this was not true regarding the national character of Koreans. Ermolenko had observed Korean houses in the Russian Ussuriysk region. They were big, clean, and had an interesting architectural style. It was impossible to compare them with the poor Korean houses in colonized Korea. The colonial Koreans only acted lazy, according to Ermolenko, because they had no reason to work hard; all the results of their work would just be taken away by the Japanese or the Korean landlords.[32]

By 1913, Japanese culture had a significant influence over Korea. First, Japan's newly adopted European culture was being brought to Korea. Second, the dominance of the Japanese language was spreading and became a required subject in Korean schools. Even highly educated Korean women liked to use the Japanese language in their everyday life. At the same time, common Korean people disapproved of the Japanese language and did not learn it. Korean traditions were preserved with little or no change. Basically, Ermolenko did not believe that in the nearest future Koreans would be assimilated by Japanese.[33]

The March First movement in 1919 changed the Russian perception of colonial Korea, so for a long time there were very few positive remarks about Japanese colonial rule. It was obvious that the Koreans did not want the Japanese to rule their country anymore and had called for absolute independence. In 1919, Russian Consul General Ya. Ya. Lyutsh sent several reports to the Russian ambassador in Japan describing the situation in Seoul during March of that year.[34]

THE RUSSIAN VIEW OF JAPANESE COLONIZATION DURING THE MID-1920s THROUGH THE EARLY 1930s

The Russian perception of colonial Korea changed once again in the mid-1920s. The significant transformation of the Russian perception toward colonial Korea starting in the mid-1920s through to the early 1930s can be explained by the following historical events: (1) the end of the Russian Civil War (1917–23), which culminated in the establishment of the Union of Soviet Socialist Republics (USSR) in 1922 and the opening of the Soviet Consulate General in Seoul in 1924; and (2) the transformation of *mudan t'ongch'i* (militarism policy) in Korea to *munhwa t'ongch'i* (cultural policy) after the March First movement. These two events resulted in heightened attention to the revolutionary movement in Korea and a temporary return to positive evaluations of Japanese colonial rule by some independent Russian professors in the mid-1920s.

Thus, in 1926, the new Soviet Consul General Toregeldy Sharmanov, wrote about the revolutionary movement in Seoul, which involved the funeral preparations for the last emperor of Korea, King Sunjong. Sharmanov evaluated the Korean trade and peasant unions as "understanding the tasks of the class revolutionary struggle."[35] On the other hand, Sharmanov saw the main field of activities of the Japanese governor-general in the liquidation of the national liberation movement of Koreans.

Simultaneously, Russian professor P. Yu. Schmidt, who visited Korea during the year 1926–27, presented in his travel records a dual-character description of Korea. Schmidt's view on Korea was different from the Soviet people, officials, etc., because he had visited Korea before and had written a book about Korea, which was neutral and contained no revolutionary theories.[36] This former Russian Empire professor continued to look at Korea with no ideological filters. Schmidt's kind of non-ideological analysis of historical events in the mid-1920s was possible because from 1921 to 1928, Soviet Russia had executed its so-called new economic policy based on involving market mechanisms and allowing limited political pluralism. This is why Schmidt's perception of Korea contains some special and very interesting commentary.

P. Yu. Schmidt wrote that the Japanese annexation of Korea was not a result of a "free-will" agreement between the Korean Emperor and Japan but was the inevitable result of the Russian defeat in the Russo-Japanese War in

1905.³⁷ Since that time, Korea changed dramatically. Korea began to lose her national peculiarities and accept American-European culture. Also, the Japanese people began to dominate the population of Korea. Japanese agriculturalists introduced artificial irrigation to Korea, and the Japanese began planting forests in the Korean mountains. A Japanese chemical engineer, Okida, who accompanied Schmidt during his visit to Seoul, told Schmidt that Koreans "are primitive and lazy and cannot achieve a higher cultural level without outside help."³⁸ Schmidt did not argue with this observation. While traveling through Korea, Schmidt discovered Korean factories and other evidence of new Korean industry, which had not been possible to see in Korea a quarter of a century before. The center of Seoul had taken on a very Europeanized look, but the suburbs of Seoul were still poor and dirty. At the end of his description of mid-1920s Korea, Schmidt asked the question, "Will Korea flourish in the future and become a new cultural center at the outskirts of Asia, as the Japanese dream, or will she have to overcome hard and stormy times?"³⁹ Schmidt gave no answer to this question; he only pointed to the Koreans' constrained protests and hatred for their conquerors. This classic Soviet description of Korea in the mid-1930s reflects the traditional Marxist class and revolutionary approach, which began to appear in the 1920s and gained strength during the 1930s with the institution of Stalinism. Soviet mariner Maks Polyanovsky, who visited Pusan on New Year's Day in 1936, saw Korea in a different way.

> Pusan was dirty. But the center of the city was paved and had a lot of illumination, trams, cars, and restaurants. Koreans wandering along the streets were like shadows; they felt like immigrants in their own land. It was not common to see Koreans in Pusan. They were all silent and secluded. What happened to the Korean population? Most of them were now peasants who had lost their land and were working for landlords. Industry in Korea was not yet developed. Recently, because of the crisis, half of all Korean workers had lost their jobs. Korea had a lot of diseases. Japanese spies were everywhere. So the "land of morning calm" changed into a "land of grave silence." But Korean workers and peasants began to declare their rights more and more, and soon their voices would be heard. The Japanese were not able to suppress the growing Korean revolutionary movement led by the Japanese Communist party.⁴⁰

After describing this hard situation in colonial Korea, Polyanovsky wrote that in the Ussuriysk region of the Soviet Union, Koreans were living happily, and all their needs were met. They were allowed to teach their children in Korean, while back in their homeland, the Korean language was prohibited. Polyanovsky also discusses his conversation with a Korean dock worker who said that he hoped that in the future Korea would become a Soviet country.[41]

Thus one can see that Soviet records describing the Korea of the early 1930s are ideologically colored and concentrated on class struggle, world revolution, and the future construction of socialism throughout the world. This prism of ideology does not allow us to find a neutral view of Korea under Japanese colonial rule in the early 1930s.

Japanese colonization of Korea was more than domestic; it was a large-scale international process, one which had a tremendous influence on neighboring countries. One of the manifestations of such influence was the growing emigration of Koreans to surrounding countries, one of which was the Soviet Union. So by studying the problems of Koreans in the USSR during the period of Japanese colonization of Korea, we can observe another point of view of colonial Korea.

THE KOREAN QUESTION IN THE RUSSIAN FAR EAST DURING THE PERIOD OF THE JAPANESE PROTECTORATE AND THE COLONIAL PERIOD

The Korean question in the Russian Far East became an actual issue for Russian internal and external policies at the end of the nineteenth century. One of the most interesting materials regarding this issue is the monograph (with "top secret" printed on the cover) prepared by Lieutenant V. D. Pesotsky and published in Khabarovsk in 1913. The book introduced the results of a Russian government expedition sent to the Russian Far East in 1909 to study the so-called *yellow* question and the *Korean* question.[42] In the first part of his book, Pesotsky analyzes the reasons for Korean immigration to the Russian Far East and the character of the Japanese colonial policy in Korea (as seen from the outside).

Reasons for Korean Migration to Russia and the Vision of Japanese Colonial Policy in Korea

Pesotsky distinguishes several reasons for Korean migration to Russia. He discusses the main reason for modern Korean migration being the continual advancement of Japan from its islands into the mainland. He also details the better living conditions provided for Koreans by local Russian and Manchurian authorities as another important factor promoting Korean migration. Pesotsky reiterates that the Japanese regime in Korea is good for the Japanese, but for the Koreans it is hard oppression, and details that since 1906 the Japanese had killed 14,566 Koreans and severely suppressed all anti-Japanese manifestations. The Japanese did not block Korean migration abroad because it gave them the opportunity to "clean the place for landless Japanese citizens."[43] By 1910, the Japanese government had already expropriated a large quantity of Korean land for their army, railway, and marine department needs. After the annexation of Korea in 1910, Japan proclaimed all Korean land belonging to the Korean government as property of Japan, including free land throughout Korea. Before annexation, the Japanese were interested in land in the southern part of the Korean peninsula, and after annexation their interests were extended to the north.[44]

When the Japanese expropriated land from Korean owners, they simply organized mandatory registration of cultivated lands. The Japanese realized they had not personally measured Korean fields, and so the sizes recorded were based on the information they received from Koreans. The Koreans thought that the Japanese were doing registration for taxation purposes and always understated the true size of their fields. Later the Japanese measured the lands and, after discovering "free" unclaimed fields, proclaimed them to be Japanese property.

The Situation of Koreans in the Russian Far East

Investigating the Korean question in the Russian Far East, Lieutenant V. D. Pesotsky tried to answer three significant questions: (1) What was the situation of Koreans in the Russian Far East? (2) How were the Koreans fairing and was their immigration to the Russian Far East useful or not? And (3) What should be done with them in the future?

In the Priamurie area of Russia, Koreans had good living conditions. They were given land as property. They formed Korean villages. Many of the Russian citizens living in the South Ussuri area lived off the labor of Koreans; that is why Russian peasants became lazy, but Koreans who were not officially registered by Russian officials were "like working cattle."[45]

Koreans who migrated to Russia before 1910 were provided all rights according to the Russia-Korea Treaty of 1884, but migrants who entered Russia later had some problems from a legal point of view because Russian authorities did not consider them Japanese. Before 1910, Koreans who migrated to Russia had Korean citizenship. After 1910, Koreans legally became Japanese citizens, but Russian authorities did not perceive Koreans who migrated to Russia to be Japanese (citizens). The national character of Koreans as seen living in Russia is a very peculiar part of the material published concerning the Korean question in Russia, because it is different from what Russian authors and journalists had seen in colonized Korea (lazy, dirty, etc.). For example, Pesotsky wrote that Koreans are good natured, honest, and trustworthy, even to foreigners. He also noted that Koreans can appear restrained and serious, but the longer you talk with Koreans, the more they become free, easy, and cheerful in conversation. According to Pesotsky, Koreans can be obstinate and hot-tempered, yet also brave, steadfast, and of great endurance. It is difficult to meet a stingy person among Koreans (if there are some, most of them are wealthy people). While in social life Koreans are always ready to help their neighbor.[46] In summary, Pesotsky felt that Korea was the most hospitable nation in the Far East.

In economic life, Koreans were evaluated by Pesotsky as "not enterprising." This he explained by way of Koreans' history of self-isolation. The Korean peasant only worked for himself and his family and did not want to do anything more and was satisfied with this. However, according to Pesotsky, hired Korean men were better than the Chinese. According to Petotsky the Koreans were more endurable, there were no criminals among them, and the Koreans had built good roads and bridges in the Posiet District. Even Korean tramps were of no threat. So the Korean question had no connection with the Yellow Peril.[47] In general, Koreans drew sympathy from the Russians.

Nevertheless, Pesotsky insisted that Russian authorities not promote Korean migration to the Russian Far East because "Korean migration [was] not good for Russia."[48] The reasons for this evaluation were as follows:

(1) Korean migration cleaned up Korea for the Japanese and contributed to the growth of Japan (not Russia); and (2) even though Korean migration to Manchuria promoted the development of China, it was not the same for Russia, as Korean migration depraved Russian peasants, and in so doing presented the illusion of a flourishing district.[49]

Pesotsky felt it was necessary to take urgent measures to solve this immigration problem and explained some possible solutions. For example, "[t]he Russian state border [with Korea] should be populated with Russians only. The Korean population should be moved from the border areas to the inner districts," and "no permission to live near the border should be given to any Korean in the future." He went on to say that it should be "necessary to verify Russian citizenship of all Koreans living in Russia and clarify every person and the rights of each of them, to check the legal positions of Korean-foreigners living in Russia and to derive their rights, and the Posiet District should be cleaned of Koreans [mostly because of economic reasons]."[50]

Through Pesotsky's report, one can see that the idea of "cleaning the Russo-Korean border" of Koreans and moving them to the inner areas of Russia was not an idea of Stalin (1937) but had appeared much earlier, during the Tsar's Russian Empire. Such a "policy" was first caused by the Japanese colonization of Korea, together with the aggressive external strategy of Japan in the Far East. On the other hand, analysis of the national character of Koreans living outside of what Pesotsky calls the "area of continuous suppression" (Korea) could provide a unique opportunity to view Koreans as they really were, unclouded by the results of Koreans suffering under the Japanese Protectorate Treaty or after the annexation of Korea.[51] Surveying Koreans living stable lives in Russian territory clearly shows the scale of tragic suppression that originated with Japanese colonization.

CONCLUSION

Russian records about Korea and Koreans during the Japanese Protectorate (1905–10) and the Colonial Period (1910–45) demonstrate the very particular Russian approach to describing Korea, which may differ from current Russian historical evaluation of events of that time.

First of all, it is necessary to point out the Russian description of the duality of the Korean perception of Japanese policies on the Korean peninsula in the early and mid-1900s. Some Koreans thought that Japanese activities in Korea could help them protect Korean independence and speed up modernization reforms. So not all of the members of the Korean population tried to fight against the growing Japanese control over Korea. This kind of duality did not allow Koreans to effectively resist Japanese colonial policy.

Many Russians who visited Korea in the early 1910s–mid-1920s described some of the positive aspects of Japanese colonization, especially in the spheres of infrastructure, industry, and the living conditions for foreigners. Being "visitors from outside" looking mostly at the visible results of "Japanese style modernization" they were unable to detect negative consequences of Japanese rule.

Another interesting aspect of the Russian view of the Japanese colonial regime are Russians' perceptions of the anti-Japanese movement before the 1919 March First Peoples' Uprising. Russians considered the movement to be not so active and unremarkable. As to the anti-Japanese resistance in Korea during the 1920s–30s, Russian descriptions of it were also very peculiar. They ignored any activities of the Korean "bourgeois" intellectuals in Korea and abroad, for example the members of the provisional government of the Republic of Korea in Shanghai, and instead concentrated especially on the description of the Korean "people's revolutionary movement" of the 1930s. For the travelers from the Soviet Union who visited Korea, the most important descriptions were manifestations of workers and peasants' resistance movement. On one hand, this kind of attention can be explained by the special attention the Soviets paid to a possible "revolutionary movement" of "suppressed people" from all around the world, as a means for figuring out the signs of a "world revolution" approaching their own borders. On the other hand, such records can demonstrate the real situation of the anti-Japanese movement in Korea in 1930s, when the leading role transferred to the workers' class and the peasants, which, finally, resulted in the establishment in 1945–48 of the socialist Democratic People's Republic of Korea in the industrially developed North.

Another interesting aspect of Russian records about Korea is the descriptions of the national character of Koreans. Those authors who derived their conclusions from an analysis of the situation in the Russian Far East, where hundreds of thousands of Korean immigrants lived, paid more attention to the positive aspects of the national character of Koreans. Russians and other visitors from the Soviet Union during the 1920s–30s presented more diverse perceptions, pointing out both the positive and the negative aspects of the Korean national character.

One of the most important results of this analysis of Russian descriptions of precolonial and Colonial Period Korea concerns the very ailing issue for Soviet Koreans: the forced resettlement of Koreans from the Soviet Far East to Soviet Central Asia in 1937. Usually this act is evaluated as being a result of Stalin's unjust policy toward non-Russian nationals. In fact, it originated from the Japanese absorption of Korea starting in 1910 and the later aggressive Japanese policy in the Far East which resulted in the Japanese invasion of Manchuria in 1932 and the Sino-Japanese War in 1937.

NOTES

1. For example, see, Maks Polyanovsky, "Trudy komandirovannoĭ po vysochaĭshemu poveleniiu Amyrskoĭ Ėkspeditsii, Prilozhenie k vypusku XI, «Koreĭskiĭ vopros v Priamur'e». Otchet poruchika pervovo Sibirskovo ctrelkovovo Evo Velichestva polka V. D. Pesotskovo" [Works of the Amur Expedition sent under His Majesty's command. Appendix to Issue XI, "Korean question in Priamurie," Report of V. D. Pesotsky, lieutenant of His Majesty First Siberian Infantry Regiment].

2. See for example, Kim Gisu's visit to Japan in 1876, Kim Hongjip's visit to Japan in 1880, and Kim Yunsik's delegation to Japan in 1881. For more details about these events see S. O. Kurbanov, *Istoriya Korei s drevnosti do nachala 21 veka* [History of Korea since ancient times to the beginning of the twenty-first century], 296–97.

3. Archimandrite Perevalov Feodosy, *Rossiĭskaya dukhovnaya micciya v Koree, Za pervoe deciatiletie ee sushchestvovaniya (1900–1925)* [Russian Orthodox Church mission in Korea during the first twenty-five years if its existence (1900–1925)], 62–63.

4. P. Rossov, *Natsional'noe samosoznanie Koreĭtsev* [National self-consciousness of Koreans], 30–31.

5. The date November 18, 1905 was indicated in the text *Natsional'noe samosoznanie Koreĭtsev* by P. Rossov. In fact, the Protectorate Treaty was signed on November 17, 1905. Russian works about Korea published at the end of the nineteenth century and the beginning of the twentieth century have many inaccuracies including transcribing Korean names. Ibid., 31–34.

6. Ibid., 34.

7. According to a biographical description of the founder of Ilchinhoe, we can suppose that P. Rossov discussed Song Byeongjun, who was a military official in Chōsen and close to Kim Okkyun, leader of the 1884 coup d'état. Yi Hŭngjik, *Chŭngbo sae kuksa sajŏn* [Enlarged new encyclopedia of Korean history], 679.

8. P. Rossov, Natsional'noe samosoznanie Koreĭtsev.

9. Ibid., 26.

10. Ibid., 27.

11. Ibid., 1.

12. Ibid., 2.

13. Ibid., 8.

14. Ibid., 40.

15. "Rossiĭskiĭ gyeneral'nyĭ konsul v Seule G. A. Planson o polozhenii Korei i ee imperatora" [Russian Consul General in Seoul to G. A. Planson about the situation in Korea and her emperor], Gosudarstvennyĭ arkhiv Rossiĭskoĭ Federatsii [State archive of Russian Federation], Fond 818, Opis' 1, Delo 163, Listy 95–96 ob. Cited in Koreya glazami Rossiyan (1895–1945), [Korea as seen by Russians (1895–1945)], 190.

16. B. D. Pak, Rossiya i Koreya [Russia and Korea], 229; and Lev Goyer, "Kopiya doneseniya agenta ministerstva finansov v Shanhae [L'va] Goyera poslu v Tokio ot 19 iyuinya (1 iyilya) 1910 g" [Copy of the report of the Ministry of Finance agent in Shanghai (Lev) Goyer to Ambassador in Tokyo on June 19 (July 1), 1910].

17. "Donesenie agenta Ministerstva finansov v Shanghai Mr. Goyer v Tokio ot," 9 iyulia 1910 [A report of an agent of the Ministry of Finances in Shanghai Mr. Goyer to Ambassador in Tokyo], June 9, 1910, Arkhiv vneshneĭ politiki Rossiĭskoĭ imperii, Fond "Chinovnik po diplomaticheskoĭ chasti pri priamurskom general-gubernatore" [Archive of external policy of Russian Empire Fund "Diplomatic official affiliated to Priamurie Governor-General"], List 579, File 54, 64–67. Cited in Koreya glazami Rossiyan (1895–1945), 223.

18. Ibid., 220.

19. Ibid., 223.

20. For example, see Carter J. Eckert, et al., Korea Old and New, 241.

21. N. V. Kuehner, Statistiko-gyeograficheskiĭ i ėkonomicheskiĭ ocherk Korei, nyne Yiponskovo general-gubernatorstva Tsiosen [Statistic, geographic and economic survey of Korea, now the Japanese Government-General of Chōsen] 1: 5.

22. Ibid., 1: 5–6.

23. Ibid., 1: 6.

24. Ibid., 1: 7–8.

25. Ibid., 1: 8.

26. Ibid.

27. Another name of the company frequently used in literature is the Oriental Development Company. See N. V. Kuehner, Statistiko-gyeograficheskiĭ i ėkonomicheskiĭ ocherk Korei, nyne Yiponskovo general-gubernatorstva Tsiosen, 2: 408–9.

28. Ibid., 2: 420.

29. Ibid., 2: 420.

30. Ibid., 2: 252–53.

31. Ermolenko, "Ot An'duna do Seula (Putevye ocherki)" [From Andong to Seoul (Travel sketches)], *Kharbinskiĭ vestnik*, July 26, 1913. Cited in *Koreya glazami Rossiyan* (1895–1945), 257–59. Quotation marks in the passage above does not mean a word for word quotation and indicate only a shortened retelling of the most important and most interesting parts from the article by Ermolenko.

32. Ibid.

33. Ibid., 260–61, and 258.

34. "Donesenie Rossiĭskovo genral'novo konsula v Seule Ya.Ya. Lyutsh Rossiĭskomu poslu v Tokio V. N. Krupenskomu" [Report of Russian Consul General in Seoul: Ya. Ya. Lyutsh to Russian Ambassador in Tokyo V. N. Krupensloy], Seoul, March 31, 1919. Cited in *Koreya glazami Rossiyan* (1895–1945), 263–74.

35. "Sekretnoe pis'mo Gyeneral'novo konsula SSSR v Seule Sharmanova v NKID ot 5 iyunya 1926 g" [Secret letter of the Consular General of the USSR in Seoul: Sharmanov to the People's Commissariat of Foreign Affairs]. In *Iyun'skaya demonstratsiya 1926 goda v Koree: Stat'i materialy* [June demonstration of 1926: articles and materials] (Moscow, ZAO ITD "Letniy Sad," 2003), 73–81. Cited in Shirman, G. V. *Istoricheskiĭ i politiko-ėkonomicheskiĭ ocherk* (1914–1923) [Korea: Historical and political and economic survey of Korea (1914–1923)].

36. P. Yu. Schmidt, *Strana utrennevo spokoĭstviya: Koreya i ee zhiteli* [Land of morning calm: Korea and her inhabitants], 2nd ed., 128.

37. P. Yu. Schmidt, "Po Koree v nashi dni (Iz poezdki v 1926/27 gg)" [Along Korea in our days (From the trip of 1926/27)]. In *Na ostrovakh Tikhogo okeana* [In the islands of the Pacific], by P. Yu. Schmidt, Leningrad, 1928. Cited in *Koreya glazami Rossiyan* (1895–1945), 289.

38. Ibid., 307.

39. Ibid., 298.

40. Maks Polyanovsky, "Strana utrenneey tishiny" [Land of morning calm]. In *Tropicheskiy reis* [Tropical sea voyage] by Maks Polyanovsky, Moscow, 193. Cited in *Koreya glazami Rossiyan* (1895–1945), 301.

41. Ibid., 289.

42. Maks Polyanovsky, "Trudy komandirovannoĭ po vysochaĭshemu poveleniiu Amyrskoĭ Ėkspeditsii, Prilozhenie k vypusku XI, «Koreĭskiĭ vopros v Priamur'e», Otchet poruchika pervovo Sibirskovo ctrelkovovo Evo Velichestva polka V. D. Pesotskovo."

43. V. D., Pesotsky, *Koreĭskiĭ vopros v Priamur'e* [Korean question in Priamurye]. Grif «sekretno» [Top secret], 16–17.

44. Maks Polyanovsky, "Trudy komandirovannoĭ po vysochaĭshemu poveleniiu Amyrskoĭ Ėkspeditsii, Prilozhenie k vypusku XI, 11, 12, and 19."

45. Ibid., 27–28.
46. Ibid., 71–72 and 73–75.
47. Ibid., 95.
48. Ibid., 106.
49. Ibid., 107.
50. Ibid., 124.
51. Ibid., 105.

8

Chinese Understandings of Colonial Korea in Modern Times, 1910–1945: Observations and Reflections

KEZHI SUN

The successful port opening between China and Korea in 1910 activated the communication between the people of these two countries. As more and more Chinese people traveled to Korea for both leisure and research, they were able to closely observe Korean society. After the annexation of Korea by Japan in 1910, tempted by the new policies implemented by the Japanese authority in colonial Korea, some Chinese people visited the country to investigate. These individuals produced many travelogues and investigation reports containing a significant amount of important information about the authors' understandings of Korea. These texts are vital references for an analysis of Chinese observations and reflections on colonial Korea in the first half of the twentieth century.

As a close neighbor country, Korea had already been communicating with China for thousands of years. Over such a long history, many Chinese had had opportunities to visit Korea and observe the country. A vast amount of knowledge about Korea had accumulated over time, much of which helped gradually shape the Chinese people's understanding of Korea. However, for many, the conditions present in pre-modern times limited access to the peninsula and visiting Korea was rare. Most Chinese gathered information about Korean society through secondhand sources. In addition, the two countries did not hold equal positions in regard to communication. The Chinese considered themselves the great kingdom of the Celestial Empire and looked down at Korea. Because of these various factors, the pre-modern Chinese understanding of Korea was not comprehensive and was largely biased.

After 1910, China and Korea opened their ports successively, which, in turn, allowed Chinese citizens to travel to Korea for any reason, be it business or pleasure. Advancements in transportation also provided opportunities to observe more of Korean society. Over time, local Chinese-language newspapers and magazines developed. Because of the traditional relationship between China and Korea, the Chinese media began to show great concern over Korea, and news coverage of the politics, economy, and society of Korea began to appear. With all of this data, the larger society in China began to acquire a better understanding of Korea.

Before the Sino-Japanese War of 1894–95, it was inevitable that the Chinese would have a bias toward Korea, considering the traditional suzerain-vassal relations between the two countries and the Chinese belief that China was the "all under heaven" (tian-guo). After the war, the Japanese forced the Qing government to sign the Shimonoseki Treaty in 1899. This treaty formally admitted the independence of Korea and established diplomatic relations with Korea under the principles of modern international relations. The establishment of such diplomatic relations ended the political dependency relationship between China and Korea. These countries became equal partners in the international society, which created opportunities for the Chinese to know, observe, and understand Korea on an equal basis.

On the basis of the above factors, not only had the Chinese media begun to release more and more information about Korea, but scholars also began to publish more books on the country after the late Qing Dynasty. Some Chinese even traveled a long way to Korea to visit or investigate. Especially after the annexation of Korea by Japan, Chinese citizens from all circles had shown great concern over the new policies implemented by the Japanese. The Chinese government at various levels also assigned many officials to produce a great number of reports. These combined with travelogues, investigation reports, information released by the media, as well as books written by Chinese are all important sources with which to study Chinese understandings of colonial Korea.[1] Considering the limitation of this volume, this chapter will limit its scope to discuss Chinese observations and reflections on colonial Korea based only on direct observations by the Chinese journalists, travelers, and government officials.

CHINESE PEOPLE WHO OBSERVED COLONIZED KOREA

The Sino-Japanese War of 1894–95 had a great impact on the Chinese people. Japan, once ignored by the Chinese, had beaten China unexpectedly and this caused Chinese intellectuals to begin to pay attention to Japan and the changes that happened in Japan after the Meiji Reform period. Many educated Chinese traveled to Japan for further study and research. On their way to Japan, they often stayed for a while in Korea. Sung Chiao-jen (April 5, 1882–March 22, 1913), who was a politician in the early period of the Republic of China, stayed briefly in many places in Korea, including Inchon and Chinnapo, on his way back to China from Japan in March 1906. He did so to directly observe the expansion of Japanese power in Korea before the annexation of the peninsula in 1910.[2] In April 1919, on his way back from a trip to investigate the educational system in Japan, Zhang Yuan stayed for a short time in Korea. His visit coincided with the 1919 Samil Independence movement. In his travelogues, Yuan describes the movement in detail using the words "fierce" and "sharp."[3]

After the Meiji Reform period, the political, economic, and social development of Japan attracted many Chinese explorers. Many stayed in Korea for a while on either end of their trip. In the summer of 1918, the anonymous author of *Chaoxian wenjianlu* (Wenjian Lu in Korea) and his friends "stayed in Korea for a while on their way to Japan as a tour group."[4] In June 1931, Ji Ping (1905–55) who was an editor of *The Shun Pao*, stayed in Korea for more than a month after his visit to Japan. During his time in Korea the Wanpaoshan Incident occurred and triggered the Koreans' hatred for China, which he describes in detail.[5]

> Our Embassy was attacked by a mob on the night of the eighth day. Everything including furniture and files has been destroyed. All the staff members found temporary shelter in the residency of the Japanese Governor-General in Korea. Among the three thousand compatriots who sought protection at the Embassy, many have died or been injured. What a miserable scene![6]

Of course, there were also Chinese who went to colonial Korea solely for the personal purpose of traveling. In July 1918, Huang Yanpei traveled with Dr. Chiang Monlin across the Chinese provinces of Liaoning, Jilin, and

Heilongjiang, as well as across Korea.[7] In 1913, Yu Shouchun also toured Korea and wrote down what he observed.[8] Wang Shuming, Tian Hexian, Ren Yueting, Yang Xixian, Zhang Xiushan, and Yang Mingpan went to Seoul for sightseeing in May 1925.[9] Indeed, during this period a large number of Chinese visited colonial Korea and left documented memories for us after their return.[10]

At the same time, Chinese government officials at both the local and national level began to visit Korea in significant numbers. Their visits were initiated by the Chinese government or the Japanese colonial government. In addition, Chinese government officials visited the colony. After Japan's annexation of Korea, in order to win the support of the international society, Japan publicized their new polices and their so-called achievements in Korea through various means in order to justify colonization. One example of such efforts was the Korean Production Overall Progress Exhibition organized by the Government-General of Korea in October 1915. The media in China clearly pointed out that the purpose of holding this exhibition was "to promote their [Japan's] achievements of colonization."[11]

Japan was attempting to demonstrate what they considered their achievements in Korea, in order to reduce anti-Japanese sentiment in China.[12] Therefore, Japan not only invited officials of the Beiyang government to visit Korea, but also facilitated the travel of ordinary people from China to Korea. On the eve of the exhibition in October 1915, in addition to asking the Chinese government to send officials, the Japanese government also promised "free transportation via the railways and steamships to Japan and Korea."[13] The Beiyang government accepted this invitation, sending a delegation of over thirty officials from the Ministry of Foreign Affairs, the Ministry of Agriculture and Commerce, and Jilin Province to visit the exhibition in Seoul. In addition to attending the exhibition, this delegation stayed in Korea for more than two weeks and created in-depth reports detailing the local government administration and security protocols, household registration, land ownership management, public infrastructure, social relief, and commercial, agricultural, and educational systems and compiled the *Chaoxian diaocha ji* (Notes of investigating Korea).

Afterward, more and more Chinese visited Korea. In September 1917, thirteen people, including Liu Bingjian, the educational inspector of Zhili Province (now Hebei Province), and Cao Hongnian (director of the second department of the primary school affiliated with the First Zhili Normal College) were sent by the military and civil governor of the Zhili Province, Cao Kun, to investigate the educational systems in Japan, Korea, and South China, including Zhejiang and Jiangsu provinces. Their first stop was Korea, and they stayed in Seoul for over ten days after their arrival on September 29, 1917. They departed for Japan on October 8. During their stay they visited many schools, including Capital Public Girls' High School, Capital High School, Capital Industry School, and Capital Middle School, as well as the Agricultural Experiment Station and the Product Exhibition Hall.[15]

Tempted by Japan's new policies, many social groups and even individuals, in addition to those sent by the government, went to Korea to research the colony or travel. In 1918, Sun Runjiang from the Chinese Society of Vocational Education decided to travel to Korea in order to study its vocational education system.[16] In 1917, Shi Haoran traveled to Korea to visit the leather factories, and in 1924, He Ciquan went to Korea to visit the leather manufacturers in Yeongdeungpo-gu.[17] With the increase of visits to Korea, the areas covered by these investigations expanded to many fields, including the development of the occupation and secondary education system, vocational education, industries, churches, and medical care facilities. Wang Hengxin went to Korea in May 1928. He not only investigated Korean churches and many industries, but also paid a special visit to a leprosy hospital in Pusan.[18]

The so-called developments and progress in Korea under Japanese colonial rule also attracted Chinese scholars. These scholars began to pay more attention to colonized Korea and spent their time and energy to explore and study the area. In October 1927, after reading a great deal of literature on Korea in the South Manchuria Railway Company library in Dalian, China, Huang Yanpei, founder of the Chinese Vocational Education Association, went to Korea in person, stayed there for more than three months, and wrote the book *Chaoxian* (Korea), which covers many aspects of colonial Korea including its politics, economy, and society.

Another reason Chinese people were interested in visiting colonial Korea under its new colonial government policies was because of their own situations at home. They harbored concern about the stagnant development of modern institutions and China's semi-feudal, semi-colonial, socio-economy. Most Chinese kept records of their visits and research, which are windows into their understanding of colonized Korea.[19]

THE TEMPTATION OF THE COLONIAL "NEW POLICIES"

As the Chinese who visited colonized Korea were from different regions and from all walks of life, their family backgrounds and upbringings varied. However, there was one shared feature in their understandings of colonial Korea, due mostly to the persuasiveness of Japan's colonial Korea propaganda. In my opinion, the opinions of the Chinese toward Japan's new policies appeared in two significantly different stages. Before the mid-1920s, most Chinese admired the so-called achievements of the new policies. Of course, this does not mean their opinions were absolutely consistent. There were also Chinese who criticized Japan's colonization, as well as those who thought positively of the colonization after the mid-1920s.

There are many descriptions of Korea in literature from every Chinese dynasty, and the emergence of modern media made successful publications on Korea possible. Both media and literature facilitated a growth in the common knowledge about Korea, therefore, Korea was not a totally unknown country to those who intended to visit. After arriving in Korea, Chinese visitors often compared colonial Korea with the historical one and discovered that great "progress" had been made under the Japanese colonial rule. After his travel and comparison, Li Jinrong concluded that

> the implementation of new policies in the past five to six years did unexpectedly make the enforcement of orders and prohibitions strict; there is no wasteland, nor homeless people; all of these result from the far-sighted planning and proper controlling. The fundamental reasons for such great progress are that the administration is executed by competent officials, and laws are obeyed by everyone.[20]

The unknown author of *Chaoxian wenjianlu* (Chronicles of Korea) went to Korea in 1918 and was deeply impressed. His comparison highlighted the strong impression the new policies had on him. In his book, the author describes that under colonial rule "no matter what the situation, once the order has been issued, no one has [an] objection," while in the past "people kept a deaf ear to the order issued by government, and the local government had no ready idea or plan to solve anything." In regards to the economy, the author wrote, "the wasted land was being cultivated; water conservancy was being built, and the agricultural production was being improved," and the "import of various industrial goods has been growing and exceeds export," while previously in Korea, "the land stayed waste; flooding always happened, and people suffering from starvation relied desperately on China's aid." Looking at transportation, this author observed that "the national and local roads were in distinctive order and the railway runs over the whole country, so people can get anywhere conveniently," while "in the past the roads laid unconstructed [and] travel was difficult." Furthermore, the author tells us that "the construction of municipal and commercial buildings has been improving day by day." Therefore, "by comparing the present with the past, distinctions between prosperity and depression are clear. None of those who come here will not praise and admire the fast speed of progress made by the Japanese administration."[21]

In the preface to *Korea*, Huang Yanpei remarked,

> I will never be cheated by the words or articles of any of those politicians with ambitions to invade other countries to ignore the advantages and the miserable situation of the colonized countries' people, nor will I follow the nowadays popular thoughts of destroying imperialism to ignore the good facilities constructed by the current government. I will think about what I hear and see to make sure they are true, then I will write them down.[22]

In other words, he was determined to objectively describe a true and real Korea without any personal prejudice. After half a year's investigation, he could not help but express his heartfelt admiration of the "marvelous achievements" of the Japanese colonial administration in Korea, "the only feeling of my two travels in Korea is my admiration of Japan's leadership." The statistics showing the increase in cultivated land, agricultural production, fishery production, industrial output, and foreign trade volume were used to make the "sharp progress" more convincing and prove that Japan's new policies were successful in colonial Korea.[23] Therefore, Huang concluded that Japan's government "treated Japanese and Korean people in the same way . . . all the facilities were constructed for the benefit of not only the Japanese but for the Koreans as well." Besides this, Huang also thought that "under the principle of coexistence and co-prosperity, the Japanese government, with a humane and just attitude, was creating and prolonging the Korean people's well-being and helped their development, and that the Koreans were not ungrateful."[24] With this in mind he advised the Korean people to obey Japan's domination and pursue their seemingly bright life by using their brains rather than arms. The Chinese people who observed these new policies in Korea were surprised by the apparent progress achieved and expressed admiration for Japan's supposed ability to govern. However, for the Chinese, the trend was to study the attractive policies of education and industry of colonial Korea.

In 1918, Cao Hongnian and others were sent to Japan and Korea to investigate Japanese education. During their stay in Korea, they visited many schools, including Public Girls' High School, Capital High School, and Capital Special School of Industry. They expressed their appreciation for the colonial educational philosophy and teaching methods. Upon seeing a globe in the classroom in the Public Girl's High School Cao commented approvingly, "no matter how enthusiastic the geography teacher is, they cannot use a flat map to convey a three-dimensional concept to the students. Therefore, the usage of a globe in this school is what makes geography worth learning."[25]

As a matter of fact, industrial education in colonized Korea left an even stronger impression on Cao Hongnian and his colleagues. While visiting the industrial schools, they saw affiliated laboratories and product displays in nearly all of the industrial schools. After their visit they concluded that the students must "not only have practical skills but must also have scientific knowledge." They further surmised that "the laboratories were established to store products and materials for inventions, and that one could predict how advanced Korea's industry would be after several years."[26]

The officials of the Ministry of Foreign Affairs and the Ministry of Agriculture and Commerce were invited to visit the exhibition. A delegation including Wang Yangbin, Wan Baoyuan, and others also visited some schools after attending the 1915 Exhibition on Production and Progress in Korea. After visiting the high schools, the authors commented on the education system in Korea,

> [t]he administration is strict, and the teaching is practical. The teachers are responsible, and the students are attentive in their studying. The relationships between teachers and students are very close.[27]

Huang Yanpei also notes that in colonial Korea,

[t]he school boys and girls are active and serious about studying and do not violate the rules. Even though the Korean education system under Japanese colonial rule does not intentionally copy the popular new system promoted by Japan, however, the teaching methods and tools I have seen have greatly improved . . . the pragmatic teaching attitudes and scholarly spirits are precious though we just see a little bit of that.[28]

Among all of these supposed achievements, the ones most admired were those in agriculture and industry. In the early period of the colonial rule, many Chinese visitors to Korea paid a visit to the Agricultural Products Exhibition Hall administered by the Government-General of Korea. This exhibition hall became a must-see destination for many visitors, including Cao Hongnian and others who arrived in Korea in September 1917 and Zhang Yuan, who visited Korea in 1919.[29] Many Chinese travelers paid special visits to Korea to investigate the demonstration farms and various factories. This apparent development in Japanese agricultural techniques and industrial inventions was quite impressive to them. These developments encouraged many, both home and abroad, to consider the idea that modern China could save itself through industry.[30]

Through the Chinese perspective, agriculture in Korea had made great progress under Japanese colonial rule. This progress can be seen firsthand by analyzing the amount of cultivated land in Korea, which in 1910 numbered a little over 2.46 million *jongbu*.[31] The amount of cultivated land doubled to over 4.50 million *jongbu* in 1924. The Chinese also perceived progress through witnessing the economic influence of agricultural products, which grew from a value of 240 million yen in 1910 to more than 1.286 billion yen in 1923—an overall increase of nearly 500 percent in thirteen years.[32]

The quality of agricultural products was also thought to have greatly improved as well. Of his visits Cao Hongnian wrote, "three years ago, most of the fruit produced in Korea was too bad to eat. The quality improved last year and this year most of the fruit are juicy and tasty." We can conclude that the Chinese visitors would have been surprised by the "advanced industry of the Japanese."[33] The development of industry was no less impressive than that of agriculture.

The sum of industrial output in colonial Korea in 1910 was just over 30 million yen. This amount increased to over 270 million yen in 1923 with an increase of eight times. Profit of all companies in colonial Korea in 1910 was just 8.6–8.7 million yen; it reached 140 million in 1923 with a growth rate of 1500 percent.[34]

The Chinese visitors were also amazed by the enthusiasm of social organizations toward industry development. Various vocational schools promoted the spread of industrial knowledge and the creation of more opportunities for students to find work in industry. Even the YMCA (Young Men's Christian Association) had established an industry department to "use new machines and the latest ideas to equip Korean young men with substantial industry knowledge."[35]

In short, many Chinese who observed colonial Korea firsthand thought the rule of Japan over Korea was successful, because they saw Korean politics being refreshed, social undertakings being developed, and productivity booming. The Chinese perspective concluded that Japan must be committed to Korea, because even though Korea was a small region (with an area just over 14,000 square li and a population of 19 million), they were profitable and had apparently established significant order and produced worthy achievements.[36]

The positive comments made about colonial rule were closely related to the underlying reasons behind why the Chinese traveled there in the first place. Most of the Chinese who admired the achievements of Japan's "governing of Korea" were sent by the Chinese government and were received and assisted by Government-General of Korea officials during their visits. Even the daily itineraries were arranged by the Government-General. So, what the Chinese saw was exactly what the Japanese colonial authorities wanted them to see. In 1917, before Liu Chongben was sent to Japan and Korea to investigate the education system, he received a letter of introduction from Japanese Consul in Tianjin Matsudaira Tsuneo. After his arrival in Korea, Liu was assisted by the Government-General of Korea Foreign Affairs Office and the Education Affairs Office. Mr. Yamatada, an education inspector from the Education Affairs Office made sure the visit followed the prepared schedules.[37] In 1917, another Chinese delegation (in which Cao Hongnian was included) traveled from Tianjin, China to Korea and Japan to investigate the colonial education system. Though they did not receive a letter from the

Japanese Consulate in Tianjin, they were introduced to and assisted by Government-General officials through the Chinese Consulate General in Korea due to their official backgrounds. The itinerary of their visit was the same as Liu Chongben's.[38]

In 1915, Wang Yangbin and Wan Baoyuan—members of the delegation sent by the Beiyang government—left for Korea to investigate the Korean Production Co-Progress Exhibition. The Government-General of Korea not only paid for all of the expenditures, it also provided an all-expense paid railway trip from Beijing to Korea. The train had special cars for the delegation and included Japanese escorts. Governor-General Terauchi Masatake held a welcome dinner for the delegation and, of course, shared with the delegation what they would visit, which had all been prepared in advance.[39] From these cases, it can be revealed that what the Chinese officials saw and heard in Korea were the very same things Japan had tried in so many ways to portray as well-known achievements. However, the Chinese were at a disadvantage, there was not enough time for them to truly investigate, for their stay was often only a couple of days and never lasted more than a week. This combined with the prearranged schedule made it difficult for them to observe the true state of Korea. Therefore, given the lack of information and the time to effectively survey the country, it is no wonder the Chinese visitors would choose to admire the achievements of Japan's governance in Korea.

SOCIAL PHENOMENA UNDER COLONIAL RULE

The supposed great changes that happened in Korea during the early stages of Japan's colonial rule attracted the attention of the Chinese. Some were sent to Korea to carry out a comprehensive study on its local administration, security, household registration, and cadastral administration; the results of which presented a high appraisal of the efficiency of the Japanese colonial system. However, with Japan's accelerated invasion of the Chinese territory, the international situation in East Asia changed dramatically, and the Chinese people began to review the Japanese colonial rule in Korea from a different perspective.

After the March First movement, Japan shifted from its stricter version of colonial governance to what they called "cultural politics." Japanese government officials allowed Korean newspapers to be published, loosened restrictions on the establishment of Korean organizations, and allowed Koreans to carry out local autonomy and to elect the members of their local councils. However, the Chinese people did not see these overtures as bringing any freedom to Koreans; rather, they felt that "police affairs, financial affairs, and internal affairs are still grasped in Japan's hands."[40] In reality, Japanese officials used this propaganda to conceal the reality of colonial domination. Although the Korean people were allowed to establish organizations, none of them could use the word "party" in the name (in reference to political affiliation), and they were restricted to using the term "association," such as in the Xingan Association. Further, these organizations were "supervised and restricted by the Japanese authority. . . . For instance, if a meeting is to be held, it is a must to apply to the Government-General of Korea for permission. Even if the permission is [given], some Japanese or military police will be sent there to keep a close eye on the meeting. Unless somebody is prepared to go to jail or to be punished, there will not be any chance to deliver any speech for revolution."[41] Therefore, even with the new cultural politics, the reality was that of the oppression of the ruled by the ruling.

Though China and Korea had had a peaceful relationship for hundreds of years, and most Chinese resented the annexation of Korea, many Chinese also admired the supposed governing achievements of the colonial Japanese rulers. Simultaneously, more Chinese began to question these so-called achievements through their in-depth observations of Korean society. They thought the colonial development did not bring good to the Korean people as a whole. One such reason was how there were very few local stores selling handicrafts made by Koreans along the streets of Seoul. The stores operated by Koreans had very low assets, while the prosperous shopping malls, markets, and various other successful enterprises were all concentrated on the Japanese streets.[42] According to Zhang Yuan's account, even in the smaller cities,

> along streets and lanes were various joint-stock corporations such as aquaculture, tobacco, liquor-making, food, and animal husbandry, all of which were owned by the Japanese, while most of the Koreans were coolies, bearing something heavy on their shoulders coming and going.[43]

Koreans in the countryside had to sell their lands and houses to the Japanese in order to pay the heavy taxes.[44] These Korean villages displayed a clear picture of the unjust situation, as hardly any Japanese lived in these areas.[45]

Modern Chinese observers think that though the economy had been developed and the city appearance had been greatly improved, the Koreans could not share in the fruits of this development. They not only lost all their economic resources but also were deprived of most of the economic development opportunities, having been reduced to targets of Japan's exploitation.

Under Japanese colonial rule, the Koreans became economic slaves and had lost their basic rights of freedom, including freedom of action. They could not travel abroad nor could they even travel domestically without obtaining permission from the police.[46] They also lost their right to freedom of speech. Seoul at that time was the media center. There were newspapers in Japanese: *Keijyou nitsupou* (Capital daily), *Chousen nitdubou* (Korea news), *Chousen nichinichi shinbun* (Korea daily news) and in Korean: *Maeil sinbo* (Korea daily news), *Chosŏn ilbo* (Korea daily), *Tonga ilbo* (East-Asia daily), and the *Chosun kyunje sinmoon* (Korea economic news). All of the newspapers in Japanese as well as in Korean were the voice of Japan—the driving force of their cultural invasion—dominating the public opinion all across the country. The Japanese even controlled the newspapers printed in Korean and only provided copies to middle-aged Koreans who could not read Japanese.[47] Though Korean journalism was highly developed, the voices and opinions of the Korean people within these various news outlets were nowhere to be found. Freedom of the press had also been stolen from the Korean people. New books written by Koreans were not allowed in bookstores without permission from the Government-General of Korea police.[48]

While many Chinese admired the growth of the colonial Korea education system, some certainly found problems with it. The Japanese owned most of the schools. Not surprisingly, the educational principles were geared toward Japanese interests. Even the few schools owned by Koreans were required to comply with the course system issued by the Government-General of Korea Educational Affairs Office. The Japanese language dominated the courses and Korean characters, language, and history were strictly limited.[49] Japanese characters and language were used in all classes, and Korean was reduced to a local dialect.⁵⁰ The Chinese who saw this commented that "it is not necessary for a nation who wants to subjugate another nation to kill all the people of this nation, but to eliminate their language and characters so that their national spirit dies out."⁵¹

Further, in Korean-owned schools there were no "courses of history and geography, which highlights the position of these courses as the inspiration for patriotism in the primary schools owned by the Japanese."⁵² On the contrary, the absence of courses of history and geography would "bury their national spirit and Japan really took great pains to assimilate the Koreans!" Therefore, some Chinese described the education in colonial Korea as "education for colonization, enslavement, and subjugation."⁵³ The direct consequence of such education was that the young Koreans who experienced this education never learned the history of Korea and had no sense of which nation they belonged to. Since everyone both spoke and wrote Japanese, it seemed to these students that using the Korean language was simply out of date.⁵⁴

Seoul, the Chosŏn Dynasty capital for 500 years, had many imperial palaces. However, with the occupying of the Japanese, everything changed. The Government-General of Korea building, erected in front of Gyeongbokgung Palace, looked like a ferocious beast, abrupt and lofty, the appearance of which fiercely shocked the Koreans. Whenever they passed by, they "involuntarily held their breath and tiptoed,"⁵⁵ and the Changgyeonggung Palace was turned into a zoo, according to observations made by Hu Shiqing: "[i]n the west corridor are displayed stone and bronze implements, while in the east corridor are animal specimens . . . the majesty of the palace [is] lost completely, [which made visitors] feel sorry as if a precious qin (a musical instrument of ancient China) was burned and a crane was cooked" (焚琴煮鶴).⁵⁶ Also, according to Zhang Mosheng, "the Japanese tried every effort to humiliate the Koreans, which means the Japanese did regard the Koreans as human beings."⁵⁷ The imperial palaces—the symbols of Korea's time-honored history and culture—had lost their previous majesty, had been ruined and now were the places where the Japanese colonists displayed Japanese achievements.

In the early stages of Japanese domination in Korea, the Koreans the Chinese witnessed in the capital were very hasty, constantly moving and in a hurry, in contrast to the people back home in Beijing who were usually casual and leisurely walking along the streets. The Chinese attributed this constant bustling to how much work was required of the Koreans, with all of the developments in industry and education.⁵⁸ A few years later however, what the Chinese saw was entirely different: Koreans relaxing in the streets, pipes in their mouths, content and carefree. Women carrying heavy baskets across town would even walk at a slower pace. The Chinese figured that the Koreans must have gained more leisure time through diligence at work, and this must have reflected a more peaceful atmosphere.⁵⁹

Though Japan had shifted from harsh, high-handed policies to "cultural politics," the atmosphere did not last long. According to Ma Boyuan, "[m]ost of the Koreans appear to be restless and anxious . . . men, women, the old and the young on trains, buses, and streets all look sallow and sad." Even the tunes of the young girls' songs were "so blue and sorrowful that people could not bear to listen, indicating the fall of their country."⁶⁰ Most of those who had been deprived of their means of living were reduced to begging on the streets, not even finding help from the poorhouses and charity hospitals that were supposed to have been established by the Government-General of Korea and provincial governments for the precise purpose of taking care of the poor. There were starving, dirty people everywhere. The military police treated these people so harshly that they naturally dared not ask for anything. They were left with no choice but to find food scraps in the garbage, causing people to die from food poisoning on a daily basis.⁶¹

According to these accounts by Chinese scholars, guests, and visitors, there was greater administrative efficiency in colonial Korea under Japanese rule than during the Chosŏn Dynasty, but the Koreans were nevertheless clearly an oppressed people whose economic resources and opportunities had been taken away by their overlords. With so few resources, it was an impossible challenge for the Koreans to fight the Japanese; their basic right of freedom had been taken from them as well. The education children received had also been influenced by colonialism. Ruled by such colonists, the lives of the Korean people continued to worsen.⁶² The Chinese admiration of the supposedly great progress and achievements of Koreans in politics, economy, culture, education, and society were difficult to see because all of these belonged to the Japanese. The Koreans could not share any of the benefits. As the Chinese visitors throughout the Colonial Period saw these dramatic changes in every aspect of Korean society, they gradually gained a more objective and rational perspective of the whole situation.

CONCLUSION

Since modern times, more and more Chinese have had opportunities to observe Korean society firsthand. In the early stages of Japanese colonial rule in Korea, out of concern for their own poverty and underdevelopment in China, the country paid close attention to the results of Japan's new policies present in the Korean colony. The Chinese had great interest in the renovation of politics, the development of the economy, and the advancement of education in what had been considered a previously underdeveloped country. They also admired and spoke highly of Japan's ways of ruling. It was inevitable that at that time Chinese visitors had a biased understanding of Korea. This was due to the fact that many of the trips were for official purposes and government funded and this often limited the duration of their stay, thereby only allowing them to see the prosperous areas of colonial Korea. However, as Japan's intention of invading China became increasingly obvious and with the growth of the Chinese people's national consciousness, more and more ordinary Chinese citizens made the effort to visit Korea. Concerned that they may end up in a similar situation under Japanese rule, the Chinese changed their focus onto the subjugated people. The Chinese became more concerned about the Korean people's political rights, economic life, and other basic rights of freedom, such as the freedom of speech and the establishment of organizations. Thus, they began to more critically analyze the nature of Japan's colonization. The Chinese observers, who themselves had been subjects in a semi-colonial and semi-feudal society and had been oppressed by imperial colonists for a long time and had lost their admiration for the so-called progress of colonial Korea as the cruelty of the Japanese rule and the sufferings of the Koreans under this domination became more apparent. These revelations awoke the Chinese people into a stark awareness of Japan's intention to invade China. On this point, the observations and reflections on colonial Korea by the Chinese in modern times are very different from those by the contemporary Japanese and Westerners.

NOTES

1. There are many Chinese descriptions of colonial Korea. These descriptions cover a wide range of topics, including politics, the economy, and Korean society. Because the

amount of literature is so large, in this chapter, only the texts written by those who had been to Korea have been selected. These texts include books of traveling notes and investigation notes and reports, as well as the travelogues published in newspapers and magazines. Additionally, some literature included in other books is presented as well.

2. Sung Jiao-jen, "Wo de lishi" [My history], 275–78.

3. Zhang Yuan, *Mingguo banian Chaoxian lüexingji* [The journals of traveling in Japan and Korea in 1919], 31.

4. Anonymous, *Chaoxian wenjianlu* [Chronicles of Korea], 1.

5. Ji Ping, "Youhan mantan II" [Thoughts about traveling in Korea II], *The Shun Pao*, July 11, 1931.

6. Ibid.

7. Huang Yanpei, *Chaoxian* [Korea], 2.

8. Yu Shouchun, "Chaoxian youji" [Notes of traveling in Korea].

9. Hu Youfei, "Hanjing jiyou" [Traveling in the Korean capitol], *Ta Kung Pao*, September 25, 1925.

10. Wang Tongling, "You Chaoxian zaji" [Miscellanies of traveling in Korea]; Huang Zonglin, "You Chaoxian minfei mu" [Visiting the mausoleum of the Korean imperial concubine Min]; and Qin Lifan, *Gaoli huangzou jiyou* [Traveling in remote areas of Korea].

11. Anonymous, "Ji Chaoxian wuchan gongjinhui" [Notes on the "Overall Progress" exhibition of Korean goods], *The Shun Pao*, October 27, 1915.

12. Ibid.

13. Ibid.

14. Wang Yangbin and Wan Baoyuan, *Chaoxian diaocha ji* [Notes of investigating Korea]; Wang Yangbin and Wan Baoyuan et al., *Chaoxian guanhuiji* [Notes on visiting exhibition in Korea]; and Wang Yangbin and Wan Baoyuan et al., *Chaoxian xingji* [Trip to Korea].

15. Cao Hongnian, *Kaocha rihan jiangzhe jiaoyu biji* [Notes on the education system in Japan, Korea and the Chinese provinces of Zhejiang and Jiangsu].

16. Anonymous, "Sheyuan Sun Runjiang hanshu diaocha riben Chaoxian shiyejiaoyu qingxing" [Report from Sun Runjiang on the vocational education in Japan and Korea].

17. Shi Haoran, "Canguan Chaoxian pige gongchan shixi biji" [Notes on visiting Korea's leather producers]; and He Ciquan, "Diaocha Chaoxian Yongdengpu zhige gongchang zhi baogao" [Report on investigating leather factories in Yeong Deung Po].

18. Wang Hengxin, "Canguan Chaoxian fushan laibingyuan jilüe" [Notes on visiting the leprosy hospital in Busan, Korea], 2.

19. Huang Yanpei, *Chaoxian*, preface.

20. Li Jinrong, "Lüxing Chaoxian ganyan" [Reflections on traveling in Korea].

21. Huang Yanpei, *Chaoxian*, preface.

22. Ibid., 7–8.

23. Ibid., 9, 10, and 14.
24. Ibid., 7–8.
25. Cao Hongnian, *Kaocha rihan jiangzhe jiaoyu biji*.
26. Ibid., 49–50.
27. Wang Yangbin and Wan Baoyuan, *Chaoxian diaocha ji*, 6.
28. Huang Yanpei. *Chaoxian*, preface.
29. Cao Hongnian, *Kaocha rihan jiangzhe jiaoyu biji*, 2; and Zhang Yuan, *Mingguo banian Chaoxian lüexingji*, 27.
30. On the thought of saving China through industry in modern China see Ding Shouhe, "Shiyejiuguo, jiaoyujiuguo he kexuejiuguo sichao de zairenshi" [A re-examination of the theories to save China through industry, education, and science], 3–5; and Liu Yisheng, "Xinhai geming yu shiye jiuguo sichao de gaozhang" [The 1911 revolution and the flourishing of the theory of saving China through industry], 73–78.
31. *Jongbu* (町步) is a measurement of land area which is used in Japan and Korea. One *jongbu* is equal to $9,917m^2$.
32. Huang Yanpei, *Chaoxian*, preface.
33. Cao Hongnian, "Rihan lüxingji" [Traveling in Japan and Korea], *Ta Kung Pao*, May 30, 1918.
34. Huang Yanpei, *Chaoxian*, 7.
35. Ma Boyuan "Chaoxian jingcheng guanchaji" [Observations on the Korean capital], *Ta Kung Pao*, August 24, 1920.
36. Huang Yanpei, *Chaoxian*, 8.
37. Liu Chongben, *Lüxing rihan riji* [Traveling journals about Japan and Korea], 27.
38. Cao Hongnian, "Rihan lüxingji."
39. Wang Yangbin and Wan Baoyuan, *Chaoxian diaocha ji*, 1–4.
40. Ji Ping, "Youhan mantan III."
41. Ji Ping, "Youhan mantan V."
42. Ji Ping, "Youhan mantan VI."
43. Zhang Yuan, *Mingguo banian Chaoxian lüexingji*, 26.
44. Ma Boyuan, "Chaoxian jingcheng guanchaji."
45. Zhang Yuan, *Mingguo banian Chaoxian lüexingji*, 26–27.
46. Ibid., 30.
47. Ji Ping, "Youhan mantan IV."
48. Zhang Yuan, *Mingguo banian Chaoxian lüexingji*, 34.
49. Ji Ping, "Youhan mantan IV."
50. Ibid.
51. Li Jinrong, "Lüxing Chaoxian ganyan."
52. Zhang Yuan, *Mingguo banian Chaoxian lüexingji*, 34.
53. Jing Hengyi, *Jing Hengyi riji* [Jing Hengyi's diary], 34.

54. Ji Ping, "Youhan mantan IV."
55. Zhang Mosheng, *Moseng zishu* [Autobiography of Moseng], 87.
56. Hu Shiqing, *Sanshiba guo youji* [Traveling in thirty-eight countries], 5.
57. Zhang Mosheng, *Moseng zishu*, 108.
58. Wang Tongling, "You Chaoxian zaji," 92.
59. Chiang Monlin, *Xichao* [The tides from the West], 187.
60. Ma Boyuan, "Chaoxian jingcheng guanchaji."
61. Anonymous, *Chaoxian wenjianlu*, 18.
62. Senzi, "Chaoxian yinxiangji: Xiangei wo suo aimude Chaoxian" [Impressions of Korea: Dedicated to my beloved Korea], 4.

9
Publicizing Colonies: Representations of "Korea" and "Koreans" in NIPPON

NAOKO SHIMAZU

In this chapter, the international impact of Japanese colonial rule in Korea is examined through the lens of Japan's cultural propaganda. My analysis focuses on a special issue on Korea featured in the iconoclastic Japanese graphic magazine, NIPPON, in July 1939. The singularity of NIPPON lies with its original publishing ethos: it was intended to function as a luxury graphic magazine created to introduce Japan and Japanese culture to Western readership. Therefore, what makes this magazine distinct from other colonial propaganda materials is that it was not a colonial propaganda addressed to the Japanese audience about Japanese achievements in the colonial empire. Instead, it was an international cultural propaganda publication which disseminated images of Japan and its empire with the aim of appealing to a wider, cosmopolitan, and international readership. A cultural analysis of NIPPON's special issue on Korea enables us to illuminate some insights on the self-perceptions of the Japanese as colonizers through the mirror of colonial Korea as the Other.

What the Korea Issue brings to the fore is the uncomfortable compromise between cultural and colonial propaganda in wartime Japan. Ultimately, this chapter reveals the ambivalent positioning of the Korea Issue, as it became—either by design or by default—NIPPON's first colonial propaganda issue, in spite of the fact that it was intended as cultural propaganda. To this end, the Korea Issue represents a transitional phase in the publication of NIPPON, from being primarily focused on Japan to one which publicized the Japanese Empire as a whole. Hence, this chapter helps to illuminate the complex nature of Japanese cultural propaganda in the age of the wartime empire, especially in terms of the formulation and implementation of the *colonial*, as opposed to the *cultural* gaze. In turn, this analysis enables us to reflect on how the exigencies of Japan's changing relations within contemporary international society mediated Japanese colonial rule in Korea.

Japan in the 1930s was a different beast from the Japan of 1910 when the island nation annexed Korea. In the 1930s, Japan's colonial empire had vastly grown geographically, from the southern Sakhalin Island all the way through to the Micronesian islands located in the central Pacific Ocean, while spreading north to include substantial territorial holdings in China through Manchukuo. Moreover, Japan's invasion into China aggravated the balance of power in East Asia, as Japan's bid for the hegemonic role in the region destabilized the underlying great power geopolitics. Japan withdrew from the League of Nations in March 1933 due to the Manchurian crisis, after what it considered to be unfair conditions imposed by the Lytton Commission, and vowed to follow an independent path in foreign policy. Having gotten rid of all the liens imposed by the Wilsonian world order under the League of Nations (in Japanese historiography this is referred to as the Versailles system), Japan triggered the second Sino-Japanese War (what is referred to as the Anti–Japanese War of Resistance in China) in July 1937. The intensity of domestic political instability mirrored the intensity of external military maneuverings, which was temporarily laid to rest with the February 26 Incident in 1936—a coup that saw the ascendancy of the Control Faction of the military in Japanese society. Meanwhile, Japan also sought new power alliances by tying itself to Germany through the Anti–Comintern Pact signed in November 1936, which fortified Japan with the encouragement it needed to attack the Soviet Union from its base in Manchuria in 1938. Between May to September 1939, Japan invaded Mongolia in what is known as the Nomonhan Incident or the Battle of Khalkhyn Gol, which ended in a total defeat for the Japanese Army. In September 1939, Germany started the Second World War by invading Poland. When the topic of Korea appeared in the July 1939 issue of NIPPON, Japan was in a state of a protracted warfare in China, while its domestic society was under the throes of the National Mobilization Law legislated in March 1938—even though it was still more than a year away from the imposition of the Imperial Rule Assistance Association in October 1940.

In this highly volatile and extremely tense, national and international context of 1939, why would Japan want to engage in cultural propaganda of its colonies? In order to make sense of the publication of the special issue in July 1939, we need to explore the correlation between the international, national, and colonial contexts. What are the intentions behind the special issue, and what utility did it have? The expansion of the Japanese colonial empire invariably complicates the Japanese perceptions of themselves and how they wished to be perceived by others. In this vein, does this special issue shed any light on the question of Japanese identity as a colonial power?

Needless to say, international contextualization plays an important role in understanding the particular focus of this study. Publicity of Japan and the Japanese empire became an increasingly important imperial mission in the 1930s, as an act of justification and legitimization for the rapid expansion of the empire. In the first half of the 1930s, we see a sudden surge of new public and semi-public or "private" (minkan) organizations created under the auspices of the Japanese Ministry of the Foreign Affairs and the Ministry of the Interior, such as the International Tourism Bureau of the Ministry of the Railways (1930), the International Tourism Committee (1931), the International Tourism Association (1931), the Japan-America Student Conference (1930–40), the Japan PEN Club (1935), and the International Students Institute (1935). Ironically, Japan's voluntary withdrawal from the League of Nations and its subsequent disengagement from the dominant international order had the effect of inducing Japan to take a more proactive role in international public relations. In part, it was undertaken as a damage limitation exercise for the negative publicity generated by the Manchurian invasion of September 1931 and the aerial bombing of Shanghai in January 1932. Yet, Japan was not an exception and was only conforming to the global trend exercised by all of the great powers, that of using cultural policy to expand its influence globally. In 1924 and 1925, the French and the Germans established cultural institutions—the Maison Franco-Japonaise (Nichi-futsu kaikan, or the French Institute on Research in Japan) and the Goethe Institute—to promote educational and cultural exchanges. Relatively speaking, therefore, the Japanese and the British were latecomers to cultural diplomacy as both the Kokusai bunka shinkōkai (KBS; Center for International Cultural Relations) and the British Committee for Relations with Other Countries (renamed the British Council in 1935) were created in 1934.[1] Indeed, Japan's KBS claimed both the external factors (the international climate and the rise of cultural agencies of other imperial powers) and the nationalistic desire to promote Japanese culture abroad, as the key determinants that led to its creation in April 1934.[2]

The KBS was established as a public interest incorporated foundation (zaidan hōjin) by a group of highly illustrious Japanese elites including cross-partisan leaders in industry, finance, arts, and the aristocracy, while boasting Prince Konoe Fumimaro as its first president. Although the KBS did not officially come under the aegis of any government ministry, it nonetheless operated like a semi-official government agency because its operation was premised on the heavy involvement of cabinet ministers and senior bureaucrats. The historian, Shibazaki Atsushi summarizes the objectives of the KBS as two-fold: "(1) to acquire a sense of cultural superiority of the Japanese toward the *uncivilized* nations (*hi-bunmeikoku*) of the East; and (2) to procure a sense of equality with the *civilized* nations (*bunmeikoku*) of the West."[3] KBS outlined its range of activities to include the following: producing publications; hosting public lectures, exhibitions, and concerts; exchanging cultural materials and students; inviting and hosting well-known foreigners; facilitating foreign research on Japanese culture; acting as a communications intermediary for organizations and individuals; producing films; and running libraries.[4] Noticeably, foreigners seemed to have consisted almost entirely of Westerners from France, the United States, Canada, and Hungary to name a few.[5] Hence, the KBS was set up primarily to promote Japanese culture to the West. It may be worth putting the KBS into the contemporary context in that it was only one of a myriad of cultural propaganda organizations set up in 1930s Japan. Indeed, the Imperial Army Publicity Section (Rikugun hōdōbu) was a much bigger and more serious player in cultural propaganda, as well as colonial cultural agencies such as the Manchukuo Film Association (Manshū eiga kyōkai). Yet, it was through the KBS, which was most closely associated with the Ministry of Foreign Affairs, that NIPPON came to forge a formal link in 1937. It is worth mentioning that in the launch issue of NIPPON in Autumn 1934, the KBS was introduced as a "movement" in Japan.[6]

NIPPON AND NATORI YŌNOSUKE

In this climate, the graphic magazine NIPPON was born in October 1934 and became an important vehicle for the promotion of Japanese culture overseas. One of the most striking aspects of NIPPON was its uncompromisingly internationalist outlook. Each issue included articles in four different languages—German, French, English, and Spanish—with German being the predominant language. Abridged versions were often provided in one another language, with Spanish being the least common. From the selection of the languages, it can be ascertained that the magazine was principally intended for Western readership. In 1936, the Japanese-language version of NIPPON (NIPPON Nihongoban) published but ceased production after the second issue, only to be relaunched in 1938 as a domestic cultural magazine, NIPPON Japan (NIPPON NIPPONban).[7] The annual subscription to NIPPON was 6 yen, or 1.5 yen, per copy and was produced four times a year. From its inception, NIPPON was distributed globally through a network of agents in North America, Latin America, Europe, and Asia:

> Universum Book Export Co., Inc, New York for USA, Canada, and Mexico; Oscar Enoch in Hamburg, Germany, for Central and Northern Europe; Azed A.-G., Basel, Switzerland, for Switzerland; Libra Rie [sic] Hachette, Paris, France for Western Europe and the Mediterranean; Livraria Delinee, Sao Paulo, for Brazil; Agencia Internacional de Diarios, Buenos Aires, for Argentina; The French Book Store, Peking, for China; Service des Grandes Revues Internationales, Tel-Aviv, for the Palestine; the Central Book Depot, Bangkok; and Maruzen Company for Japan.[8]

Any story of NIPPON cannot be told in isolation from the central personality of its founding editor, Natori Yōnosuke (1910–62).[9] In 1928, at the age of eighteen, he went to study graphics and photography at the Munichen Kunstgewerbeschule (Munich School of Art and Craft), much influenced by his German mentor, Sigmund von Weech who was professor of design at the Berlin Kunstgewerbeschule (Berlin National Crafts School). Natori took to Germany like a duck to water, making extensive connections and exuding youthful confidence and resourcefulness. In 1931, the highly prestigious *Berliner Illustrirte Zeitung* (Berlin graphic newspaper), then the largest graphic magazine in the world with a circulation of two million, published Natori's first photographs. In the following year, he was commissioned by the *München Illustrierte Presse* (Munich graphic press) to take photographs of Austria and Yugoslavia, and thereafter he became a professional photographer. In November 1931, some three months after the Japanese invasion of Manchuria,

Ullstein Verlag, the largest German publishing firm of the time contracted Natori as their first Japanese photographer. This took him to Japan on a special assignment in February 1932, where he took some 7,000 photographs on thirty different themes in three months for a special issue on Japan. These photographs became foundational to his portfolio of Japan-themed photographs in the 1930s, as the thirty thematic sets were used 270 times through distribution globally and were featured in many different publications worldwide before 1939.[10]

Arguably, therefore, Natori dominated the world media as the most influential visual image-creator of "Japan" at the time. When Natori ended his special assignment to Manchukuo in early 1933, Ullstein Verlag instructed him to remain in Tokyo as their correspondent in Japan as the assent of Hitler had made it difficult for foreigners to work in Germany. Thereafter, he continued with his international assignments from Tokyo, and his famous photograph of young Japanese soldiers exercising was featured on the front cover of *Life* magazine on January 11, 1937, the first Japanese photographer to receive such an accolade.[11] The outbreak of the Second Sino-Japanese War in 1937 triggered a second wave of demand for Japan-related photographs. This kept him busy as the photographs taken by him and staff photographers at NIPPON Kōbō (NIPPON studio, a limited company which Natori had set up in 1933) were featured in *Life* magazine and distributed by Black Star Publishing.[12] Most notably, he was the only Japanese photographer to be chosen for the major exhibition, "Photography, 1839–1937," curated by Alfred Stieglitz at the Museum of Modern Art (MOMA) in New York.

What made young Natori such a highly coveted photographer for these major international publishers? When Natori first started taking photographs of Japan for *Berliner Illustrirte Zeitung*, his policy was to take photographs of Japan *as if he were a German*.[13] He was not interested in presenting Japan through Japanese eyes mainly because he believed that such photographs would not interest Western readers. This meant that he was analytical in his perspective of capturing Japan, by emphasizing the differences between Japanese and Western everyday practices and material culture.[14] Moreover, he understood the importance of producing photographs that the German readership desired because he regarded photographs as commercial products rather than artistic works. This commercially driven attitude toward photography led to a fall out with some of his Japanese photographer colleagues.

Ironically, however, his German employers found him useful precisely because of his Japanese sensibilities. He was even sent on a special assignment to take photographs of the United States as a Japanese photographer for Fortune in 1937. In Japan, it was his Western-gaze and Western sensibilities that had made his creed of photography distinct, giving his output a cutting edge. His sensitivity toward cross-cultural representations of Japan accounted for his precocious success. In this way, he made himself indispensable as the Japanese photographer in the West. As if fate had smiled on him, many of the influential connections in the creative sector, which he had made in Germany, ended up migrating to the United States with the ascent of Hitler. Therefore, Natori's international operation similarly moved to the United States together with the German émigré networks after 1933.[15]

In 1933, at the age of twenty-three, Natori returned to Japan, full of youthful enthusiasm and ambition, and caused a stir in Japanese journalism by introducing Western-style photojournalism. He approached the avant-garde group that had started the magazine, Kōga (which included photographers Kimura Ihee, Ina Nobuo, Hara Hiromu, and Okada Sōzō among others) in 1932 and persuaded them to join him in the establishment of NIPPON Studio in Tokyo. According to Ina Nobuo, a photography critic of the time, "[u]nder his [Natori] leadership, we gathered with a burning ambition and determination to start some new artistic movement."[16] In 1934, NIPPON launched as a luxurious, high-end, graphic magazine introducing Japanese culture to the Western world, with Natori at the helm as both the publisher and editor. He was convinced that Japan needed to have a world-class graphic magazine that could compete with the best that the West had to offer, such as the *Berliner Illustrirte Zeitung*. More importantly, Natori had a grand vision that NIPPON, the first "proper" graphic magazine in Japan, was to act as the "maternal body" of photojournalism in Japan. In his own words, he hoped "to give birth to independent Japanese photojournalists, the type that one sees abroad."[17] NIPPON was especially cosmopolitan in its outlook, borne out of the transnational networks of the creative industries—graphic designers, planners, illustrators, photographers, photojournalists, producers, and publishers—of the interwar world in which its founder, Natori Yōnosuke, operated. In this climate of cross-cultural currents, the Japanese creative world was highly attuned to developments in the West.

Natori dominated the magazine in every aspect of its production—not only as photojournalist but also as its graphic designer, magazine editor, and fundraiser. Everything about Natori was new and exciting to the contemporary Japanese: his very being, including his lifestyle, became the embodiment of the spirit of the magazine. Being a highly Westernized bon viveur who dressed with sartorial elegance, Natori spoke strange Japanese in a somewhat high-pitched feminine tone and seemed more comfortable conversing in German with his German wife, Erna Mecklenburg, who was the backbone of his creative genius and supported him as an editor of the magazine. The studio issued work contracts to his subordinates, a practice unheard of in this line of work in contemporary Japan and provided a workspace which was like a design showroom with the most fashionable Bauhaus furniture shipped in from Europe. Many young aspiring photographers, graphic designers, and magazine editors were attracted to NIPPON Studio because of Natori's charismatic larger-than-life character, as well as for the studio's reputation for cutting-edge photojournalism. One of the most famous was Domon Ken who came to NIPPON Studio in 1936, and who later fell out of favor with Natori over copyright issues.[18] NIPPON Studio was the place where serious photojournalism was first practiced in Japan and was considered by many as the origin of editorial and graphic designs of today's Japan.[19] Natori himself reminisced later that "[t]ogether with the knowledge of photojournalism I brought back from Germany, and centering on modern art that incorporated graphics, crafts, and photographs, I wanted to engage in some concrete movement."[20]

However, Natori's work and that of his studio were not projects conceived with any commercial sense. His "no expenses spared" attitude toward the production of the magazine meant that "each issue had cost the equivalent of a house."[21] This was due to Natori's financial backing from his family and family connections, particularly his mother who was the daughter of Asabuki Eiji of the Mitsui Group (zaibatsu), the funding from which had enabled the magazine to exist at all.[22] Tsuda Shingo, chairman of Kanebō (textiles) and a family friend of Natori's, also funded much of the production, providing 10,000 copies for 6,000–7,000 yen. Tsuda shared Natori's concern about the unfavorable images of Japan that the Western countries held, one that viewed Japan as a country that produced low quality goods. He even went on to say that "[t]he key to world peace lies with showing the true image of Japan to foreigners and correcting their sense of superiority in all things as a matter

Publicizing Colonies: Representations of "Korea" and "Koreans" in NIPPON 267

of urgency."²³ In a sense, Natori had hoped that NIPPON, as the most luxurious and beautiful magazine produced in pre-war Japan, would come to symbolize the Japan he had desired to project to Western readership. In 1937, this expensively produced magazine was adopted by the aforementioned KBS as a semi-official organ of the Japanese government to promote Japanese culture, hence, guaranteeing its survival.

THE KOREA ISSUE

Let us now turn our attention to NIPPON's Korea Issue, which was published in July 1939. By then, NIPPON Studio Ltd had reinvented its Japanese name as Kokusai Hōdō Kōgei, marking its more formal integration as a publication of the KBS. Accordingly, the NIPPON reflected its aims as those that mirrored the expanded interests of Imperial Japan, in its stated role to "represent actual life and events in modern Japan and the Far East."²⁴ It is important to note that Natori became central to official Japanese government propaganda (both army and non-army) from 1938 onwards. In April 1938, the Naikaku jōhōkyoku (Information Division, Cabinet Office) created the Shashin kyōkai (Photography Association). In the same month, NIPPON Studio produced a new graphic magazine, *Commerce Japan*, which it published in three languages—French, Italian, and Spanish. In terms of the layout, the aesthetic bent, and the overall quality of production, *Commerce Japan* was very similar to NIPPON. In September 1938, Natori created the South China Photo Service under the oversight of Japan's South China Army's Information Bureau and launched his first Shanghai-based, English-language, luxury, graphic magazine—*Shanghai*—in November 1938. This was followed by another graphic magazine, *Canton* in April 1939, the English-language version of NIPPON which targeted the audience of Western expatriates in China. To complicate matters, it was set up to make it look as though the Chinese had published it for their domestic market. In the same month, Natori launched yet another illustrated magazine though of inferior production quality, called *Kanan Gahō South China Graphic* in English and Chinese via the South China Photo Service.²⁵

The success of NIPPON's Korea Issue seems to have led to reforming the KBS's propaganda policy. Previously, the KBS's main target were Western audiences. However, from September 1939, it turned its attention toward "the East and Latin America" and proceeded to publish the NIPPON special issue on Manchukuo (Volume 19) in October 1939.[26] The Manchukuo Issue appears to have come to the attention of the Kwantung Army who immediately assigned Natori to launch yet another luxury graphic magazine *Manchukuo*, in April 1940, under the Manchukuo Photo Service. In the meantime, NIPPON Studio continued to produce NIPPON, staying more or less true to Natori's original editorial ethos. Even as late as September 1944, NIPPON was published in the color format. The list of publications under the NIPPON Studio continued to expand as it launched new magazines throughout the war years, even venturing into Southeast Asia after December 1941. Most intriguingly, six days before the Japanese Imperial Army invaded Southeast Asia on December 7, 1941, NIPPON Studio launched, under Natori, the monthly Thai-language graphic magazine, *Kaupaapu Tawan'ōku Tōa Gahō* (East Asia graphic magazine) on December 1, 1941. Hence, the Korea Issue must be analyzed in this broader context of an all-out international publicity offensive launched by the KBS, which was by then under the auspices of the Cabinet Office (having moved from the Foreign Ministry control), in order to publicize Japan's imperial and colonial mission to the wider world. The change of policy in September 1939 brings about the publication of magazines in East Asian languages writ large.[27]

To prepare for the Korea Issue, Erna Mecklenburg (Natori's wife and editor), Shinoda Tomio (marketing), Mori Takayuki (photographer), and Takamatsu Jinjirō (designer) visited Korea. Few detailed records of the trip exists, with the exception of that of Takamatsu who reminisced about the unpleasant occasion of being escorted back by the police to Seoul when they went to visit a ginseng farm.[28] Back in Tokyo, Kamekura Yūsaku (1915–97) who was the art director and a designer of NIPPON, was in charge of the layout for the issue. Natori did not personally lead the Korean visit, and there is no evidence to suggest that the editorial team attempted to coordinate their visit with the colonial administration. Although NIPPON was an official organ of the KBS by this time, NIPPON still operated more or less independently with very little intervention.

The Korea Issue is comprised of fifty-three pages printed in large format (14.67" x 10.5"), and the table of contents includes the following articles: "Tyōsen: Sketches of Modern Korea and Her People"; "The Culture of Two Thousand Years Ago"; "Market Places" (this article used *kumijashin*, a method of mounting different pictures together to create a graphic effect, a method

Publicizing Colonies: Representations of "Korea" and "Koreans" in NIPPON

that has been attributed in Japan to Natori); "Transfiguration during a Twenty-Nine-Year Period"; "Map of Korean Industry"; "Zylinkerhüte und Mullröcke" (Tophats and muslin skirts); "A Selection of Celebrities"; "Korean Handicraft"; and "Houses with Ondoru." It also included a short story, "Nukute: *The Wolf*" and a section devoted to book reviews. In general, the Korea Issue describes Korea and Koreans through clothing, objects, and habitus. Apart from the short piece on Korean celebrities, none of the other articles focus on the Koreans as people. Overall, it is possible to delineate four themes used to characterize "Korean-ness" in this special issue: colors, dress, objects, and women.

At the visual level, thematically, the Korea Issue is woven together through the use of two key colors—blue and white. The finest example is the

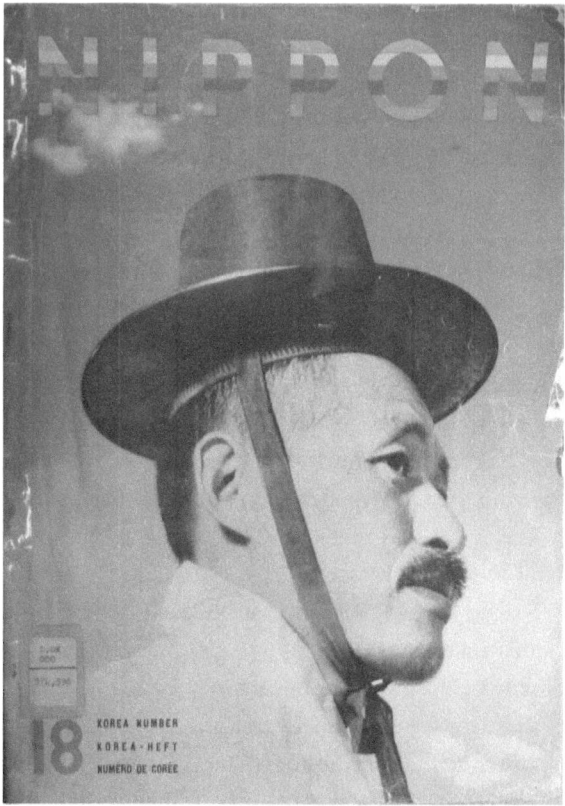

Fig. 9.1 Cover of the Korea Issue, NIPPON, Volume 18 (July 1939).

cover page of the magazine (see Figure 9.1), featuring a profile of a distinguished-looking old man with the traditional black top hat (ca).[29] The shot is taken up toward the face with the strikingly blue sky as a backdrop. The opening gambit informs the reader: "[w]hen I [S. Tutihashi] looked at the bright azure of the sky that hung over the Korean peninsula [Tyōsen], I understood the reason for the exquisite kōrai [Koryŏ] pottery being produced in this land. Its glorious color is an exact reflection of the Korean sky."[30] Then, it introduces the other color scheme, white: "[t]he present Koreans, both men and women wear white almost exclusively, and they call themselves the 'white-clothed race.'"[31] Interestingly, both of these color schemes adopted in the Korea Issue have their origins in the colors associated with different styles of Korean pottery—the blue representing the Koryŏ pottery and the white representing the Yi pottery of the Chosŏn period. In Korean culture, the color blue (palan) symbolizes many important virtues: first, blue denotes the east direction where the sun rises, which represents purity; second, the color blue represents "rejuvenation, happiness, and virtue" and serves as a color which wards off evil.[32] Similarly, the color white denotes the rays of the sun and its brightness and is therefore a sacred color, and a color that brings good omens. White is often referred to in popular Korean sayings such as "[w]earing white clothes, one gets invited often," or "[i]f one wears white clothes, one gets respect in dreams"[33] and, according to Daoism, white is the color of death. The text accompanying the visuals describe the Koreans as "dreamy," possessing "an air of grand leisureliness" left behind the times, as represented by "the sight of a Korean gentleman sitting at the corner of a busy Keizyō street, dressed in ca (a big hat) and tlmaki (outer garment) and smoking the livelong day a pipe of prodigious length is something to be envied by persons nerve racked by the hurry of modern civilization."[34] This theme of Korea as a land of nostalgia, one of bygone days, is a recurring theme.

Ethnic dress is commonly used as a visible manifestation of identity politics and is often taken up by various groups to assert their ethnic and or national identity.[35] The Korea Issue is no exception. Korean clothing is deployed as a constant visual leitmotiv of Korean-ness throughout the issue, often represented in the female figure. In the article "Zylinkerhüte und Mullröcke" (Tophats and muslin skirts), the author attempts to explain the origins of the color white:

The custom of wearing white has different interpretations. It is said to have come from the Chinese as the fashionable color of the Sung Dynasty. While others assume that the tradition comes from the imperial times when white was prescribed as a funeral color. It was said that because several emperors died quickly one after another and subjects wore for white clothing for years white clothing seems to have become the norm.[36]

It goes on to explain, "The task of women is to always keep a supply of spotless white clothes. Therefore, doing laundry plays a large role in the Korean household."[37] The Koreans were historically known as the "white-clad people" because of their tradition of sun-worship.[38] In the article, there is no mention of Korean male clothing, not even elaborations on the top hat featured so prominently in the title. Metaphorically, if one were to interpret the Japanese Colonial Period as a period of mourning, the Korean insistence on wearing white against the instructions of the colonial regime makes much symbolic sense and can be seen as a persistent reminder to the Japanese regime and to the Koreans themselves of the Korean colonial resistance.

According to the author, the cut or the design of Korean clothing had not been influenced by Western fashion and had remained unchanged.[39] This was also true of the *kimono* and the *qipao*. Arguably, the notion of East Asia as steadfastly loyal to its tradition through its unchanging clothing styles is an oversimplification of the complex processes in which dress becomes the site of cultural negotiations. For instance, Finnane has argued that the Chinese woman's dress, the *qipao*, acted quintessentially as a site of various influences that came into Republican China, particularly in the 1920s and 1930s, as the constant, and radical, evolution of the *qipao*, which changed its design almost every other season, shows.[40] Therefore, the argument made in the NIPPON's Korea Issue can be interpreted as a simplistic binary of the East and the West, in which the East remained static and unchanging, while the West remained dynamic and evolving. Accordingly, no hybridization of Korean or East Asian dress ever took place, because the categorical distinction between the East and the West remained unbridgeable, as represented in these two distinct paradigms.[41]

Foreign fascination with the color white was a constant feature in the portrayals of Korea. Earlier in 1897, the intrepid Scottish traveler, Isabella Bird, wrote about the white clothes in her *Korea and Her Neighbours*.

"Everywhere in Korea, one saw Korean women being slaves to the colour white by washing and pounding the clothes at all times."[42] In 1919, the Japanese artist, Ishii Hakutei wrote in his travelogue that "[t]he white clothing of the Koreans are said to be sad and, in a way it is sad, but when it is placed against the landscape, it is striking. It is especially beautiful when placed against the green background."[43] In 1932, Kurahashi Tōjirō, a publisher, who traveled to Korea wrote, "[t]hose who travel in Korea are likely to see the scene of people in white clothing working slowly on the reddish-brown terrain."[44] This was also repeated by Willard Price who penned an article on Korea in *National Geographic* in October 1945, explaining that "the national costume is white because white is the mourning color of Korea.... During one period of Korean history royalty died off so fast that the people were continually in white and became used to it."[45] His use of the term "costume" to describe Korean clothing reflects his gaze as an outsider, categorizing it as exotic and theatrical. Intriguingly, Willard proceeded to inform the reader, "[a] statistician figured Korean women spent three billion hours a year washing, ironing, and sewing. To get more work, Japanese ordered Koreans to be practical and wear darker clothes but they refused."[46] Hence, the color white served as an important signifier for Korean-ness and became closely bound with gender in the eyes of foreign observers.

Fascinatingly, Price has a section in the aforementioned *National Geographic* article "Fantastic Costume has a 'Bible Pocket'" which subverts the apparent Korean-ness of the clothing. The article informs readers that Koreans carry the Bible as good Christians should and, in order to do so, traditional Korean clothing (in this case men's clothing) had been altered to include a hidden feature in the way of the Bible-carrying pocket. This immediately closes the cultural distance between Koreans as the exotic Other because viewing the Koreans as Christians allowed them to become one of "us," hence, closer to "Americans."[47] Implicit in this argument is also the fact that the Japanese colonizers were not Christians and, moreover, forced their colonial subjects to adopt the Japanese civic religion of State Shinto. Ironically, though, this subversion of the Koreans as the Other through the Bible pocket was only possible through reading the article, as this pocket is not visible in the photographs featured.

All of the above discussion on Korean clothing and its whiteness was premised on Korean women as the principal agency that enabled the white-clad people to exist. Images of Korean women were used liberally to convey Korean-ness in the issue. The leitmotiv of a Korean woman carrying a pot or a basket on her head recurs throughout the different sections of the issue, but if one pays closer attention, these Korean women were almost without exception hard at work, if not pounding dirt out of white laundry, they would be carrying pots, selling their produce in markets, and so on and so forth. Indeed, this was a common feature of NIPPON which mobilized "woman" frequently to convey "Japanese-ness," though it must also be stressed that depictions of Japanese women, like their Korean counterparts, were often at work. The insistence of portraying women at work might have been due to Erna Mecklenburg's role in the magazine. Although it became a cliché, Natori knew that using Japanese women as a vehicle for promoting Japanese

Fig. 9.2 Korean women carrying pots, NIPPON, Volume 18, (July 1939): 27.

culture was a highly saleable formula to win Western interest. In this sense, NIPPON effectively adopted whichever "gaze" satisfied the Western readership, even if it meant that it pandered to the archetypal Western Orientalist desire for the feminine East. In wartime, however, this female-as-protagonist formula became less persuasive as a propaganda instrument because "Japan" now had to resonate power and might. Hence, Japanese men became more prominent, particularly in the Japanese-language version of NIPPON (NIPPONban), where articles such as "The Significance of the China Affair," "Sekijuji no shita ni" (Under the Red Cross), featuring Red Cross nurses and their daily routine, and the pictorial representation of the "Toyo heiwa seisaku" (Peace policy in the Orient), feature propaganda material for the Japanese domestic audience.[48]

The second major thematic strand of the Korea Issue is that of objects and through them, heritage. What is stressed is the notion that Korea is a fount of history and art, a land of ancient treasures, and customs and one which has been left behind for hundreds of years. In this sense, NIPPON seems guilty of implicitly ascribing the notion of the "hermit kingdom" to Korea. In the Korea Issue, there are two articles on history and art: "The Culture Two Thousand Years Ago" about the excavation made in the early twentieth century of the artifacts from the Lolang period. The main argument is that Korea had a fine ancient culture as evidenced in these findings, but that it was "illustrative of how oriental culture flourished two thousand years ago."[49] This statement has a two-pronged message: (1) it was a message to Western readers that the Orient possessed an impressive ancient culture as seen by these excavations; and (2) it indicated that Korea's artistic significance took place two thousand years ago.

Similarly, the article "Koreanische Volkskunst" on Korean handicraft, waxes lyrically about the Korean sensitivity to beauty:

> This sense of beauty, peculiar to the Korean race, stands out in their arts and crafts. It is commonly said that one has only to look at Korean craftsmanship to understand ancient Korea. The ancient traditions are vividly alive here, enabling articles of a high standard still to be produced, even as they were in bygone times.[50]

It goes on to describe the beauty of the pottery, particularly those of the Yi Dynasty, lacquer ware, wooden articles, stone ware, bamboo work, silver and brass ware, and handmade paper and concludes, "[t]hey are, to our great regret, quickly passing away from the world's general attention."[51] It is true that contemporary Japanese art connoisseurs were very interested in the Yi pottery, with Yanagi Sōetsu as the most active modern promoter and interpreter of Korean art at the time, the leading figure of the Mingei Movement.[52] In all, Korea was a repository of ancient culture, "the land of historical charms and activities" as advertised by the Government Railways of Tyōsen tourist promotional material.[53] Needless to say, all the superlatives used to praise the beauty of ancient art, culture, and handicraft only had the effect of reifying Korea as a premodern society.

"Transfiguration during a Twenty-Nine-Year Period" stands in stark contrast to the rest of the content, because it reflects most closely the official colonial policy of *naisen ittai* (the unity of Japan and Korea), advocating the vision of Korea as colonial modernity. It starts off with a quote from an Italian special envoy on a mission to Korea, "I have been able to see the true form of Japan in Korea." Then, the article goes on to say, "[w]hy doesn't Japan try to tell the world more about Korea?" The author argues that Japan, Korea, and China were often lumped into one category of "Asia" but, as soon as the Westerners witness Japan's developmental efforts in Korea and Taiwan, they would understand immediately that Japan was in a class of its own, distinctly apart from and superior to the rest of Asia, reminiscent of the argument made by the Meiji educationalist publisher, Fukuzawa Yukichi in his "Datsu-A" [Escape-Asia] theory of 1885.[54] His argument focuses on the rupture in Korean history brought about by the annexation of 1910, at which point the Japanese invested "formidable proportions" of expenditures into the colony to bring it up to scratch. In fact, the Japanese efforts were so spectacular, the author dares to opine, that had the Lytton Commission known about how modernized Korea had become under Japanese colonial rule, the League of Nations might have responded differently to the Manchurian Incident.[55] The type of argument, where the colony is used as a mirror to reflect the achievements of the colonizer, was also evidenced in Japanese travel writing on colonial Taiwan.[56] Not surprisingly, it shares comparatively with the colonial mentality betrayed in Western colonial writings.[57] This article contains quantitative diagrams that demonstrate the improvements that had been made under the Japanese rule. Of particular interest is a pictorial table titled "Statistics of Japanese-Korean Inter-Marriages" as if to demonstrate statistically how Korea and Japan were coming closer together.[58]

The only section of the Korea Issue that introduces Korean individuals is "A Selection of Celebrities." Four Korean "celebrities" are introduced: Son Ki-tei, who was an Olympics gold medalist runner in the 1932 Los Angeles Olympic Games; Genzirō Nagata, an opera singer studying at the Tokyo Music School; Sai Syō-ki, a dancer with a "healthy physique" who introduced stronger "physicality" to Japanese dancing; Tyō Kaku-Tyū, a novelist who had his piece published in Kaizō.[59] All of them are dressed differently: the Olympian in casual Western wear, the dancer in a traditional Korean dancing costume, the novelist in a kimono, and the opera singer in a Western suit. These celebrities were young people, who were trained under Japanese teachers or coaches. This section of the Korea Issue intended to demonstrate how much the Japanese colonizers were supporting the development of colonial talent, even introducing them into mainstream Japanese culture. Of note, Tyō Kaku-Tyū's short story, "Nukute: *The Wolf*" is given four-pages near the end of the special issue, making it one of the longest pieces in the issue.[60]

CULTURAL OR COLONIAL PROPAGANDA?

Having examined the Korea Issue in some detail, what observations can we make from it? Generally, the Korea Issue suffers from a one-dimensional conceptualization of Korea and its people, as a place of nostalgia and repository of objects of beauty. To be sure, the strong, aesthetically driven editorial ethos of NIPPON had turned the Korea Issue into one of the most visually stunning issues. Indeed it is almost lyrical in its beauty. Photographs and lithographs of Korean women carrying pots on their heads were laid out to give an appearance that they were meandering through the pages of the issue. Evidently, much thought had gone into the choice of the colors blue and white, which worked as a thematic strand, giving the entire issue a visual coherence. The articles focused mostly on dress and objects, which were then presented as objects of desire with a nostalgic longing for an ancient culture of some two thousand years ago. This one-dimensionality was augmented by the general lack of interest in Koreans as real people. The exception was the piece on Korean celebrities but, even that preferred to dwell on the Korean cultural elite who had been successfully integrated into mainstream Japanese culture. By not giving voice to the Koreans, NIPPON did not have to deal with the complexities of their colonial existence.

It has been argued by Ryang that "there was a peculiarity in the Japanese colonial discourse embodied in travel writing, in that many travellers held the view, amongst other very diverse understandings of the colony, that Korea was similar to Japan."[61] Arguably, one could interpret the allusions of Korea as a place of nostalgia or as a reminder of Japan's lost innocence, which enabled the positioning of Japan as the symbol of modernity and Korea as the premodern Other. This dichotomy fascinates as it can be found even in the disjuncture between the hyper "modern" materiality of the Korea Issue, which deployed up-to-date graphic and printing technology as well as to the use of super-luxury quality paper, and the predominantly premodern representations of Korea featured within it. However, this binary does not come across explicitly in the issue, as the magazine does not introduce the Self (that is, Japan) as a contrasting point in its portrayals of colonial Korea as the Other.

Significantly, the Japanese colonial authority is visually not represented in the Korea Issue (apart from Japanese company advertisements). This is a highly intriguing omission, if the Korea Issue is to be considered a piece of colonial propaganda. Surely, one of the main purposes of colonial propaganda during this period was to showcase colonial development? Whatever became of the colonial modernity of the 1930s Korea?[62] Even the archetypal colonialist, Tokutomi Sohō opined that "Korea was a civilized nation and that it would be 'a laughable act of ignorance' if one were to talk of Korea in the same terms as the colonial rule of Africa by European nations."[63] Sure enough, there is one article which struck a chord with the more mainstream colonial argument about Japan's investments in Korea, but, it remained an anomaly.

As an interesting counter-reference, Natori included two photographs of Korea in the 1937 German-language publication, *Grosses Japan Dai NIPPON* (Great Japan)— a luxury book of 144 photographs, which he had compiled, published by Karl Specht. Natori's photographs on Korea are replete with colonial symbolism: one consists of the newly constructed Western-style, neo-classical Government-General Building built by the Japanese in 1936. It was a large structure with a huge dome and pillars placed in the forecourt of the Kyonbokkun Palace in Seoul, surrounded by forbiddingly high iron railings.⁶⁴ In the foreground to the left of the photograph stands a group of white-clad Korean women chatting in the midday sun. The other photograph is visually more interesting, taken from a low-angle just above the street level, focusing on the backs of Koreans again clad in white, both men and women, and children, with one Japanese official in uniform (also with his back to the camera) and a young boy clad in Western clothes (hence, presumably Japanese) all standing in front of a building.⁶⁵ In these photographs, Natori had set up a rigid binary between the Self and the Other, which helped to create tension, hence, giving it a critical edge. In this way, his selected photographs of Korea emphasized the Japanese as the *modern* colonials, juxtaposed strikingly against the Koreans as the *premodern*. However, when we examine the Korea Issue, Natori's typology of the visual binary was not in evidence, because "Japan" and the "Japanese" are visually absent from the issue.

So what do the above analyses of the representations of Korea and Koreans, and of the absence of the Japanese colonial authority, in the Korea Issue imply? The most plausible explanation is that NIPPON, as a luxury graphic magazine and an organ of the KBS, was still identified primarily as *cultural* propaganda and not a *colonial* propaganda mouthpiece. If we recall the original publishing ethos of NIPPON, its mission was the promotion of Japanese culture to Western readership. As Natori did not conceptualize culture politically but rather aesthetically, he was primarily concerned with the overall aesthetic quality of NIPPON, which had to compete with the top Western graphic magazines. In the Korea Issue, the high aesthetic standard is in ample evidence both at the expense of realism and in the choice of subjects of photographs.

Moreover, the Korea Issue was formulaic in its representation of Korea and Koreans. It was a formula Natori had developed during his editorship of NIPPON, one that reflected his own philosophy of how to introduce Japanese culture to the uninitiated Western readership. From his first assignment for the *Berliner Illustrierte Zeitung*, Natori recognized the importance of coming up with themes which interested Western readers. This worked best when he focused on the differences between Japan and the West. His photographs would show close-up shots of Japanese women, with explanations of how the *kimono* was worn and descriptions of the interior of a Japanese house for example. The initial success of his method meant that it became a staple formula for NIPPON. Another example of the repetitive use of this successful formula is the photograph of Korean artisan's tools featured in the Korea Issue (see Figure 9.3).⁶⁶ This adopts an identical layout to the photograph of Japanese artisan's tools that Natori produced for the catalog of the International Handicraft Exhibition held in Berlin in May 1938, which would also be published in the NIPPON special issue on Japanese handicraft in June 1938.⁶⁷

Therefore, I argue that the way in which Korea was visualized in the special issue was not too different from the way Japan was visualized in other issues of NIPPON. According to Weisenfeld, NIPPON can be read as a magazine that exhibited Japan to the Western readership, as if it were a portable museum.⁶⁸ In the same vein, therefore, in the pages of the special issue,

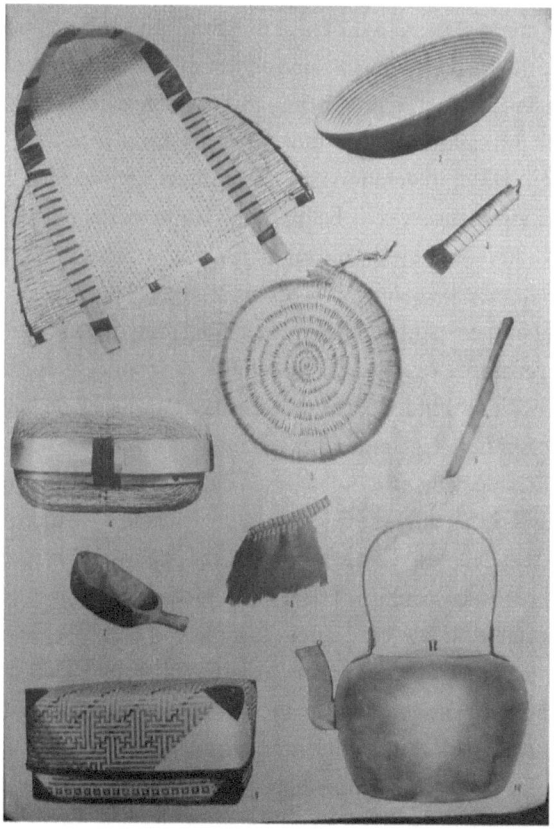

Fig. 9.3 Photograph of the Korean artisans' tools, NIPPON 18 (July 1939): 33.

Korea was beautified as a portable museum to be marketed to the West. True enough, Natori's pandering to the tastes and desires of the Western readership meant that many issues of NIPPON invariably featured images of Japanese women and scenery—not such a radical departure from the stereotypes of geishas and Fujiyamas. In that sense, we can argue that Natori was either the victim or the perpetuator of the Western orientalist gaze on Japan and, by extension, on Korea, because of his understanding that one had to produce magazines that would appeal to Western sensibilities. Arguably, therefore, it may be more accurate to categorize NIPPON's treatment of Korea in its special issue as one of being orientalist.

Above all, what is most paradoxical about the images of Korea and Koreans presented in the special issue is that much of the representations went against the grain of the colonial policy of *naisen ittai*—the central plank of the Government-General of Korea at this time. According to a recent study by Mark Caprio on the assimilation policies of the Japanese in Korea, the Counterplan Proposal of September 1938 sought to strengthen further the fundamental principle of *naisen ittai*, in order for Korea and Koreans to achieve an even closer integration into the Japanese Empire.[69] As the Japanese evidently pitched themselves as being the Asian moderns, ideally, the Korea Issue ought to have portrayed Koreans as Asian near-moderns. If the purpose of colonial cultural propaganda vis-à-vis other colonial powers was to impress upon them how successful Japan had been in turning these under-developed, semi-feudal territories into visions of colonial modernity, then, flooding the special issue with beautiful images of Koreans exotically clothed and carrying clay pots on their heads in some rural setting, was not going to persuade their Western readership. What the Korea Issue did, therefore, was emphasize the distance between the Japanese and Koreans, instead of closing the distance between the two peoples, as the policy of *naisen ittai* would have dictated. As such, the Korea Issue could not have been produced, at least as far as the NIPPON editorial team was concerned, as a piece of colonial propaganda but was instead a cultural promotion of traditional Korea. This explains the absence of the Japanese colonizer as the Self in the issue. After all, it was the first foray of NIPPON into the uncharted territory of promoting the Japanese colonial empire. The lack of know-how on how to deal with the thorny subject of colonies was evident in the way the Korea Issue was conceived.

Hence, the special issue presents an ambiguous period of transition where the needs of wartime colonial propaganda had not been easily met and accommodated by the existing structures of cultural propaganda. Underneath it all, we see a more ambivalent, and complex, image of Japan as the colonizer, grappling with the changing regional context, initiated by their military ambitions.

NOTES

The author thanks Kokusho Kankai for their permission to use the images in this article.

1. The KBS remained in operation until September 1972 when it was disbanded to make way for its successor, the Japan Foundation.
2. Kokusai bunka shinkōkai, KBS: Sanjūnen no ayumi [KBS: Its thirty years], 10–12.
3. Shibazaki Atsushi, Kindai Nihon to kokusai bunka kōryū: Kokusai bunka shinkōkai no sōsetsu to tenkai [Modern Japan and international cultural exchange: The establishment and development of the Center for International Relations], 18 and 56.
4. Kokusai bunka shinkōkai, KBS: Sanjūnen no ayumi, 14.
5. Ibid., 17.
6. NIPPON 1 (October 20, 1934), inside front cover. No author given.
7. Shirayama Mari, "Natori Yōnosuke no shigoto—1931–45" [Natori Yonosuke's work—1931–45], 18–19.
8. NIPPON 10 (March 15, 1937), inside front cover. No author given.
9. For Natori's biographical information, consult the following: Shirayama Mari, "Natori Yōnosuke no shigoto: 1931–45," 5–33; Natori Yōnosuke, Shashin no yomikata [How to read photographs]; Ishikawa Yasumasa, Hōdō shahin no seishun jidai: Natori Yōnosuke to nakamatachi [Photojournalism's early years: Natori Yosuke and his comrades]; and Mikami Masahiko, Wagamama ippai: Natori Yōnosuke [Totally selfish: Natori Yonosuke].
10. "Eizō ni yoru kiroku to dentatsu: Shashin sakokushugi o toranakkata senkusha—Natori Yōnosuke: Taidan: Tsurumi Shunsuke, Hani Susumu" [Recording and dissemination through moving images: The avant-garde who did not choose photographic isolationism—Natori Yonosuke: Conversation: Tsurumi Shunsuke, Hani Susumu," n. p.
11. LIFE 2, no. 2 (January 11, 1937).
12. For instance, LIFE 2, no. 23 (December 6, 1937), front cover; and "Photographer Natori at the Japanese Front," LIFE 2, no. 25 (December 20, 1937): 60–61.

13. Natori Yonosuke, Shashin no yomikata, 124.

14. "Eizō ni yoru kiroku to dentatsu: Shashin sakokushugi o toranakkata senkusha," n. p.

15. Natori Yōnosuke, Shashin no yomikata, 19–22.

16. Shirayama Mari and Hori Yoshio eds., Natori Yōnosuke to NIPPON Kōbō [1931–45] [Natori Yonosuke and the NIPPON studio], 6.

17. Shirayama Mari, "Natori Yōnosuke no shigoto: 1931–45," 5–8.

18. There is an interesting discussion by contemporaries of the legendary fallout between Natori and Domon in Ishikawa Yasumasa, Hōdō shahin no seishun jidai: Natori Yōnosuke to nakamatachi, 78–81.

19. Kaneko Ryūichi, "'NIPPON' to wa nandattanoka: Fukkokuban kanketsu ni attate [What is NIPPON: On the occasion of its reprint], 2.

20. For his philosophy on photography, see Natori Yōnosuke, Shashin no yomikata [How to read photographs].

21. Natori Yōnosuke, Shashin no yomikata, 172–73.

22. Shirayama Mari, "Natori Yōnosuke no shigoto: 1931–45," 6–10.

23. Shirayama Mari and Hori Yoshio eds., Natori Yōnosuke to NIPPON Kōbō [1931–45], 10 and 14.

24. Korea Issue, NIPPON 18 (July 1, 1939), 3.

25. Shirayama Mari and Hori Yoshio eds., Natori Yōnosuke to NIPPON Kōbō [1931–45], 70–91.

26. There is extensive coverage of the Manchukuo issue in Gennifer S. Weisenfeld, "Touring Japan-as-Museum," 774–81.

27. Ibid., 98–103 and 127–31.

28. Ibid., 96.

29. On the history of ca, consult Kim Young-suk, Kankoku fukushoku bunka jiten [Dictionary of Korean clothing culture], 29–31.

30. Tutihashi S. "Tyosen," NIPPON 18 (July 1, 1939), n. p.

31. Ibid.

32. Itō Ahito, Kankoku bunka shinboru jiten [Dictionary of Korean symbols], 12–15.

33. Ibid., 374–77.

34. On the history of tlmaki, consult Kim Young-suk, Kankoku fukushoku bunka jiteni, 142–43.

35. There is a growing corpus of literature in this field, for instance, Joanne Bubolz Eicher, ed. Dress and Ethnicity.

36. "Zylinderhuete und Mullrueke" [Top hats and muslin skirts], NIPPON 18 (July 1, 1939): 25.

37. Ibid.

38. Itō Ahito, Kankoku bunka shinboru jiten, 565–68.

39. "Zylinderhuete und Mullrueke," 24.
40. See, for instance, Antonia Finnane, *Changing Clothes in China*.
41. Korea Issue, NIPPON, 18 (July 1939); and Shirayama Mari, "Natori Yōnosuke no shigoto: 1931–45," 96–98.
42. Isabella Lucy Bird, *Korea and Her Neighbours*, 26 and 45.
43. Ishii Hakutei, "Natsu no Kongōzan" [Summer in Mount Kongo], 75.
44. Quoted from Kim Brandt, "Objects of Desire," 736.
45. Willard Price (1887–87), an American, traveled to Japan many times in the 1930s, and again during the postwar, and wrote numerous books on Japan. He is also known as a children's author, having written a series of adventures novels. Willard Price, "The Jap Rule Hermit Kingdom [Korea]," 437.
46. Willard Price, "The Jap Rule Hermit Kingdom [Korea]," 444.
47. My use of the term "cultural distance" is taken from Peter Burke's chapter "The Discreet Charm of Milan: English Travellers in the Seventeenth Century," in *Varieties of Cultural History*, 94–110.
48. Ota Saburo, "The Significance of the China Affair: Shina jihen no igi," 8–9; "Sekijuji no shita ni" [Under the Red Cross], 10–11; and Yokoyama Ryuichi, "Toyo heiwa seisaku" [Peace policy in the Orient], 52–53.
49. "The Culture of Two Thousand Years Ago," NIPPON 18 (July 1, 1939): 45.
50. "Koreanische Volkskunst," [Korean handicraft], 44.
51. Ibid., 44.
52. Yuko Kikuchi, *Japanese Modernisation and Mingei Theory*; and Kim Brandt, *Kingdom of Beauty*.
53. "Tyosen Beckons You this Year" (advertisement), NIPPON 18 (July 1, 1939): 51.
54. "Transfiguration during a Twenty-Nine-Year-Period," NIPPON 18 (July 1, 1939): 18.
55. Ibid., 20.
56. Naoko Shimazu, "Colonial Encounters," 21–37.
57. On colonial mentality of the Western traveler, see, for instance, Alison Blunt, *Travel, Gender, and Imperialism*, 64–65.
58. "Statistics of Japanese-Korean Inter-Marriages," NIPPON 18 (July 1, 1939): 21.
59. "A Selection of Celebrities" NIPPON 18 (July 1, 1939): 28–29.
60. In fact, this short story is an intriguing story about the murder of an official by a young man of a village, over having his fiancé "stolen" by the official. It is possible to read the subtext of colonial resentment and anger against the Japanese as represented by the official. Tyo Kaku-Yu, "Nukute: The Wolf," NIPPON 18 (July 1, 1939): 37–40.
61. Sonia Ryang, "Japanese Travellers' Accounts of Korea," 138.
62. See Tani E. Barlow's "Introduction: On 'Colonial Modernity'" in *Formations of Colonial Modernity in East Asia*, 1–20; on recent debates on colonial modernity, confer the special issue of *Cultural Studies* 26, no. 5 (2012), with the lead article by Hyunjung Lee

and Younghan Cho, "Introduction: Colonial Modernity and Beyond in East Asian Contexts," 601–16.

63. Sonia Ryang, "Japanese Travellers' Accounts of Korea," 138.

64. Jung-sun Han, "Japan in the Public Culture of South Korea."

65. From a reprint of *Grosses Japan Dai NIPPON*, n. p.

66. "Koreanische Volskunst," 33.

67. Natori's know-how in creating highly acceptable images of Japanese craftsmanship for Japanese officialdom led to his appointment as the official representative at the Berlin International Crafts Exhibition in May 1938. Shirayama Mari and Hori Yoshio eds., *Natori Yōnosuke to NIPPON Kōbō (1931–45)*, 58–59; and Nagashima Yoshizo, "The Hand as a Tool," NIPPON 15 (June 1, 1938): 16.

68. Gennifer S. Weisenfeld, "Touring Japan-as-Museum," 747–93.

69. Mark E. Caprio, *Japanese Assimilation Policies in Colonial Korea, 1910–1945*, chapter 5 deals with the period under discussion.

Bibliography

INTRODUCTION

An Pyŏngjik. "Han'guk kŭnhyŏndaesa yŏn'gu ŭi saeroun p'aerŏdaim" [New research paradigm for Korean modern history]. *Ch'angjak kwa pip'yŏng* 25, no. 4 (Winter, 1997): 39–58.

Duus, Peter. *The Abacus and the Sword: The Japanese Penetration of Korea, 1895–1910*. Berkeley: University of California Press, 1995.

Eckert, Carter J. *Offspring of Empire: The Koch'ang Kims and the Colonial Origins of Korean Capitalism, 1876–1945*. Seattle: University of Washington Press, 1991.

Kim, Hakjoon. "A Devil Appears in a Different Dress: Imperial Japan's Deceptive Propoganda and Rationalization for Making Korea Its Colony." In *The International Impact of Colonial Rule in Korea, 1910–1945*, edited by Yong-Chool Ha, 19–48. Seattle: Center for Korea Studies/University of Washington Press, 2019.

Ku, Daeyeol. [Ku Taeyŏl, Ku, Dae-Yeol]. "The British and American Perceptions of Korea during the Colonial Period." In *The International Impact of Colonial Rule in Korea, 1910-1945*, edited by Yong-Chool Ha, 179–217. Seattle: Center for Korea Studies/University of Washington Press, 2019.

Ku Taeyŏl [Ku, Daeyeol, Ku, Dae-Yeol]. *Han'guk Kukche kwan'gyesa yŏn'gu* [A study of the history of Korean international relations]. Sŏul: Yoksa wa Pip'yŏngsa, 1996.

Lee, Hong Yung, Yong-Chool Ha, and Clark W. Sorensen. *Colonial Rule and Social Change in Korea*. Seattle: University of Washington Press, 2015.

Myers, Ramon Hawley, Mark R. Peattie, and Jingzhi Zhen. *The Japanese Colonial Empire, 1895–1945*. Princeton, NJ: Princeton University Press, 1984.

Schmid, Andre. "Japanese Propaganda in the United States from 1905." In *The International Impact of Colonial Rule in Korea, 1910–1945*, edited by Yong-Chool Ha, 73–102. Seattle: Center for Korea Studies/University of Washington Press, 2019.

Shimazu, Naoko. "Publicizing Colonies: Represenations of "Korea" and "Koreans" in NIPPON." In *The International Impact of Colonial Rule in Korea, 1910–1945*, edited by Yong-Chool Ha, 259–284. Seattle: Center for Korea Studies/University of Washington Press, 2019.

Shin, Gi-Wook, and Michael Robinson, eds. *Colonial Modernity in Korea*. Cambridge, MA: Harvard University Press, 1999.

Sin Yongha. "Singminji kŭndaehwaron chaejŏngnip sidae e taehan pip'an" [A critique of the attempt to reinterpret colonial modernity]. *Ch'angjak kwa pip'yŏng* 25, no. 4 (Winter 1997): 8–38.

Sun, Kezhi. "Chinese Understandings of Colonial Korea in Modern Times, 1910–1945: Observations and Reflections." In *The International Impact of Colonial Rule in Korea, 1910–1945*, edited by Yong-Chool Ha, 239–257. Seattle: Center for Korea Studies/University of Washington Press, 2019.

CHAPTER 1

Allen, Horace Newton. *Korea: Fact and Fancy*. Seoul: Methodist Publishing House, 1904.

Bhom, Fred C., and Robert R. Swartout, Jr., eds. *Naval Surgeon in Yi Korea: The Journey of George W. Woods*. Berkeley: Institute of East Asian Studies/University of California, 1984.

Bishop, Isabella L. Bird. *Korea and Her Neighbours*. New York: Fleming H. Revell Co., 1897.

Brown, Arthur Judson. *The Mastery of the Far East: The Story of Korea's Transformation and Japan's Rise to Supremacy in the Orient*. New York: Charles Scribner's Sons, 1919.

Cavendish, Alfred Edward John. *Korea and the Sacred White Mountain: Being a Brief Account of a Journey in Korea in 1891*. London: George Philip and Son, 1894.

Chang Chiyŏn. "Siirya pangsŏng taeyok" [Tonight I weep loudly and bitterly]. *Hwangsŏng sinmun*. November 20, 1905.

Ch'oe Ch'anggu. *Kŭndae Han'guk chŏngch'i sasangsa* [A history of modern Korean political thoughts]. Sŏul: Iljokak, 1972.

Ch'oe Munhyŏng. *Han'guk kŭndae ŭi segyesajŏk ihae* [An understanding of modern Korea from the perspective of world history]. Sŏul: Chisiksanŏpsa, 2010.

———. *Myŏngsŏng hwanghu sihae chinsil ŭl palk'inda* [I expose the truth about the assassination of Queen Min]. Sŏul: Chisiksanŏpsa, 2001.

Chŏng Chinsŏk. *Daehan maeil sinbo wa Paesŏl* [The Korea daily newspaper and (Ernest) Bethell]. Sŏul: Chisiksanŏpsa, 1987.

Chōsen Sōtokufu [The Japanese Governor-General office], ed. *Chōsen hito no shinsō to seikaku* [Koreans' thoughts and character]. Keijo: Chōsen Sōtokufu, 1927.

Conroy, Hilary. *The Japanese Seizure of Korea, 1868–1910: A Study of Realism and Idealism in International Relations*. Philadelphia: University of Pennsylvania Press, 1960.

Cook, Harold F. *Korea's 1884 Incident: Its Background and Kim Okkyun's Elusive Dreams*. Seoul: Royal Asiatic Society/Korea Branch, 1972.

Denny, Owen N. *China and Korea*. Shanghai: Kelly and Walsh, 1888.

Diosy, Arthur. *The New Far East*, 4th ed. London: Cassell and Co., 1904.

Fukujawa, Yukichi. "Ajia shoku to no wasen to ga eijoku no setsu" [Debates on Japan's war and peace with Asian countries]. In *Fukujawa Yukichi zenshu* [Collected works of Fukujawa Yukichi], edited by Keio University. Tōkyō: Iwanamishoten, 1961.

———. *The Autobiography of Yukichi Fukujawa*. Revised and translated by Eiichi Kiyooka. New York: Schocken Books, 1972.

———. "Chōsen toritono shokei" [The execution of the Korean independence party leaders]. In *Fukujawa Yukichi zenshu* [Collected works of Fukujawa Yukichi], edited by Keio University. Tōkyō: Iwanamishoten, 1961.

———. "Dastsu a ron" [On escaping from Asia (or, On leaving Asia behind)]. *Jijishinp'o*. March 16, 1885.

Griffis, William Elliot. *Corea: The Hermit Nation*. New York: Charles Scribner's Sons, 1882.

———. *Corea: The Hermit Nation*. 8th edition. New York: Charles Scribner's Sons, 1907.

Hamilton, Angus, Herbert H. Austin, and Masatake Terauchi. *Korea: Its History, Its People, and Its Commerce*. Boston and Tokyo: J. B. Millet Co., 1910.

Hawley, Samuel, ed. *Inside the Hermit Kingdom: The 1884 Korea Travel Diary of George Clayton Foulk*. New York: Macmillan and Co., 1895.

Heard, Augustine, Durham White Stevens, and Howard Martin. "China and Japan in Korea." *The North American Review* 54, no. 454 (September 1894): 300–20.

Hŏ Tonghyŏn. "Chŏnp'al paekp'alsip yŏndae kaehwap'a insadŭl ŭi sahoe chinhwaron suyong yangt'ae pigyo yŏn'gu: Yu Kiljun kwa Yun Ch'iho" [A comparison of the reception of social Darwinism by Korean progressive leaders in the 1880's: Yu Kiljun and Yun Ch'iho]. *Sach'ong* 55 (September 2002): 173–74.

Honma Kyusuk'ae. *Chōsen zakki* [Miscellaneous notes on Korea]. Tōkyō: Nirokusinp'o, 1894.

Hwang, In K. *The Korean Reform Movement of the 1880s: A Study of Transition in Inter-Asian Relations*. Cambridge, MA: Schenkman Publishing Co., 1978.

Hwang Zunxian. *Chosŏn ch'aengnyak* [Korean policy]. Translated with annotations by Cho Ilmun. Sŏul: Kŏnkuk Taehakkyo Chulp'ansa, 1977.

Hyŏn Kwangho. *Taehan cheguk kwa Rōsia kŭrigo Ilbon* [The great Korean empire, Russia, and Japan]. Sŏul: Sŏnin, 2007.

Kang Tongjin. *Ilche ŭi Han'guk ch'imnyak chonch'aeksa yŏn'gu* [A study on the history of imperial Japanese policies for the aggression of Korea]. Sŏul: Hankilsa, 1980.

Kennan, George. "Korea: A Degenerate State." *The Outlook* (October 7, 1905): 307–15.

Kim, C. I. Eugene, and Hankyo Kim. *Korea and the Politics of Imperialism, 1876–1910.* Berkeley: University of California Press, 1967.

Kim Changch'un. *Semirhan illŏsŭt'ŭ wa huigwi sajin ŭro pon kŭndae Chosŏn* [Modern Yi Chosŏn Korea seen through rare pictures]. Sŏul: Sallim, 2008.

Kim Ch'ŏngkyun. "Chosŏn munyerane nat'anan Hangukŭi yimji" [Korea's image appeared in Chosŏn]. In *Chekukŭi yitong kwa sikminji Chosŏnŭi ilbonindŭl* [The transfer of the empire and Japanese in colonial Korea], edited by Chŏng Pyŏngho, 151–61. Sŏul: Mun, 2010.

Kim P'yongmuk. "Ŏyangnon." [On defense of the country from the West]. In *Kŭndae Han'guk chŏngch'i sa sangsa* [A history of modern Korean political thoughts], edited by Ch'oe Ch'anggyu, 40–45. Sŏul: Iljokak, 1972.

Kim T'aejun. "Yu Kiljun ŭi kaehwa sasang kwa minjokjŏk cha-a-insik ŭi hyŏngsŏng" [Yu Kiljun's thoughts on civilizations and the formation of national self-identity]. In *Han'guk kŭndae chisigin ŭi minjokchŏk chaa hyŏngsŏng* [The formation of the national self-identity by Korea's modern intellectuals], edited by Sŏ Yŏnho. Sŏul: Sohwa, 2004.

Kim Tujin. "Tong-Ajia hwairon ŭi pyŏnyong" [A change in the thesis of civilized countries and uncivilized countries among East Asian countries]. *Han'guk chŏngch'i hakhoebo* 44, no. 3 (Fall 2010): 15–18.

Kim Yongku. *Kŏmundo wa Vladivostok* [Kŏmundo and Vladivostok]. Sŏul: Sŏgang Jesuit Taehakkyo Chulp'ansa, 2008.

Koryŏ Taehakkyo Asea Munje Yŏn'guso [Asiatic Research Center, Korea University], ed. *Kuhankuk oegyo munsŏ* [Diplomatic documents of late Chosŏn Korea]. Sŏul: Koryŏ Taehakkyo Asea Munje Yŏn'guso, 1964.

Kuksa P' yŏnch'an Wiwonhoe [The national history compilation committee], ed. *Yun Ch'iho ilgi* [The diary of Yun Ch'iho]. Sŏul: T'amkudang, 1971.

Ladd, George Trumbull. *In Korea with Marquis Itō.* London: Longmans, Green, and Co., 1908.

Longford, Joseph H. *The Story of Korea.* New York: Charles Scribner's Sons, 1911.

Lowell, Percival. *Chosön: The Land of the Morning Calm.* Boston: Ticknor and Co., 1886.

Miln, Louise Jordan. *Quaint Korea.* New York: Charles Scribner's Sons, 1895.

Nahm, Andrew C. "Kim Ok-kyun and the Reform Movement of the Progressives." *Korea Journal* 24, no. 12 (December 1984): 38–62.

———, ed. *Korea under Japanese Colonial Rule: Studies of the Policy and Techniques of Japanese Colonialism: Proceedings of the Conference on Korea, November 12–14, 1970.* Korean Studies Series 2. Kalamazoo: Western Michigan University, 1973.

Oguma Eiji. *Danitzu minjoku sinwano kigen* [The origins of the myth of the homogeneous nation]. Tōkyō: Shinyosha, 1995.

Oppert, Ernst Jakob. *A Forbidden Land: Voyages to the Corea.* New York: G. P. Putnam's Sons, 1880.

Pak, Chihyang. *Ilgŭrŏjin kŭndae* [Distorted modern times]. Sŏul: P'urŭn Yŏksa, 2003.

Parker, E. H. *China: Her History, Diplomacy, and Commerce.* London: Hazell, Watson, and Viney, 1901.

Ross, John. *History of Corea: Ancient and Modern.* London: Paisley: J. and R. Parlane, 1879.

Saaler, Sven, and Christopher W. A. Szipilman, eds. *Pan-Asianism Volume 2: A Documentary History.* Lanham, MD: Rowman and Littlefield, 2011.

Sands, William F. *Undiplomatic Memories: The Far East, 1896–1904.* New York: Whittlesey House, McGraw-Hill Book Co., 1930.

Shin Yongsuk. "Late Chosŏn Dynasty Korea in Contemporary French Newspapers." *Korea Journal* 26, no. 6 (June 1986): 51–60.

Sin Yŏnggil. *Chosŏnjo mangkuk chŏnyagi* [On the eve of the fall of the Korean kingdom]. Sŏul: Chisŏndang, 2008.

Sin Yongha. *Ilche singminji chŏngch'aek kwa singminji kŭndaehwaron pip'an* [A critical study of Japanese colonial policy and colonial modernity]. Sŏul: Munhak kwa Chisŏngsa, 2006.

———. *Pak Ŭnsik ŭi sahoe sasang yŏn'gu* [A study of Pak Ŭnsik's social thoughts]. Sŏul: Sŏul Taehakkyo Chulp'ansa, 1982.

———. *Sin Ch'aeho ŭi sahoe sasang yŏn'gu* [A study of Sin Ch'aeho's social thoughts]. Sŏul: Han'gilsa, 1984.

Song Kŏnho. *Han'guk hyŏndae inmulsaron* [Treaties on personalities in Korea's modern history]. Sŏul: Han'gilsa, 1984.

Tarui Tokich'i. *Daitō gappō ron* [Thesis on the union of great East] Nara: n.p., 1885. Tōkyō: Chŏryoshoin reprint, 1975.

Urquhart, E. J. *Glimpses of Korea.* Mountain View, CA: Pacific Press Publishing Association, 1923.

Walker, Dale L. "Jack London's War." *The World of Jack London.* www.jacklondons.net.

Weems, Benjamin B. *Reform, Rebellion, and the Heavenly Way.* Tucson: University of Arizona Press, 1964.

Whigham, Henry James. *Manchuria and Korea.* New York: Charles Scribner's Sons, 1904.

White, Trumbull. *The War in the East: Japan, China, and Corea*. Philadelphia: P. W. Ziegler and Co., 1895.

Yang Kiwung. "Kim Okkyun kwa Fukujawa Yukichi" [Kim Okkyun and Fukujawa Yukichi]. *Hallym Ilbonhak yŏn'gu* 4 (November 1999): 107–21.

Yates, Charles L. *Saigo Takamori: The Man Behind the Myth*. New York: Kegan Paul International, 1995.

Yi Hyang, and Kim Chŏngyŏn. *P'uredŭrik Puresuteksŭ ch'akhan migaein tongyang ŭi hyŏnja* [Frederick Boulesteix's "A Good Uncivilized Man and a Wise Oriental Man"]. Sŏul: Ch'ŏngyŏnsa, 2001.

Yi Kwangrin. "Kaehwa sŭng Yi Tongin" [Yi Tongin, an enlightened monk]. *Ch'angjak kwa pip'yŏng* [Creation and criticism] 18 (Fall 1970): 461–72.

Yi Taejin. *Ilbon ŭi Taehan cheguk kangchŏm* [Imperial Japanese forced occupation of the great Korean empire]. Sŏul: Kkach'i, 1995.

———. "Was Korea Really a 'Hermit Nation'?" *Korea Journal* 38, no. 4 (Winter 1998): 5–35.

Yi Yongju. "Munmyŏngnon ŭl kŏchy'ŏ t'araron e irŭnŭn kil" [A road to the theory of "escaping from Asia" via the theory of civilization: Fukujawa Yukichi's perception of Asia and the "mission to civilize"]. In *Kŭndae chŏnhwan'gi tongasia sok ŭi Han'guk* [Korea in East Asia in the period of modern transformation], edited by Yi Kyusu, Yim Kyŏngsŏk, and Chin Chekyo, 249–68. Sŏul: Sungkyunkwan Taehakkyo Chulp'ansa, 2004.

Yu Kiljun Chŏnsŏ P'yŏnch'an Wiwonhoe [Committee for the collection and compilation of works by Yu Kiljun], ed. *Yu Kiljun chŏnsŏ* [The collected works of Yu Kiljun]. Sŏul: Iljokak, 1971.

Yu Tongjun. *Yu Kiljun chŏn* [A biography of Yu Kiljun]. Sŏul: Iljokak, 1987.

CHAPTER 2

Chang Insŏng. *Chang So ŭi kukche chŏngch'i sasang* [Confucianism topics on international relations]. Sŏul: Sŏul Taehakkyo Ch'ulp'anbu, 2002.

Chŏn Pokhŭi. *Sahoe chinhwaron kwa kukka sasang: Ku Hanmal ŭl chungsim ŭro* [The theory of social evolution and a spirit of nationalism]. Sŏul: Hanul, 1996.

Chŏn Sangsuk [Jeon, Sang Sook]. "Chosŏn Ch'ongdok chŏngch'i cheje wa kwallyoje: 1910-yŏndae rŭl chungsim ŭro" [Japanese "politics of the Korean Government-General" and its bureaucracy: Focused on the 1910s]. *Han'guk chŏngch'i oegyosa nonch'ong* 31, no.1 (2009): 5–36.

———. *Chosŏn Ch'ongdok chŏngch'i yŏn'gu: Chosŏn Ch'ongdok ŭi "sangdae-jŏk chayulsŏng" kwa Ilbon ŭi Han'guk chibae chŏngch'aek t'ŭkchil* [Japanese "politics of the Korean governor-general," 1910–1936: "Political autonomy" of the Korean governor-general and the "specialty" of Japanese colonial control of Korea]. Sŏul: Chisik Sanŏpsa, 2012.

———. "Chosŏn t'ŭksusŏng'ron kwa Chosŏn singmin chibae ŭi silje" [Theory of Korean uniqueness and Chosŏn colonial reality]. In *Singminji kŭndaehwa-ron e taehan pip'an-jŏk sŏngch'al* [Critical reflections on the theory of colonial modernity], edited by Shin Yongha et al. Sŏul: Nanam, 2009.

———. "Ilche ŭi singminji Chosŏn haengjŏng irwŏnhwa wa Chosŏn Ch'ongdok ŭi 'chŏngch'i-jŏk chayulsŏng'" [The colonial administrative unification of Japanese imperialism and the "political autonomy" of the governor-general in Korea]. *Ilbon yŏn'gu nonch'ong* 21 (2005): 281–310.

———. "Kukkwŏn sangsil kwa Ilbon ŭi Hanbando chŏngch'aek" [Japan's policy toward the Korean peninsula and the deprivation of Korean sovereignty]. *Tonga yŏn'gu* 59, (August 2010): 5–41.

———. "Kŭndae 'Sahoe Kwahak' ŭi Tong Asia suyong kwa Meiji Ilbon 'Sahoe Kwahak' ŭi t'ŭkchil: Bluntschli's kukkahak suyong ŭl chungsim ŭro" [East Asia's acceptance of modern social sciences and modern the characteristics of Japanese social sciences: With priority given to the reception of Bluntschli's political thought]. *Ihwa sahak yŏn'gu* 44 (2012): 181–220.

———. "Rŏ-Il chŏnjaeng chŏnhu Ilbon ŭi taeryuk chŏngch'aek kwa Terauch'i [Terauchi Masatake]" [Terauchi and Japan's continental politics in the Russo-Japanese War]. *Sahoe wa yŏksa* 71 (2006): 5–33.

———. "Yugyo chisigin ŭi 'kŭndae' insik kwa Sŏgu 'Sahoe Kwahak' ŭi ihae: Kaeguk chŏnhu Kim Yunsik ŭi kaehwa insik kwa sŏyang hangmun suyongnon ŭl chungsim ŭro" [Confucian intellectual's conception of "modernity" and understanding of Western social sciences: Focused on Kim Yunsik's recognition of Kaewha and the reception of Western knowledge]. *Sahoe iron* 42 (2012): 275–308.

Chōsen Sōtokufu [Governor-General of Korea]. *Furoku 1* [Appendix 1]. Keisei (Seoul): Chōsen Sōtokufu, 1912.

Dobe Ryoichi. *Kŭndae ilbon ŭi kundae* [The modern Japanese military]. Translated by Yi Hyunsoo and Kwon Taehwan. Sŏul: Yuksa Hwarangdae Yŏnguso, 2003.

Duus, Peter. *The Abacus and the Sword: The Japanese Penetration of Korea, 1895–1910*. Berkeley: University of California Press, 1995.

Fujiwara Akira. *Ilbon kunsasa* [Japanese military history]. Translated by Seo Yungchik. Sŏul: Sisa Ilbonusa, 1994.

Editorial. *Keijō Nippō*, June 4, 1911.

Gaimushō [Ministry of Foreign Affairs of Japan], ed. "Kankoku heigō ni kansuru jōyaku" [Treaties on Korean annexation]. In *Nihon gaikō nenpyō narabini shuyō bunsho* [Japanese diplomatic chronology and important documents Vol. 1]. Tōkyō: Hara Shobō, 1965.

———. "Taikan hōshin ni kansuru kette" [Decision on Korean policies]. In *Nihon gaikō nenpyō narabini shuyō bunsho* [Japanese diplomatic chronology and important documents Vol. 1]. Tōkyō: Hara Shobō, 1965.

Hihara Toshikuni. *Kandai shisō no kenkyū* [Research on Chinese thought of the Han time]. Tōkyō: Kenbun Shuppan, 1986.

Ichimata Masao. "Nihon no kokusaihō o kizuita hitobito" [Figures who constructed Japanese international law]. *Kokusai mondai shinsho* 37 (1973): 15–27.

Inoue Kiyoshi. "'Kaikoku' to kindai kokka no seiritsu" [Open door and establishment of the modern state]. In *Kindai Nihon shisōshi* [History of modern Japanese thought], edited by Arakawa Ikuo and Ikimatsu Keizō. Tōkyō: Yūhikaku, 1973.

———. *Nihon no gunkokushugi III* [Japanese militarism III]. Tōkyō: Gendai Hyōronsha, 1975.

Iriye Akira. *Ilbon ŭi woegyo* [Diplomacy of Japan]. Translated by Yi Seonghwan. Sŏul: Purŭnsan, 1993.

Isida Tak'esi [Ishida Takeshi]. *Ilbon ŭi sahoe kwahak* [Japanese social sciences]. Translated by Han Yŏnghye. Sŏul: Sohwa, 2003.

Jeon, Sang Sook. *See* Chŏn Sangsuk

"Kankoku wo teikoku ni heigō no ken" [The matter to annex Korea to the Japanese Empire]. *Shōsho* [Imperial rescript] August 29, 1910.

Kitaoka Shin'ichi. *Nihon rikugun to tairiku seisaku: 1906–1918 nen* [The Japanese Army and its continental politics, 1906–1918]. Tōkyō: Tōkyō Daigaku Shuppankai, 1978.

Kobayashi Michihiko. *Nihon no tairiku seisaku, 1895–1914: Katsura Tarō to Gotō Shinpei* [Japanese continental politics 1895–1914: From Katsura Tarō to Goto Shinpei]. Tōkyō: Nansōsha, 1996.

Kurachi Tetsukichi. *Kurachi Tetsukichi-shi jutsu Kankoku heigō no keii* [Kurachi Tetsukichi's statement on Korean annexation]. Tōkyō: Gaimushō Chōsabu Daiyonka, 1939.

Matsushita Yoshio. *Nihon gunbatsu no kōbō Vol. 1* [The rise and fall of Japanese warlords Vol. 1]. Tōkyō: Jinbutsu Ōraisha, 1967.

Moriyama Shigenori. *Kindai Nikkan kankeishi kenkyū: Chōsen shokumichika to kokusai kankei* [A study of modern Japan-Korea Relations: Colonization of Korea and international relations]. Tōkyō: Tōkyō Daigaku Shuppankai, 1987.

Motoyama Yukihiko. *Meiji kokka no kyōiku shisō* [Educational thought of Meiji Japan]. Kyoto: Shibunkaku Shuppan, 1998.

Mutō Shūtarō. *Kindai Nihon no shakai kagaku to Higashi Ajia* [Social sciences of modern Japan and East Asia]. Tōkyō: Fujiwara Shoten, 2009.

Nakatsuka Akira. *Kindai Nihon no Chōsen ninshiki* [Modern Japan's perception of Korea]. Tōkyō: Kenbun Shuppan, 1993.

Oguma Eiji. *Tan'itsu minzoku shinwa no kigen* [The origin of the myth of a single race nation]. Tōkyō: Shin'yōsha, 1995.

Okita Yukuji. *Nihon kindai kyōiku no shisōshi kenkyū: Kokusaika no shisō keifu* [A study on educational history of modern Japan: Genealogy of globalization thought]. Tōkyō: Gakujutsu Shuppankai, 2007.

Pusan Fu [Office of the Pusan district]. *Pusan fushi genkō Vol. 6* [Documents of the Pusan official district Vol. 6]. Pusan: Pusan Fu, 1937.

Shunjō Tokio. *Kankoku heigō shi* [History of Korean annexation]. Keijō: Chōsen oyobi Manshū Sha, 1926.

Sim Kichae. *Bakumatsu ishin Nitchō gaikōshi no kenkyū* [A study on the history of Japan-Chōsen foreign policies from the last period of Japan's feudal government to the Meiji Restoration]. Tōkyō: Rinsen Shoten, 1998.

———. "Mangmal Myŏngch'i ch'ogi e issōsŏ ŭi Ilbon ŭi tae-Chosŏn taeŭng" [The early Meiji government's foreign policy toward Korea]. *Oriental Studies* 13 (2000): 232–46.

Sūben Saarŏ [Sven Saaler]. "Kukche kwangye ŭi pyŏnyong kwa naesyŏnŏl aident'iti hyŏngsŏng" [The influence of changes in international relations on the formation of national identity: The creation of Asianism]. *Han'guk munhwa* 41 (2006): 135–57.

Watanabe Hiroshi. *Higashi Ajia no ōken to shisō* [East Asian royal authority and thought]. Tōkyō: Tōkyō Daigaku Shuppankai, 1997.

Wei Yuan. *Haiguo tuzhi* [Illustrated gazetteer of countries beyond the seas]. Yangzhou: 1847. Reprinted by Zhengzhou: Chinese Old Book Publishers, 1999.

Yamagata Aritomo. "Gaiko seiryaku ron" [Political strategy of foreign policies]. (March 3, 1890). In *Yamagata Aritomo iken sho* [Statements of Yamagata Aritomo], edited by Ōyama Azusa. Tōkyō: Hara Shobō, 1966.

———. "Gunbi iken sho" [Opinion on military preparedness]. (December, 1893). In *Yamagata Aritomo iken sho* [Statements of Yamagata Aritomo], edited by Ōyama Azusa. Tōkyō: Hara Shobō, 1966.

———. "Teikoku no kokuze ni tsuite no enzetsu" [A speech on the empire's national policy]. (December 6, 1890). In *Yamagata Aritomo iken sho* [Statements of Yamagata Aritomo], edited by Ōyama Azusa. Tōkyō: Hara Shobō, 1966.

Yi Hangi. "Han'guk mit Ilbon ŭi kaeguk kwa kukchebŏp" [International law and the open door of Korea and Japan]. *Haksurwŏn nonmunjip inmun sahoe kwahak p'yŏn* 19 (1980): 185–210.

Yosijawa Seich'iro [Yoshizawa Seiichirō]. *Aegukchuŭi ŭi hyŏngsŏng* [Formation of Jingoism]. Translated by Chŏng Chiho. Sŏul: Nonhyŏng, 2006.

CHAPTER 3

An, Ch'ang-ho. "A Korean Appeal to America." *The Nation* 108, no. 2807 (April 19, 1919): 228–29.

Asakawa, K. "Korea and Manchuria under the New Treaty." *Atlantic Monthly* 96 (November 1905): 699–711.

Baldwin, Elbert F. "Korea and Japan at The Hague." *The Outlook* (September 7, 1907): 26–28.

Barstow, Marjorie, and Sydney Greenbie. "Korea Asserts Herself." *Asia* (September 1919): 921–26.

Brown, Arthur Judson. "The Japanese in Korea." *The Outlook* 63 (November 12, 1910): 591–95.

———. "Unhappy Korea." *The Century Magazine* 68, no. 1 (May 1904): 147–50.

Brudnoy, David. "Japan's Experiment in Korea." *Monumenta Nipponica* 25 (1970): 155–95.

Casserly, Gordon. "From Chemulpo to Seoul." *The Living Age* 23 (June 4, 1906): 613–21.

Chong, Prince Ye We. "A Plea for Korea." *The Independent* 63 (August 22, 1907): 423–26.

Chung, Henry. *The Case of Korea: A Collection of Evidence on the Japanese Domination of Korea, and on the Development of the Korean Independence Movement*. New York, Chicago: Fleming H. Revell, 1921.

———. "Korea Today: A Korean View of Japan's Colonial Policies." *Asia the American Magazine on the Orient* 19 (January–December 1919): 467–74.

———. *The Oriental Policy of the United States*. New York: Fleming H. Revell, 1919.

Clark, Donald N. *Living Dangerously in Korea: The Western Experience, 1900–1950*. Norwalk, CT: Eastbridge, 2003.

Cooper, Frederick, and Ann Laura Stoler, eds. *Tensions of Empire: Colonial Cultures in a Bourgeois World*. Los Angeles: University of California Press, 1997.

Cumings, Bruce. "Archaeology, Descent, Emergence: Japan in British/American Hegemony, 1900–50." In *Japan in the World*, edited by Masao Miyoshi and H. D. Hartoonunian, 79–111. Durham NC: Duke University Press, 1993.

———. *The Origins of the Korean War Volume 1*. Princeton, NJ: Princeton University Press, 1981.

Curzon, George H. *Problems of the Far East: Japan, Korea, China.* London: Longmans, Green, and Co., 1894.

De Forest, H. H. "The Moral Purpose of Japan in Korea." *The Independent* 70 (January 1911): 13–17.

Duus, Peter. *The Abacus and the Sword: The Japanese Penetration of Korea, 1885–1910.* Berkeley: University of California Press, 1998.

Eliot, Charles William. *Some Roads Towards Peace: A Report to the Trustees of the Endowment on Observations Made in China and Japan in 1912.* Publication of the Carnegie Endowment for International Peace. Division of Intercourse and Education. No. 1. Washington, DC: Endowment, 1914.

Ellis, William T. "An Interview with Prince Itō." *The Independent* 67 (November 1909): 1068–70.

Gluck, Carol. *Japan's Modern Myths: Ideology in the Late Meiji Period.* Princeton, NJ: Princeton University Press, 1985.

Goette, John. "One Roosevelt Proposes, Another Disposes." *The Saturday Review.* (September 8, 1945): 26–27.

Government-General of Chōsen. *Annual Report on Reforms and Progress in Chōsen (Korea), 1916–17.* Seoul: Government General of Chōsen, 1918.

———. *Annual Report on Reforms and Progress in Chōsen (Korea), 1917–18.* Seoul: Government General of Chōsen, 1920.

———. *Annual Report on Reforms and Progress in Chōsen (Korea), 1918–21.* Seoul: Government General of Chōsen, 1922.

Grajdanzev, Andrew. "Korea in the Postwar World." *Foreign Affairs* 22 (April 1944): 479–83.

———. "Problems of Korean Independence." *Asia and the Americas* 44 (September 1944): 416–19.

Griffis, William Eliot. "An American View." *The Nation* 108, no. 2812 (May 24, 1919): 830–31.

———. "Japan's Absorption of Korea." *North American Review* 192 (1910): 516–26.

Henkle, Rae D. "The Benevolent Assimilation of Korea." *The Nation* 109 (October 11, 1919): 505–6.

Henning, Joseph. *Outposts of Civilization: Race, Religion, and the Formative Years of American-Japanese Relations.* New York: New York University Press, 2000.

Hirobumi, Itō. "Japanese Policy in Korea." *Harper's Weekly* 52 (January 11, 1908): 27.

"Ilbon sinmunji" [Newspapers in Japan]. *TaeHan maeil sinbo*, August 14, 1906.

"Japan as Colonial Administrator" (editorial). *The Nation* 100, no. 2608 (June 24, 1915): 702.

Jordan, David Starr. "Japan's Task in Korea." *The American Review of Reviews* 66 (July 1912): 81–82.

Kawakami, Kiyoshi Karl. *American-Japanese Relations: An Inside View of Japan's Policies and Purposes.* New York: Fleming H. Revell Co., 1912.

———. *Japan Speaks on the Sino-Japanese Question.* New York: MacMillan, 1932.

———. *Japan and World Peace.* New York: MacMillan, 1919.

———. *The Real Japanese Question.* New York: MacMillan, 1921.

———. *What Japan Thinks.* New York: Macmillan, 1921.

Keeton, George W. "Background for War: The White Man of the Orient." *Travel* 81 (November 1942): 34.

———. "Korea and the Future." *The Contemporary Review* (June 1942): 354–58.

Kennan, George W. "Are the Japanese Honest?" *The Outlook*, 101, no. 8 (August 31, 1912): 1011–16.

———. "Is Japan Persecuting Christians in Korea?" *The Outlook* 102 (December 14, 1912): 804–10.

———. "The Japanese in Korea." *The Outlook* 81, no. 11 (November 11, 1905): 609–16.

———. "The Korean People: The Product of a Decayed Civilization." *The Outlook* 81, no. 8 (October 21, 1905): 409–16.

———. "The Land of the Morning Calm." *The Outlook* 78 (October 8, 1904): 363–69.

———. "Prince Itō and Korea." *The Outlook* 93 (November 27, 1909): 665–69.

Kent, George. "Korea: Exhibit 'A' in Japan's New Order." *Asia* 42 (April 1942): 230.

"Kinaenssi jiron Nanjŏng" [The situation of Korea by Keenan]. *TaeHan maeil sinbo,* October 23, 1906.

Kinnosuke, Adachi. "The Japanese in Korea." *The American Review of Reviews* 36 (October 1907): 472–75.

"Korea: A Tribute to Japanese Administration" (editorial). *The Review of Reviews* (August 1915): 232–33.

"Kumigaek kwa Han'gugin" [Western visitors and Koreans]. *TaeHan maeil sinbo.* April 5, 1910.

Ladd, George Trumbull. "The Annexation of Korea: An Essay in 'Benevolent Assimilation.'" *Yale Review* (July 1912): 639–56.

———. *In Korea with Marquis Ito.* London: Longmans, Green, 1908.

———. "Letter to the Editor: America and Japan." *New York Times,* March 22, 1907.

Larsen, Kirk, and Joseph Seely. "Simple Conversation or Secret Treaty: The Taft Katsura Memorandum in Korean Historical Memory." *Journal of Korean Studies* 19, no. 1 (Spring 2014): 59–92.

MacKenzie, F. A. *The Unveiled East.* London: Hutchinson and Co., 1907.

Makoto, Baron Saitō. "A Message from the Imperial Japanese Government to the American People: Home Rule in Korea?" *The Independent* (January 31, 1920): 167–69.

Masatake, Terauchi. "Reforms and Progress in Korea." In *Korea: Its History, Its People, and Its Commerce*, edited by Angus Hamilton, Herbert Henry Austin, and Masatake Terauchi, 215–390. Boston: J. B. Millet, 1910.

Maxey, Edwin. "Korea: An Example of National Suicide." *The Forum* 39, no. 2 (October 1907): 281–90.

———. "The Reconstruction of Korea." *Political Science Quarterly* 25 (December 10, 1910): 673–87.

Menefee, Selden C. "Our Korean Allies." *The Nation* 155 (November 14, 1942): 509.

Nelson, M. Frederick. *Korea and the Old Orders in Eastern Asia*. Baton Rouge: Louisiana State University Press, 1946.

"Oein ŭi nune yŏnghanŭn Chosŏn" [Korea in the eyes of foreigners]. *TaeHan maeil sinbo*, March 10, 1910.

Oishi, Kuma. "The Causes Which Led to the War in the East." *The Arena* 10, no. 60 (November 1894): 721–35.

Okuma, Count. "Japan's Policy in Korea." *The Forum* 37 (April 1906): 571–80.

Park, Jihang. "Land of the Morning Calm, Land of the Rising Sun: The East Asia Travel Writings of Isabella Bird and George Curzon." *Modern Asian Studies* 36, no. 3 (July 2002): 513–34. Stable URL: http://www.jstor.org/stable/3876646.

Peffer, Nathaniel. "Korea." *The New Republic* (March 10, 1920): 56.

Pierson, Arthur T. "First Impressions of Korea." *Mission Review* New Series 24, Old Series 34 (March 1911): 183–90.

Pieters, Albertus. "Editorial: The Korean Conspiracy Case." *The Independent* 74 (February 27, 1912): 443.

———. "The Korean Conspiracy Case: A Review." *The Outlook* 103 (January–April 1913): 120–24.

Piggot, F. T. "The Itō Legend: Personal Recollections of Prince Itō." *The Nineteenth Century and After* 67 (January 1910): 173–88.

Powell, E. Alexander. "Japan's Policy in Korea." *Atlantic Monthly* 129 (March 1922): 395–412.

Rea, Bronson Geo. "Saito: The Man Who Stood by Dewey at Manila; His Work in Korea; An Appreciation." *The Far Eastern Review* (December 1924): 565–68.

"Rhee's Revival." *Newsweek* (December 13, 1943): 60.

Rhee, Syngman. *Japan Inside Out: The Challenge of Today*. New York: F. H. Revell, 1941.

Schmid, Andre. *Korea Between Empires, 1895–1919*. New York: Columbia University Press, 2002.
——. "Two Americans in Seoul: Evaluating an Oriental Empire, 1905–1910." *Korean Histories* 2, no. 2 (2011): 1–23.
Sherrill, Charles H. "Korean and Shantung versus the White Peril." *Scribner's Magazine* (March 1920): 367–72.
Stead, William Thomas ed. "The Honest Broker' Between East and West: A Japanese View." *The Review of Reviews* 26 (July–December 1902): 66.
Tendon, A. "Korea, the Cockpit of the East." *Review of Reviews* 29 (February 1904): 176–81.
Valliant, Robert B. "The Selling of Japan: Japanese Manipulation of Western Opinion, 1900–1905." *Monumenta Nipponica* 29, no. 4 (Winter 1974): 415–38.
Weyl, Walter E. "Korea: An Experiment in Denationalization." *Harper's Magazine* (March 1919): 392–401.
Wheeler, Edward. "The Assentation of Itō." *Current Literature* (December 1909): 613–14.
Wilde, Harry Emerson. *Japan in Crisis*. New York: MacMillan, 1934.
"Will There be War in East Asia?" (Editorial). *The Outlook* 96, no. 5 (October 1, 1910): 258–60.
Willoughby, W. W. "Japan and Korea." *Unpartisan Review* 13, no. 25 (January 1920): 24–42.
Yamagata, I. "The Korean Annexation: A Japanese View." *The Outlook* (February 1, 1922): 185–87.
Yoon, P. K. "The Present and Future of Korea." *The Review of Reviews* 36 (December 1907): 580.

CHAPTER 4

Bhabba, Homi. *The Location of Culture*. London: Routledge, 1994.
Chŏn Sangsuk. "Che 1-ch'a Segye tajŏn Ihu kukche chilsŏ ŭi chaep'yŏn kwa minjok chidojadŭl ŭi Taeoe insik" [Reorganization of international relations after World War I and the understanding of Korean national leaders]. *Hanguik chŏngch'i oegyosa nonch'ong* 26, no. 1 (2005): 313–49.
Chŏng Yonguk. "1920-yŏndae kongsanjuŭi undong yŏn'gu" [A study of the Communist movement in the 1920s]. In *Nam-pukhan yŏksa insik pigyo kangŭi (Kŭnhyŏndae p'yŏn)* [Comparison of historical perceptions between the North and South Koreas], edited by Chŏng Yonguk. Sŏul: Ilsongjŏng, 1989.
"Chŏngsin haptong ŭi sirhyŏn" [Realization of combining political affairs with new things]. *Chosŏn ilbo*, July 7, 1929.

"Chumokhal nonongro sŏa ŭi tae chung ch'aek" [The Russian Soviet Federative Socialist Republics' noteworthy policy toward China]. *Chosŏn ilbo*, January 4, 1927.

Chung, Chin O. *Pyongyang between Peking and Moscow: North Korea's Involvement in the Sino-Soviet Dispute 1958–75*. Tuscaloosa: University of Alabama, 1978.

"Chungguk kukche kwalliron ŭi ch'ulch'ŏ" [The origin of the Chinese international management theory]. *Chosŏn ilbo*, August 18, 1921.

"Chungguk ŭi p'ungun (sang)" [Chinese storm (1)]. *Chosŏn ilbo*, August 30, 1924.

"Chunghwain sŏn'gakcha chekun ege yŏham" [Chinese pioneers are allowed]. *Chosŏn ilbo*, October 14, 1923.

"Dankotaru socihi o yōsu" [Require strong measures]. *Keijō Nippō*, May 21, 1921.

"Gisil ihae ŭi Pangyŏk 1" [Prevention of actual profits and losses]. *Chosŏn ilbo*, August 20, 1920.

"Gunshuku kaigi no kōka" [The outcome of the disarmament conference]. *Keijō Nippō*, March 7, 1922.

"Hainichi hōan shikō [The enforcement of the anti-Japanese bill]. *Keijō Nippō*, May 8, 1924.

Hoffmann, Stanley. "An American Social Science: International Relations." *Daedalus* 106, no. 3 (Summer 1977): 41–60. Stable URL: http://www.jstor.org/stable/20024493.

Hunter, Helen-Louise. "North Korea and the Myth of Equidistance." *Korea and World Affairs* 4, no. 2 (Summer 1980): 268–79.

"Hwainul pojanghan chungguk ui tongnan" [Disaster containing Chinese civil war]. *Chosŏn ilbo*, October 7, 1924.

"Hyŏnha sasang ŭi aidia choryu" [The two ideological currents in the contemporary world]. Editorial. *Chosŏn ilbo*, May 17, 1924.

Im Kyŏngsŏk, and Cha Hyeyŏng. *Kaebyŏk e pich'in singminji Chosŏn ŭi ŏlgul* [The colonial Korea's face in journal *Kaebyŏk*]. Sŏul: Mosinŭn Saramdŭl, 2007.

"Jōyaku ihan o kōgi seyo" [Protest the violation of the treaty]. *Keijō Nippō*, May 7, 1924.

Kim Hyŏndae. "Ilcheha *Tonga ilbo* ŭi minjok undongsajŏk koch'al: Munhwa chŏngch'i kigan (1920–1928) ŭi sasŏl punsŏk ŭl chungsim ŭro" [A study of the nationalistic movement of the *Tonga ilbo* under Japanese imperialism]. Master's thesis. Hanyang Taehakkyo, 1987.

Kim Younghee. "Ilche chibae sigi Han'gugin ŭi sinmun chŏpch'ok kyŏnghyang" [The trends in newspapers' exposure of Koreans under Japanese imperialism]. *Hanguk ŏllon hakpo* 46, no. 1 (2001): 39–71.

Ko Pongjun. "1920-yŏndae chisigin ŭi kukche chŏngch'i insik e kwanhan yŏn'gu: 'Kaebyŏk' ŭi sahoejuŭijŏk kukche chŏngch'i kwannyŏm ŭl chungsim ŭro" [A study

on the intellectuals' recognition of international relations in Korea in the 1920s].
Master's thesis. Sŏul Taehakkyo Taehagwŏn, 1998.

Koh, Byung Chul. *The Foreign Policy of North Korea*. Praeger Special Studies in International Politics and Public Affairs. New York: F.A. Praeger, 1969.

———. *North Korea and the World: Explaining Pyongyang's Foreign Policy*. Seoul: Kyungnam University Press, 2004.

"Kukka, minjok, keyegŭp" [The state, nation, and class]. Editorial. *Chosŏn ilbo*, June 19, 1926.

"Kunbi ch'ukso wa Ilbon yoron" [Arms reduction and Japanese public opinion]. *Chosŏn ilbo*, November 29, 1921.

"Kungmin chŏngbu ŭi oegyo chŏngch'aek" [Foreign policy of the nationalist government]. *Chosŏn ilbo*, January 27, 1929.

Kwak, Tae-Hwan, Wayne Patterson, and Edward E. Olsen, eds. *The Two Koreas in World Politics*. Seoul: Institute for Far Eastern Studies, Kyungnam University Press, 1983.

"Kyŏngje palchŏn ŭi sin sigi wa sinbangmyŏn" [New era and the way of economic development]. *Chosŏn ilbo*, December 16, 1921.

"Kyŏngsiji mothal Il-Mi kwang'gye" [Deteriorating US-Japanese relations]. Editorial, *Chosŏn ilbo*, July 5, 1925.

"Miguk ŭi kŭktong" [US policy toward the Far East]. *Chosŏn ilbo*, July 5, 1925.

"Miguk ŭi kyŏngjejok chinch'ul: Chungguk e taehan kihoe ŭi kyundŭng undong" [Economic entry of the United States: The movement of equal opportunity for China]. *Chosŏn ilbo*, May 20, 1929.

Neuman, Stephanie G. ed. *International Relations Theory and the Third World*. Basingstoke: Macmillian, 1998.

"Nichi beisensō" [Japan-US war]. *Keijō Nippō*, March 10, 1922.

"Nisshi kyōei-ron" [The co-existence of Japan and China]. *Keijō Nippō*, January 28, 1920.

"Pujŏn choyak ŭi mosun" [Contradictions of the anti-war treaty]. *Chosŏn ilbo*, April 19, 1928.

"P'yŏnghwa wa chŏnjaeng: Puchŏn choyak kwa kunbi ch'ukso" [Peace and war: Antiwar treaty and arms reduction]. *Chosŏn ilbo*, September 23, 1928.

Ryu Ki Du. "Kwagŏ illyŏn ŭi taep'yŏngyang chungsim ŭi kukche chŏngso" [Past one year's international situation in the Pacific]. *Chosŏn ilbo*, January 1, 1929.

Saaler, Sven, and Christopher W. A. Szpilman. *Pan-Asianism: A Documentary History*. Landham, MD: Rowman and Littlefield Publishers, 2011.

"Segye chongse ŭi hyŏnse i" [The current trend in world politics]. Editorial. *Chosŏn ilbo*, March 22, 1925.

"Segye p'yŏnghwa nŭn hŏ-sik ŭi mun'gu" [World peace is the ostentatious slogan]. *Chosŏn ilbo*, June 28, 1921.

"Segye p'yŏnghwa nŭn ŏnje toel kŏtin'ga" [When will world peace be coming?]. *Chosŏn ilbo*, January 2, 1929.

"Segye wa Chosŏn" [The world and the Chosŏn nation]. *Chosŏn ilbo*, January 21, 1924.

"Segyejŏk minjok" [The nation in the world]. *Chosŏn ilbo*, December 12, 1921.

"Shiberia taisku no shōrai" [The future of the Siberia policy]. *Keijō Nippō*, May 21, 1921.

"Shuppei no igi o mattou seyo" [Let's fulfill the original meanings of military dispatch]. *Keijō Nippō*, May 31, 1927.

Smith, Steve. "Six Wishes for a More Relevant Discipline of International Relations." In *The Oxford Handbook of Political Science*, edited by Robert E. Goodin. New York: Oxford University Press, 2011.

Sŏ Chungsŏk. "Ilche sidae sahoejuŭjadŭl ŭi minjokkwan kwa kyegŭp kwan: 1920-yŏndae rŭl chungsim ŭro" [Socialists' perception on the nation and class under the rule of Japanese imperialism]. In *Han'guk minjokchuŭiron III* [Korean nationalism Vol. 3], edited by Park HyunChae, 272–342. Sŏul: Changjak kwa pip'yong, 1985.

Son Chunsik, "Singminji Chosŏn ŭi taeman insik: Chosŏn ilbo (1920–1940) kisa rŭl chungsim ŭro" [The perception of colonial Chosŏn on Taiwan: Focusing on *Chŏson ilbo*'s articles, 1920–1940]. *Chungguk kun-hyŏndae sa yŏn'gu: Han'guk Chungguk kun-hyŏndae sa Hakhoe* 34 (2007): 113–32.

"Sŏyang kwa tongyang (sang)" [The West and the East (I)]. *Chosŏn ilbo*, August 22, 1920.

"Suraksŏkch'ul ŭi chungguk chŏngse" [Chinese circumstances become clear]. *Chosŏn ilbo*, October 1, 1929.

Sylvester, Christine. "African and Western Feminisms: World-Traveling the Tendencies and Possibilities." *Signs: Journal of Women in Culture and Society* 20, no. 4 (Summer 1995): 941–69. doi: 10.1086/495027.

"Taedong isang ŭi yoksajok tongŭ" [Historical consensus on grand jury]. Editorial. *Chosŏn ilbo*, December 8, 1929.

"T'aep'yŏngyang hoeŭi wa Il-Yŏng Mi haegun ryŏk [The Pan-Pacific conference and naval power of Japan, Britain, and the United States]. *Chosŏn ilbo*, August 3, 1921.

"Taep'yŏngyang ŭi hyŏnjae wa changnae" [The here and the hereafter of the Pacific]. *Chosŏn ilbo*, May 15, 1921.

"T'aep'yŏngyang ŭi yangmyŏnjŏk ch'ungdol" [Double-sided clashes in the Pacific]. *Chosŏn ilbo*, January 7, 1929.

"Tai Manshū konpon taisku no juritsu?" [The establishment of the fundamental countermeasures against Manchuria]. *Keijō Nippō*, February 9, 1921.

Tickner, Arlene. "Seeing IR Differently: A Note from the Third World." *Millennium* 32, no. 2 (2003): 295–324.

"Tongyo rŭl chŏnhanŭn chungguk chŏngse" [The chaotic news from Chinese circumstances], *Chosŏn ilbo*, September 24, 1929.

Yi Hojae. *Han'guk ŭi kukche chŏngch'igwan: Kaehang hu 100-yŏn ŭi oegyo nonjaeng kwa pansŏng.* [International political views of Korean people: Diplomatic disputes and self-examinations over one hundred years after the opening of a port]. Sŏul: Pŏmmunsa, 1994.

"Yŏng-Mi ŭi 250ŏk t'uja kyehoek: Chungguk kŏnsŏl saŏp ŭl wihayŏ," [Twenty-five-billion-dollar investment plan of Britain and the United States]. *Chosŏn ilbo*, October 24, 1928.

Yu Chaech'ŏn. "Ilche ha Han'guk chapchi ŭi kongsanjuŭi suyong e kwanhan yŏn'gu" [The study of the accommodation of Communism in Korean magazines during the Japanese Colonial Period]. *Tonga yŏn'gu* 15 (1998): 17–52.

CHAPTER 5

An Insik. "Siguk kwa oin ŭi kago" [The current state of affairs and our resolution]. In "Chŏnsiha ŭi siguk yŏnsŏl" [Wartime political speeches]. *Samch'ŏlli* 9, no. 5 (October, 1937). Accessed August 21, 2018. http://db.history.go.kr/id/had_160_0280.

An Pyŏngju. "Miguk ŭn ŏdiro kana: Rujŭbelt'ŭ ron" [Where is the United States heading?: A theory on Roosevelt]. *Pip'an* (September 1937): 18–34.

Aydin, Cemil. *The Politics of Anti-Westernism in Asia: Visions of World Order in Pan-Islamic and Pan-Asian Thought*. New York: Columbia University Press, 2007.

Ch'a Sangch'an. "Sasang ŭro pon Chosŏn kwa miguk ŭi kwan'gye" [Korea: US relations from a historical perspective]. *Chogwang* (May 1941): 98–107.

———. "Sinmi tae yangyoran: Yuwŏl sahwa?" [What was the great Korean-American War of 1971?]. *Chogwang* (June 1940): 66–71.

Ch'ae P'ilgŭn. "Tonga ŭi yusin, miyŏng kyŏngmyŏl ŭi p'yŏngyang taeyŏnsŏlhoe sokki" [The record of the great speech assembly in P'yŏngyang for the restoration of the Orient and the extermination of the United States and the United Kingdom]. *Samch'ŏlli* (January 1942): 38–43.

Chaha Sanin. "Miguk kyŏngjech'aek ŭi p'asyohwa: Ch'ŏngch'i hyŏngmyŏnk ŭi naeyong kŏmt'o" [Fascitization of the US Economic Policies: Reviewing the contents of the political revolution]. *Chungang* (February 1933): 19–21.

Chang Tŏksu. "Chŏksŏng kukka ŭi chŏngch'e" [The true identity of the enemy states]. In "Taedonga chŏnjaeng kwa pando ŭi mujang, kyŏlchŏn taeyŏnsŏl sokkirok ŭi tŭkchip" [The Great East Asian War and arming the Korean Peninsula: The special issue of recording the great speeches for the decisive war]. *Samch'ŏlli* 14, no. 1 (1942): 24–27.

"Chang Tŏksu." In *Han'guk minjok munhwa taebaekkwa sajŏn* [Encyclopedia of Korean culture]. www.encykorea.com. Accessed August 21, 2018.

Chin Uhyŏn. "Nyu ttŭil miguk ŭi tonghyang" [The situation of the new deal America]. *Chungang* (January 1935): 21–25.

Ch'inil Panminjok Haengwi Chinsang Kyumyŏng Wiwŏnhoe, ed. *Ch'inil panminjok haengwi kwan'gye saryojip* [Compilation of historical sources on pro-Japanese activities and treason]. Vol. 10. Sŏul: Ch'inil Panminjok Haengwi Chinsang Kyumyŏng Wiwŏnhoe, 2009.

Chŏng Irhyŏng. "Amerik'a munmyŏng ŭi chonghoenggwan" [A comprehensive overview of the American civilization]. *Chogwang* (October 1936): 136–49.

"Chŏng Irhyŏng." In *Han'guk kŭnhyŏndae inmul charyo* [The biographical database of Koreans in the modern and contemporary period]. Accessed August 21, 2018. http://db.history.go.kr/id/im_109_01168.

"Chŏng Irhyŏng." In *Han'guk minjok munhwa taebaekkwa sajŏn* [Encyclopedia of Korean culture]. Accessed August 21, 2018. www.encykorea.com.

"Chŏnsiha ŭi siguk yŏnsŏl" [Wartime political speeches]. *Samch'ŏlli* (October 1937): 6–9.

Chu Yohan. "Tongyang ŭi ch'imnyakcha yŏngmi t'ado ŭi taesajahu!" [Invasion of the Orient and the brave roars for overthrowing the United Kingdom and the United States!]. *Samch'ŏlli* (January 1942): 44–59.

——— et al. "Tae miyŏngjŏng kwa uriŭi kago" [The Great War against the United States and the United Kingdom and our resolution]. *Chogwang* (January 1942): 72–74.

Cumings, Bruce. *The Origins of the Korean War: Liberation and the Emergence of the Separate Regimes*. Princeton, NJ: Princeton University Press, 1981.

Duus, Peter, and Kenji Hasegawa, eds. *Rediscovering America: Japanese Perspectives on the American Century*. Berkeley: University of California Press, 2011.

Gaddis, Lewis. *We Now Know: Rethinking Cold War History*. Oxford: Clarendon Press, 1997.

"Ham Sanghun." In *Han'guk kŭnhyŏndae inmul charyo* [The biographical database of Koreans in the modern and contemporary period]. Accessed August 21, 2018. http://db.history.go.kr/id/im_114_00389.

Ham Sanghun. "T'aep'yŏngnyang t'ŭkchip: Miguk ŭi t'aep'yŏngnyang chŏngch'aek" [A special issue on the Pacific: The US policies on the Pacific]. *Chogwang* (December 1941): 26–29.

Han Ch'ijin. "Amerik'a munmyŏngnon" [A perspective on American civilization]. *Chogwang* (July 1940): 146–55.

———. "Miguk sahoejŏk sasang ŭi hyŏndan'gye" [The current stage of US sociological thoughts]. *Chogwang* (May 1940): 122–29.

"Han Ch'ijin." In *Han'guk kŭnhyŏndae inmul charyo* [The biographical database of Koreans in the modern and contemporary period]. Accessed August, 21, 2018. http://db.history.go.kr/id/im_114_10112.

"Han Ch'ijin p'an'gyŏl" [The verdict on Han Ch'ijin] (1945). In *Konghun chŏnja saryogwan* [Digital archives of the national merits]. Accessed August 21, 2018. http://e-gonghun.mpva.go.kr/user/IndepMeritsDataDetail.do. (Note: to find source, search for title of document; an exact URL is not available).

Han Hŭkku. "Chaemi yungnyŏn ch'uŏk p'yŏnp'yŏn" [Remembering my six-year stay in the United States]. *Sinin munhak* (March 1936): 117–21.

———. "Munhaksang ŭro pon migugin ŭi sŏnggyŏk" [The characters of Americans in their literature]. *Chogwang* (April 1942): 142–47.

"Han Poyong." In *Han'guk kŭnhyŏndae inmul charyo* [The biographical database of Koreans in the modern and contemporary period]. Accessed August 21, 2018. http://db.history.go.kr/id/im_114_00156.

Han Poyong. "Ilchi punjaeng kwa yŏngmi ŭi tonghyang" [The China-Japan dispute and the trends in the United Kingdom and the United States]. *Chogwang* (October 1937): 52–59.

———. "Sin tongnip piyulbin taegwan" [An overview of the new independent Philippines]. *Chogwang* (December 1935): 139–46

———. "Sinch'un kukche chŏngguk ŭi tonghyang: Sisa munje" [The trends of international politics in this spring: Current affairs]. *Chogwang* (January 1936): 306–19.

———. "Sŭngsehan miguk ŭi nodong undong: CIO ŭi yakchin kwa AFL ŭi mollak" [The US labor movement on the winning side: The great advancement of CIO and the fall of AFL]. *Chogwang* (June 1937): 163–75.

Harootunian, Harry. *Overcome by Modernity: History, Culture, and Community in Interwar Japan*. Princeton, NJ: Princeton University Press, 2000.

Hong Chŏngwan. "Ilche ha haebang hu Han Ch'ijin ŭi hangmun ch'egye chŏngnip kwa minjujuŭiron" [Han Ch'ijin's scholarly development and his theory of democracy during the Colonial Period and after Liberation]. *Yŏksa munje yŏn'gu* (October 2010): 157–202.

"Hong Sŏngha." In *Han'guk kŭnhyŏndae inmul charyo* [The biographical database of Koreans in the modern and contemporary period]. Han'guksa Database. Accessed August 21, 2018. www.db.history.go.kr.

Hong Sŏngha. "Sanŏp puhŭngbŏp kwa miguk kyŏngje ŭi changnae" [The national industrial recovery act and the future of the US economy]. *Chungang* (January 1933): 23–24.

Iriye, Akira. *Power and Culture: The Japanese American War, 1941–1945*. Cambridge, MA: Harvard University Press, 1981.

Kim Hoch'ŏl. "Hwanggŭm ŭi nara miguk ŭi imyŏnsang" [The other side of the golden country the United States]. *Pip'an* (February 1932): 74–76.

Mitarai Tatsuo. "Kinjanghan t'aep'yŏngnyang hyŏngse: Miguk ŭi chŏksŏng ŭl pora" [Tense political situation in the Pacific: Recognize the enemy state America]. *Samch'ŏlli* 13, no. 3 (March 1941): 8–15.

Mogya Hongil [Yi Hongjo]. "Ilmi oegyo p'alsimnyŏnsa" [The eighty years of Japan and the US relations]. *Chogwang* (January 1942): 58–67.

Pak Indŏk. "Miju kangyŏn'gi: Hŭgin hakkyo wa widaehan yŏin kyoyukka" [My lecture travels in the United States: A black school and a great woman educator]. *Samch'ŏlli* 10, no. 8 (August 1938): 59–62.

Pae Sŏngnyong. "Miguk nongjobŏp p'ajŏng kwa nyu ttŭil ŭi unmyŏng" [The breakdown of the Agricultural Adjustment Act and the destiny of the New Deal in the United States]. *Chungang* (March 1936): 38–41.

———. "Sinjŏngch'i chŏngse ŭi kusang, t'ŭkchip: Sinjŏngch'i chŏngse ŭi yŏksasŏng [A vision of the new political situation, the special report: The history of the new political situation]. *Minju Chosŏn* 1, no. 1 (November 1947): n. p.

———. "T'aep'yŏngyang sang e saero tongnip han piyulbin konghwaguk ŭi changnae: Miguk ŭi kŭktong chŏngch'aek e yŏn'gwan haya" [The future of the Philippines emerging as a new independent republic in the Pacific]. *Sahae kongnon* (December 1935): 28–33.

Robinson, Michael. *Cultural Nationalism in Colonial Korea, 1920–1925*. Seattle: University of Washington Press, 1988.

———. "Ideological Schism in the Korean Nationalist Movement, 1920–1930: Cultural Nationalism and the Radical Critique." *Journal of Korean Studies* 4, no. 1 (1982): 241–68.

"Sijo." In *Han'guk Minjok munhwa taebaekkwa sajŏn* [Encyclopedia of Korean culture]. Accessed August 21, 2018. www.encykorea.com.

"Silchae haeyŏ innŭn yut'op'ia: Miguk teksasŭ kin [Keene] ch'on ŭi ip'unggyŏng" [On utopia in this world: Keene Village, Texas, United States]. Sijo (July 1937): 31–35.

Simdang Hagin. "Wŏsingt'ong ŭi ch'uŏk" [Remembering my days in Washington DC]. Chogwang (November 1938): 60–65.

"Sin Hŭngu." In Han'guk kŭnhyundae inmul charyo [The biographical database of Koreans in the modern and contemporary period.]. Accessed August 21, 2018. http://db.history.go.kr/id/im_107_20554.

Sŏ Chaep'il. "Chaeryu osimnyŏn: Miguk sahoe ŭi tongt'ae" [Living abroad for fifty years: The dynamics of the American society]. Chungang (April 1935): 12–14.

Sŏ Ch'un. "Che ich'a segye taejŏnnon" [A theory of World War II]. Chogwang (January 1936): 94–98.

"Soyŏnbang ch'ongyŏngsagwan ch'uripcha kŏmgŏ ŭi kŏn." [On arresting the visitors of the USSR Consulate-General in Seoul]. Sasang e kwanhan chŏngbo 8 (January 14, 1938). Accessed August 21, 2018. http://db.history.go.kr/id/had_160_0280.

Taylor, Charles. "Modern Social Imaginaries." Public Culture 14, no. 1 (Winter 2002): 106–7.

US Department of State. Peace and War: United States Foreign Policy 1931–1941. Washington, DC: United States Government Printing Office, 1943.

"Wŏn Sehun." In Han'guk kŭnhyŭndae inmul charyo [The biographical database of Koreans in the modern and contemporary period]. Accessed August 21, 2018. http://db.history.go.kr/id/im_108_00924.

Wŏn Sehun. "Ilchung yangguk aegukcha ŭi nonjŏn" [A debate between a Chinese patriot and a Japanese patriot]. Samch'ŏlli (January 1937): 82–94.

Yi Ch'ŏng. "Miguk sŏn'gyohoe ŭi Chosŏn kyoyuk pangch'im e taehaya" [The policy of American missionaries on Korean education]. Pip'an (January 1932): 66–70.

Yi Hongjo. See Mogya Hongil.

Yi Myomuk. "Miguk ŭi ŏje wa onŭl" [The past and present of the United States]. Chogwang (June 1941): 64–71.

Yi Tonhwa. "Tongyang p'yŏnghwa ŭi kŭnbonch'aek." [A fundamental solution for peace]. In "Chŏnsiha ŭi siguk yŏnsŏl" [Wartime political speeches]. Samch'ŏlli 9, no. 5 (October, 1937). Accessed August 21, 2018. http://db.history.go.kr/id/had_160_0280.

"Yŏ Unhong." In Han'guk kŭnhyundae inmul charyo [The biographical database of Koreans in the modern and contemporary period.]. Accessed August 21, 2018. http://db.history.go.kr/id/im_108_00503.

Yu Kwangnyŏl. "Wae miyŏng ŭl ch'ina?" [Why do we strike the United States and the United Kingdom?]. *Chogwang* (January 1943): 37–42.

Yun Chi'ho et al. "Taedonga chŏnjaeng kwa pando ŭi mujang: Kyŏlchŏn taeyŏnsŏl kirok ŭi t'ŭkchip" [The great East Asian War and the armament of the Korean peninsula]. *Samch'ŏlli* (January 1942): 18–36.

CHAPTER 6

Baldwin, Frank Prentiss. "The March First Movement: Korean Challenge and Japanese Response." PhD diss. Columbia University, 1969.

Bergamini, Davis. *Japan's Imperial Conspiracy*. London: Pocket Books, 1972.

The Conspiracy Case in Chosen. Seoul: Seoul Press, 1912.

Darity, William A., Jr. *International Encyclopedia of the Social Sciences*. Macmillan, 1968.

Division of Historical Policy Research US Department of State. *United States Policy Regarding Korea, 1834–1950*. Seoul: Hallim University, 1987.

Documents on British Foreign Policy (DBFP). First Series. Vol. 6. http://diplomatic-documents.org/editions/united-kingdom.

Dougherty, James E., and Robert L. Pfaltzgraff. *American Foreign Policy: FDR to Reagan*. New York: Harper & Row, 1986.

Duverger, Maurice. *An Introduction to the Social Sciences with Special Reference to Their Methods* (Minera series of Student's Handbooks: No. 10). New York: Frederick A. Praeger, 1964.

Esthus, Raymond A. *Theodore Roosevelt and Japan*. Seattle: University of Washington Press, 1967.

Foreign Relations of the United States (FRUS). https://history.state.gov/historicaldocuments/pre-truman.

Harrington, Fred H. *God, Mammon, and the Japanese: Dr. Horace N. Allen and Korean-American Relations, 1884–1905*. Madison: University of Wisconsin Press, 1944.

Kennedy, Malcom D. *The Estrangement of Great Britain and Japan 1917–35*. Manchester, UK: Manchester University Press, 1969.

Ku, Dae-Yeol. [Ku Taeyŏl, Ku Daeyeol]. *Korea under Colonialism: The March First Movement and the Anglo-Japanese Relations*. Seoul: Royal Asiatic Society–Korean Branch, 1986.

Kuksap'yŏnch'an Wiwŏnhoe, ed. *Hanminjok tongnip undonsa charyojip I–105 in sagŏn kongp'an simalso* [One hundred and five persons incident trials: Materials of the history of the Korean Independence movement]. Sŏul: Kuksap'yŏnch'an Wiwŏnhoe, 1986.

MacNair, Harley Farnesworth, and Donald. F. Lach. *Modern Eastern International Relations*. New York: Van Nostrand Co., 1955.

Manicas, Peter T. *A History and Philosophy of the Social Sciences*. Oxford, UK: Blackwell, 1987.

Nish, Ian H. "Korea between Japan and Russia, 1900–1904." Paper presented at the sixth annual conference of the Association of Korean Studies Europe (AKSE). Seoul: Republic of Korea. August 2–5, 1982.

Pak Yongsŏk. *Manbosan sagŏn yŏn'gu* [Study of the Manbosan incident]. Sŏul: Asea munhwasa, 1978.

Tonga Ilbosa, ed. *3.1 undong 50 chunyŏn kinyŏm nonjip* [Collection of articles in commemoration of the fiftieth anniversary of the March First movement]. Sŏul: Tong ilbosa, 1969.

CHAPTER 7

Eckert, Carter J., Ki-baik Lee, Young Ick Lee, Michael Robinson, and Edward W. Wagner. *Korea Old and New: A History*. Cambridge, MA: Harvard University, 1990.

Feodosy, Archimandrite Perevalov. *Rossĭskaya dukhovnaya micciya v Koree. Za pervoe deciatiletie ee sushchestvovaniya (1900–1925)*. [Russian Orthodox Church mission in Korea during the first twenty-five years of its existence (1900–1925)]. Harbin: Kratkiĭ istoricheskiĭ ocherk s prilozheniem statisticheskikh dannykh o veroispovedanii koreĭtsev, 1926.

Goyer, Lev. "Kopiya doneseniya agenta ministerstva finansov v Shanhae [L'va] Goyera poslu v Tokio ot 19 iyuinya (1 iyilya) 1910 g"—AVPR, f. Yaponskiy stol, Doneseniya poslannika v Tokio, 1910, d. 917, l. 8. [Copy of the report of the Ministry of Finance agent in Shanghai (Lev) Goyer to Ambassador in Tokyo on June 19 (July 1), 1910. Archive of Foreign Policy of Russia, Japan Dept. Reports from the Envoy in Tokyo, 1910, File 917, Sheet 8].

Greve, V. V. *Kitaĭtsy, Koreĭtsy i Yipontsy v Priamur'e* [Chinese, Koreans, and Japanese in Priamurye: A report by V.V. Grave (Special envoy of the Ministry of Foreign Affairs) // V.V. Grave; Works of Amur Expedition]. Issue No 11. St. Petersburg: Tip [ografiya]. F.V. Kirschbauma, 1912.

Kim, N. *Pod gnetom Yiponskovo imperializma. Ocherk sovremennoĭ Korei* [Under oppression of Japanese imperialism: Survey of modern Korea]. Vladivostok: Izdatel'stvo Dal'nevostochnogo gosudarstvennogo universiteta, 1926.

Koreĭtsy na Rossĭskom dal'nem vostoke. Dokumenty i materialy (1917–1923). [Koreans in Russian Far East (1917–1923). [(Archive) documents and materials]. Vladivostok: Izdatel'stvo Dal'nevostochnogo gosudarstvennogo universiteta, 2004.

Koreĭtsy na Rossiĭskom dal'nem vostoke. Vtoraya polovina XIX—nachalo XX v. Dokumenty i materialy [Koreans in Russian Far East: Second half of the nineteenth century—beginning of the twentieth century, (Archive) documents and materials]. Vladivostok: Izdatel'stvo Dal'nevostochnogo gosudarstvennogo universiteta, 2001.

Koreya glazami Rossiyan (1895–1945). [Korea as seen by Russians (1895–1945)]. Moscow: Moskva, 2008.

Kuehner, N. V. Statistiko-gyeograficheskiĭ i ėkonomicheskiĭ ocherk Korei, nyne Yiponskovo general-gubernatorstva Tsiosen. [Statistic, geographic, and economic survey of Korea, now the Japanese Government-General Chōsen]. Vladivostok: Izdanie i pechat' Vostochnovo instituta, 1912.

Kurbanov, S.O. Istoriya Korei s drevnosti do nachala 21 veka [History of Korea since ancient times to the beginning of the twenty-first century]. St. Petersburg: Izdatel'stvo Sankt-Peterburgskogo Universiteta, 2009.

Pak, B. D. Rossiya i Koreya [Russia and Korea]. Moscow: Izdatel'stvo Nauka, 1979.

Pesotsky, V. D. Koreĭskiĭ vopros v Priamur'e [Korean question in Priamurye]. Grif «sekretno» [Top secret]. Khabarovsk: Printing House of the Amur Governor-General Office 1913.

Polyanovsky, Maks. "Trudy komandirovannoĭ po vysochaĭshemu poveleniiu Amyrskoĭ Ėkspeditsii. Prilozhenie k vypusku XI. «Koreĭskiĭ vopros v Priamur'e». Otchet poruchika pervovo Sibirskovo ctrelkovovo Evo Velichestva polka V. D. Pesotskovo" [Works of the Amur Expedition sent under His Majesty's command. Appendix to Issue XI. "Korean question in Priamurie." Report of V. D. Pesotsky, lieutenant of His Majesty First Siberian Infantry Regiment].

Rossov, P. Natsional'noe samosoznanie Koreĭtsev [National self-consciousness of Koreans]. St. Petersburg: Tipo-litografiya «Gerold», 1906.

Schmidt, P. Yu. Strana utrennevo spokoĭstviya: Koreya i ee zhiteli [Land of morning calm: Korea and her inhabitants]. 2nd edition. St. Petersburg: Tipografiya Arteli Pechatnogo Dela, 1904.

Shirman, G. V. Istoricheskiĭ i politiko-ėkonomicheskiĭ ocherk (1914–1923). [Korea: Historical and political and economic survey of Korea (1914–1923)] Moscow: Moskva, 1923.

Yi Hŭngjik. Chŭngbo sae kuksa sajŏn [Enlarged new encyclopedia of Korean history]. Sŏul, Gyohaksa, 1992.

CHAPTER 8

Anonymous. Chaoxian wenjianlu [Chronicles of Korea]. n.p., n.d.

———. "Ji Chaoxian wuchan gongjinhui" [Notes on the "Overall Progress" exhibition of Korean goods]. *The Shun Pao*, October 27, 1915.

———. "Sheyuan Sun Runjiang hanshu diaocha riben chaoxian shiyejiaoyu qingxing" [Report from Sun Runjiang on the vocational education in Japan and Korea]. *Jiaoyu yu zhiye* [Education and vocation] 3 (1918): 3.

Cao Hongnian. *Kaocha rihan jiangzhe jiaoyu biji* [Notes on the education system in Japan, Korea, and the Chinese provinces of Zhejiang and Jiangsu]. Tianjin: Zhili Shuju, 1918.

———. "Rihan lüxingji" [Traveling in Japan and Korea]. *Ta Kung Pao*, May 30, 1918.

Chiang Monlin. *Xichao* [The tides from the West]. Tianjin: Tianjin Education Press, 2008.

Ding Shouhe. "Shiyejiuguo, jiaoyujiuguo he kexuejiuguo sichao de zairenshi" [A re-examination of the theories to save China through industry, education, and science]. *Wenshizhe* [Journal of literature, history, and philosophy] 5 (1993): 3–11.

He Ciquan. "Diaocha chaoxian Yongdengpu zhige gongchang zhi baogao" [Report on investigating leather factories in Yeong Deung Po]. *Gongxue* [Industrial studies] 1, no. 2 (1924): 1–4.

Hu Shiqing. *Sanshiba guo youji* [Traveling in thirty-eight countries]. Kaifeng: Zhonghua shuju, 1933.

Hu Youfei. "Hanjing jiyou" [Traveling in the Korean capital]. *Ta Kung Pao*, September 25, 1925.

Huang Yanpei. *Chaoxian* [Korea]. Shanghai: Shangwu yinshuguan, 1929.

Huang Zonglin. "You Chaoxian minfei mu" [Visiting the mausoleum of the Korean imperial concubine Min]. *Nansheshilu* [Anthology of south society] 18 (1916): 265.

Ji Ping. "Youhan mantan I–III" [Thoughts about traveling in Korea]. *The Shun Pao*, July 10–12, 1931.

———. "Youhan mantan IV–X" [Thoughts about traveling in Korea]. *The Shun Pao*, July 14–20, 1931.

Jing Hengyi. *Jing Hengyi riji* [Jing Hengyi's diary]. Hangzhou: Zhejiang guji chubanshe, 1984.

Li Jinrong. "Lüxing Chaoxian ganyan" [Reflections on traveling in Korea]. *Dongfang zazhi* 13, no. 7 (1916): 81–83.

Liu Chongben. *Lüxing rihan riji* [Traveling journals about Japan and Korea]. In *Guowai youji huikan* Vol. 1 [Collections of traveling journals about foreign countries Vol 1], edited by Yao Zhuxuan. Shanghai: Chung Hwa Book Company, n. d.

Liu Yisheng. "Xinhai geming yu shiye jiuguo sichao de gaozhang" [The 1911 revolution and the flourishing of the theory of saving China through industry]. *Huanan shifandaxue xuebao* 2 (1993): 73–78.

Ma BoWon. "Chaoxian jingcheng guanchaji" [Observations on the Korean capital]. *Ta Kung Pao*, August 24, 1920.

Qin Lifan. *Gaoli huangzou jiyou* [Traveling in remote areas of Korea]. *Dongwu* 1, no.3 (1919): 3.

Senzi. "Chaoxian yinxiangji: Xiangei wo suo aimude chaoxian" [Impressions of Korea: Dedicated to my beloved Korea]. *Sishi niandai* 5 (1935): 4.

Shi Haoran. "Canguan chaoxian pige gongchan shixi biji" [Notes on visiting Korea's leather producers]. *Anhui shiye zazhi* 3 (July 1917): 1–11.

Sung Jiao-jen. "Wo de lishi" [My history]. In *Sung Jiao-jen wenji* [Collected works of Mr. Sung Jiao-jen: Part I], 275–78. Taipei: Committee of Party History, Central Committee of Kuomintang, 1982.

Wang Hengxin. "Canguan chaoxian fushan laibingyuan jilüe" [Notes on visiting the leprosy hospital in Busan, Korea]. *Mafeng jikan* 2 (1928): 14–15.

Wang Tongling. "You chaoxian zaji" [Miscellanies of traveling in Korea]. *Dongfang zazhi* 18, no. 14 (1921): 91–94.

Wang Yangbin, and Wan Baoyuan. *Chaoxian diaocha ji* [Notes on investigating Korea]. Beijing: Quanguo tushuguan wenxian suowei fuzhi zhongxin, 2004.

Wang Yangbin, and Wan Baoyuan et al. "Chaoxian guanhuiji" [Notes on visiting exhibition in Korea]. In *Chaoxian diaocha ji* [Notes on investigating Korea], 1–62. Beijing: Quanguo tushuguan wenxian suowei fuzhi zhongxin, 2004.

———. "Chaoxian xingji" [Trip to Korea]. In *Chaoxian diaocha ji* [Notes on investigating Korea], 1–21. Beijing: Quanguo tushuguan wenxian suowei fuzhi zhongxin, 2004.

Yu Shouchun. "Chaoxian youji" [Notes of traveling in Korea]. *Hujiang daxue yuekan* 2, no. 1 (1913): 28–30.

Zhang Mosheng. *Moseng zishu* [Autobiography of Moseng]. Shanghai: Jidong yinshushe, 1948.

Zhang Yuan. *Mingguo banian chaoxian lüexingji* [The journals of traveling in Japan and Korea in 1919]. Nanjing: Gonghe shuju, 1919.

CHAPTER 9

Barlow, Tani E. *Formations of Colonial Modernity in East Asia*. Durham, NC: Duke University Press, 1997.

Bird, Isabella Lucy. *Korea and Her Neighbours*. New York: Elibron Classics, 2005.

Blunt, Alison. *Travel, Gender, and Imperialism: Mary Kingsley and West Africa*. London: Guildford Press, 1994.

Brandt, Kim. *Kingdom of Beauty: Mingei and the Politics of Folk Art in Imperial Japan.* Durham, NC: Duke University Press, 2007.

———. "Objects of Desire: Japanese Collectors and Colonial Korea." *Positions: East Asia Cultures Critique* 8, no. 3 (2000): 711–46.

Burke, Peter. *Varieties of Cultural History.* London: Polity Press, 1997.

Caprio, Mark E. *Japanese Assimilation Policies in Colonial Korea, 1910–1945.* Seattle: University of Washington Press, 2009.

"The Culture of Two Thousand Years Ago." *NIPPON* 18 (July 1934): 45.

Eicher, Joanne Bubolz. *Dress and Ethnicity: Change across Space and Time.* Oxford: Berg, 1999.

"Eizō ni yoru kiroku to dentatsu: Shashin sakokushugi o toranakkata senkusha—Natori Yōnosuke: Taidan: Tsurumi Shunsuke, Hani Susumu." [Recording and dissemination through moving images: The avant-garde who did not choose photographic isolationism—Natori Yonosuke: Conversation: Tsurumi Shunsuke, Hani Susumu]. In *Shashin sakokushugi o toranakkata senkusha—Natori Yōnosuke no shigoto: 1930nendai* [The Avant-garde who did not choose photographic isolationism—Natori Yonosuke's work: The 1930s], edited by. Inubuse Eiji, Hani Susumu, and Yamagishi Shōji, n.p. Tōkyō: Seibu Bijutsukan, 1978.

Finnane, Antonia. *Changing Clothes in China: Fashion, History, Nation.* London: Hurst and Company, 2007.

"Grosses Japan Dai NIPPON." In *Shashin sakokushugi o toranakkata senkusha: Natori Yōnosuke no shigoto: 1930nendai* [International visual communication: 1930s], edited by Inubuse Eiji, Hani Susumu, Yamagishi Shōji, n.p, n.d.

Han, Jung-sun. "Japan in the Public Culture of South Korea: Conflicting Images Attached to Colonial Sites." In *Imagining Japan in Post-War East Asia: Identity Politics, Schooling and Popular Culture,* edited by Paul Morris, Naoko Shimazu, and Edward Vickers, 106–26. Abingdon: Routledge, 2013.

Inubuse Eiji, Hani Susumu, and Yamagishi Shōji eds. *Shashin sakokushugi o toranakkata senkusha—Natori Yōnosuke no shigoto: 1930nendai* [The Avant-garde who did not choose photographic isolationism—Natori Yonosuke's work: The 1930s]. Tōkyō: Seibu Bijutsukan, 1978.

Ishii Hakutei. "Natsu no Kongōzan" [Summer in Mount Kongo]. In *Sekai kikō bungaku zenshū* [Collection of world travel writing] Vol. 13, compiled by Shiga Naoya, Satō Haruo, and Kawabata Yasunari, 67–73. Tōkyō: Shūdōsha, 1960.

Ishikawa Yasumasa. *Hōdō shahin no seishun jidai: Natori Yōnosuke to nakamatachi* [Photojournalism's early years: Natori Yonosuke and his comrades]. Tōkyō: Kōdansha, 1991.

Itō Abito. *Kankoku bunka shinboru jiten* [Dictionary of Korean symbols]. Tōkyō: Heibonsha, 2006.

Kaneko Ryūichi. "'NIPPON' to wa nandattanoka: Fukkokuban kanketsu ni attate" [What was NIPPON: On the occasion of its reprint]. In *Fukkokuban Nippon: Bessatsu* [Reprint NIPPON: Separate volume], edited by Kaneko Ryūichi. Tōkyō: Koku kankōkai, 2005.

Kikuchi, Yuko. *Japanese Modernisation and Mingei Theory: Cultural Nationalism and Oriental Orientalism*. London: RoutledgeCurzon, 2004.

Kim Young-suk. *Kankoku fukushoku bunka jiten* [Dictionary of Korean clothing culture]. Osaka: Toho shuppansha, 2008.

Kokusai bunka shinkōkai. *KBS: Sanjūnen no ayumi* [KBS: Its thirty years]. Tōkyō: Kokusai bunka shinkōkai, 1964.

"Koreanische Volkskunst" [Korean handicraft]. NIPPON 18 (July 1, 1939): 34.

Korea Issue. NIPPON 18 (July 1, 1939).

Lee, Hyunjung, and Younghan Cho. "Introduction: Colonial Modernity and Beyond in East Asian Contexts." *Cultural Studies* 26, no. 5 (2012): 601–16.

LIFE 2, no. 2 (January 11, 1937).

LIFE 2, no. 23 (December 6, 1937).

LIFE 2, no. 25 (December 20, 1937).

Mikami Masahiko. *Wagamama ippai: Natori Yōnosuke* [Totally selfish: Natori Yonosuke]. Tōkyō: Chikuma shobō, 1988.

Nagashima Yoshizo, "The Hand as a Tool." NIPPON 15 (June 1, 1938): 6–7.

Natori Yōnosuke. *Shashin no yomikata* [How to read photographs]. Tōkyō: Iwanami shoten, 1963.

Newhall, Beaumont. *Photography 1839–1937*. New York: The Museum of Modern Art, 1937.

NIPPON 1 (October 20, 1934), inside front cover.

NIPPON 10 (March 15, 1937), inside front cover.

Ota Saburo. "The Significance of the China Affair: Sina jihen no igi." NIPPON (December 17, 1937): 8–9.

"Photographer Natori at the Japanese Front." LIFE 2, no. 25 (December 20, 1937): 60–61.

Price, Willard. "The Jap Rule Hermit Kingdom [Korea]." *National Geographic* 88, no. 4 (October 1945): 429–51.

Ryang, Sonia. "Japanese Travellers' Accounts of Korea." *East Asian History* nos. 13/14 133–52.

"Sekijui no shita ni" [Under the Red Cross]. NIPPONban 1, no. 1 (July 15, 1938): 10–11.

Shibazaki Atsushi. *Kindai Nihon to kokusai bunka kōryū: Kokusai bunka shinkōkai no sōsetsu to tenkai* [Modern Japan and international cultural exchange: The establishment and development of the center for international cultural relations]. Tōkyō: Yūshindō, 1999.

Shimazu, Naoko. "Colonial Encounters: Japanese Travel Writing on Colonial Taiwan." In *Refracted Modernity: Visual Culture and Identity in Colonial Taiwan*, edited by Yuko Kikuch, 21–38. Honolulu: University of Hawai'i Press, 2007.

Shirayama Mari. "Natori Yōnosuke no shigoto: 1931–45" [Natori Yonosuke's work: 1931–1945]. In *Fukkokuban Nippon: Bessatsu* [Reprint NIPPON: Separate volume], edited by Kaneko Ryūichi, 5–33. Tōkyō: Koku kankōkai, 2005.

Shirayama Mari, and Hori Yoshio, eds. *Natori Yōnosuke to Nippon Kōbō* [1931–45] [Natori Yonosuke and the Nippon Studio]. Tōkyō: Iwanami shoten, 2006.

"A Selection of Celebrities." NIPPON 18 (July 1, 1939): 28–29.

"Statistics of Japanese-Korean Inter-Marriages." NIPPON 18 (July 1, 1939): 21.

"Transfiguration during a Twenty-Nine-Year Period." NIPPON 18 (July 1, 1939): 18.

Tutihashi, S. "Tyosen." NIPPON 18 (July 1, 1939): n. p.

Tyō, Kaku-Tyu. "Nukute: The Wolf." NIPPON 18 (July 1, 1939): 37–40.

"Tyosen Beckons You This Year" (advertisement). NIPPON 18 (July 1, 1939): 51.

Weisenfeld, Gennifer S. "Touring Japan-as-Museum: Nippon and Other Japanese Imperialism Travelogues." *Positions: East Asia Cultures Critique* 8, no. 3 (Winter 2000): 747–93.

Yokoyama Ryuichi. "Toyo heiwa seisaku" [Peace policy in the Orient]. NIPPON (December 28, 1938): 52–53. (no volume number)

"Zylinderhuete und Mullrueke" [Top hats and muslin skirts]. NIPPON 19 (July 1, 1939): 24–26.

Contributors

YONG-CHOOL HA is the Korea Foundation Professor of Korean Social Science at the University of Washington–Seattle. His primary academic interests have been comparative politics and society with a particular focus on late coming nations (Korea, Japan, Prussia, China and the Soviet Union), Soviet and Russian politics, Russian Far East Korean domestic and international politics, inter-Korean relations and East Asian regional politics, and international theories in East Asia.

SANG SOOK JEON is a research professor for the Institute of East-Asian Studies KwangWoon University. His recent works include: Hangukin ŭi kŭndae kukkakhwan "minjugongwhaguk" chaego (Reconsideration of Korean's viewpoints of state and democratic republic; Sunin, 2017) and Chosŏn ch'ongdok chungch'i yŏn'gu 1910–1936 (Japanese politics of the Korean Governor-General, 1910–1936; Chisik Sanŏp Publishing Co. Ltd., 2012).

HAKJOON KIM has been a distinguished professor of Dankook University since 2015. Dr. Kim currently serves as the chairman of the Board of Trustees for Incheon National University. He was president of the Northeast Asian History Foundation (2012–15), chairman of the Board of Trustees of Dankook University (2011–13), chairman of the Donga ilbo (East Asian daily, 2001–11), and president of the Korean Political Science Association (2000). He also served as president of the Korean Federation of Teachers' Association (1999–2001) and chancellor of the University of Incheon (1996–2000).

DAEYEOL KU is an emeritus professor of the Department of Political Science and Diplomacy at Ewha Womans University. His publications include *Korea under Colonialism: The March First Movement and Anglo-Japanese Relations* (Royal Asiatic Society, 1985); *Cheguk juui wa oellon* (Journalism and imperialism; Ewha University Press, 1986); *Hanguk kuken kwan gyesa yŏngu I and II* (A study on the history of Korean international relations; Yoksa Bipyongsa, 1995); and *Samguk t'ongil ŭi chŏngch'ihak* (Unification politics of the Three Kingdoms; Kkach'i, 2010).

SERGEY O. KURBANOV is professor and chair of the newly established Department of Korean Studies at St. Petersburg University. His spheres of interest are wide, including the general history of Korea, Korean Confucianism, and the everyday lives of North and South Koreans from 1987–2000s. Currently, Professor Kurbanov has undertaken a project to write a book on the history of North Korea 2000–2018.

JUNG HWAN LEE is an assistant professor in the Department of Political Science and International Relations at Seoul National University. He received a PhD in political science from the University of California–Berkeley in 2010. He is the author of a number of articles and books on the political economy and foreign policy in contemporary Japan including *Ilbin e issŏsŏ ul t'alchipchunghwa kaehyŏk kwa kong-sa kongban kwang'gye* (Decentralization reforms and public-private partnership in contemporary Japan).

YUMI MOON is associate professor of history at Stanford University. Her most recent work includes *Populist Collaborators: The Ilchinhoe and the Japanese Colonization of Korea, 1896–1910* (Cornell University Press, 2013) and "Immoral Rights: Korean Populist Collaborators and the Japanese Colonization of Korea, 1904–1910" (*The American Historical Review*, February 2013).

ANDRE SCHMID is associate professor and chair of the Department of East Asian Studies at the University of Toronto. He has published work in various journals including the *Journal of Asian Studies*, *Yoksa munje yon'gu*, *South Atlantic Quarterly*, and *SAI* among others. His work also includes two winners of the John Whitney Hall Award, *Korea Between Empires, 1895–1919* (Columbia

University Press, 2002) and the co-authored work *Nation Work: Asian Elites and National Identities* (University of Michigan Press, 2000).

NAOKO SHIMAZU is associate dean of faculty and professor of humanities (History) at Yale-NUS College, Singapore. Before coming to Singapore, she taught for twenty years at Birkbeck College, University of London. She is a global historian with a regional focus on Asia. Her publications include *Imagining Japan in Post-War East Asia* (co-editor, Routledge, 2013); *Japanese Society at War: Death, Memory, and the Russo-Japanese War* (Cambridge University Press, 2009); *Nationalisms in Japan* (editor, Routledge, 2006); and *Japan, Race, and Equality: Racial Equality Proposal of 1919* (Routledge, 1998). Her current work is on the cultural history of diplomacy, centered on her monograph, *Diplomacy as Theatre: The Bandung Conference and the Making of the Third World*.

KEZHI SUN is a professor in the Department of History at Fudan University. His research field is modern Korean history and Sino-Korean history. His representative work is *Sanghaei Hanin Sahoesa, 1910–1945*. (A study of the Shanghai Korean Association, 1910–1945; Sŏul: Hanul Ak'ademi, 2001).

Index

A-B-C (America, Britain, China) entente, 211
active imaginations and wishful strategies: of colonized nations, 108; comparing *Chosŏn ilbo* and *Keijō Nippō* and, 133–34; of international cooperation, 114–16; during the 1920s, 107–9; overview of, 105–7; rise of destructive dreams and, 116–19. *See also* Koreans under colonial rule
Adachi Kinnosuke, 75–76, 85–86
African Americans, Powell's depiction of colonized Koreans vs., 94
Aginaldo, Emilio, 145
Agricultural Adjustment Act (AAA) (US, 1933), 158
agriculture: art of, Japanese propaganda on teaching Koreans about, 35; in Korea, Chinese on Japanese colonial rule and, 247; in Korea, Japanese colonization policy and, 225
Allen, Horace N., 41
Allies common policy: issue of Korea and, 205. *See also* Western powers; World War II
Alston, Beilby, 191
American mainstream magazines: disparaging articles on Korean traditions and history in, 89–90; on Japanese mistakes in Korea, 94–95; on Japan's colonization of Korea, 89–92; on Korea as outlet for Japanese population pressures, 93; *Life*, 264; *National Geographic*, 272; not questioning Japanese colonization of Korea, 93–94; as public face of Japanese colonialism, 81. *See also* English-language writing; Japanese propaganda in the US; United States; Western readership
American-Japanese Relations: An Inside View of Japan's Policies and Purposes (Kawakami), 86–88
Amoy (Xiamen), Japanese failure to occupy, 59
An, Ch'ang-ho, 100n46
An Chunggŭn, 40, 82
An Insik, 165
An Pyŏngju, 159–61, 170, 175n80
Analects, The (Confucius), 153
Andong-Shenyang railway line, 185
Anglo-Japanese Alliance (1902): end of, 37; Japan's northern continental policy and, 62–64; Russo-Japanese War and, 74–75; third revision (1911), 184–86; Triple Intervention (1895)

and, 60; US support for KMT in China and, 124
annexation of Korea: Great Britain as helpful ally in, 43; international law and, 49–50, 61–62; Japanese imperialistic modernization project and, 51; justifying, 32–34; Schmidt on, 228–29; temporary cessation among powers to seize regional hegemony and, 183–84. *See also* Colonial Period; colonization of Korea; Government-General of Korea; Japan-Korea Protectorate Treaty
"Annexed (Federated) Great East Theory," 32–34
annual reports, English-language, as public face of Japanese colonialism in Korea, 80–82
anti-Japanese Koreans: exile of, to engage in movement against Japanese, 39; as guerillas, political groups in Korea and, 171; as guerillas abroad, 170; Japanese encouraging eradication of, 19; Poanhoe (Society for keeping tranquility) and, 220; Tarui Tokich'i on existence of, 33. *See also* Korean Independence movement; nationalists, Korean
Anti–Japanese War of Resistance in China (1937–45), 260
art of Korea, Korea Issue, NIPPON depicting, 274–75
Asabuki Eiji, 266
Asian solidarity and Asianism: Fukujawa's thesis on, 20–21; Yellow Peril and, 60–61. *See also* Japan and Korea as one body
assassinations: of Itō Hirobumi, 40, 82; of Kim Okkyun, 36; of Queen Min, 36–37; of Stevens by Chang Inhwan, 41; as tradition in Korea, American press on, 100n29

Atlantic Monthly, 94–95
Aydin, Cemil, 139–40

Bakufu Central government, *han* administrative unit and, 53
Balkans, wartime colonial Korea compared with, 170–71
Bergholz, Leo A., 193
Berlin International Handicraft Exhibition, 279, 284n67
Berliner Illustrirte Zeitung (Berlin graphic newspaper), 263–65, 278
Bhabha, Homi, 107
Bible-carrying pocket, Korean clothing and, 272
Bigot, Georges Ferdinand, 35
Bird, Isabella, 37, 40, 271–72
blue color, virtues in Korean culture of, 270
Blue Eagle Revolution, in US, Chaha Sanin on social control and, 156–57
British Committee for Relations with Other Countries, 261
British Empire: maintaining control of, as postwar British objective, 206. *See also* Great Britain
British Foreign Office: "On the Japanese Policy in Corea" (memorandum), 191; on Korean independence (1941), 207; on Korean independence (1945), 211; on March First Independence movement, 190. *See also* Great Britain
Brown, Arthur J., 40, 89

Cable Act (US, 1921), 122
Cairo Declaration (1943), 7, 98, 207–210
Canton (magazine), 267
Cao Hongnian: education system fact finding in Korea (1917) by, 242–43, 246, 248–49; on Korean agriculture and Japanese colonial rule, 247–48
Cao Kun, 243

capitalist modernity. *See* modernity or modernization
Caprio, Mark E., 280
Cavendish, Alfred, 40
Ch'ae P'ilgŭn, 166
Chaha Sanin, 156, 170
Chang Chiyŏn, 38–39
Chang Inhwan, 41
Chang Tŏksu, 141, 166–68, 170
Changgyeonggung Palace, 252
Ch'aoxian ceLué (Korean policy), by Hwang Zunxian, 27
Chaoxian diaocha ji (Notes of investigating Korea, 1915), 242
Chaoxian wenjianlu (Chronicles of Korea, Wenjian Lu in Korea) (anonymous), 241, 244–45
Cheam-ri massacre by Japanese, 191
Cheondoism (Religion of the heavenly way), 33. *See also* Tonghak
Chiang Kai-Shek, 119, 127–28, 130, 162
Chiang Monlin, 241–42
Chicago Poems (Sandburg), 155
Chin Uhyŏn, 157–58
China: Anglo-Japanese Alliance (1911) and, 186; Asian solidarity thesis and, 20–21; balance of international power shifting to the Pacific and, 117; Cairo Declaration (1943) and, 209; *Chosŏn ilbo* on stability of, 127–28; Communist Revolution (1949), Cold War and, 168; Ganghwa Treaty (1876) and, 57; Hu Shih–Murahuse Kōshin debate on Japan's relations with, 162–64; Japanese interests in, 119; Japanese military actions against, 133–34; Japanese rationalization for its war against, 34–36; Japanese relations in 1920s with, 120; Japanese vs. Koreans on future of, 121–22; Japan-Korea Treaty (1876) and, 25, 56; Japan's use of "Shina" and cultural and political superiority over, 52; *Keijō Nippō* on stability of, 129–30; Korea as vassal state of, 21; Korean army mutiny (1882) and, 25; Korean newspaper editorials (1920–30) on, 112, 131; as Korean rival, Griffis on, 26; Lenin and anti-imperialistic atmosphere in, 196; Mogya Hongil on US imperialism and, 154; Northern, international focus on Japan's actions in, 147; port opening between Korea and, 239–240; on Provisional Government of Korea (Chongqing), 207; as regional power, Koreans on, 129; Russophobia and, 27; Tarui Tokich'i on Great East State and, 32; US and UK on Japanese expansion into, 181; US support for Kuomintang government in, 124; US talks on Korean question with, 210–11; US vs. Japan and tension over, 108–9; wartime colonial Korea compared with, 170–71; weakened, Japanese colonization of Korea and, 4; World War II British policy toward Korea and, 205–6. *See also* Chinese understandings of colonial Korea; First Sino-Japanese War; Manchuria; Northeast Asia; Second Sino-Japanese War
Chinda Sutemi, 191
Chinese intellectuals or scholars: Sino-Japanese War (1894–95) and, 241; study of Korea by, 243
Chinese understandings of colonial Korea: Chinese people who observed colonized Korea, 241–43; historical, geographical, and geopolitical issues in, 11–13; history of observing Korean society by, 254; literature by Chinese visitors to Korea for study of, 254–

55n1; overview of, 239–40; social phenomena under colonial rule, 249–53; temptation of colonial "new policies," 244–49
Cho Pyŏngse, 38
Ch'oe Chewu, 24
Ch'oe Ikhyŏn, 23, 38
Ch'oe Namsŏn, 37
Ch'oe Sihyŏng, 24
Chogwang (The morning light): anti-American essays after 1941, 154–55, 173n58; anti-American essays prior to 1941, 153–54; "The Crisis of 1936" (Han Poyong), 146–47; Han Ch'ijin article on American civilization, 152–53; Han Ch'ijin article on US sociology, 151–52; Han Poyong article on US interests in China (1937), 147–48; Han Poyong article on US labor movements, 150–51; Korean wartime discourse on the US in, 141–42; Pacific War and portraits of US in, 143–45; on Philippine independence, 145–46; *Pip'an* and discourse on democratic US by, 159; *Samch'ŏlli* compared with, 162; socialists' writings in, 155; US civilization, essays on nature of, 148–50; US military occupation and writers for, 169–70
Chŏn Pongjun, 34, 36
Chong, Ye We, 100n46
Chŏng Hangyŏng, 192. *See also* Chung, Henry
Chŏng Irhyŏng, 144–45, 148–50, 169–70
Ch'ŏngnyŏnhoe (Young Men's Association, YMA), 222
Chōsen kaikano kigen (The origin of Korean civilization, 1895), 28
Chōsen Nokaiho (Chōsen agricultural association), 225

Chōshū Domain: differences and conflict in, 71n50; Japanese Army and, 62; Japan's northern continental policy and, 64; Russo-Japanese War and, 63
Chosŏn Chungang Ilbo Company. See Chosŏn ilbo Company
Chosŏn Dynasty: Japan's propaganda for colonizing, 19; Koreans' black-and-white view of the world and, 132; negative international perceptions of, 182. *See also* Chosŏn issue; Colonial Period; Japanese propaganda; Korea
Chosŏn ilbo Company, 143, 155–56
Chosŏn ilbo (newspaper): on Asian ethnic conflicts and US interests in Asia, 123–24; on China and East Asian future, 126–30; on Communist revolution in Russia, 124–25; editorials on international affairs (1920–30), 110–13, 110t, 111t; editorials passively watching world affairs, 114–16; Japanese banning of, 143; *Keijō Nippō* compared with, 133–34; published during Colonial Period, 251; on shifts in balance of international power, 116–17; understanding Koreans' international perceptions and, 109, 110; on US as imperialistic with conflicting principles, 117; on US importance to future of Korea, 124–25; on Yellow Peril in the US, 123
Chosŏn issue: interest line and, 58–62; Japanese crisis consciousness and perception of, 54–58; Japanese national identity development and, 49, 68–69. *See also* Chosŏn Dynasty; Japanese national identity; Korea
Chosun kyunje sinmoon (Korea economic news), 251
Chousen nichinichi shinbun (Korea daily news), 251

Chousen nitdubou (Korea news), 251
Christian Koreans, 90, 187–88, 272
Chu Yohan, 154, 166, 170
Chung, Henry (Chŏng Hangyŏng), 100n46, 192, 194
Chungang (The central post): Chaha Sanin on dictatorship in US, 156–57; Chin Uhyŏn on Roosevelt 1935 electoral victory, 157–58; launch of, 155–56; Pae Sŏngnyong on US Supreme Court and the New Deal, 158; *Pip'an* and coverage of Rooseveltian US by, 159; *Samch'ŏlli* compared with, 162; Sŏ Chaep'il on US evolution as social experiment, 157; as socialist voice, 141–42
Churchill, Winston, 209
civilization: developmental stage of, 182; Western powers on falsity of Japanese as bearer to Korea of, 188. *See also* Social Darwinism
civilization transition: opening of East Asia and, 51–54; Treaty of Ganghwa (1876) and, 58, 67. *See also* Japan-Korea Protectorate Treaty; Japan-Korea Treaty
civilizing by colonizing: Japanese propaganda on, 20–22, 76–77; in Korea, Adachi article on Japan's intent in, 85; in Korea, Itō's English-language propaganda on, 82–85; in Korea, Japanese English-language propaganda on, 80–82; in Korea during 1930s, Western powers admiration of, 200; Western powers on, 20. *See also* colonial governance or rule; colonization of Korea; modernity or modernization
clothing, Korean, 270–72
cognition, use of term, 213n2
Cold War, 132, 168, 208, 212

colonial gaze, cultural gaze compared with, 13–15, 260, 276–81
colonial governance or rule (colonialisms): Japanese adoption of European methods of, 224; Korean self-rule question and, 201–2; in the Philippines vs. Korea, Kennan on, 91; Powell on hierarchy of, 95; questions of legitimacy of, 180–81; Saitō compared with American critics on, 96–97; Western perception of Korea and, 183
Colonial Period (1910–45): Chinese on "new policies" of, 244–49; Chinese on social phenomena during, 249–53; international influence during, 1; international perspectives of, 7–8; Kim Man Gyem on, 226; Korean international relations during, 179; Koreans as economic slaves under, 250–51; Koreans wearing white during, 271; Korea's global importance during, 180; Kuehner on dual aspects of, 224–25; late, ideological landscape of, 168–69; scope of international impact during, 2. *See also* Chinese understandings of colonial Korea; colonization of Korea; Government-General of Korea; Great Britain's perception of Korea during Colonial Period; Japanese propaganda; Japanese propaganda in the US; Koreans under colonial rule; NIPPON; post–Colonial Period; pre-Colonial Period; United States' perception of Korea during Colonial Period
colonization of Korea: American mainstream magazines on, 89–92; colonial historiography and, 4–5; critics of, criticisms of US rule and, 101n60;

as experiment in colonialism, 78; as good for Japanese but not Koreans, Pesotsky on, 231; Japanese as belonging with Western powers and, 73; Japanese methods for, 19; Japanese rationalization for, 27; Japan's justification for, 3–4; Korean Production Overall Progress Exhibition, 242; Koreans on Russo-Korean border and, 232; questions about international impact of, 3; Saitō on policy issues and advancements made by Koreans, 96. See also history of Korea; Japanese propaganda; Japan-Korea Treaty; *Keijō Nippō*; Koreans under colonial rule

colonized nations: as nations without state status, 107–8; newspapers of, as sources for their international perspectives, 109–13

colors in Korean culture, Korea Issue, NIPPON on, 269–71

Commerce Japan (magazine), 267

communism: appeal to the colonized of, 114; colonial Korea influenced by, 131–32; Han on US labor movement and, 150–51; Independence movement in Korea and, 204; Korean political scene (1920s) and, 196; Korean's fascination with, 8; revolution in China (1949) and, 168; underground movement in Korea, 203. See also Soviet Revolution

Company Law (1911), 189

Confucian scholars, traditional, Japan-Korea Treaty (1876) opposed by, 23

Confucius, Han Ch'ijin on American ideals and teachings of, 153

Congress of the Philippines, 146

Corea: The Hermit Nation (Griffis), 25–28

Counterplan Proposal (1938), 280

"The Crisis of 1936" (Han Poyong), 146–47

cultural gaze, colonial gaze compared with, 13–15, 260, 276–81

cultural nationalists: *Chogwang* (The morning light) as voice of, 142; ideological schism between revolutionaries and, 141, 169. See also nationalists, Korean

cultural policy, Japan's: adoption of Saitō's, toward Korea, 195; to expand influence globally, 261–62; Russian perception of colonial Korea and, 228

cultural rule, Japan's: after March First movement, Chinese on, 13

"The Culture of Two Thousand Years Ago" (Korea Issue, NIPPON), 269, 274

Cumings, Bruce, 141, 168

Curzon, George N., 77–78, 99n9, 191

Daito gappo ron (Thesis on the union of the great East) (Tarui Tokich'i), 32

"Dass-a-ron" (On escaping from Asia) (Fukujawa), 29

"Datsu-A" (Escape-Asia) theory (Fukujawa Yukichi , 1885), 275

Declaration of Independence, US, Chŏng Irhyŏng on, 149

democracy: Chŏng Irhyŏng on US civilization and, 148, 149; Han Ch'ijin's theory of, 170

Democratic People's Republic of Korea (DPRK), 179. See also North Korea

Denny, Owen N., 41

Dewey, George, 97

dictatorship, Chaha Sanin on social control and, 156–57

Diet (Japanese Empire), interest line plan and, 59

Diosy, Arthur, 43

diplomacy/diplomatic activities: colonial rule of a nation state and, 106;

Japan's, mediating conflict between Korea and the West and, 55–56
Domon, Ken, 266
dresses, different, Japanese propaganda acting as, 44
Duus, Peter, 142

East Asia: Anglo Americans and Japan as power in, 75; China-oriented international system in, 49; *Chosŏn ilbo* on international conflict due to US-Japanese rivalry, 128–29; Japanese relations in 1920s with other Great Powers on, 120; Korean newspaper editorials on situations in (1920–30), 112; opening of, Japanese search for national identity and, 51–54
East Asia as one family (*toyo ikka*), 202
Eastern China Railway, 124
Eden, Anthony, 207–8
Edo Period or government, Japan: Japanese delegation to Korea from, 55; separating civilization and modernization from Western civilization, 52–53
education: in Japan, Meiji national policy on, 53; Japan's Ordinance (1911) on, Western powers on falsity of, 188; in Korea, Chinese study visit during Colonial Period of, 242–43, 246–47; in Korea, "for colonization, enslavement, and subjugation," Chinese on, 252; in Korea, Japan's discriminatory system of, 13
Emancipation Proclamation, Lincoln's, Chŏng Irhyŏng on, 149
Emergency Quota or Immigration Act (US, 1921), 122
enemy, simplistic Korean perception of, 8, 132
England. See Great Britain
English-language writing: about Korean history, 79–80; on colonization of Korea in early twentieth century, 77–79, 99n12; by Japanese authors, 99–100n27; publicizing Japanese colonial government efforts in Korea, 80–82. See also American mainstream magazines
Ermolenko (Russian reporter), 226–27, 237n31
ethnic dress, for Korea Issue, NIPPON, 270–71
Eulsa Treaty (1905), 38
European powers. See Western powers
Exhibition on Production and Progress in Korea (1915), 246–47

Far Eastern Affairs, US Division of, 208
fascism: Chin Uhyŏn on Roosevelt and, 158; in Italy, international retaliation against Japan and, 147; Mussolini's statement (1932) on, 156; An Pyŏngju's debate on Franklin D. Roosevelt, 159–61. See also National Socialism
fatalism and nihilism, Korean's inferiority complex and, 42–43, 48n102
February 26 Incident (1936), Japan, 260
Finnane, Antonia, 271
First Sino-Japanese War (1894–95): China's perception of Korea before, 240; China's perception of Korea during Colonial Period and, 13; impact on Chinese people, 241; Japan on liberating Korea from China and, 29; Japanese Army's political influence and, 62; Japanese influence over Korea and, 49–50; Japanese rationalization for, 34–36; Japan's interest line and, 59, 67–68; Triple Intervention (1895) and, 60

forestry, art of, Japanese propaganda on teaching Koreans about, 35
Fortune (magazine), 265
Fourteen Points, Wilson's, 192–93
France: campaign against Korea (1866), 55; cultural institutions and diplomacy by, 261; East Asia and, 213n1; international politics of 1920s and, 115; Korean 1880s treaty with, 25; Triple Intervention (1895) and, 59–60
Friends of Korea (in US), 194
Fukujawa Yukichi, 20, 22–25, 29,
Fukuzawa Yukichi, 275

Gaddis, John Lewis, 168
Gale, James Scarth, 79
Ganghwa, Treaty of (1876). See Japan-Korea Treaty
Ganghwa Island Incident (1875), 57
Gauss, Clarence E., 206–7
gaze: colonial or cultural, comparison of, 13–15, 260; as outsider, Price and, 272; Western, Natori and, 265; Western, NIPPON's adoption of, 274
Geneva Convention, nations without state status excluded from, 115
Genzirō Nagata, 276
geopolitical location: Corea on Korea as inevitable victim and, 26; Minami on national border of Japan and, 199–200; as powerful resource for Korea, 223–24; Seoul-Ŭiju railway and, 185
Germany: cultural institutions and diplomacy by, 261; East Asia and, 213n1; Japan's Anti–Comintern Pact with, 260; Korean 1880s treaty with, 25; Natori's studies in, 263; Nazi, international retaliation against Japan and, 147
Gotō Shinpei, 65
Government Railways of Tyōsen, tourist promotional material, 275

Government-General of Korea (Chosŏn): Agricultural Products Exhibition Hall and, 247; Chinese government visitors and, 248–49; Japanese rule in colonial Korea and, 50–51; Keijō Nippō as newspaper of, 110; modernization and assimilation policies of, 186–87; permission for meetings of Korean organizations and, 250; political affairs in Japan and, 66, 68; Saitō as, relations with Westerners and, 195; sales of new books written by Koreans and, 251; Seoul headquarters building for, 252, 277–78; as unbridled despotism, 201. See also annexation of Korea
Goyer, Lev, 223
The Graphic (London-based weekly), 40
Great Asian Federation, 32–33
Great Britain: cultural institutions and diplomacy by, 261; as great power, 212–13n1; Han on potential Far East choices (1937) for, 147–48; Hu Shih on Japan's alliance with, 164; international politics of 1920s and, 115; Japanese annexation of Korea and, 43; Japan's China strategy vs., 128; Japan's northern continental policy and, 65, 66; Japan's relationship with US and, 75–76; Korean 1880s treaty with, 25; Korean Independence movement and, 190–91; negative perception of Korea and, 183; not supporting Liberation or Korean independence, 180; on Provisional Government of Korea (Chongqing), 207; Russophobia and Kŏmundo occupation by, 27–28; shift of power to US from, 116–17; Treaty of Portsmouth and, 38; Triple Intervention (1895) and, 59–60; US State Department on Korean question

and, 210–11; World War II Chinese policy toward Korea and, 205–6. *See also* Anglo-Japanese Alliance; British Foreign Office

Great Britain's perception of Korea during Colonial Period: before 1910, 182–83; international relations of Korean Peninsula (1920s), 195–97; international relations of Korean Peninsula (1930s), 197–204; issues of the 1910s, 183–89; Korean liberation and independence, 204–12; March First movement and Western policies, 189–95; overview of, 10–11, 179–81

"Great East State," Tarui Tokich'i on, 32

Great Eastern Union (*daitō gappō*), 4

Great Korean Empire, 36

great powers (*yŏlgang*): Adachi Kinnosuke on Japan among, 85; Itō Hirobumi and Japan among, 82; Japan in the 1920s as, 120; on Japanese colonial rule in Korea, 187; use of term, 212–13n1. *See also* Great Britain; major powers; United States; Western powers

Greater East Asian Co-Prosperity Sphere, 153–54, 202

Greece, wartime colonial Korea compared with, 170–71

Greene, William Conyngham, 188

Griffis, William E.: disparagement of Korea by, 42; on First Sino-Japanese War, 35; on "Hermit Kingdom," 77; on Itō Hirobumi as Japanese resident-general in Korea, 39; on Japan colonizing Korea, 78, 92; misinformation for US society about Korea by, 25–28; on Queen Min's assassination, 37

Grosses Japan Dai NIPPON (Great Japan), 277–78

Guomindang (Kuomintang), China, 124, 128, 196, 207

Ha, Yong-Chool, 2, 7–8

Hague, The: International Peace Conference (1907), 40; Korean delegation to, article on, 88–89

Haiguo tuzhi (Illustrated gazetteer of countries beyond the seas), 52

Ham Sanghun, 144–45, 153–54, 169, 170

han administrative unit, Bakufu Central government and, 53

Han Ch'ijin, 144–45, 151–53, 169–70

Han Hŭkku, 155, 174n64

Han Poyong: on American life, 173n42; on British and US choices in the Far East (1937), 147–48; *Chogwang*'s coverage of the US and, 144; "The Crisis of 1936" by, 146–47; on new Philippines constitution, 145–46; on US labor movements, 150–51; wartime mobilization and silence of, 169

Han River bridge, *Annual Report* feature on, 80

handicraft, Korean, 270, 274–75

Han'guk tongsa (Painful history of Korea) (Pak Unsik), 79

Harootunian, Harry, 139

Harper's Weekly, 82–85, 91

Hasegawa, Kenji, 142

Hasegawa Yoshimichi, 187, 195

Hawai'i, Japanese ties with the US and tensions over, 75

He Ciquan, 243

"Hermit Kingdom," 77, 274

history of Korea: American mainstream magazines disparaging, 89–90; colonization of Korea and development of, 4–5; Japanese representations of, English-language products and, 79–82; nationalist Korean perspectives on, 79; Korea Issue, NIPPON depict-

ing, 274; Soviet and Chinese perceptions of colonial Korea and, 11–13
Hitler, Adolf, 147
Hong Chongwil, 36
Hong Sŏngha, 156, 170, 174n66
Hŏnpŏp Yŏn'guhoe (Society for research constitution), 221
"Houses with Ondoru" (Korea Issue, NIPPON), 270
Hu Shih, 162–64, 175n88
Hu Shiqing, 252
Huang Yanpei, 241–43, 245–247
Hulbert, Homer, 79–80, 87, 92
humanism, Han Ch'ijin article on US sociology and, 151–52
Hwang Zunxian, 27

Ilchinhoe (Association for progress), 33, 38, 43, 221, 235n7
Immigration Act (US, 1924), 121–22
immigration of Asians to US. See Yellow Peril
Imo Incident (1882), 59
Imperial Army. See Japanese Army
Imperial National Defense Policy (Japan, 1907), 184–85
Imperial Rule Assistance Association (Japan, 1940), 260
imperialism: Korean socialists on, 155. See also British Empire; Great Korean Empire; Japan; Japanese Empire
Ina Nobuo, 265
The Independent, 92, 96–97
India, British special rights over frontiers of, 186
Inoue Kakukoro, 34, 38
intellectuals. See Chinese intellectuals or scholars; Japanese intellectuals; Korean intellectuals; Western intellectuals
Inter-American Conference for the Maintenance of Peace (Buenos Aires, 1936), 150

interest line (J. riekisen), 58, 63–65, 67–68
international affairs: colonial rule in Korea and Korean interest in, 7–8, 106, 131. See also international politics
international law: Japan on China's treatment of Korea as violation of, 35; Japanese annexation of Korea and, 49–50, 61–62; Japanese annexation of Taiwan and, 50; Japanese society on limitations of, 54; opening of East Asia and, 51; Perry and Japan's opening to the West and, 52; Treaty of Ganghwa (1876) and, 57–58, 67; Yamagata on, 59. See also Japan-Korea Protectorate Treaty; Japan-Korea Treaty
International Peace Conference (The Hague, 1907), 40
international politics: "The Crisis of 1936" (Han Poyong) on, 147; Japanese reality vs. Koreans' perspective on, 119–21, 131; Korea during Colonial Period and, 179; Koreans' destructive vision of, 116–19, 131–32; nations-without-state status excluded from, 115; passivity of colonized nations and, 107–8. See also international affairs
international relations: Ham Sanghun's articles on, 153–54; Japan's withdrawal from League of Nations and, 261; Korean Peninsula (1920s), 195–97; Korean Peninsula (1930s), 197–204
Iriye, Akira, 139
Ishii Hakutei, 272
Italy: Chaha Sanin on dictatorship in, 157; Fascist, international retaliation against Japan and, 147; Korean 1880s treaty with, 25
Itō Hirobumi: assassination, 40, 82; assassination attempts on, 222;

Chang questioning Oriental peace of, 39; "Great East Federation" and, 33–34; on integrating East Asian nations into Japan, 21; on invading Korea before Western powers, 56–57; Japanese propaganda and, 6, 77; Japan's embellishment of, 38–40; writing for US publications on Korean colonization, 82–85, 100n34

Iwakura Embassy officials, studying Western systems, 54

Iwakura Tomomi, 56–57

James, William, 152

Japan: American anxiety about, 92; American newspaper correspondents writing on Korea from, 78–79; Asian solidarity thesis and, 20–21; attempts to separate Korean government from its people by, 28–29; China's defeat in the Opium War and, 52, 67; colonial intention of Korean assimilation by, 14; economic interests in Manchuria, territorial expansion and, 184; Griffis on modernization of, 25–26; Hu Shih–Murahuse Kōshin debate on China's relations with, 162–64; Kennan on mistakes in Korea by, 90; Korean and Chinese culture transfers to, 224; Korean newspaper editorials on (1920–30), 131; as Korean rival, Griffis on, 26; Manchuria's strategic importance (1930s) for, 198–99; nationalists and socialists on possible US conflict with, 9–10; Nomonhan Incident (1939) with Soviet Union, 203; post–World War I balance of power and, 108–9; post–World War I strained relations between US and, 192–94; Russophobia of, 27, 37–38; Social Darwinism justifying colonial rule over Korea by, 30; Soviet Union treaty with (1925), 196–97; strategic view of Korea in its international identity, 5; US challenges to Pacific power and, 116–17; Western perception of Korea and, 183; Westernizing in, Meiji Restoration (1868) and, 20; Yellow Peril and national crisis of consciousness in, 60; Yellow Peril in the US and, 123. *See also* annexation of Korea; colonization of Korea; Government-General of Korea; Japanese Army; Japanese intellectuals; Japanese national identity; Japanese propaganda; Meiji Restoration; Pearl Harbor attack

Japan and Korea as one body (*naesŏn ilch'e, naisen ittai*) ideology, 10, 169, 202

Japan-China friendship (*ilchung ch'insŏn*), 163

Japanese and Koreans are the same (*naisen ichiyo, naeson iryang*), 60–61

Japanese and Koreans, shared ancestry among (*J. Nissen dōsō*), 60–61

Japanese Army: annexation of Korea and, 62; modern, Yamagata and, 58; northern continental policy and, 63–64; Publicity Section, cultural propaganda by, 262; at Russian border (1916) and in Korea (1919), 185; *Samch'ŏlli*'s publication of wartime speeches cheering, 164–65; Southeast Asia invasion by, 268; Taishō democracy period and, 66

Japanese Empire: of the 1930s compared with 1910s, 260; northern continental policy of, 63–64

Japanese Government-General of Chōsen (*J. Chōsen Sōtokufu*). *See* Government-General of Korea

Japanese intellectuals: "Annexed (Federated) Great East Theory" of, 32–34; books on Korea by, 28; Europe and pre-World War II discourse of, 142; on half-civilized or uncivilized Korea, 22; on how Japan would survive in competitive world, 30; on Japan as civilized nation, 20; on Korea as never independent, 26; Korean self-rule question and, 202; Pan-Asianist internationalism and, 139–40

Japanese national identity: Chosŏn issue and the interest line, 58–62; continental state plan of Japan and Chosŏn, 62–66; crisis consciousness and Chosŏn issue perception, 54–58; East Asian international system and, 49–51; opening of East Asia and, 51–54; Western powers' expansion into East Asia and, 67–69

Japanese Navy, northern continental policy and, 63–64

Japanese Pan-Asianist discourse. *See* Pan-Asianism, Japan's

"Japanese Policy in Korea" (Itō Hirobumi, 1907), 82–85, 91

Japanese propaganda: "Annexed (Federated) Great East Theory," 32–34; Chinese understandings of colonial Korea and, 250; as control on Korean people, 42–44; disparagement of Korea and its emperor, 40–42; governmental, Natori and, 267; international vs. colonial, in NIPPON (magazine), 15; Japanese attempt to separate Korean government from its people, 28–29; for Japanese domestic audience, 274; Japanese promotion of Social Darwinism, 30–31; Japanese rationalization for its war against China, 34–36; Japanese rationalization for its war against Russia, 36–38; Japan's promotion of Hermit nation and Russophobia, 25–28; Korean colonization and, 19–20; Korean response to, 23–25; as mission to civilize the uncivilized, 20–22; as mission to "protect" Asian neighbors from Western powers, 22–23. *See also* Korea Issue, NIPPON; NIPPON

Japanese propaganda in the US: Adachi article on Japan's intent in Korea, 85, 86; American mainstream magazines and the limits of critique, 89–97; history and annual reports, 79–82; Itō on "Japanese Policy in Korea" in, 82–85; Kawakami's book, 85–88; Korean writers and, 88, 100n46; motives for, 74–79; overview of, 73–74; Pearl Harbor attack and, 97–98

Japan-Korea Protectorate Treaty (1905): anti- and pro-Japanese Koreans and, 221; disparagement of Koreans after, 90; as invalid, Yi Taejin on, 47n75; Japanese propaganda in relation to Korea and, 76–77; Korean assertion of coercion by Japan in, 88–89; Korean court's signing of, 38–39; Korean international relations and, 179; Russo-Japanese War and, 61; US and British perceptions prior to, 179; writings about Korea after, 78. *See also* annexation of Korea

Japan-Korea Treaty (1876, signed at Gangwha/Kangwha): on "independent state," 21–22, 35; international law, Asian interests, and Japanese expansion under, 57–58, 67; Korean elites studying Japanese modernization after, 220; Korean response to, 23–25

Japan's South China Army's Information Bureau, 267

Jeon, Sang Sook, 2, 5
Ji Ping, 241
Jo Heeyoon, 221
jongbu (Japanese and Korean land measurement), 256n31
Jordan, David Starr, 93
Jordan, John N., 184
June 10 movement, 195
Jungle, The (Sinclair), 155

Kaehwadang (Party of reforms), 220
Kamekura Yūsaku, 268
Kanan Gahō South China Graphic (magazine), 267
Kanazawa Shosaburo, 225
Kaneko Kentaro, 77
Kapsin Coup (1884), 59
Karakhan, Lev, 196
Katsura Tarō, 62–65, 184
Kaupaapu Tawan'ōku Tōa Gahō (East Asia Thai-language graphic magazine), 268
Kawakami, Karl Kiyoshi, 85–88, 92
KBS (Kokusai bunka shink), (Japan's Center for International Cultural Relations), 261–62, 267–68, 281n1
Kei Kyo Saenmyeonhoe (Society of self-education and personal inviolability), 221
Keijō nippō (Japanese colonial newspaper): on America as the enemy state, 165–66; on China and East Asian future, 129–30; *Chosŏn ilbo* compared with, 133–34; editorials on international affairs (1920–30), 110–13, 112t, 113t; Japanese vs. Korean perceptions of international affairs and, 8; merger of other newspapers resulting in, 47n76; on modernization under Japanese guidance (*Khanjosinp'o* in text), 36; on possible US-Japan war, 120; on Soviet Russia and East Asian affairs, 126; on Washington Navel Conference, 121; on Yellow Peril in the US, 122–23
Keijon ipbo (The capital city daily): as Japanese propaganda tool, 39
Keijyou nitsupou (Capital daily), 251
Keio University, Fukujawa and, 20
Kellogg-Briand Pact (1928), 146
ken (prefecture) system, Meiji national policy on, 53–54
Kennan, George, 38, 42, 90, 91
Khalkhyn Gol, Battle of, 260
Kido Koin (J. Kido Takayosi), 21
Kim, Hakjoon, 2–4
Kim Gisu, 235n2
Kim Hoch'ŏl, 158–59
Kim Hongjip, 235n2
Kim Il-Sung, 133, 162, 171
Kim Jonkan, 221
Kim Kyushik, 192
Kim Man Gyem, 226
Kim Okkyun: assassination of, 36; coup d'état planned by, 220; progressive group oriented toward Japanese enlightenment and, 24; pro-Japanese/anti-Chinese rebellion (1884) and, 29; Song Byeongjun and, 235n7; Tarui Tokich'i meeting of, 32
Kim P'yŏngmuk, 23
Kim Yunsik, 235n2
kimono, as symbol of East Asian dress, 271
Kipling, Rudyard, 168
Ko Changil, 192
Kodama Gentarō, 63
Kōga (magazine), 265
Kojong, King, later Emperor, 23, 36, 83, 193, 223
Kokusai Hōdō Kōgei, NIPPON Studio reinvented as, 267
Kŏmundo, British occupation of, Russophobia and, 27–28

Komura Jūtarō, 61
Konoe Fumimaro, Prince of Japan, 262
Korea: Asian solidarity thesis and, 20–21; Chinese residents persecuted in, 198, 241; development in, Japanese *Annual Reports* on, 80–82; English-language writing in early twentieth century about, 77–78; First Sino-Japanese War and, 34–36; as hermit nation, 25–28, 77, 274; history of, 79–80, 89–90, 274; Japanese criticism of, 39; Kawakami on his book and role of businesses in, 87; Liberation (1945) and, 179; port opening between China and, 239–40; as potential US ally after Pearl Harbor attack, 98; pro-Japanese/anti-Chinese rebellion (1884) in, 28–29; as uncivilized, 182–83; Yamagata's planned railways through, 59. *See also* annexation of Korea; Chosŏn Dynasty; Chosŏn issue; Colonial Period; colonization of Korea; history of Korea; Japanese propaganda; Japanese propaganda in the US; Japan-Korea Treaty; Korean Independence movement; Koreans under colonial rule
Korea and Her Neighbours (Bird), 271–72
Korea Issue, NIPPON: content, 268–76; cover of, 269f; as cultural or colonial propaganda? 276–81; Korean artisans' tools depicted in, 279, 279f; Korean women depicted in, 273f; overview of, 259–62. See also NIPPON
Korean army, 22, 24–25, 59. *See also* Korean restoration army; Korean Righteous Army
Korean Christians, 141–43
Korean Congress (Philadelphia, 1919), 194
Korean Democratic Party, 170, 174n66, 175n88

"Korean Handicraft" ("Koreanische Volkskunst") (Korea Issue, NIPPON), 270, 274–75
Korean Independence movement: British response to, 190–91; communist movement in Korea and, 204; Japanese suppression of, 201; major powers' perception of, 11; 105-Person Incident (1911), 88, 187–88; pro-Japanese sentiment (late 1930s) and, 203; Soviet Union and, 196–97; on trusteeship possibility, 210; US State Department on all organizations representing, 207; Western perception of, 187. *See also* anti-Japanese Koreans; March First Independence movement; nationalists, Korean
Korean intellectuals: as bourgeois, Russians on, 234; international perspectives of, 134n5; on Itō Hirobumi and "Oriental peace," 39; as newspaper readers, 109–10; Tonghak (Eastern learning) and anti-foreign inclination of, 24; underground communist movement and, 203; wartime discourse on the US by, 140–41; young, Japan-Korea Treaty (1876) supported by, 23–24. *See also* active imaginations and wishful strategies; *Chungang*; socialists
Korean Liberation (1945), Cumings on civil war and, 168
Korean National Association in the United States, 192
Korean Production Overall Progress (Co-Progress) Exhibition (1915), 242, 249
Korean restoration army, 207. *See also* Korean army
Korean Righteous Army, 40. *See also* Korean army

Index

Korean students: admiration for US life, 173n42; disobedience by, 203
Korean War (1950–53), 168
Korean-American War (1871), 153
Koreans under colonial rule: active imaginations, wishful strategies, and passive actions (1920s) of, 107–9; imagined perception of international order, 114–19; Japanese reality vs. perspective of, 119–21; Japanese vs. Koreans on international concerns, 121–30; newspapers as sources for international perspectives, 109–13; observations on international perspectives of, 131–34; overview of, 105–7. *See also* colonization of Korea
"The Koreans Who Are Being Trampled Under Foot by the Imperialist Party of Japan" (Karakhan), 196
Korea–United States Treaty (1882), 25
Koryŏ pottery, blue representing, 270
Ku, Daeyeol, 2, 10–11
Kuehner, N. V., 223–25
kumijashin (graphic design effect), 268–69
Kumpei Matumoto, 35
Kuomintang (KMT or Guomindang), China, 124, 128, 196, 207
Kurahashi Tōjirō, 272
Kurbanov, Sergey, 2, 11–13
Kwangmuje, Emperor: disparagement of, 40–41; "Great East State" and, 33; Great Korean Empire under, 36; Japanese criticism of, 39; Japan–Korea Protectorate Treaty and, 38, 40
Kwangseo faction, China, 128
Kwantung Army, 268. *See also* Japanese Army
Kyŏngjaeng-ron (On competition, Yu Kiljun, 1883), 30

Ladd, George Trumbull, 39–40, 92
Langer, William, 214n25
language, Japanese theory of common roots of Japanese and Korean, 225
League of Nations: Japan's withdrawal from, 147, 260–61; Korean appeals for autonomy to, 118–19; Korean Independence leaders in US and, 194–95; Korean petition for independence to, 203–4; Manchurian Incident (1931) and, 275; nations without state status excluded from, 115; newspaper editorials on ineffectiveness of, 117; US failure to join, Japanese and Koreans on, 123; US liberal expansionism and proposal for, 149. *See also* The Hague
Lee, Jung Hwan, 2, 7–8
legal rights of accused, 105-Person Incident and, 188
Lenin, Vladimir, 196
Li Jinrong, 244
liberal expansionism, by US, Chŏng Irhyŏng on, 149
Life magazine, 264
Lincoln, Abraham, 149
Liu Bingjian, 242–43
Liu Chongben, 248–49
London, Jack, 38
London Conference, 115
Longford, Joseph H., 43
Lowell, Percival, 42
Lytton Commission, 260, 275
Lyutsh, Ya. Ya., 227

Ma Boyuan, 253
MacDonald, Claude, 188
Machtpolitik (power politics), Western perception of Korea and, 183
MacKenzie, F. A., 101n68
Maeil sinbo (Korea daily news), 47n62, 251
magazines. See American mainstream magazines; NIPPON

major powers: Japanese colonization of Korea and, 19; March First Independence movement (1919) perceived by, 11. *See also* Great Britain; great powers; United States; Western powers
Manchukuo (magazine), 268
Manchukuo Photo Service, 268
Manchuria: *Chosŏn ilbo* on Korean ties with, 125–26; exiled anti-Japanese Koreans in, 39; Japan and "self-rule government" in, 147; Japan on British expansionist interests in, 186; Japan on Korea as bridge to, 5–6, 11–13; Japanese interests in, 119; Japanese invasion (1932) of, 235; Japan's northern continental policy and, 64–66; Japan's occupation of, 147; Jordan observing Japanese expansion into, 184; *Keijō Nippō* on interconnecting stability of Korea and, 130; propaganda in US and Japanese invasion of, 73; US and UK on Japanese expansion into, 181; Western powers on Korea as bridge to, 197–98. *See also* Northeast Asia
Manchurian Incident (1931), 197, 198–99, 201–3, 275
Manchurian-Koreans, Mobaoshan Incident (1931) and, 198
"Map of Korean Industry" (Korea Issue, NIPPON), 270
March First Independence movement (1919): Americans on Japanese in Korea vs. US in the Philippines and, 91; Chinese understandings of colonial Korea and, 249–50; criticisms of colonial government reform and, 95; English-language writing challenging Japanese assertions after, 102n78; failure of, 196; Japanese propaganda in US and, 88; Korean migration to Russian Far East and, 12; major powers' perception of, 11; as organized resistance, 214n25; Powell on Japanese mistakes in Korea after, 94–95; Russian perception of colonial Korea and, 227; Russian perceptions of anti-Japanese movement before, 234; as unfortunate occurrences, Saitō on, 96–97; Western powers' attitudes toward Korea and, 181; Western powers' reexamination of policies and, 189–95; Zhang Yuan visit to Korea and, 241
"Market Places" (Korea Issue, NIPPON), 269–70
Married Women's Independent Nationality Act (US, 1921), 122
Marxism: Japanese intellectuals' fascination (1920s) with, 142; as prism for Russian view of Korea, 229–30
Marxists, class-based, imagining Korea's independence, 114
Matsudaira Tsuneo, 248
Maxey, Edwin, 78
McKenzie, Frederick, 80
McKinley, William, Jr., 145–46
Mecklenburg, Erna, 266, 268, 273
Meiji period: colonization of Korea as reform process of, 78; Itō and reforms of, 82; Itō comparing Korea to, 84; Japanese propaganda during, 73, 76; modernity and reforms under, 182; racialism and, 60–61
Meiji Restoration: Hu Shih on glory of, 163; imperial expansionist policies, 50; Japanese diplomacy with Korea and, 56; Japanese intellectuals on Social Darwinism after, 30; modernization from above during, 53; open-door modernization during, 54;

reforms after, 59; Westernizing in Japan and, 20
men, Japanese, Korea Issue, NIPPON depicting, 274
military power: as essential for independence, Koreans on, 8; of Japan during 1910s, 184–85; of Japan vs. Korea during Colonial Period, 133; Japanese, Chosŏn issue and, 55; Japanese, modernization and, 58; Japan's civilization and modernization and, 53–54; newspaper editorials on arms race and, 118
Miller, Ransford, 195–96
Miln, Louise J., 41
Mimana on the Korean peninsula (K. Imna): as Japanese colony AD 100–500, 4, 16n5, 26–27; Japanese vs. Korean pronunciation of, 80
Min, Queen, 36–37
Min Yŏnghwan, 38
Minami Jiro, 198, 199–200, 202
Mingei Movement (folk art), 275
Minju Chosŏn (Democratic Korea), 170, 176n112
missionaries: in China, 148; in Korea, 87–88, 90, 193
Mitarai Tatsuo, 165–66
Mitsui Group (zaibatsu), 266
Mobaoshan Incident (1931), 198. See also Wanpaoshan Incident
modernity or modernization: capitalist, colonization's role in, 91; Chŏng Irhyŏng on US civilization and, 148–49; Japanese intellectuals questioning meaning of, 139; in Korea during Colonial period, China's observation of, 13; stagnant development in China and, 243; US and UK on Korea before 1910 and, 182. See also civilizing by colonizing; Korea Issue, NIPPON; Social Darwinism

Mogya Hongil (Yi Hongjo), 154
Le Monde illustré (The illustrated world), 35
Mongolia, 119, 260
Monroe Doctrine, 117, 149, 154–55, 165
Moon, Yumi, 2, 8–10
More, Thomas, 142
Mori Takayuki, 268
mudan t'ongch'i (militarism policy) in Korea, 228
Muller, G. W. Max, 191
München Illustrierte Presse (Munich graphic press), 263
munhwa t'ongch'i (cultural policy) in Korea, 228
Murahuse Kōshin, 162–64
Museum of Modern Art, New York, "Photography, 1839–1937" exhibition, 264
Mussolini, Benito, 156

Nagamori, law by, 220
Naikaku jōhōkyoku (Information Division, Cabinet Office, Japan), 267
naisen ittai (unity of Japan and Korea), 275, 280. See also Japan and Korea as one body
Nakada Takeo, 30
The Nation, 81, 93
National Geographic, 272
National Labor Relations Act, US (1935), 151
National Mobilization Law, Japan, 260
National Recovery Administration, US, 156–58
National Socialism (Nazi Party), 142, 147. See also Germany
nationalists, Korean: cultural, Chogwang (The morning light) as voice of, 142; ideological split between socialists and, 141, 169; imagining Korea's independence, 114; Pearl Harbor attack and sympathetic hearing of,

Index   335

98, 100n102; US as perceived by (1930s–40s), 9, 142. See also anti-Japanese Koreans; Korean Independence movement
nations without state status, 107–8. See also Koreans under colonial rule
Natori Yōnosuke: Berlin International Handicraft Exhibition and, 284n67; formulaic layouts by, 278–80, 279f; NIPPON and, 262–67; Korea Issue, NIPPON and, 268; as photographer, 263–65; photographs of Korea in German-language publication and, 277–78
Neutrality Act (Chungnippŏp), US, 148
New Deal, US: Chaha Sanin on Fascistization of US economy and, 156; Chin Uhyŏn on Roosevelt 1935 electoral victory and, 157–58; Japanese intellectuals' indifference to, 142; Korean socialists on, 155; Pae Sŏngnyong on, 158; An Pyŏngju's debate on Franklin D. Roosevelt, 159–61
New Republic, The, 88
newspapers or magazines: Americans writing on Korea from Japan for, 78–79; Berliner Illustrirte Zeitung, 263–65, 278; colonial, as voice of Japan in Korea, 251; editorials on arms race and military power, 118; editorials on international topics, 110t; editorials on League of Nations ineffectiveness, 117; Korean, Japan closes down (1941), 141; Maeil sinbo, 47n62, 251; as sources for Koreans' international perspectives, 109–13; in US and Europe, Japanese propaganda and, 76–77. See also American mainstream magazines; Chosŏn ilbo; Chungang; Keijō Nippō; Tedong sinbo

Nicholas II, Emperor of Russia, 223
Nihon hyōron (Japan commentary), 163. See also Murahuse Kōshin
NIPPON (magazine): colonial intention of Korean assimilation and, 14–15; cultural or colonial propaganda? 276–81; internationalist outlook of, 262–63; Japanese-language version, 274; Korea Issue, 267–76; Manchukuo Issue, 267–68; Natori Yōnosuke and, 262–67. See also Korea Issue, NIPPON
NIPPON Studio, 265–68
Nomonhan Incident (1939), 203, 260
Non-Aggression Pact, 118
North Korea, 133, 170, 179, 234
Northeast Asia, 7, 57–58. See also Manchuria
northern continental policy, Japan's, 62–66
"Nukute: The Wolf" (Korea Issue, NIPPON), 270, 276, 283n60

Objects: Korea Issue, NIPPON depicting, 269, 274. See also handicraft, Korean
Okida (Japanese chemical engineer), 229
Ōkubo Toshimichi, 56–57
"On the Japanese Policy in Corea" (British Foreign Office memorandum), 191
105-Person Incident (1911), 88, 187–88
Open Door Policy, US, 87, 117, 148, 154
Opium War, 52, 67
Oriental Colonization Company, 225
Oriental Development Company, 236n27
Oriental Information Bureau, Washington DC, 39
Oriental peace: Chang questioning Itō Hirobumi on, 39; Japanese claim to stand for, 37; Japanese use of term, 34
Orientalism, as racist viewpoint, 89–90
Origins of Species, The (Darwin), 183
Origins of the Korean War, The (Cumings), 141

Other: colonial Korea as, 259; cultural distance of Koreans as, 272; *Grosses Japan Dai NIPPON* photographs of, 278; Korea Issue, *NIPPON* portrayals of, 277–78

Outlook, The: editors of, on Japanese propaganda in, 88; Japanese propaganda on Korean colonization in, 81; on Korea as outlet for Japanese population pressures, 93; on Korean nationalists, 88, 100n47; "Will there be War in East Asia?" editorial in, 92

Pacific Ocean: balance of international power shifting from Europe to, 116–17; rivalry over expansion in, 92

Pacific War, 139, 143–45, 153, 206

Pacific War Council, 208

Pact of Paris (1928), 146

Pae Sŏngnyong, 145, 158, 170, 174n74, 176n112

Pak Indŏk, 175n97

Pak Ŭnsik, 31, 79

Pak Yŏnghyo, 24

Pan-Americanism, Chŏng Irhyŏng on, 149

Pan-Asianism, Japan's: Americans on contradictions in, 98; comprehensive study of, 175n86; internationalist, as Japan's alternative worldview, 139–41; Itō on "Japanese Policy in Korea" and, 84; Japan's, *Chogwang* essays and, 153–54; Koreans writing during wartime on US and writers on, 169; official war narratives on US-Japanese confrontation and, 9; *Samch'ŏlli* as voice of, 142, 161–68

Paris Peace Conference (1919), 190, 192–93

Parker, E. H., 35

passive actions: of colonized nations, 108; during the 1920s, 107–9. *See also* Koreans under colonial rule

Patriotic Enlightenment movement (Aeguk Kyemong Undong), 79

Pearl Harbor attack, 74, 143–44, 154, 166, 169

perception or perceptions: facts compared with, 182; use of term, 213n2. *See also* Great Britain's perception of Korea during Colonial Period; Russian perception of Koreans and Japanese colonial rule; United States' perception of Korea during Colonial Period

Permanent Court of International Justice, 149. *See also* The Hague

Perry, Matthew C., 52–53

Pesotsky, V. D., 230–33

Philippine Autonomy Act (1916), 146

Philippine Independence Act (1934), 145–46

Philippines: Japan–US understanding about, 75; Koreans on US granting independence to, 142, 145–46; Mogya Hongil on US imperialism and, 154; US and independence of, 9; US comparing Japanese in Korea to US in, 90–91

Pierson, Arthur T., 92

Pip'an (Criticism): Kim Hoch'ŏl on Great Depression in the US, 158–59; An Pyŏngju's debate on Franklin D. Roosevelt's policies, 159–61; *Samch'ŏlli* compared with, 162; as socialist voice, 141–42; Yi Ch'ŏn on US missionaries and their schools, 159

Poanhoe (Society for keeping tranquility), 220

Political Science Quarterly, 78, 81

Polyanovsky, Maks, 229–30

Portsmouth, Treaty of (1905), 38

post–Colonial Period: colonial historiography development during, 4–5; international perspectives on colonial rule and, 106; Koreans' view of ene-

mies or friends in, 132. *See also* active imaginations and wishful strategies
Powell, E. Alexander, 94–97
pragmatism, Han Ch'ijin on American philosophy of, 152
pre–Colonial Period (late nineteenth century to 1910): "Chosŏn issue" for Japanese national development and, 49
present-day Korean peninsula, intellectualization effort of 1920s and, 133
Price, Willard, 272, 283n45
pro-Japanese Koreans: anti-Chinese rebellion and, 28–29; Ham Sanghun as, 144; Japanese supporting and fostering, 19; just before the Protectorate Treaty, 219–21; Kim Jonkan as, 221; *Samch'ŏlli* and wartime speeches of, 161–62; Second Sino-Japanese War and, 203; Yun Ch'iho as, Social Darwinism influence on, 31. *See also* Ilchinhoe
propaganda. *See* Japanese propaganda; Japanese propaganda in the US; NIPPON
Protectorate Treaty (1905). *See* Japan-Korea Protectorate Treaty
Provisional Government of Korea: Chongqing, Cairo Declaration (1943) and, 208–9; Chongqing, US requested to recognize, 206–7; Shanghai, establishment of, 189; Shanghai, Russian view of, 234
Pusan, Korea, 27, 55, 229

Qingdao, German-held, Japanese occupation of, 190
qipao, as symbol of East Asian dress, 271
Quezón, Manuel, 145–46

Racial affinity: Japanese claims of Koreans and, 4–5. *See also* Japan and Korea as one body

racial discrimination (racism): of British and US, *Samch'ŏlli* writers on, 166–67; Han Hŭkku on Americans and, 155; in the US, Han Ch'ijin article on American civilization and, 152
racial rivalry theory, Japan on Korea joining in war against Russia and, 37
racialism, Japanese: development of, 60–61; justifying annexation of Korea and, 68
railways: Eastern China, 124; Government Railways of Tyōsen, tourist promotional material for, 275; Japanese, into Manchuria, 185; through Korea, Yamagata on, 59; Trans-Siberian, 58–59
Rediscovering America: Japanese Perspectives on the American Century (Duus and Hasegawa), 142
Ren Yueting, 242
Republic of Korea (ROK, South Korea): establishment of, 179. *See also* Provisional Government of Korea
Review of Reviews, 81, 85
Rhee, Syngman, 100n46, 100n102, 192, 194, 203–4
Rizal, Jose, 145
Robinson, Michael, 141
Roosevelt, Franklin D.: Chŏng Irhyŏng on leadership of, 149–50; Eden on Korea question and, 207–8; Korean nationalists and socialists on, 141; Korean socialists on New Deal and working class under, 155–56, 169; oral understanding with Stalin on Korea, 211; Philippine Independence Act and, 146; An Pyŏngju's debate on policies of, 159–61; on Soviet cooperation with Cairo Declaration, 209; wartime diplomacy, 205
Roosevelt, Theodore, 38, 90, 183
Rossov, Piotr (Peter), 220, 222, 235n5

Royds, William M., 190, 200, 204
Russia: *Chosŏn ilbo* on East Asian balance of power and, 129; Civil War (1917–23), 228; geopolitical ambition of, 4; Japan on national security threat of, 185; Japanese military actions against, 133–34; Japanese rationalization for its war against, 36–38; Japanese relations in 1920s with, 120; Japanese tensions in late Meiji period with, 76; Korea Treaty with (1884), 25, 232; Korean border with, cleaning Koreans from, 233; move eastward, Japan's anxiety and, 5; perception of Korea during Colonial Period, 12; Soviet Revolution in, Koreans' dream of change and, 109; Tarui Tokich'i on Asian colonization intentions of, 32; Triple Intervention (1895) and, 59–60; Tsushima Island occupation (1861) by, 54–55; Yamagata on interest line to check, 58–59. *See also* Russian perception of Koreans and Japanese colonial rule; Russo-Japanese War; Soviet Revolution; Soviet Union
Russian Far East, 12–13, 39, 219, 230–33, 235. *See also* Siberia
Russian perception of Koreans and Japanese colonial rule: duality of Korean perception of Japanese policies and, 233–34; during early Protectorate period, 221–23; focus on "people's revolutionary movement" of 1930s, 234; just before the Protectorate Treaty, 219–21; from mid-1910s to early 1920s, 226–27; during mid-1920s through early 1930s, 228–30; national character of Koreans and, 234–35; overview of, 219; reasons for Japanese colonization, 223–24; in Russian Far East, 230–33; transformation of, 224–26

Russo-Japanese War (1904–5): Asian solidarity and Asianism after Japanese victory in, 60; English-language writing on Korea after, 88; Itō on "Japanese Policy in Korea" in, 83–84; Japanese influence over Korea and, 49–50; Japanese propaganda and, 77; Japanese rationalization for, 36–38; Japan's interest line and, 59, 67–68; Kennan as war correspondent during, 90; Korea named as Japanese protectorate after, 61; Korea's loss of independence after, 220; Russia's perception of, 12; Schmidt on Japanese annexation of Korea and, 228–29; second Anglo-Japanese Alliance concluding with, 185; Western perception of Korea and, 183
Ryang, Sonia, 277

Sahae kongnon (Cosmopolitans), 142, 145
Sai Syō-ki (dancer), 276
Saigo Takamori, 21, 32
Saionji Kinmochi cabinet, sociopolitical system of Japanese society and, 184
Saitō Makoto, 96–97, 191, 195, 200–202
Samch'ŏlli (The Korean peninsula): Hu Shih–Murahuse Kōshin debate in, 162–64; name changed to *Taedonga*, 175n85; as Pan-Asianist voice, 141–42, 161; on US as enemy after 1941, 165–66; war-mobilizing speeches in, 166–68
Samil Independence movement (1919), 241. *See also* March First Independence movement
Sandburg, Carl, 155
Sands, William F., 40–41
Schmid, Andre, 2, 6–7
Schmidt, P. Yu., 228–29

"Scorched-Earth Diplomacy" (Ch'ot'o oegyo), 163
Scribner's Magazine, 81
Second Sino-Japanese War (1937–45): Chogwang's coverage of US position prior to, 142; demand for Japan-related photographs and, 264; forced resettlement of Korean immigrants from Soviet Far East to Soviet Central Asia (1937) and, 235; Han updating choices for British and US in the Far East after, 147–48; Japan triggering, 260; Japanese victory in, pro-Japanese sentiment and, 203; Samch'ŏlli as Pan-Asianist voice and, 161–62; Western powers' reassessment of Korean peninsula after, 197
Second World War. See World War II
Segye chisik (World knowledge), idealized portraits of US by, 142
Seikanron (Japan invading Korea before Western powers), 21, 56–58, 60–61, 67
Seinan War (1877), 58
"A Selection of Celebrities" (Korea Issue, NIPPON), 270, 276
Self, Japanese colonizer as, Korea Issue, NIPPON and, 277–78, 280
self-determination of nations doctrine, US and at Paris Peace Conference and, 192–93
Seoul: Europeanized look of, 229; Japanese delegation to Korea through, 55; Korean army mutiny (1882) and Japanese legation in, 25; Soviet Consulate General opened in, 228. See also Government-General of Korea
Seoul Press, 39
Seoul-Ŭiju railway, Japanese extension into Manchuria of, 185
Seventh-Day Adventist Church, 142

Shanghai (magazine), 267
Shanghai, Provisional Government of the Republic of Korea in, 189, 234
Sharmanov, Toregeldy, 228
Shashin kyōkai (Photography Association, Japan), 267
Shi Haoran, 243
Shibazaki Atsushi, 262
Shidehara Kijuo, 191
Shimazu, Naoko, 2, 13–15
Shimonoseki Treaty (1899), 240
Shinoda Tomio, 268
Shinto Shrine Worship policy, implementation of, 102n87
Shufeldt Treaty (1882), 25
Siberia, Keijō Nippō on dispatching Japanese military forces to, 126
"Siirya pangsŏng taeyok" (Tonight I weep loudly and bitterly) (Chang Chiyŏn), 38–39
Sijo (Trends), 142–43
Sin Ch'aeho, 31, 79
Sin Hŭngu, 166, 168, 176n103
Sinclair, Upton, 155
singminji sagwan (colonial historical perspectives), 79–80
Sino-Japanese conflict, Chogwang's coverage of, 146
Sino-Japanese War. See First Sino-Japanese War; Second Sino-Japanese War
Sino-Soviet conflicts, North Korea's equidistance policy and, 133
Sŏ Chaep'il (Philip Jaisohn), 157, 194
Sŏ Ch'un, 146
Social Darwinism, 4, 30–31, 83–84, 183. See also social evolution theory
Social Democratic Party (Sahoe Minjudang), 176n100
social evolution theory, 54. See also Social Darwinism
social imaginary, Taylor on, 140

social sciences, origin of notion of perception in, 182
socialism: as Japanese and Chinese power source, 125; as prism for Russian view of Korea, 229–30. See also Soviet Union
socialists: ambivalence toward Franklin D. Rooseveltian America by, 155–61; *Chungang* and *Pip'an* as voice of, 142; ideological split between cultural nationalists and, 141, 169; US as perceived by (1930s–40s), 9
sociology of knowledge, 182
Sŏhak (Western learning), 24. *See also* Tonghak
Son Ki-tei (Olympics gold medalist runner), 276
Son Pyŏnghi, 33
Song Byeongjun, 235n7
Song Ziwen, 208
South China Photo Service, 267
South Korea, establishment of, 179
South Manchuria Railway Company library, Dalian, China, 243
South Pacific islands, 147, 172n27, 190
Southeast Asia, Japanese Imperial Army's invasion of, 268
sovereignty line (J. *shukensen*), 58–59. See also interest line
Soviet Revolution: *Chosŏn ilbo* editorials on, 125–26; Japanese vs. Koreans on, 121–22; Koreans' dream of change and, 109, 131; as negative factor to Japan's future interests, 119; self-determination principle suggested by, 114. *See also* communism
Soviet Union: Chaha Sanin on dictatorship in, 157; Cold War and, 139, 168; East Asia and, 213n1; Japanese treaty with (1925), 196–97; Japan's move in Northern China and, 147; Nomonhan Incident (1939) with Japanese, 203;

perception of Korea during Colonial Period, 11–12; propaganda and support for Koreans by, 196; An Pyŏngju accused of contacting, 175n80; An Pyŏngju's debate on FD Roosevelt and, 160; Soviet Consulate General opening in Seoul, 228; US clarification of Korean policy with, 209–10; World War II British, Chinese, and US policies toward Korea and, 205–6. *See also* Russia; Russian Far East; Russian perception of Koreans and Japanese colonial rule; Stalin, Joseph
Spanish Civil War, 160–61
Spanish-American War, 145
Specht, Karl, 277
speeches: praising Japanese Army, 164–65; in US, as Japanese propaganda, 77; war-mobilizing, 166–68
stagnated Korea theory, Japanese propaganda and, 22
Stalin, Joseph: Cairo Declaration (1943) and, 209–10; forced resettlement of Koreans to Soviet Central Asia (1937) and, 13, 235; Koreans on Russo-Korean border and, 233; oral understanding with Franklin D. Roosevelt on Korea, 211; An Pyŏngju's debate on Franklin D. Roosevelt and, 160. *See also* Soviet Union
State Department, US: Cairo Declaration (1943) and, 208–9; interdivisional research on the Korean question, 210–11; on Korean nationalist movement, 193; on Korean participation in war against Japan, 206–7; personnel increases during World War II at, 212; on route from Japan's industrial center to Manchurian capital, 199. *See also* United States
"Statistics of Japanese-Korean Inter-Marriages" (Korea Issue, NIPPON), 276

Stevens, Durham White, 34, 41
Stieglitz, Alfred, 264
Suematsu Kenchō, 77
Sultans, Islamic, Japan's colonial rulers in Korea compared with, 182
Sun, Kezhi, 2, 11–13
Sun Runjiang, 243
Sung Chiao-jen, 241
Sunjong, Emperor, 195, 228
Suzuki Keiroku, 88–89
Sylvester, Christine, 109

T*aedonga* (formerly *Samch'ŏlli*), 175n85
TaeHan maeil sinbo (newspaper), 79
Taft-Katsura understanding, Philippines and, 75
Taishō democracy period (1912–26), Japan's, 66
Taiwan, 50, 57, 275
Takamatsu Jinjirō, 268
Tarui Tokich'i, 32–34, 37
Taylor, Charles, 140
Tedong sinbo (Great East newspaper), 37, 47n76
Tehan ilbo (The Korea daily), 37, 47n76
Tehran Conference (1943), 206, 209
Terauchi Masatake: Chinese delegation to Korean Production Co-Progress Exhibition and, 249; Japan's northern continental policy and, 63–66; Korean resistance to administration of, 186–87; military rule in Korea and, 195; Western perception of, 187
Third Communist International, US branch of, 151
Third World, African and Asian former colonies and formation of, 107
Tian Hexian, 242
Tickner, Arlene, 107
Toksa sillon (A new reading of history) (Sin Ch'aeho), 79

Tokutomi Sohō, 277
Tonga ilbo (East-Asia daily), 251
Tonghak (Eastern learning), 24, 33, 221
torture, 105-Person Incident and, 188
Toyama Mitsuru, 32
Toynbee, Arnold, 211, 214n25
Toyotomi Hideyoshi, 22, 33
"Transfiguration during a Twenty-Nine-Year Period" (Korea Issue, NIPPON), 270, 275–76
Trans-Siberian Railway, 58–59
travel writing, Japanese colonial discourse in, 277
Treaty of Peace, Amity, Commerce, and Navigation (1882), 25
Triple Intervention (1895), 59–60, 74–75
trusteeships: Eden's talks with Franklin D. Roosevelt on, 207–8; for Korea, Koreans lack of political experience and, 202; for Korea, mandatory rule system and, 180; for Korea, US planners on implementation of, 209–10; for Korea, US planners on "in due course" and, 210–11; for Korea, vague consensus on, 11; multilateral, Franklin D. Roosevelt's wartime diplomacy on, 205; post–World War II universal application of, 208
Tsuda Shingo, 266
Tsushima Island: Japanese trading with Chosŏn through, 57; Russian occupation (1861) of, 54–55, 61, 67
Twenty-One Demands (Japan, 1915), 184
Tydings-McDuffie Act (1934), 145
Tyō Kaku-Tyū, 276
"Tyōsen: Sketches of Modern Korea and Her People" (Korea Issue, NIPPON), 269

Uchida Yasuya, 188
Ugaki Kazushige, 199

ŭipyŏng (righteous army), 39, 222
Ullstein Verlag, 264
underground revolutionaries, voices of, 170
Union of Soviet Socialist Republics (USSR). *See* Soviet Union
United Automobile Workers (UAW), 151
United Kingdom (UK). *See* Great Britain
United Nations: guarantee of Korean independence and, 209; Franklin D. Roosevelt's wartime diplomacy and, 205
United States: anti-Japanese sentiment in, 75, 92–93; Chaha Sanin on dictatorship in, 156–57; *Chogwang* articles about, 143–53; Chŏng Irhyŏng on civilization in, 148–50; Cold War and, 168; exiled anti-Japanese Koreans in, 39; expanding influence in Asia, Japan and, 119; as great power, 212–13, 213n1; Han on potential Far East choices (1937) for, 147–48; Hu Shih on Japan's alliance with, 164; Japanese belligerent discourse and antagonism before 1929 toward, 139–40; Japanese propaganda from 1905 in, 6; Japanese relations (1920s) with, 120; Japanese wartime discourse on, 141; Japan's move in Northern China and, 147; Japan's northern continental policy and, 65–66; Korean Independence movement and, 192–93; Korean perceptions of (1930s–1940s), 9–10; Korean socialists' writings on, 155–56; Korean students' admiration for life in, 173n42; Korean wartime discourse on, 140–41, 169; Natori's international operation moves to, 265; not supporting Liberation or Korean independence, 180; post-World War I international power of, 108; *Samch'ŏlli*'s reporting (1937–40) on, 162; Senate, Japan on Korean issue raised in, 193–94; shift of power from Britain to, 116–17; Supreme Court, Roosevelt's New Deal and, 158. *See also* American mainstream magazines; Japanese propaganda in the US; Roosevelt, Franklin D.; Roosevelt, Theodore; State Department, US; US Army Military Government in Korea; Yellow Peril
United States' perception of Korea during Colonial Period: before 1910, 182–83; international relations of Korean Peninsula (1920s), 195–97; international relations of Korean Peninsula (1930s), 197–204; issues of the 1910s, 183–89; Korean liberation and independence, 204–12; March First movement and Western policies, 189–95; overview of, 10–11, 179–81
Unpartisan Review, 81
Unyō Incident (1875), 57
US Army Military Government in Korea (USAMGIK) (1945–48), 7
Ussuriysk region: Korean immigrants to, 230, 232. *See also* Russian Far East
Utopia (More), 142
utopia, Japan's Pan-Asianist discourse advocating, 139–40

Versailles, Treaty of, 194–95
Versailles system, 260
violence, used by the Japanese colonial authorities, international questioning of, 11
Wagner Act (1935), 151
Wan Baoyuan, 246, 249
Wang Hengxin, 243
Wang Shuming, 242
Wang Yangbin, 246, 249
Wanpaoshan Incident (1931), 198, 241

war: destructive vision for change based on, 131–32; Japanese colonization of Korea and, 19; Korean exclusion from international talks on, 118; in Northeast Asia, Korean anticipation of, 7; predictions of, changes of balance of international power and, 117. See also specific wars

Washington Navel Conference: Japanese anger at Yellow Peril in US and, 123, 133; Japanese expansion after, 197; Japanese naval arsenal reduction and, 120–21; Japan's withdrawal from, 147; Keijō Nippō editorials on, 112; limitations of, 195; newspaper editorials on arms race and, 118

Weech, Sigmund von, 263

Wei Yuan, 52

Weisenfeld, Gennifer S., 279

Western correspondents, Japanese on Russo-Japanese War and, 38

Western gaze: Natori and, 265; Korea Issue, NIPPON and, 274

Western intellectuals, on Korea's failure to modernize and loss of sovereignty, 26

Western modern international law system. See international law

Western powers: advance into Chosŏn, as Japanese national crisis, 67; on civilizing by colonizing, 20; as colonizers, Japan as new competitor with, 73–74; investments in Korea, Japan's Company Law and, 189; on Japanese bridge and railroad construction in Korea, 185; Japan's civilization and modernization and, 52–53; Japan's mission to "protect" Asian nations from, 22–23; opening of East Asia and, 51; perception of Korea before 1910, 182–83; Tarui Tokich'i on Asian colonization intentions of, 32; as threat to Japan, Tsushima Island seizure and, 54–55; Treaty of Ganghwa (1876) and, 57–58; unequal treaties with Japan and, 56. See also Great Britain; great powers; major powers; United States

Western readership, NIPPON (magazine) and, 259, 263–65, 267, 274–75, 278–80

Whigham, Henry James, 43

White, Trumbull, 35

white clothes, foreign fascination with, 271–72

white color, virtues in Korean culture of, 270–71

Wijŏngch'ŏksap'a (conservative group), 23

Wilson, Woodrow, 11, 114, 146, 190, 192

wire services, in US and Europe, Japanese propaganda and, 76–77

women, Korean, Korea Issue, NIPPON depicting, 269, 272–74, 273f

Wŏn Sehun, 162–64, 175n88

world traveling, understanding Koreans' international perceptions and, 109

World War I, 108, 180, 184, 189

World War II: Allies' common policy during, 205; in Europe, Ham Sanghun on, 153; German invasion of Poland and, 260; Japanese intellectuals' discourse prior to, 142; Korea as strategic base for Japan during, 204; Sŏ Ch'un's prediction of, 146; system of mandatory rule and trusteeship after, 180

Yalta Conference (1945), 206, 209, 211

Yalu River railway bridge, Japanese completion of, 185

Yamagata Aritomo: annexation of Korea and, 62; on integrating East Asian nations into Japan, 21; Japan's northern continental policy and, 64–65;

modern Japanese Army and, 58; Russo-Japanese War and, 63; on safeguarding Japan's interest in Korea, 23, 35
Yamaguchi Prefecture, Japanese Army and, 62
Yamatada, Mr. (Education Affairs Office), 248
Yanagi Sōetsu, 275
Yang Mingpan, 242
Yang Xixian, 242
Yellow Peril: Anglo-Saxons in Canada and, 166–67; as international concern for Japanese and Koreans, 121–25; Japanese countering Western idea of, 5; Russians on Korean question and, 76–77, 230, 232; Russo-Japanese War and, 60; spread of, in the West, 68. *See also* Japan and Korea as one body; Japanese propaganda; racial discrimination
Yi Ch'ŏn, 159
Yi Dinasty: handicraft of, 270, 275. *See also* Chosŏn Dynasty
Yi Hangno, 23
Yi Hŏnyŏng, 30
Yi Kwangsu, 166, 170
Yi Taejin, 47n75
Yi Tongin, 24
Yi Tonhwa, 165
Yi Yongku, 33, 43
Yidach'i Kenjo, 36
Yŏ Unhong, 166, 176n100
Yŏ Unhyŏng, 155–56
Yoon, P. K., 100n46
Young Men's Association (YMA, Ch'ŏngnyŏnhoe), 222
Young Men's Christian Association (YMCA), 222, 248
Yu Kiljun, 24, 27, 30–31
Yu Kwangyŏl, 154
Yu Shouchun, 242

Yun Ch'iho: fatalism and nihilism of, 42–43; as Pan-Asianist voice, 170; racial rivalry theory used by, 37; on Social Darwinism and Japan, 31; speech praising Japanese Army by, 165; war-mobilizing speeches of, 166–167
Yun Hae, 192
Yun Pong-gil Incident (1932), 203

Zhang Mosheng, 252
Zhang Xiushan, 242
Zhang Yuan, 241, 247, 250
"Zylinkerhüte und Mullröcke" (Tophats and muslin skirts) (Korea Issue, NIPPON), 270–71

www.ingramcontent.com/pod-product-compliance
Lightning Source LLC
Chambersburg PA
CBHW021341300426
44114CB00012B/1028